Gandhi
The Master Communicator

GANDHI
The Master Communicator

Kusum Lata Chadda

KANISHKA PUBLISHERS, DISTRIBUTORS
NEW DELHI-110 002

KANISHKA PUBLISHERS, DISTRIBUTORS
4697/5-21 A, Ansari Road, Daryaganj
New Delhi-110 002
Phones : 2327 0497, 2328 8285
Fax : 011-2328 8285
E-mail: kanishka_publishing@yahoo.co.in

Gandhi The Master Communicator
First Published 2010

ISBN 978-81-8457-242-1

PRINTED IN INDIA

Published by Madan Sachdeva for Kanishka Publishers, Distributors, 4697/5-21A, Ansari Road, Daryaganj, New Delhi-110 002, Typeset by Sunshine Graphics, Delhi, and Printed at Rajdhani Printers, Delhi.

Preface

Speaking at Gandhi Smriti and Darshan Samiti, Delhi, Prof. BR Nanda, one of the finest biographers of Gandhi, rued the lack of interest among the youth of India in Gandhi. He warned the audience that it would be a sad day for India if it had to someday 'import' Gandhi from the West. He was not far from truth because in India Gandhi is flaunted as a trophy but when it comes to following his ideals, most of us think them to be too impractical or beyond ordinary mortals. In spite of innumerable books on Gandhi this misconception remains. It would seem immodest to claim, or even suggest, that another addition to this already overflowing pool would make any difference. Yet one is ready to take a chance drawing inspiration from Gandhi's words that truth and non-violence have to be repeated many times as long as there are people who doubt their efficacy. The saga of Gandhi has to become a part of Indian consciousness so that we are able to redeem our debt to Gandhi.

The present work examines Gandhi as a communicator because it is in this capacity that he straddled India and later the world, both in terms of time and space. Ever since he started speaking and publishing on public issues he engaged his readers/audiences in a continuous dialogue. His writings contained in the hundred volumes published by the Government of India of which volumes 98 to 100 contain indices *(Collected Works of Mahatma Gandhi)* need to be dusted and brought out to speak to the people for whom they were meant. The best way to know Gandhi is through his own words. Gandhi cannot be paraphrased for he chose his words with great caution and after good deal of deliberation. The present work, therefore, presents Gandhi in his own words with only bare outlines to suggest the context in which he was speaking/writing.

In the present age when the media makes or mars a person Gandhi's deft handling of the media speaks volumes about his realistic assessment of men and events. Also, in the age when the print media was the only source of widespread communication Gandhi made maximum use of it for the dissemination of his ideas, for organising the movements that he led, for educating the people, while at the same time building a nation. Gandhi also made a fine distinction between liberty and license in so far as media was concerned. His responsible handling of the press set standards of journalism. Public men (read politicians), who thrive on media can learn a lesson or two from him as to how to use the media judiciously. His wide repertoire of communication skills was supplemented and complemented by his use of the print media.

Gandhi played an important role in our history, specifically our freedom movement. What were his tools for mobilizing such a huge population, one needs to know. Was he thinking only about freedom from the foreign rule and mobilised people for that or did he go beyond this short term goal? Was there a definite strategy that he followed in the communication process to bring desired results? Why were people ready to be persuaded by him? Was it his personality, was it his demeanour or was it the content and intelligent timing of his communication that helped? These questions are sought to be answered in the present work.

There are other reasons also for recounting Gandhi. Gandhi wrote about almost everything under the sun. The level of personal evolution that he had achieved makes his opinions valuable. One may not agree with all that he said but at least one can get an altogether different perspective on the problem at hand by reading him. After trying a wide variety of methods of conflict resolution, the world has recognised the worth of Gandhian method of non-violent Satyagraha and the use of soul-force. Similarly in the recent concern for global warming and environmental pollution his views on sustainable development are becoming more relevant. People world over have awakened to the evil of irresponsible and thoughtless consumerism and industrialism. Gandhi not only voiced his concerns but also offered doable solutions to most of these problems. These may be worth looking into and giving a fair trial.

In this ambitious venture I have had the good fortune of being guided and encouraged by a very able and committed set of people. Since this work is an adaptation of my Ph.D thesis entitled 'Gandhi's Communication Strategy: the Use of Print Media', first and foremost I would like to thank my Ph.D guide Dr. Jai Narain from the

Department of Gandhian Studies, Panjab University, Chandigarh who helped me choose to work on the topic of my choice and provided me useful inputs. My co-guide, Dr. Radhakrishnan former Director, Gandhi Smriti and Darshan Samiti being stationed in Delhi where I live, was more accessible and therefore always available for any guidance. My association with Dr. Radhakrishnan was most rewarding as he is both an activist and a scholar and helped me understand Gandhi in the right perspective. Moreover, like a true Gandhian, if he found that my arguments were not cogent enough he would simply ask me to defend my stand. If I succeeded in doing so, whether he agreed with my viewpoint or not, did not matter to him. Like his idol Gandhi, Dr. Radhakrishnan worked round the clock and expected his students to do the same. I also benefited immensely from the international workshops and talks held at Gandhi Smriti during his tenure and later. He suggested and facilitated my conducting interviews with some of the contemporaries of Gandhi like Sadiq Ali and Dr. Usha Mehta. He also helped me meet and interact with practising Gandhians like Dr. Fatima Meer and Professor Glenn Paige (who entrusted me with the translation of his book 'Global Nonkilling Political Science', which I eventually did).

My friends and colleagues from PGDAV College (University of Delhi) made important contributions to this work. Dr. Sunder Raman, was instrumental in helping me zero-in on this topic and persuaded me to take Dr. Radhakrishnan as my guide. Needless to say, both his suggestions proved to be very useful. He also very painstakingly went through my manuscript and made valuable suggestions. Dr. ND Arora gave me the benefit of his long experience in teaching and guiding research on Gandhi, to clarify my doubts on various issues. Sushil Gupta, my colleague from the Department of English, volunteered to look into my language and punctuation in particular with zero tolerance for error. Still if some errors remain, the lapse is on my part. I would also like to place on record my thanks to Prof. Surendra Chopra who despite his advanced age and poor health volunteered to read my manuscript and corrected me on some critical details Sadly, while the first draft of this manuscript went to the publisher, Dr. Chopra breathed his last. His advice will be sorely missed in future. The person, however, who really helped me bring out the book was Ashok Sahay who edited my thesis and smoothened out what he called the 'research-ish' part of the work to make it more readable. I am indebted to him for that. Last but not least I cannot put in words the help given to me by my husband Dr. Somesh Chadda and the trust bestowed in my capability by my children, Richa and Pranav who all along encouraged me in this time-consuming venture with an unspoken 'you can do it'.

My special thanks are due to the library staff of Gandhi Museum Library, Indian Institute of Public Administration Library and Nehru Museum Library, Delhi. I am particularly thankful to Aruna Tandan, the Research Officer of the Nehru Museum Library for her help and support.

Finally, I am thankful to my publishers who committed to publish this book in record time as soon as I made the manuscript available.

I dedicate this book to my father who read my thesis but is not around to see it published as a book. Though an army officer, he was a staunch Gandhian and would recall with emotion how he travelled over a thousand kilometres by train to be present at Gandhi's funeral in Delhi.

Delhi, 2010

Kusum Lata Chadda

e-mail: kusumchadda 56 @ rediffmail.com

Contents

Introduction

Rarely has history gifted the world with a person who has won the willing obedience of so vast a number of people with such diversity of background as did Mohandas Karamchand Gandhi. It was on the strength of this ability to influence people that he managed to mobilize the ill-organized and ill-equipped masses – first of South Africa and then of India – to take on the might of the British Empire. Such an accomplishment was possible only for a man with an unerring gift of communication. And Gandhi, if anything, was a powerful communicator.

Communication, as it is understood today, 'involves the transfer of information from sender to the receiver with the information being understood by the receiver in the same sense in which the sender wants it to be understood'.[1] Thus any communication process involves three factors: the sender of the communication, the transmission of the message and the receiver of the communication. Relevant also is the concept of 'noise' signifying anything that interferes with pure communication. In the overall process of communication feedback is important because only through feedback can the sender know whether what he tried to communicate has been received and correctly understood. Situational factors may also affect communication. These include the educational, sociological, legal, political or economic situations in which the communication is conducted. Finally, since the goal of communication is 'to reach out' and come into contact with one of the cognitive senses of the people, the process can be verbal or non-verbal, intentional or unintentional, provided the goal is achieved.

Gandhi has been described as a great persuader.[2] In fact, the very first theory of communication recorded, attributed to a Greek named Corax and later refined by his student Tisias, dealt with courtroom speaking and the craft of persuasion. Tisias became convinced that persuasion could be taught as an art and encouraged instructors to train the people in the art of rhetoric.[3] To our associative memory, however, 'rhetoric' implies a certain heaviness of pomposity and didacticism. Gandhi's rhetoric was free of any such empty artifice. It came spontaneously to him — from the heart — in the form of gently marshalled, relevant data aimed at appealing to the heart.[4]

Communication involves 'all human behavior'.[5] Gandhi exemplified this. Each and every activity of his had a hidden or obvious message in it. Time-management, an essential part of his daily routine, conveyed the importance of discipline and value of time. Similarly, his message on goodness of exercise and correct diet in an individual's life came through loud and clear by his emphasis on daily walks and a series of diet experiments. His decision to drink only goat's milk as he thought that cow and buffalo milk was procured by torturing the animal showed his concern for subhuman life and was an appeal to others to respect it. His insistence on maintaining a meticulous record of income and expenditure emphasized the importance of transparent and well thought out economic planning. Regular spinning of the *charkha* was his way of being one with the poor in the quest for a respectable livelihood. The same reason went into his wearing minimal and homespun clothes. In fact Gandhi's style of dressing up always attracted comments, both adulatory and scornful. Choosing particular attire reflected the inner change in Gandhi and thus struck a responsive chord in the people who came into contact with him. An American researcher has brought out this aspect to great effect in her thesis where she observes:

> Engaged in the simple labour of spinning, dressed as one of the poor in loincloth and chadar, this important and powerful man communicated the dignity of poverty, the dignity of labour, the equality of all Indians, the greatness of Indian civilization, as well as his own saintliness. The communicative power of costume transcended the limitations of language in multilingual and illiterate India. His impact on the West was enhanced by his resemblance, in his simplicity of dress and saintly manner, to Christ on the Cross.... When Gandhi tried to convince all Indians to wear plain white khadi, he threatened not only regional industry and caste hierarchy but also the roles of separation of the roles of daughter, wife and widow which are central to the perception of female identity.[6]

Gandhi communicates through dramatic changes in his attire over the years

Gandhi as a practicing lawyer in South Africa (Johhanesburg, 1900)

Gandhi in Kathiawadi dress on his return to India (1915)

Gandhi adopts the loin cloth to identify himself with the poorest of the poor (Madura, 1921)

Gandhi moved closer to the common man by opting for village life and living in a cottage. In this way he was communicating to the world the necessity of living in harmony with nature and emphasizing the self-sufficiency of villages.[7] His cottages were built invariably with the material available in the village itself.

Gandhi's hut at Segaon where he lived in 1936 was built totally of material obtained locally

Gandhi's lifestyle emphasized the discipline of both body and mind and need for restraint and *tapasya* (that is, physical suffering accepted or taken up willingly for positive goal one desires intensely). As Jawaharlal Nehru aptly put it, 'The idea of some kind of penance, *tapasya,* is inherent in Indian thought, both among the thinkers at the top and the unread masses below. It is present today as it was present some thousands of years ago, and it is necessary to appreciate it in order to understand the psychology underlying the mass movements which have convulsed India under Gandhiji's leadership.'[8] This insistence on *tapasya* was the essential ingredient of Gandhi's charisma.

Gandhi recognized the fact that India was a country rich in the tradition of communication through symbols and parables. The *puranas* and the epics Indians grow up with, talk in terms of symbols. These symbols are derived from Hindu mythology, Islamic tradition, folklore and a host of other traditions which are a part of India's diverse culture. Bhikhu Parekh has beautifully summed up this aspect of Gandhi's communication skill in the following words:

> After a long reflection and experimentation he [Gandhi] evolved a distinct mode of discourse that was also a form of praxis. Convinced that human actions derived their emotional energy from 'heart' which could only be addressed and activated by judiciously selected language of symbols, and recognizing that Hindu culture was deeply symbolic, he evolved a powerful cluster of culturally evocative symbols including such things as the spinning wheel, the *khadi,* the cow, and the 'Gandhi cap'....Partly by conscious design and partly as spontaneous expressions of his own way of life, his dress, language, mode of speaking, food, bodily gestures, ways of sitting, walking and talking, humour and staff, became a symbol of a specific way of life. Each evoked deep cultural memories, spoke volumes and conveyed highly complex messages.[9]

The unique contribution of Gandhi lay in the fact that he modernized the traditional symbols and thus made them more relevant to the times. Thus, his idea of religion was free from bigotry and more close to the ethical practice rather than being a set of rituals. The Prophet Mohammed was for Gandhi a symbol of compassion, and Islam, a religion preaching equality and tolerance. Christ and

Christianity contained the message of passive resistance against evil. He initially attacked untouchability without disturbing the caste system as he thought that once untouchability goes the hierarchical nature of the caste system would vanish, giving place to a horizontal division of labour. Similarly, with regard to the interpretation of popular epics, Gandhi declared that the great Hindu epic, the *Mahabharata,* recounted not the war between cousins but a struggle between justice and injustice guided by Truth itself. Rudolph and Rudolph have made a penetrating study of Gandhi as a modernizer of tradition. In their book, *Gandhi, the Traditional Roots of Charisma* which is a sequel to their earlier work, *The Modernization of Tradition: Political Development in India,* the authors illustrate how social and political change in India involved adaptation of past inheritance as much as displacement of that inheritance. In the context of this, they see Gandhi's leadership as historically determined, rooted in the aspects of tradition, which he interpreted for his times. The Rudolphs concede that similar attempts had earlier been made by leaders like Bipin Chandra Pal and Bal Gangadhar Tilak to arouse national consciousness by giving identity to Indians. The search for roots, however, made these leaders associate more with Hindu symbols, thus cutting off followers of other religions, especially the Muslims, from the main movement. Gandhi also did borrow from the rich Hindu symbols, but interpreted them in a manner that they became universal in nature. He may not have fully succeeded in this effort, but he certainly re-established the secular tradition.[10] The former President of India, V.V. Giri, corroborates this. Describing Gandhi as an 'enlightened pathfinder', Giri opines that Gandhi 'embodied in himself, as few have done in Indian history, the soul of India. If, as Max Mueller once said, one finds oneself everywhere in India between an immense past and an immense future, the chasm could be bridged in our age by none other than Mahatma Gandhi.'[11]

Romain Rolland, one of the best biographers of Gandhi, also conceded that, had Gandhi's genius not seen the need to adapt or source his present ideology in the past, he would not have succeeded as a communicator. Rolland is of the opinion:

> Nations have short memories, and I should have but slight faith in India's power to remain true to the Mahatma's teachings if his doctrines were not an expression of the deepest and the most ancient longings of the race. For if there is such a thing as genius, great by its own strength,

whether or not it corresponds to the ideals of its surroundings, there can be no genius of action, no leader, who does not incarnate the instincts of his race to satisfy the need of the hour, and requite the yearning of the world.[12]

Gandhi was successful because he had the insight to understand these longings of the Indians and give expression to them.

Apart from the above-mentioned non-verbal and possibly unintentional methods of communication, Gandhi's genius lay in evolving an effective network of communication through his 'extended family'. This was a multi-layered network of relations at

DIAGRAMMATIC REPRESENTATION OF GANDHI'S COMMUNICATION NETWORK

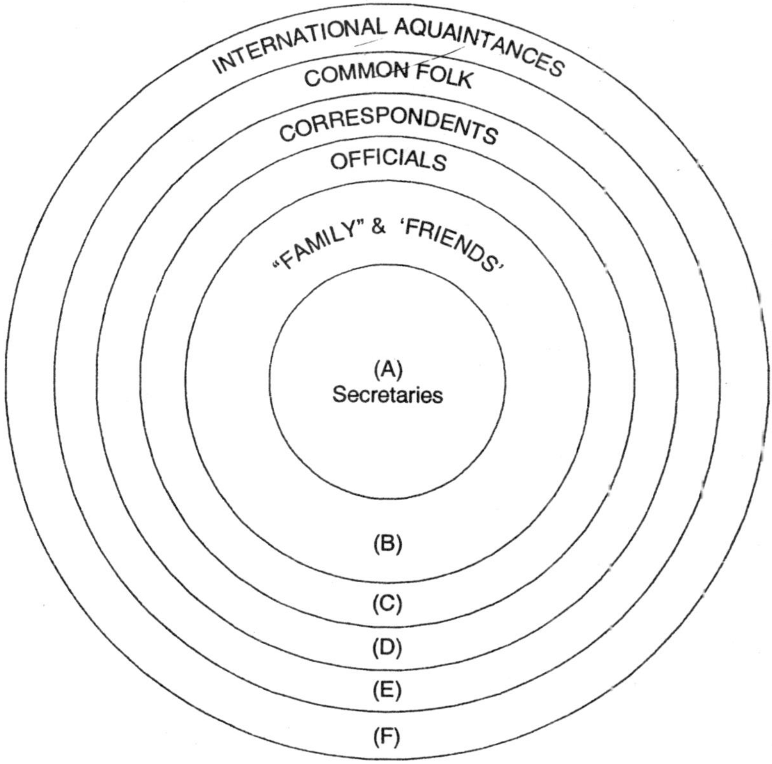

DIAGRAM-I

the center of which was Gandhi himself (see Diagram-I). If this network is represented through concentric circles, close to the center of this network was: *(a)* his innermost circle of associates, mostly comprising his secretaries or those who attended to his daily needs. In the succeeding circle *(b)* his 'family' of 'elder brothers', 'brothers', 'sisters', 'sons' and his numerous 'daughters', besides his own biological family existed. In the same category were also his 'friends' with whom he corresponded on a regular basis. Some of Gandhi's 'elder brothers' were Motilal Nehru.[13] V.N. Srinivasa Sastri,[14] Madan Mohan Malaviya,[15] Swami Shraddhanand[16] and Rabindranath Tagore.[17] Gandhi's illustrious 'brothers' were the Ali Brothers[18] and Sardar Vallabhbhai Patel[19] who were important figures in the national life. His equally worthy 'sons' were Jamnalal Bajaj,[20] Subhas Chandra Bose[21] and Jawaharlal Nehru,[22] all of whom played significant roles in the freedom movement of India. His 'sisters' like Sarojini Naidu,[23] Urmila Devi,[24] Gangabehn Vaidya,[25] Prema Kantak[26] and innumerable others were the most famous women leaders of their time. His illustrious 'daughters' like Mirabehn,[27] Amtulassalam,[28] Zohra Ansari,[29] and Raihana Tyabji[30] were his associates and messengers in the most difficult phases of the national movement.

The list of Gandhi's 'friends' is equally impressive. It included personalities like M.A. Ansari,[31] Rajkumari Amrit Kaur,[32] G.D. Birla,[33] Charles Andrews,[34] Horace Alexander,[35] Agatha Harrison,[36] H.S.L. Polak[37] and many others with whom Gandhi at times shared his innermost thoughts, and at times discussed political situations asking for their responses. In this circle were also included leaders and politicians who differed with Gandhi on various issues such as Mohammad Ali Jinnah,[38] B.R. Ambedkar[39] and Subhas Chandra Bose in the forties. In fact a volume of *The Collected Works of Mahatma Gandhi,* running into 583 pages is devoted solely to the people who Gandhi met or referred to in his writings. This does not include mythological figures or people of doubtful historical authenticity. From this one can imagine the vast network of communications Gandhi managed.

These were also the very people whose lives had been changed in varying degrees by the impact of Gandhi's personality or words. In his inimitable prose, Nehru has compared this metamorphosis of peoples' lives to the impact of Socrates on his pupils. Like Socrates,

Gandhi too left one 'staggered and bewitched', 'smitten by a kind of sacred rage' so that 'one simply could not go on living the way one did.'[40]

An important result of Gandhi's network of communication was that he was able to win over most of the local leaders of the time and this made mass mobilization easier. An Indian scholar writing on the impact of Gandhi avers:

> Gandhi had powerful influence over the Indian leaders of his time and this strengthened Gandhi's hold over the masses because each of them had his own base in society.... Motilal conceded to Gandhi, 'Our difficulty is that in politics you beat us at our own game'. Maulana Abul Kalam Azad found in Gandhi a profound religious thinker. To Vinoba Bhave, Gandhi's *satya, sadhana, Bhagawadbhakti* and *tapascharya* were reminiscent of the Vedic rishis of the old. Rajaji found in him clarity of thinking and marvelous grasp of the opponent's case. Rajendra Prasad found in him a personification of the passion for service of the poor. MA Ansari found in him a fellow savant with a scientific approach to the question of health and disease. Sarojini Naidu discovered in him a poet in action. Birla and Jamnalal Bajaj were drawn to him by his shrewdness in practical affairs. Acharya Kripalani loved to follow the rebel in Gandhi.[41]

This was a fine example of the two step flow theory of communication developed by Elihu Katz and Paul Lazarsfeld in their book *Personal Influence* in 1955. The model was based on the earlier research in which they found that information presented on the mass media did not reach and have an impact on the receivers, as previous views of communication seemed to suggest. Specifically, their research indicated that political radio and print messages seemed to have little impact on individuals' voting decisions. After further research they came to the conclusion that 'ideas often *flow* from radio and print *to* opinion leaders and *from them* to less active sections of the population' – in a two step flow.'[42] The leaders who were in Gandhi's close knit extended family were the 'opinion leaders' who spread his ideas in their own 'constituencies'.

The next circle (c) ranged from grassroot officials such as the town clerk to the 'nobility', such as the Viceroy of India or a member of the British Parliament. More often than not they were duty bound to oppose Gandhi, but as individuals were as vulnerable to Gandhi's charms or charisma as were others. Their 'conversion' was usually one of the goals of Gandhi and in this, he, more often than not, succeeded. The outer circle (d), which was wider than these three earlier circles, included those nameless correspondents who wrote letters to Gandhi on personal or public matters. Their letters found place in the 'letters'column of Gandhi's journals. Gandhi sought to impart his ideas and entered into a seemingly never-ending dialogue with them on a footing of equality. These correspondents included admirers, skeptics and even critics of Gandhi. It is instructive to note here that an important factor in the communication process is how the receivers interpret the messages because most of the time 'meanings are in people not in words'.[43] Gandhi saw the need to correct such misinterpretations and opened a permanent column in his journals where he would respond to the letters sent by the common people, officials and even leaders. How far this helped resolve issues have been examined in due course. Still wider was circle (e), comprising the common people for whom Gandhi was the *Daridranarayana*[44] incarnate, whose allegiance was based on emotions rather than rationality, but who were his largest and most volatile constituency. These were the people whom Gandhi met during his tours, whom he described as the 'real India', whose uplift was the most important of his dreams, and with whose plight he sought to identify himself. They were also the foot soldiers of his non-violent army.

The outer-most circle (f) included international admirers, detractors or simply observers of Gandhi who were the messengers of his thoughts in foreign lands. These included heads of states, politicians, public men, intellectuals, artists, journalists and correspondents, who, intrigued by his methods and ideas, wrote to Gandhi. They were sometimes cultivated by Gandhi consciously to publicize his cause throughout the world.

The circles represented in the diagram were not always mutually exclusive. They at times overlapped or converged with each other because for Gandhi no issue was less important as was no person, whatever his social or economic status. Many of such contacts were born through the various ashrams Gandhi had established in India and South Africa during his life-time.

Gandhi complemented and supplemented the above mentioned forms of communication with extensive use of print media. On the basis of the evidence available now one can safely say that using the print media for the dissemination of his ideas was part of a clear strategy with Gandhi.

The dictionary meaning of strategy is 'the art of planning operations in war, especially the movement of armies and navies into favourable positions of fighting; skill in managing an affair'.[45] In other words, a strategy is the art of conducting a campaign and manoeuvring an army involving a long—term plan. Strategy stands for making plans in the light of what the adversary may or may not do. To be effective, strategies and policies must be put into practice by means of plans, increasing in detail until they get to the nuts and bolts of operations. Tactics, which are generally confused with strategy, then are the action plans through which strategies are executed. Effective tactics must support strategies.

Gandhi followed a clear cut strategy because, one, he wrote with a purpose. He was not a journalist in the commonly accepted sense of the term. His life and his writings had a symbiotic relationship with each other. Writing, for him, was not a writer's pursuit for creativity or a role he was duty bound to perform. Neither was writing a proselytizing mission with him. Writing satisfied his need to share his ideas with others, 'a two-way dialogue, between himself and his readers on a joint journey on the path leading to the Truth'.[46] In the July 2, 1925, issue of his journal *Young India* Gandhi wrote:

> I have taken up journalism not for its sake but merely as an aid to what I have conceived to be my mission in life. My mission is to teach by example and present under severe restraint the use of the matchless weapon of satyagraha which is a direct corollary to non-violence....It is a solvent strong enough to melt the stoniest heart. To be true to my faith, I may not write in anger or malice. I may not write merely to excite passion. The reader can have no idea of the restraint I have to exercise from week to week in the choice of the topics and my vocabulary. It is training for me. It enables me to peep into myself and make discoveries of my weaknesses.[47]

The term 'strategy' used in the present context, therefore, refers to the 'purpose' coupled with 'common-sense planning' on the part of Gandhi in his writings. The ensuing discussion, therefore, would focus on the strategy with regard to the use of communication through print media and not the strategy per se employed by Gandhi in his movements.

Predisposed as he was to organized work it can be taken for granted that Gandhi's use of the print media would also be along carefully thought out lines. In this connection Gandhi's frequent reference to 'one step is enough for me' or this belief in the authenticity of the 'small voice' have been trotted by some critics as evidence of the lack of planning in his activities. Gene Sharp's well-known thesis on Gandhi as a political strategist convincingly silences such doubts.[48] Therefore, the present work rests on the premise that Gandhi followed a deliberate strategy in so far as his writings were concerned. One, he envisaged a clear goal in his mind as to the purpose for which he wrote, and, secondly, he made discreet use of print media aware of its quality as a double edged weapon.

Strategy, as referred to earlier, is always with reference to some goal or end in view. Gandhi wanted to bring a change in the thinking of the people. He wanted those people who, under the illusion of power and honour embrace violence and unjust behaviour, to realize the immorality of their actions. He wanted to awaken the sense of pride and self respect in those who, as a result of centuries of oppression, had lost the courage and will to fight injustice. He wanted those who belonged to neither of these two categories to shake off their sense of complacency and work for the regeneration of society and weed out all evil practices that led to fear and inertia.

Gandhi also made discriminate and discreet use of the print media. As retreat is a strategy in war, similarly to publicize or not to publicize an issue is a part of strategy of communication. This restraint aimed at laying the tradition of responsible reporting in India.

Strategy is also an exercise in choosing the right objective from several available goals. The choice of the right goal, right time and right place not only motivate the 'soldiers'; but also contribute to the success of the plan. Finally, a good strategy gives the leader the initiative to dictate terms in any negotiation. It would be worth examining whether Gandhi's communication strategy had the above-mentioned qualities or not.

Gandhi has left behind a vast body of articles and books now compiled in hundred volumes of *The Collected Works of Mahatma Gandhi* (Publications Division, Government of India, New Delhi). It includes a mind-boggling number of letters, drafts, petitions and circulars written by him.

This compilation is a clear testimony to the fact of Gandhi's long journalistic career that spanned nearly half a century. Beginning with his unpublished *London Diary* (written in 1889) his first publications were a series of articles published in *The Vegetarian* (1891-95), a journal of the Vegetarian Society of England. These attempts have been noticed only in retrospect. What established Gandhi as a journalist was his editorship of the weekly *Indian Opinion* (1904) published from South Africa. Similarly, the *Green Pamphlet* on the conditions of Indians in South Africa followed by a *Note* on the same topic (both of which preceded the launching of *Indian Opinion)* were the most widely distributed propaganda material on a matter of public interest at that time.

While the *Indian Opinion* was devoted to the cause of Indians in South Africa, Gandhi also utilized his writing skills to argue against the cult of violence in Indian freedom struggle in the first decade of the twentieth century. He held the western civilization responsible for the spread of violence and wrote a scathing attack on it in a booklet entitled *Hind Swaraj* (1909).

On his return to India in 1915 Gandhi was already a known figure. He had acquired the image of an activist journalist through the columns of *Indian Opinion* and his famous *Green Pamphlet*. Yet on the advice of his political guru, Gopal Krishna Gokhale, the well-known Moderate leader of his times, Gandhi chose to remain away from political activities. The infamous Rowlatt Act passed by the British government in 1919 curbing the freedom of expression, gave birth to the new 'avatar' of journalist Gandhi. In defiance to the Act, Gandhi started an unregistered weekly appropriately named *Satyagraha* (April 7, 1919) as 'a weapon of civil disobedience'.[49] This was followed by his taking over the editorship of *Young India* (English) and *Navajivan* (Gujarati) in the first week of July 1919. At one stage the circulation of the two newspapers reached 40,000, a remarkable achievement in those days. The milder tone of *Indian Opinion* was now replaced by a stronger voice, though without any trace of rancour. So powerful was the impact of his writings that the

British Government was compelled to silence him. He was sentenced to imprisonment in 1922. Emphasizing the importance of *Young India,* Bhabani Bhattacharya writes: 'In point of fact, the first great Gandhian decade in India was, in its broad outlines the *Young India* story'.[50]

With characteristic insight, Gandhi soon realized that though political freedom was in sight India would have to go a long way in getting social and economic freedom. Removal of social and economic evils now became a mission with Gandhi fructifying in the form of journals like *Harijan* (English), *Harijan Sewak* (Hindi) in February 1933 and *Harijanbandhu* (Gujarati) in March 1933.These journals initially avoided discussion on political developments and focused on social evils like untouchability, rural poverty, illiteracy and the like with heavy doses of articles on cottage industries, health, hygiene and cleanliness. These were also the last journals edited by Gandhi.

Besides the above-mentioned journals Gandhi also wrote a number of books. Reference has already been made to *Hind Swaraj* written in 1909. He translated Ruskin's *Unto This Last* into Gujarati and serialized it in *Indian Opinion* under the title *Sarvodaya.* Other original works of Gandhi were *Satyagraha in South Africa* (published in the form of a book in 1928), and his *Autobiography,* appropriately titled *The Story of My Experiments with Truth* (1929). As shall be discussed later, Gandhi chose the timing for the serialization of these two when the national movement in India was losing its hold. *The Story of My Experiments with Truth* proved to be a masterstroke of communication. It was soon translated into various foreign and Indian languages and still continues to change lives. The other books attributed to Gandhi are mostly compilation of his articles on subjects such as *Key to Health, Discourses on the Gita,* and *All Men Are Brothers*

Considering the range and impact of Gandhi's writings spanning nearly fifty years, one is amazed that not a single systematic and comprehensive study on the subject of Gandhi as a communicator has been attempted. The need to correct this lapse, to fill this gap—as it were—led to this study.

Also, on reviewing some literature connected to the subject, it would appear that no scholar has yet dealt specifically and purely with the subject. Thus the present work—which stands on the premise that Gandhi planned all his moves after a good deal of deliberation, and that he found communication to be an important part of his strategy and that he was fully aware of how he could use the print media as a part of his strategy for communication—seems to be an area for fruitful research.

Gandhi's written and spoken words are well documented. Hence, largely, the method of content analysis is followed. The data thus gathered is represented through appropriate graphical representations wherever required. A few interviews of Gandhi's co-workers, contemporary journalists and common people who were participants in his movements are also undertaken to get a first hand view of the period under review. Since the data in question is not available in an organized form, for the purpose of the present work it has been suitably sifted for a meaningful presentation. This is done in the form of item analysis and thematic analysis in terms of the structure of ideas. Also, because the content is addressed to readers/public, spoken or written material in terms of response is studied.

The study though rooted in history is not a historical study. At times it may seem to lean more heavily on political movements and developments. This is because, for Gandhi, politics was a means to the end of achieving *swaraj* in its multidimensional form.[51] Care, however, has been taken to focus mainly on the communication part of these developments. The political developments are discussed only in so far as they provide the backdrop for the communication strategy adopted by Gandhi.

The sequence of discussion is chronological. This sequence seemed more appropriate because throughout his life Gandhi was striving for personal evolution and this was reflected in his writings. Another reason is that Gandhi was always building on his past experiences and referring to them. Hence events and actions can be better understood if they are discussed chronologically.

Data for the book is culled mainly from the hundred volumes of his *Collected Works*. The original writings of Gandhi in form of books are also referred to. Secondary sources, such as his biographies or books on different aspects of his life, activities, and philosophies are consulted for their impact on the original writings of Gandhi

The book apart from the introduction and conclusion is divided into seven chapters. The first chapter deals with the use of print media by Gandhi during his stay in South Africa. This chapter deals with how he made use of pamphlets, circulars, letters to newspapers and finally the journals edited by him and the books written by him for purposes of communication. The second chapter discusses how Gandhi used the experience he gained in South Africa to conduct three local movements in India making a discriminate and discreet use of print media. The third chapter deals with the use of print media by Gandhi to educate Indians on Rowlatt Bills and organizing the Non-Cooperation Movement. The fourth chapter examines the use of print media during the interregnum between the Non-Cooperation Movement and the Civil Disobedience Movement in preparation for the Civil Disobedience Movement. The fifth chapter is devoted to Gandhi's communication strategy during the Salt Satyagraha and the Round Table Conference. The sixth chapter covers the phase of exclusive social journalism in the writing career of Gandhi, which marked the apolitical phase of the Gandhian discourse a phase generally considered less important. This is the lengthiest chapter of the book because it is through social journalism that Gandhi managed to mobilize the masses in India for his political and constructive work.

The seventh and the final chapter is about the different roles Gandhi was called upon to play as a communicator in the last phase of his life. First, he took on the role of an advisor when the Congress Ministries were formed in 1937. Later, he was the organizer of the last of the movements launched by him, namely the Quit India Movement. This chapter also throws light on Gandhi's participation in the negotiations for freedom and his efforts at retaining an undivided India Finally, the most tragic period of Gandhi's life, when he wore himself out in dousing the fires of communal hatred throughout the country, an attempt that culminated in his martyrdom, is analyzed.

Though the present work covers a wide field, it does not claim to be exhaustive. In fact, written words constitute only half of Gandhi's repertoire of communication. One however draws solace in Gandhi's words: 'I flatter myself with the belief that some of my writings will survive me and will be of service to the causes for which they have been written.'[52] This indicates that Gandhi knew that the dialogue he had initiated would not end with his death. The spirit of his words will continue to carry weight. Encouraged by this, with full awareness of the vastness of the topic and the epochal nature of Gandhi's personality, the present venture has been undertaken.

REFERENCES

1. Harold Koontz and Heinz Weihrich, *Essentials of Management* (McGraw-Hill Book Co., Singapore, 1990) p. 365.
2. Indira Gandhi, *Foreword, CWMG,* XC, p. vi.
3. Brent D.Reuben, 'History: the Traditions of Communication Studies', *Communication and Human Behaviour,* (Macmillan Publishing Company, New York, 1984), p. 41.
4. For a detailed discussion on this see Mark Lindley, 'Gandhi's Rhetoric', *Gandhi and the World Today (1998),* (Centre for Gandhian Studies, Kerala, India, 1999), pp. 57-90.
5. Claude E. Shannon and Warren Weaver, *The Mathematical Theory of Communication,* (University of Illinois Press, 1949), p. 3.
6. Emma Tarlo, *Clothes Matter, Dress and Identity in India,* (Viking Penguin India, 1997) p. 73.
7. Rajni Bakshi, *Bapu Kuti,* (Penguin India, 1999) for instance, believes that Gandhi's hut at Sevagram Ashram in Wardha is the temple where those who share Gandhi's dreams and believe that the answers to the world's ills lies with Gandhian values, go.
8. Jawaharlal Nehru, *The Discovery of India,* (Asia Publishing House, New Delhi, 1960), p. 82.
9. Bhikhu Parekh, *Gandhi,* (Oxford University Press, 1997), pp. 8-9.
10. Susanne Hoeber Rudolph and Llyod I. Rudolph, *Gandhi, The Traditional Roots of Charisma,* (Orient Longman, India, 1987).
11. V.V. Giri, 'Enlightened Pathfinder', in S. Radhakrishnan, *Mahatma Gandhi 100 Years,* (Gandhi Peace Foundation, 1968) pp. 93-94.
12. Romain Rolland, *Mahatma Gandhi* (Publications Division, Ministry of Information and Broadcasting, Government of India, New Delhi, 1990) p. 119.
13. Father of Pt. Jawaharlal Nehru, the first Prime Minister of India. Motilal Nehru was a renowned lawyer of his times who gave up his practice to join Gandhi in his struggle against the British in India. He was also the founder of the Swarajist Party and, most importantly, the author of the first blueprint of India's Constitution prepared by Indians, popularly known as the Nehru Committee Report (1928).
14. President of Servants of India Society, a Liberal Member of Executive Council.
15. Founder of Banaras Hindu University.
16. Leader of Arya Samaj who founded the Gurukul Kangri University based on the Vedic system of education.
17. Poet Laureate of India, author of India and Bangladesh's national anthems, winner of Nobel Prize in Literature for his collection of poems, *Gitanjali.* Also the founder of an unconventional university, Shanti Niketan (presently known as Vishwa Bharati).

18. Muhammad Ali and Shaukat Ali, the leaders of the Khilafat Movement in India.
19. Patel successfully led the peasant movement in Bardoli (Gujarat) in 1928, helped in the integration of Princely States in the Indian Union and was the first Home Minister of independent India.
20. Noted industrialist and philanthropist who was considered by Gandhi as his "fifth son."
21. Popularly known as 'Netaji', the leader, was a Congress Party leader from Bengal who broke away from the party on policy matters and formed the Forward Bloc and later organized the Indian National Army to fight the British.
22. Gandhi's chosen heir and the first Prime Minister of independent India.
23. Poetess and Congress leader who led the movement for the capture of Dharasana Salt Works during the Civil Disobedience Movement of 1930.
24. Wife of CR Das, an important Congress leader from Bengal, who coordinated the picketing of liquor shops and foreign goods in Bengal.
25. An ashram associate of Gandhi who faced police lathi charge during the Salt Satyagraha. Gandhi used to have regular correspondence with her on personal and ashram matters.
26. A close confidante of Gandhi in his experiments regarding self–control.
27. Madeleine Slade, the daughter of a British Admiral who had access to the British Viceroys and other officials and at times presented Gandhi's case before them.
28. This Muslim women accompanied Gandhi on his trip to Noakhali and undertook fast unto death to restore communal harmony in 1946.
29. Daughter of M.A. Ansari, a Nationalist Muslim.
30. Daughter of Abbas Tyabji, the brother of Badruddin Tyabji, the first Muslim to become the President of the Congress Party. At her instance, Gandhi introduced recitations from the Qoran in his daily prayers. She was also a strong advocate of Hindustani as a link language in India and favoured Devanagari script for Urdu.
31. A Nationalist Muslim leader who was regularly consulted by Gandhi on the Hindu-Muslim question.
32. A Christian-Sikh scion of the royal family of Kapurthala who had wide political links.
33. Industrialist and philanthropist and later owner of the nationalist paper, *The Hindustan Times.*
34. A Christian priest, popularly known as *deenbandhu,* i.e., friend of the poor, was a common friend of Rabindranath Tagore and Gandhi and a useful link between the British and the Indian leaders.
35. An American friend of Gandhi whom Gandhi consulted on public opinion in America.

36. A British lady appointed by Gandhi in 1931 to act as interpreter of Indian movement to the British public and leaders.
37. Gandhi's associate in South Africa and also his publicist of plight of Indians in South Africa.
38. Leader of the Muslim League credited with the formation of Pakistan.
39. Leader of the Depressed Classes who disputed Gandhi's claim of being the representative of the "untouchables."
40. Jawaharlal Nehru, *The Discovery of India, op. cit.,* pp. 362-3
41. M.M. Verma, *Gandhi's Technique of Mass Mobilization* (R.K. Gupta and Co., New Delhi, 1990) p. 112.
42. Elihu Katz and Paul S Lazarsfeld, *Personal Influence: The Part Played by People in the Flow of Mass Communication* (Free Press, New York, 1956), p. 32.
43. *Ibid.,* pp. 53-54.
44. God appearing in the form of the poor.
45. *Oxford Advanced Learner's Dictionary of Current English* (Oxford University Press, Eighth edition, 1979).
46. D.S. Mehta, *Mass Communication and Journalism in India* (Allied Publishers Private Limited, Bombay, 1979) p. 11.
47. 'My Incapacity', *Young India,* 2-7-1925, *CWMG,* XXVII, p. 322.
48. Gene Sharp, *Gandhi as a Political Strategist* (Porter Sargent Publisher, Inc. Boston, USA, 1979).
49. M. Chalapathi Rau, *The Press in India* (Allied Publishers Private Limited, 1968) p. 72.
50. Bhabani Bhattacharya, *Gandhi, the Writer* (National Book Trust, New Delhi, 1969) p. 76.
51. Gandhi used the term *swaraj* to mean *(a)* establishment of a nonviolent society based on independence from foreign rule, *(b)* participatory government granting full political rights to all, *(c)* economic self-sufficiency ensuring decent standard of living, *(d)* perfect social equality, and *(e)* self-control leading to deliverance from the cycle of births and deaths.
52. *Harijan,* 24-4-39.

1
The South African Years (1893-1914)

> Writing about the impact of the South African experience on Gandhi, Khushwant Singh made this interesting observation: 'It was a metamorphosis from a crawling caterpillar, turning into a chrysalis and emerging as a butterfly – a monarch butterfly with wings made of *khadi*.'
>
> 'Gandhi Forever', *Hindustan Times*, January 29, 2000

Gandhi's public life began when he arrived in South Africa as a twenty-three year old barrister in May 1893. He came here on a one-year assignment to assist an Indian merchant in a civil suit. During this period there were four Colonies in South Africa – the Natal, the Cape, the Transvaal and the Orange Free State. The original discoverers and colonizers of South Africa were the Dutch. Later the British arrived and took over the Cape in 1806 and Natal in 1843. Thus were sown the seeds of friction between the Dutch and the British, leading to the Boer War (1899-1902) later. As a result of the Boer War the whole of South Africa became part of the British Empire. The British had professed that they had fought the War primarily to secure the British and Indian settlers in Dutch territories their legitimate rights – the promise they failed to honour. The Whites (the British and the Dutch living in South Africa) had earlier arranged with the British rulers of India to have Indian labour exported to South Africa under contract. After the period of contract was over such labourers were to be allowed to live under the ordinary law of the land and not be subjected to any kind of legislative or administrative discrimination. Racial prejudice and trade jealousies, however, led to the passage of discriminatory laws. When Gandhi

MAP OF SOUTH AFRICA
(Source: Collected Works of Mahatma Gandhi, Vol. I)

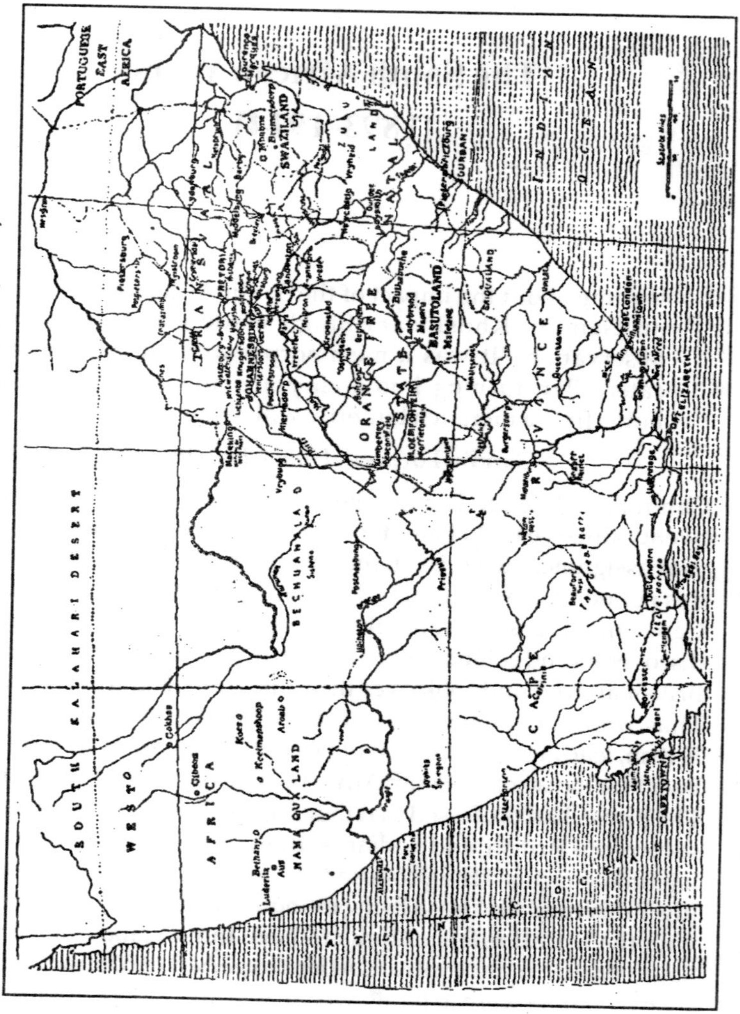

was about to leave South Africa in 1894 after completing his legal assignment, he came across a reference in the local newspapers to a Bill disenfranchising Indians. When Gandhi informed the Indians settled there of the implications of the law they persuaded him to stay on and fight against the South African Government on behalf of the Indian settlers.

As Indians were mostly concentrated in Natal and Transvaal, Gandhi initially addressed their problems in these two Colonies alone. In Natal the main problems they faced and on which Gandhi campaigned were connected with the franchise, immigration, licenses to trade, and tax on indentured labourers who wished to stay on in South Africa after expiration of their indentures. After the Boer War the main thrust of Gandhi's campaigning shifted to Transvaal. The reason for this was that it was expected that after the defeat of the Boers, and the change in the constitutional position, Indians would be treated as equals. But the change of the government did not help matters. A law, by which Indians were confined to separate locations for trade and residence, with exception being made to highly educated Indians who conformed to the European life-style, was enacted. This was just the beginning of the discriminatory policies the government was to launch later. A judgment of the Cape division of the Supreme Court declared that any marriage which was not in accordance with the Christian rites and not recorded by the Registrar was illegal. This made all Hindu, Muslim and Parsi wives nothing but mistresses and rendered their children illegitimate. This forced women to come together and protest for the first time. It was against this background that Gandhi set out to ameliorate the sufferings of his compatriots and provide them a life of dignity.

Probably Gandhi would not have so deeply empathized with the Indian settlers had he not suffered personal humiliation on his arrival in South Africa because of racial discrimination. The 'steel' that had entered his soul on being thrown out of his railway compartment at the Petermaritzburg station, as he recounts in his autobiography, was to be soon wrought into the weapon of Satyagraha, and the issue of individual self-respect broadened into that of the self-respect of the community. Over a period of time Gandhi's satyagraha would extend even to the protection of all living beings. He realized that though he felt his humiliation so acutely, the Indian settlers had got used to it and had learnt to swallow it. They needed to be made conscious of their dignity and rights. He decided to stay on in South Africa and fight for the rights of Indian settlers and educate them about their plight.

A way to do what he had in mind was to form an organisation and make extensive use of the media. Gandhi founded the Natal Indian Congress in 1894 with the intention of organizing the disparate groups of Indians under one banner and thus strengthening them so that their voice had effect on the government. Gandhi supplemented this by maintaining a list of friendly newspapers and individuals and utilized these contacts for distribution of open letters on Indian problems. He also kept in touch with the London-based British Committee on Indian National Congress and contributed reports on the situation in South Africa to its journal *India*. In South Africa he used the White press for ventilating the grievances of Indians.

Gandhi's brush with the South African press was not something new but his use of the press henceforth was deliberate and planned. When Gandhi had just arrived in South Africa in 1893, he had attended the first day in court wearing his turban and on being asked by the judge to remove it, had refused to do so. This was reported in *The Natal Mercury*[1] and another paper on the basis of this report, described him as 'An Unwelcome Visitor'[2] Gandhi gave suitable reply to this through a letter to the editor of the paper. Thereafter, Gandhi became a regular writer to the paper on issues concerning the misrepresentations regarding the Indian community. The paper was prejudiced against the Indian settlers terming them as 'barbaric', recommending their repatriation and disenfranchisement.[3] It is clear, therefore, that Gandhi had already been using the press to express his views on questions that mattered to the Indians. In line with his earlier practice, his strategy on learning about the disenfranchisement of Indians was to use the press to educate Indians on the implications of the Act and to put pressure on the government to reconsider it.

As indicated earlier, the White press in South Africa was in the habit of publishing articles maligning the Indian community and describing India in a state of political infancy. At one time it went to the extent of advocating that Indians did not deserve to get voting rights as they did not have the same in their own country,[4] and that

Indians should not be allowed to vote as they were less intelligent. Earlier such allegations would have gone unanswered but now Gandhi made it a point to rebut every such misinformation by either marshalling facts[5] or gently reminding the paper of its Christian and British traditions.[6]

Not content with writing only responses to articles Gandhi ventured an open letter to members of the Natal Legislature in early December 1894 on the problems of Indians in Natal, highlighting the ignorance in South Africa about India and its people. This letter was printed in the form of a pamphlet and circulated among Europeans on December 19, 1894 along with a covering letter.[7]

The Green Pamphlet

Gandhi' first major attempt at using the print media for mass communication, however, was the publication of the *Green Pamphlet* (so called because its cover was green) in which he described in detail the condition of the Indian settlers in South Africa. Gandhi wrote the piece while he had come home to Rajkot in India on a brief visit in 1896. Ten thousand copies of the pamphlet were published. Its success gave Gandhi confidence in the efficacy and publicity value of the media. Gandhi came to be recognized as an expert on the condition of Indian South Africans and a votary of their rights. Open letters from Gandhi to public men in India followed. India's English press solicited letters and articles from Gandhi on South African affairs. *The Times of India, The Hindu, The Statesman* and *The Englishman* vied with each other in publishing Gandhi. In 1899/1900 *The Times of India*'s weekly edition published a series of articles by Gandhi. Influenced by this, GA Natesan, the editor of *Indian Review*, volunteered to give financial assistance for the upkeep of Indians deported from Transvaal because of the hostile attitude of the Whites there. He also helped get donations from other wealthy Indians for the cause.

Back in South Africa, the *Green Pamphlet* was a subject of publicity, though of a different kind. In India, the pamphlet had turned Gandhi into a hero but in South Africa it had made him a villain in the eyes of the White settlers. On his return to South Africa with his wife and others a White crowd tried to prevent them from setting foot on the South African soil. Gandhi was beaten up and but for the cunning of his friend in the police department, would have lost his life. At the same time there was a strong denunciation of the violence in the White press and Gandhi returned the favour by refusing to book the culprits. The violence against Gandhi was largely because of the way in which the British news agency, the *Reuters* had distorted the contents of the pamphlet thus instigating the Whites of South Africa against Gandhi.[8] On the positive side, such a despatch by *Reuters* and the subsequent reaction of the people, made the international community aware of Gandhi and his activities.

Methods of Political Publicity Adopted by Gandhi Prior to the Publication of Indian Opinion: May 29, 1893 to June 3- 1903

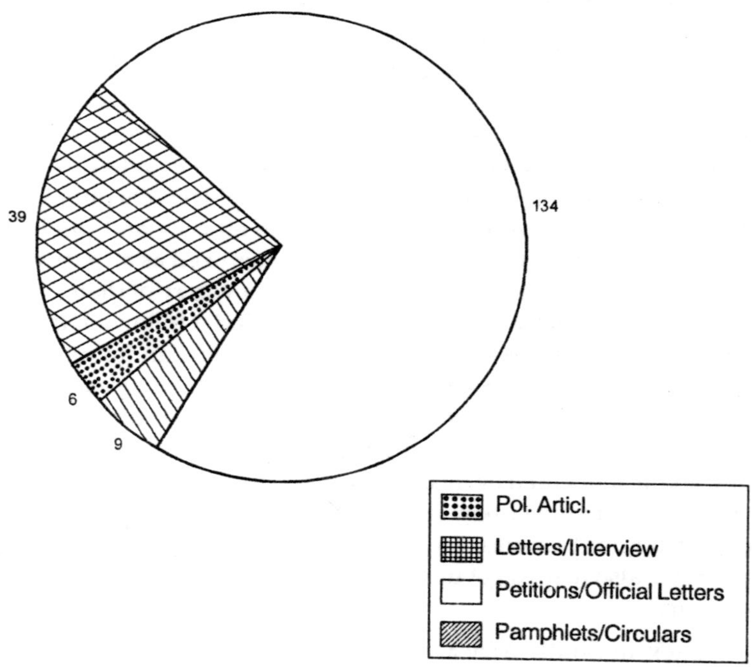

Chart-I

The Indian Opinion (IO)

By 1903 Gandhi had realized that occasional writings and open letters or articles were not enough to meet the grand campaign strategy he had in mind. A newspaper devoted solely to the cause of Indians was the need of the hour.

One such paper, the *Indian Opinion,* was already being published since 1903 and Gandhi took over as its editor in 1904. From now it became the 'views paper' of Gandhi.

The *Indian Opinion* soon became very popular among Indian settlers. According to Gandhi's own estimate the number of Indians who could read the paper was a little more than 20,000 and therefore the circulation of 3,000 copies was quite satisfactory. The paper was so popular among Indians that if it did not reach on time Gandhi would be flooded with complaints. The paper generally reached Johannesburg on Sunday morning. Gandhi tells us: 'I know of many, whose first occupation on receiving the paper would be to read the Gujarati section through from beginning to end. One of the company would read it, and the rest would surround him and listen. Not all who wanted to read the paper could afford to subscribe to it by themselves and some of them therefore club together for the purpose.'[9] It is interesting to imagine today how the unlettered also were reached by Gandhi in this manner. This also explains why Gandhi took every care to be direct and clear in his writings. Since the paper was bilingual (for a brief period, also had a Tamil section) the content of the writings in Gujarati and English were very different. For the English section Gandhi chose subjects he wanted the British rulers to ponder over whereas in Gujarati section, the subject matter concerned advice, education and encouragement to Indians.

Gandhi had adopted a deliberate plan, a carefully thought out strategy, like a general in the army in his battle against the government in South Africa. It was a 'war without violence'[10] in which the morale of the 'soldiers' had to be constantly boosted by right publicity, and the 'weapon' of the 'war' was the journal. Gandhi admits, ' I believe that a struggle which chiefly relies upon internal strength cannot be carried on without a newspaper, but it is also my experience that we could not perhaps have educated the local Indian, nor kept Indians all over the world in touch with the course of events in South Africa in any other way, with the same ease and success as through Indian Opinion, which therefore was certainly a most potent weapon in our struggle'.[11]

The paper reflected the evolution of Gandhi's thought. His early admiration for British sense of justice was soon to give way to the sense of disillusionment and subsequently, to the resolve to fight against the unjust system. The subject matter of the articles was also reflective of the determination of Gandhi to fight to the end.

In the first half of 1903, Gandhi's writings showed his respect and faith in the British Constitution, his appreciation of the privileges of British citizenship and his trust in the Empire as the family of nations. In a very subtle appeal to this sense of justice, Gandhi wrote: 'The European lion bids fair to swallow up the Indian lamb in British South Africa, while the arbiter of the Downing Street is looking on!'[12]

Then, in the second half of the year, when the Immigration Registration Act, Natal was given the royal assent, a deeply disappointed Gandhi wrote an article in the *Indian Opinion*, which, in sum, argued that the new Act was harsher than the older one.[13] The manner in which Gandhi dealt with the issues in his journal shows the precision of a lawyer as well as the sensitive nature of the writer. He pointed out the anomaly in the thinking of the local officials that on the one hand, the Asian labour was clearly needed by the farmers and industrialists, while on the other hand they resented the flooding of South Africa by immigrants. He pointed out how just out of trade jealousies permits were not issued to many Indian traders.[14]

Apart from specific issues of law, Gandhi also took upon himself to fight back against any incident demeaning Indians. Pointlessly pricking the self-respect of Indians was a common occurrence. Gandhi took objection to the comment made by a judge in a court that if Indians took off their boots they could hardly be visible. And what made it even more tasteless was that this comment was made while discussing as to what constitutes respect to the court![15]

Gandhi was tireless in his efforts to point out cases of injustice. He wrote about the unsuitability of the sites chosen for bazaars for Indians, pointing out that objections had been raised by the sanitary officials themselves.[16] Through the columns of his journal Gandhi also made an appeal to the Indian National Congress due to meet in Madras, to consider the plight of South African Indians.[17]

The journal also brought out various facets of Gandhi's personality and his leadership qualities. In March 1904 when plague broke out in the Colonies of South Africa, the columns of the paper (from March 1904 to September 1904) were devoted to educating the people on how to prevent the pestilence from spreading further and on taking care of the sick alone. But Gandhi, much to his dismay, found that the South African Government was using plague as an excuse to heap more indignities on Indians and to impose more and more restrictions on their movement. Gandhi wrote a sharply worded article on this to draw the attention of the Government to this hypocrisy.[18] One such ludicrous restriction was that the non-White cyclist should wear badges to show that they were not Whites![19]

In October 1904 Gandhi became the editor of *Indian Opinion.* The paper was not financially viable and therefore in order to run it Gandhi had to put in all his personal earnings. With the spread of plague in Johannesburg he was more inclined to serve the people in the field and could not devote all his time to the paper. In such a situation AR West, a rich man gave him land to set up his printing press and helped him out financially. Incidentally, during the same time Gandhi met his lifelong friend HSL Polak who was instrumental in bringing about a major change in his life. Polak lent him Ruskin's book *Unto this Last* and the contents of the book deeply impacted Gandhi, leading him to set up the Phoenix Settlement wherein he could put into practice the idea of bread labour described in Ruskin's book. All these developments had far reaching consequences in the philosophical development of Gandhi, which was in turn, reflected in his contributions to the paper he edited. Partly to meet the financial burden of printing the paper, and partly in tune with the new thinking of Gandhi, *Indian Opinion* was reduced to foolscap size so that it could be printed manually. The message therefore that went to the readers was that newspapers should pay for themselves and that even with the minimal resources one can run a paper if one is determined to do so.

During this period (1905-06) Gandhi shifted his attention from Natal to Transvaal. The Indian population of Transvaal was only 11,321 composed of chiefly merchants, as opposed to 299,000 Whites and 945,000 Natives according to the 1904 census.[20] He took up the problem of the Indian community in Transvaal by making representations through the British India Association and highlighting these in the columns of the *Indian Opinion*.

In August 1906 the Transvaal government passed an ordinance making it compulsory for all Indians to register themselves afresh.

Earlier the Indians had refused to do so and, on the assurance of Lord Milner, who was the first Governor of Transvaal and Orange Free Country, had agreed to voluntary registration. The Ordinance was thus a breach of promise on the part of the government. The British Indian Association protested against the ordinance on August 6, 1906. On September 8, Gandhi condemned the ordinance as a 'crime against humanity' and a means devised by the Transvaal government for compelling the Indians to leave Transvaal.[21] Gandhi explained the impact of the Ordinance at a private meeting and asked the people not to re-register. The mass meeting of September was a landmark. Gandhi called on the community to refuse to submit to the ordinance even if it meant going to jail. This speech delivered by Gandhi at the Hamidiya Islamic Society was reproduced in *Indian Opinion* for wider circulation. It was at this meeting that a Muslim member vowed to resist the Ordinance at all cost and a spiritual content of the protest was introduced. In his speech Gandhi had promised: 'If the Government sends us to gaol I shall be the first to court imprisonment. And if any Indian is put to trouble because of his refusal to register afresh in accordance with the Draft Ordinance, I will appear for his case free of charge.'[22] Further in an article entitled 'Some Questions', it was stated that reports of these cases and of others that may be instituted will be cabled to the whole world.[23]

Gandhi's words gave strength to the Indians to fight ahead. It was decided by the Indian community to send to England a delegation headed by Gandhi to represent the case of Indians. Gandhi made full use of the time at his disposal and his status as the representative of his people. Gandhi met and tried to influence every person who could help his case. He is reported to have used 5000 penny stamps while in London, and preparing over 2000 notices for Members of Parliament.[24]

The positive response that he received in London, made the deputation hopeful of success. The delegation had also received during their voyage a cable informing them that the British Government had withheld its sanction to the Ordinance. However, on December 6,1906, when the Transvaal was granted self-government, the new government re-enacted the Ordinance. The Ordinance became a law after receiving Imperial sanction on May 9, 1907. On returning to South Africa, Gandhi reminded the Indians of their earlier resolve. He used his entire intellectual and moral resources to rouse and sustain the spirit of resistance and willingness for any kind of sacrifice. Referring to the Suffragette Movement in England, he exhorted the Indians to salvage their honour in articles with telling titles like, 'When Women Are Manly Will Men Be Effeminate?'[25]

The symbiotic relationship between his life and writings had already become clearer when in the later half of 1905 Gandhi adopted the austere life of the Phoenix Settlement and *brahmacharya* and began writing on self-discipline, sanitation and good citizenship. This was also to prepare himself and the people for Satyagraha against the injustices heaped by the government. Later, he sought to inspire his readers by recounting the lives of great men and women.[26] These assorted group of greats included writers and poets ranging from Gorky to Tolstoy and public figures like Curzon, Lincoln, T. Madhav Rao, Munro and many others. The last in this series, on Tyler, Hampden and Bunyan, ends with the lines, 'A people that has produced such a trinity—why should it not enjoy self-rule? If these men suffered so much hardship, it would not be too much for the Transvaal Indians to go to gaol or to suffer some loss in trade.' This series was followed by the life-sketch of members of the deputation, including that of Mahatma Gandhi, who were to visit England to present the case of Indians. This is an example of Gandhi's perspicacity in planning. The last such word portrait was published in the November of 1906, just when he was in the thick of negotiations with the White authorities for the betterment of South African Indians and–probably knowing which way the talks were going—was preparing the Indians to get ready for the struggle if the negotiations failed.

Another significant fact to be noted is that from 1906 onwards one finds that Gandhi gradually increased the number of articles in Gujarati. From 1906 when he started writing in Gujarati for his paper, out of the total of 1850 articles that he had penned 907 were in Gujarati. Over a period of time, the number of pages devoted to Gujarati articles was increased from 4 to 8 to 10 to 12 and consequently from 12 to 13 to 14 and finally to 16, on public demand. His English articles were written on subjects that he wanted the British to be familiar with.[27] Thus while most of his writings on political subjects was in English (translated into Gujarati at times), his famous speech at the Hamidiya Society calling for Satyagraha was published in Gujarati. Similarly, articles on health and hygiene and the shortcomings of the community were in Gujarat . In 1907 when the Satyagraha was at its peak, 90 per cent of his political writings were in Gujarati. This was a clear strategy adopted by Gandhi.

It is instructive to note that during this time Gandhi chose in the Gujarati columns of *Indian Opinion* to summarize some chapters from Salter's *Ethical Religion*, in a way emphasizing the moral basis of his struggle. He gave signal for the next step in the protest against registration with words backed by action. He took the pledge of passive resistance in a historic letter addressed to *Indian Opinion* entitled 'Mr. Gandhi's Pledge'.[28] Following this, Gandhi made use of the press more intensely than ever before to clarify the Indian viewpoint and to refute hostile and false allegations. He also contemplated action in the form of Satyagraha if his efforts at negotiations failed. As ES Reddy sums up, Gandhi had come to 'recognize that petitions could help only when they had some sanction behind them–either physical force or the immensely superior soul force, Satyagraha.'[29]

Gandhi dwelt at length, especially in the Gujarati articles, with every aspect of the struggle, its causes and consequences, techniques and procedures, and prospects of failure and success. The names of the black sheep—'the piano players'—as they were called for giving the imprint of all their fingers for registration, were published in *Indian Opinion* as much to warn others as to shame the cowardly. The journal also at times proudly displayed the photographs of satyagrahis. In response to a letter from a reader as to what should be done with the old copies of *Indian Opinion*, Gandhi advised the questioner that people should 'maintain a file of issues' or 'post it to a friend in India' because it was the ' easiest and the cheapest way to publicize in India the facts of our struggle here'.[30]

Gandhi supplemented his writings in *Indian Opinion* with personal letters, petitions and letters to the South African press. When some Indians, tired of the stalemate, drafted a surrender proposal, Gandhi conceived and executed the idea of presenting a monster petition signed by over 4500 Indians, showing the power of numbers by sheer number of Indians who opposed the law. His efforts were rewarded when at the end of the year he had the satisfaction of noting that an increasing number of newspapers controlled by Whites published cartoons making fun of Government's impotence.[31]

Gradually, Gandhi was getting convinced that his struggle was universal in nature because it was based on the principle of truth and nonviolence. His self-confidence is reflected in the statement: 'Indians in Transvaal will stagger humanity without shedding a drop of blood' as none less than Leo Tolstoy was impressed by the nonviolent nature of the struggle.[32]

Gandhi made use of his training as a lawyer to carry forward the movement and appeared in defence of passive resisters. He advised his clients to plead not guilty so that courts heard their version of the story. These hearings were later reported in the *Indian Opinion.*[33]

It had become clear to the South African Government by now that Gandhi was the force behind the strength of the Indian community. On December 28, 1907, Gandhi, the source of disaffection, was sentenced to quasi-exile, i.e., sentenced to leave the Colony on the pretext that he had refused to register under the Asiatic Registration Act. Predictably, Gandhi refused to obey the order. This refusal invited a two months imprisonment (starting January 12, 1908). Cartright, a well-known journalist and a sympathizer was sent to meet Gandhi in jail with a draft letter for compromise, which had been approved by General Smuts. Gandhi suggested some changes in the draft so as 'not to shock the Whites.' Off the record, verbal promises were also part of the compromise if the 'Asiatics' identified themselves afresh.

The Indians and the Chinese carried out their part of the agreement, but not the Government. Gandhi must have known that this would happen. He had prepared himself and the community for such an eventuality. He had kept the Indians abreast of every thing in the daily columns of *Indian Opinion*. People had already been warned of the failure of voluntary registration and asked to be ready to burn their certificates. The Asiatics assembled at the mass meetings of August 16 and 23, 1908 to burn their voluntary certificates and thus invalidate themselves. The impressive unanimity during this action showed conclusively that the campaign against the Act was not 'manufactured' as the Government claimed. In fact, Gandhi never allowed Satyagraha to lose touch with reality. It was both an effort to protest and show anomalies of the law—such as the sheer irrelevance of thumb impressions when identification had already been secured from the traders.

Satyagraha received fresh momentum and acceptance when Sorabji, an eminent Parsi from Durban, crossed over from Natal to Transvaal to assert his right of entry as an educated Indian. Arrests of passive resisters that time round were followed by sentences of hard labour. Gandhi was imprisoned twice for crossing into the Transvaal and failing to produce registration certificate which Gandhi had already burnt at the famous bonfire of certificates.

Even in the jail, Gandhi, the reformer, was not inactive. He used the 'opportunity' to highlight through the columns of *Indian Opinion* the hardships faced by prisoners, such as inadequate diet and ill-treatment and protested and petitioned for their rectification. About his own hardships he spoke with humour, free from any bitterness. But the news of his ill-treatment leaked out through HSL Polak and created a stir in the South African press, leading to questions in the British Parliament.

The Government's hope that, with Gandhi behind bars the movement would lose momentum, proved futile. In point of fact, the movement's base broadened. For the first time the Indian women emerged from their seclusion setting up associations in support of passive resistance and later on, some of them even courted arrest. Similarly, the upper class Indians, including several leading merchants, surrendered their stock-in- trade and other assets to their European creditors rather than submit to the humiliation of producing registration certificates in order to obtain trading licenses.

Persistent publicity coupled with disciplined action won over a section of European opinion as well. William Hosken, a member of the Transvaal Assembly from Johannesburg, openly supported the demand of Indians for equal treatment. He had to pay dearly for this. He earned the wrath of General Smuts and lost his seat in the Assembly in the coming elections.[34] A Committee led by Hosken took up the cause of Indians. It made representations at home and wrote letters to the British press. These efforts though never rewarded with concrete results managed to create a mild thaw in a section of the South African press. In May 1909 when Gandhi came out of jail, the Pretoria News pleaded that the Transvaal Government should desist from arresting Gandhi as it would amount to making a man suffer for following his conscience.[35] The first biography of Gandhi, *Gandhi-A Patriot in South Africa,* written by Reverend Joseph J Doke appeared during this period serialized in *The London Indian Chronicle.* In the introduction to the biography Lord Ampthill, a pro-Indian member of the British House of Lords, wrote that the purpose behind the publication was to dispel from the minds of the Whites the notion that Gandhi was 'an ordinary agitator' bent on 'vulgar defiance of law' because 'with a better knowledge of the man must come a better knowledge of the matter'.[36] The author of the biography went at length to describe that Gandhi could be persuaded to allow him to write his biography only when the author assured him that it would help publicize his cause.

After coming out of jail Gandhi would have preferred to continue with the movement, but his co-workers had other plans. They urged him to go to London, where a final shape was being given for a Union of South African Colonies. In London Gandhi held a meeting with Lord Ampthill, the Chairman of the South African British Indian Committee. Gandhi had prepared a statement of demands of the Indian community in South Africa which he held back from publication on the request of Lord Ampthill. He released it only when the negotiations did not make any headway.

When Gandhi came back from London on November 30, 1909, the situation seemed dismal on the political front. The rank and file, taking victory for granted, had relaxed its guard and the Government, knowing the actual state of affairs, was all too ready to act in a repressive manner. Gandhi met this repression with a confidence in soul-force stronger than ever. He strove to disarm opposition from the common White people by removing their groundless fears and putting the Indian demands in their right perspective.[37] Addressing Indians, he sought to keep their will to resist.[38] While urging them to fight for their rights, he was far from reticent in telling them first to set their house in order. In an article entitled 'Indian Traders' who were described as plague by a White daily, Gandhi implored the traders not to smuggle in illegal migrants, and to keep their stores clean and not sleep in the rooms where goods were kept.[39] While refuting a White magistrate's contention in the press that Indians were habitual liars, Gandhi in his article, 'Are Indian Liars?' almost in the same breath, strongly exhorted his countrymen to stick to the truth because 'God will protect those who follow truth'.[40] Similarly, Gandhi lashed out at his people for demanding equality in South Africa while practising untouchability based on caste[41] and religion[42] at home.[43] Gandhi was of the firm belief that if the opponent was to be converted to reason, the wrong he had done should be brought home to him without any trace of ill-will or exaggeration. Through his columns he protested against the ill-treatment of the Indian passive resistors in jail, the discrimination against Indian teachers and pupils in Natal schools,[44] and the disenfranchisement of Coloured people in the South African Union Act.[45]

On June 1, 1910, the Union of South Africa was born, but the sufferings of the Indians did not end. In a 'Letter to the Press' Gandhi reiterated the Indian demand for equal treatment.[46] The Government, however, was unrelenting. New areas of discrimination were discovered and tried against Indians. In a ridiculous move, the Government challenged the right of a minor, the son of a merchant of long standing, to remain in the Union after attaining the age of sixteen. The matter was taken to the courts where it was ultimately decided in favour of the minor. In another instance Gandhi was constrained to charge the Government with 'legalized murder' when a number of South African Indians were refused permission to land, and as a result of the severity of life on the deck, Narayanswamy, one of the deportees, died.

The Union Parliament was to be inaugurated in November 1910 and, in an effort to bring about a settlement for closing the struggle, Gandhi outlined a proposal known as *Proposed New Immigration Bill*. The Government paid no heed to Gandhi's suggestions and on February 25, 1911 the *Immigrants Restriction Bill* was published. This Bill retained most of the features of the earlier laws against which the Indians had been struggling. General Smuts wanted an early passage of the Bill in view of the impending coronation of the king of England and also did not want any agitation. As a result, a mediation known as Provisional Settlement was arrived at. Satyagraha was temporarily suspended. Gandhi was optimistic about the settlement as reflected in his articles, 'At Last',[47] and 'What Has Satyagraha Achieved?'[48] In the latter article Gandhi enumerated twenty-nine achievements of satyagraha.

Towards the end of 1911, the term of the Provisional Settlement expired. A new *Immigrants Restriction Bill* was drafted and shown to

Gandhi. However, when it was published in the *Gazette*, Gandhi discovered some alterations. He found that the clause requiring a declaration on oath from educated Asiatics entering the Orange Free State that they would not farm or trade in the state, was retained. Following an exchange of letters between Gandhi and Smuts some amendments were made and some assurances were given. On June 24, the Parliament was prorogued when the Bill had its second reading, and on July 19, Gandhi was informed that the Provisional Settlement would continue, pending the legislation.

The question of immigration and domicile though seemed to be put at rest, the harassment and persecution of Indians continued unabated. One such attempt to harass the Indians was the introduction of the Gold Law and Townships Act, which were used to destroy the hitherto tacitly accepted practice of equitable ownership and use by Indians of property nominally held by friendly Whites. One by one in the townships, White owners of stands were served notices to evict their Coloured tenants. Traders were refused transfers of trade licenses. Even the Provisional Settlement was violated in spirit. Women and children of domiciled Indians were not allowed to land in South Africa. Gandhi was fully aware of the need to revitalize the struggle. In a piece published under the heading 'Gandhi under Detention', which was signed by Gandhi the following exhortation was made: 'Two things need to be done: must rid the community of its defects which may have brought about the present condition and two, everyone of us must fight against injustices perpetrated by the whites'.[49]

One of the greatest blows to the Indian community came when, in early 1913, the Supreme Court of the Cape Colony declared the marriages solemnized according to Muslim custom did not satisfy the immigration laws. This finally forced Gandhi to take notice of the change in Government's attitude and therefore get ready for a fresh struggle on a larger scale than ever before. In an article captioned, 'To the Readers of Indian Opinion', Gandhi wrote: 'We hope to print, for the most part, writings of two kinds: those which will provide the community with full information, in so far as that is possible, of the hardships we suffer, and we will [also] consider and suggest remedies; secondly, those that deal with an ethic of public conduct or contain, in essence, thoughts of great men on this problem. We hope that *Indian Opinion* will thus become an instrument of education'.[50] And Gandhi honoured his promise to the last word.

Analysis of the Nature and Volume of Articles Written by Gandhi

Gandhi used *Indian Opinion* for a variety of inter-related causes. Diagram on the facing page(Chart-II) would give an idea of the nature and volume of articles written by him between the years 1903 to 1914 i.e., during his stay in South Africa. The maximum number of articles written by Gandhi, were devoted to political issues affecting Indians (1291). In the second place came articles specifically dealing with education of Indians with regard to conducting their affairs in South Africa and guiding them on the conduct of satyagraha as well as giving them small tips on good living (292). Next in decreasing order were articles dealing with personalities such as life sketches of eminent people, obituaries, or pen portraits of people and their achievements (202). At distant fourth were articles dealing with international events or affairs, including political developments in India, characterized in the Pie Chart under the category 'miscellaneous'(158). Articles on health (86) and moral or philosophical issues (40) were very few. This distribution clearly shows that Gandhi was more preoccupied with the political, social and economic rights of Indians than anything else.

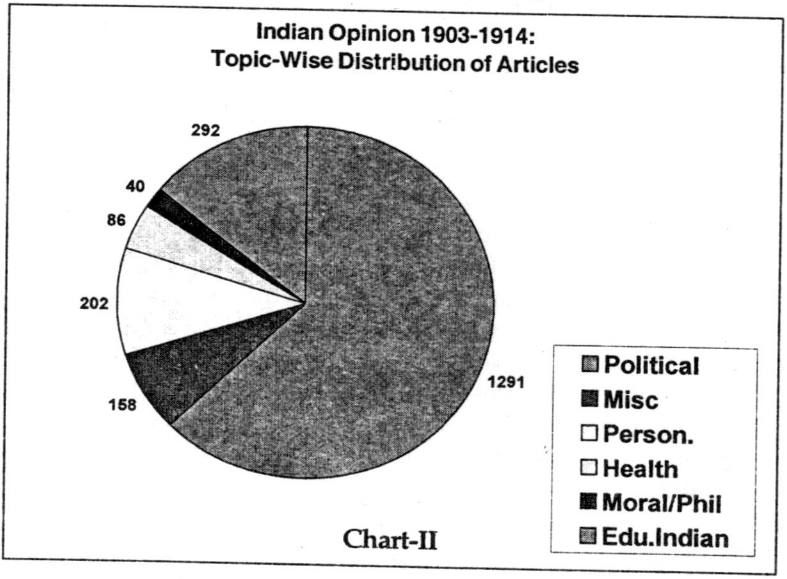

Chart-II

Chart–III which shows the year-wise distribution of articles, clearly indicates that in the period of Satyagraha (1907-08) the articles on political matters reached their peak as did the articles on educating the Indians. In the year 1909 the number of petitions and official letters show a sudden rise because Gandhi was in England writing to and meeting every influential British official. The increase in the number of articles on health in the years 1903 was because of the outbreak of plague and in 1913 because of the serialization of articles under the heading 'General Knowledge on Health'. It would seem that Gandhi could teach today's journalists what, when and how to write good, meaningful articles.

Hind Swaraj

Another important and well-known writing by Gandhi during his South African years was his seminal work entitled *Hind Swaraj* which was mainly addressed to the youth in India who believed that violent means would drive out the British from the Indian soil. Gandhi was very disturbed and concerned about this development and wrote the inspired piece and promptly sought to publicize its contents.

Hind Swaraj was originally written between 13 and 22 November 1909 on board the ship, Kildonan Castle, on Gandhi's return trip from England to South Africa. It was published in two instalments in the Gujarati section of *Indian Opinion* on 11 and 12 December, 1909, respectively. The following year (1910), it was published in a book form from Gandhi's International Printing Press, Phoenix, Natal, South Africa. Later in the same year Gandhi translated it into English and published it in his press on March 20, 1910. The English title of the book was *Indian Home Rule.* On the title page of the English translation Gandhi changed the Gujarati title from *Hind Swarajya* to *Hind Swaraj*. It was through the English text that the book reached the world public and elicited diverse responses.

The urgency with which Gandhi wrote the *Hind Swaraj* shows that it was written with definite purpose in mind. In his book, *Satyagraha in South Africa* Gandhi writes:

> During my stay in England I had occasion to talk to many Indian anarchists. My booklet *Indian Home Rule* ...had its birth from the necessity of having to meet their arguments as well as to solve the difficulties of Indians in South Africa who held similar views.[51]

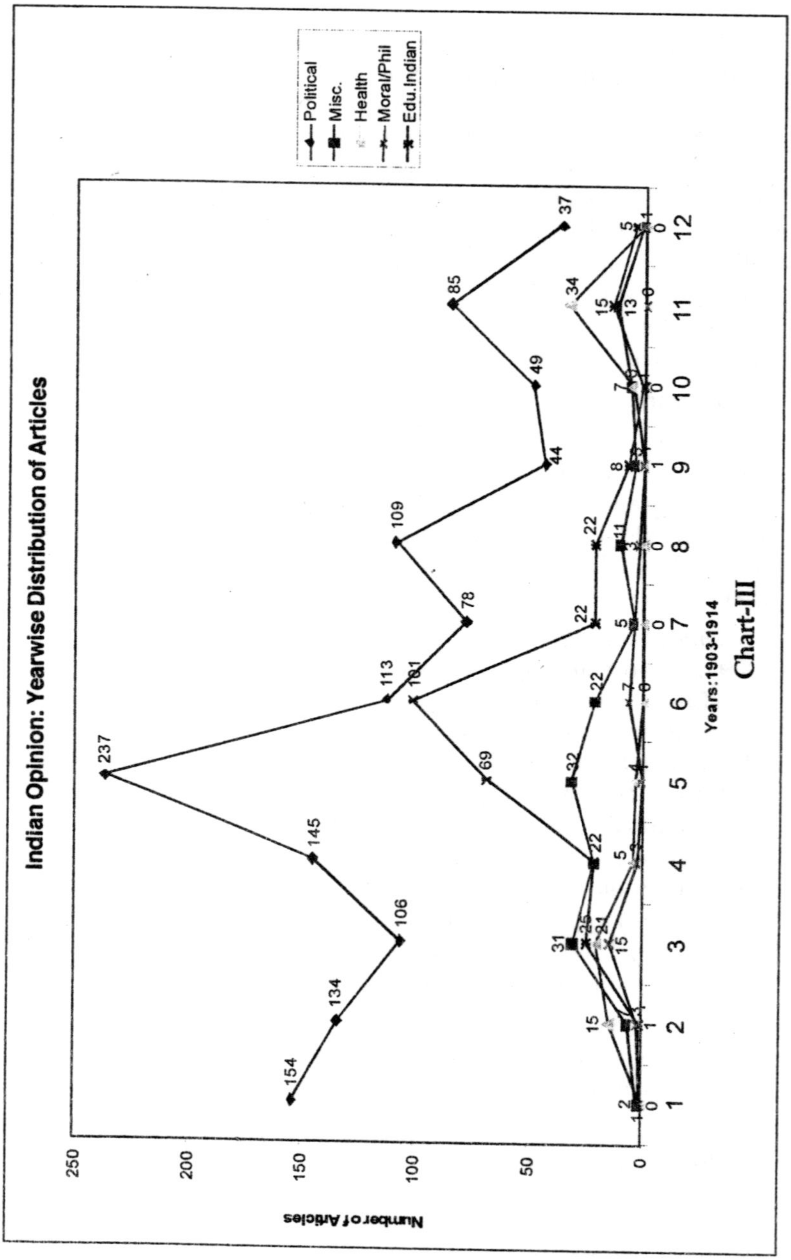
Indian Opinion: Yearwise Distribution of Articles
Political
Misc.
Health
Moral/Phil
Edu.Indian
Number of Articles
Years:1903-1914

Chart-III

Anthony J Parel has very convincingly elaborated upon the reasons that impelled Gandhi to write this pamphlet. According to Parel

> The book is addressed to a mixed audience: the expatriate Indians greatly attracted to terrorism and political violence, the Extremists and Moderates of the Indian National Congress; the Indian nation, and 'the English'. By the Indian nation Gandhi means ordinary Indians, irrespective of their religious, linguistic, regional or caste differences as well as the new emerging middle class, referred to in the text as 'doctors', 'lawyers', and the 'the wealthy'. And by 'the English' he means both the British ruling class living in India and *Britons* living in Great Britain.[52]

As to the urgency of writing it, Gandhi had confided in his friend, Polak, a month in advance about the ideas that had taken 'possession' of him.[53] Certainly Gandhi was going through an inner turmoil but the roots of it were outside. In anticipation to the criticism of his booklet Gandhi had stated with his characteristic candour:

> ...having had the position of a publicist practically forced upon me by circumstances; I felt bound to write for those for whom *Indian Opinion* caters. The choice lay between allowing the readers of *Indian Opinion*, anxious though they were for guidance, to drift away in matter of the insane violence that is now going on in India, or giving them, no matter how humble, a lead that they are asking for. The only way I saw of mitigating violence was the one sketched in the pamphlet.[54]

The politics of expatriate Indians had greatly disturbed Gandhi. These Indians had ideas and were involved in activities totally contrary to the values Gandhi cherished. Most of them believed in violence, narrow nationalism with a marked anti-Muslim tilt and preached the doctrine of hatred towards the British. Holding modern civilization responsible for this state of affairs, he wrote a scathing criticism of its flaws. Years of scholarship and experience were brought to bear upon his writing. It was in fact the quintessence of his life experience, reading and thinking till that point of time.

The other factor that culminated in the book was that when Gandhi visited England in 1909,the public mind, both Indian and

British, was exercised over the assassination of Curzon-Wyllie by Madan Lal Dhingra, an Indian. Dhingra was greatly influenced by the writings of another Indian, VD Savarkar. Subscribing to the same philosophy was Taraknath Das, the editor of *Free Hindusthan,* a penny monthly published from Vancouver, Canada. The Das doctrine was simple: violence was the only means to freedom. On the other hand, around the same time Tolstoy had penned the famous 'Letter to a Hindoo', which argued that nonviolence was the only means available to the morally upright conscience. The letter somehow fell into Gandhi's hands. It was edited and translated in the very week *Hind Swaraj* was written. It all appears to be far more than just a curious coincidence. Rajmohan Gandhi describes how Gandhi was impressed with the message of this letter and got twenty thousand copies of the letter printed in England with money received from the Pranjivan Mehta who had passed on this letter to him.[55]

Another point of view is given by Dennis Dalton who says: 'The aim of *Hind Swaraj* was to confront the anarchists and violence prone Indian nationalists with an alternative to violence, derived from Gandhi's earliest experiments with satyagraha. Equally important is the book's concern with the concept from which it takes its title: this is Gandhi's first extensive statement on swaraj, his idea of freedom'.[56]

Hind Swaraj as a Dialogue

Hind Swaraj is written in the form of a dialogue between a 'reader' and an 'editor'. Parel writes that this form is deliberate because dialogues are inconclusive in nature and, therefore, there is scope for further discussion. Besides, the choice of 'reader' and 'editor' as main protagonists is also significant because they represent two modern participants instead of the traditional, wise 'guru' and the submissive 'shishya'. It permits the reader to be bold in his assertions. According to Gandhi he chose this form because this was the general practice in Gujarati literature. Here Gandhi forgets that this practice was followed in ancient Sanskrit texts as well. Apart from the reasons assigned by Parel and Gandhi himself, Gandhi's legal background may also have influenced him to choose the dialogue medium: two sides presenting their cases, marshalling a wide range of facts and figures in support of their divergent stands.

The Content

Hind Swaraj is divided into twenty chapters with chapter headings not necessarily indicating the contents. Chapter I, 'The Congress and its Officials', contains the now celebrated paragraph on the 'objects of a newspaper'. Besides the chapter acknowledges the contribution of the Moderates in the Congress, who were at that point of time being derided as 'political mendicants' while at the same time pointing out that their time had ended in 1909. In the subsequent chapters Gandhi deals with entire range of India's burning issues: the effects of the Partitition of Bengal and its effect on the Congress; the problem of terrorism; the real meaning of Swaraj; the evil effects of the materialistic civilization; the reasons why India came under British domination; the economic situation in India; the problem of co-existence between Hindus and Muslims; the dysfunctional role of doctors, lawyers and modern machinery as the evil agents of 'soulless' modern civilization ; leaders of Italy; passive resistance and, the value of education. The concluding chapter, virtually reads like an exhortation to Indians to reform themselves. No wonder it was made into a manifesto after the fashion of the *Communist Manifesto* in 1919 (The first Indian edition of *Indian Home Rule* was published in Madras in 1919 and was adopted as the manifesto of the Gandhian revolution and the basis of his *Constructive Programme* later).

On the face of it *Hind Swaraj* seems to be an innocuous document living up to the title *Sermon on the Sea* given to its American edition in 1924. A careful reading, however, shows it to be a work representing the whole gamut of Gandhian values.

After putting the book in black and white, Gandhi went on to communicate to people known to him and elicit their responses on his booklet. On April 4, 1910 he wrote a letter to Leo Tolstoy urging him to 'go through the booklet' and send the 'criticism of his writing'.[57] Tolstoy sent in his reply on May 8, 1910 addressing Gandhi as 'Dear Friend' and further stating: ' I read your book with great interest because I think that the question you treat in it – the passive resistance – is a question of the greatest importance not only for India but for the whole humanity'.[58] Tolstoy's response is important because it was the only positive response Gandhi received then.

One comes across an altogether different response from WJ Wybergh. Wybergh was a theosophist, a member of the Transvaal

Legislature and the Commissioner of Mines for Transvaal. He had also been criticized by Gandhi in *Indian Opinion* for being the first to propose the segregation of Indians. Wybergh did not find the arguments given in booklet 'coherent' and certainly 'at variance with ordinary opinion'. In line with the British Government's policy, Wybergh also believed : 'Granting that you do not intend to be disloyal, yet I am sure that the average plain ignorant man without intellectual subtlety would suppose that you were preaching against British rule in India, for you attack everything which the plain man would identify with this rule'. Refuting Gandhi's criticism of civilization, Wybergh held that civilization was a 'necessary step in the evolution of mankind'. Perhaps as a forerunner of Erikson's line of thinking, Wybergh pointed out, 'What you call 'soul- force' and 'passive resistance' have nothing to do with love or spirituality in them-selves. In advocating these things instead of physical force, you are only transferring the battle and violence from the physical to the mental plane. Your weapon is mental and psychic, not physical, but also not spiritual.' Wybergh also did not agree with Gandhi's views regarding the non-utility of governmental institutions. He believed that: 'To undermine them without being ready to substitute something else a little better but still of the same character is simply to destroy the possibility of all advance'. Saying the last word on the subject, Wybergh opined: 'When all humanity has reached sainthood Governments will become unnecessary, but not till then'.[59]

Hind Swaraj was generally not received well in 1909. Since the dominant mood in India was in favour of the action of those who supported violent means to achieve independence for India, the leaders of the movement rightly perceived it as being addressed to them. As such they were the most vocal in lambasting *Hind Swaraj*. Shyamji Krishnavarma in his journal *The Indian Sociologist* saw in Gandhi's idea an extension of 'extreme Christian theory of suffering'. The irony was that while these people thought it was too soft, the Government of India considered it a revolutionary document preaching sedition. Hence it was banned in March 1910. Gandhi's political 'guru' dismissed it as being written in haste and believed that Gandhi would later modify it. Gokhale was wrong. Gandhi stuck to his views to the end of his life.

After several decades of its publication, *Hind Swaraj* was able to get some good reviews during the life time of its author. A special issue of the *Aryan Path,* exclusively devoted to *Hind Swaraj* came out in September 1938 (Volume IX, No. 9). Gandhi was requested to write a message for it. In reply he wrote, 'after the interval of thirty years through which I have passed, I have seen nothing to make me alter the views expounded in it'. The contributors of the special issue included eminent western thinkers such as Fredrick Soddy, GDH Cole, CD Burns, John Middleton Murray, Hugh I' Anson Fausset, Gerald Heard and Irene Rathbone. Though none of them found themselves totally in agreement with the thesis advanced in *Hind Swaraj,* they nevertheless saw the importance of the great work. Fredrick Soddy, for instance, though disagreeing with Gandhi, suggested that 'anyone who wished to change the world will do well to study' the book. To GDH Cole Gandhi's case against the West looked 'infinitely stronger' than it did in 1908, when the 'ephemeral civilization of the West looked stable under the Western eyes'. CD Burns saw the highest merit of *Hind Swaraj* 'in its emphasis upon moral issues and opposition to the pursuit of private wealth and power'. John Middleton Murry considered *Hind Swaraj* a 'great book', and 'one of the spiritual classics of the world' and compared Gandhi's vision of real swaraj to the Christian vision of the Kingdom of Heaven. Gerald Heard thought *Hind Swaraj* was superior to Rousseau's *Social Contract* and Karl Marx's *Das Capital,* for it did not mark the end of an age but the beginning of a new order. Irene Rathbone found the book 'enormously powerful', the language of which forced her 'by its tremendous honesty to search my own honesty'. She thought that the work was 'simple and logical, economical, condensed, poetic'. Hugh Fausset summed *Hind Swaraj* as a book whose purpose was 'to save India not from Englishmen, but from the modern civilization which was eating into the vitals of the West'. He had enough trust in the indestructible vitality of the human spirit to be sure that it would not allow itself to be lastingly mechanized. The machine was exposing ruthlessly the consequences that may befall upon men and nations who had lost their integrity. *Hind Swaraj* was an attempt at restoring man to his true estate, and was for this reason 'one of the best modern books to that real revolution which must happen to us all, if we were to fulfill the creative purpose of life'.[60]

These observations were, significantly, made during the life time of Gandhi, when the full impact of his writings was still not properly assessed. The debate on the book continues today, with powerful arguments being marshalled forth by both sides.

Reflecting on his long sojourn in South Africa, where he passed a major part of his youth, Gandhi had expressed the hope that though the South African problem had not completely been resolved, over a period of time things will be better for Indians because of the pressure of Indian and British public opinion. He expressed satisfaction over the fact that the 'attitude of South Africa has changed' and that 'is our greatest asset'[61] In this connection it would be worthwhile to quote Joseph J Doke, the first biographer of Gandhi:

> Mr. Gandhi is a dreamer. He dreams of an Indian community in South Africa welded together by common interest and common ideals, educated, moral, worthy of that ancient civilization of which it is heir, remaining essentially Indian, but so acting that South Africa will eventually be proud of its Eastern citizens, and accord them as of right their privileges which every British subject would enjoy.[62]

Gandhi attempted to realize this dream by the effective use of his writings and was fairly hopeful of doing so. He used the print media actively during his stay in South Africa and with good effect. He began by writing letters to the editors of newspapers in South Africa as well as in Indian papers. Later he graduated to printing pamphlets to argue his cause. The most famous of such pamphlets was the *Green Pamphlet*, which even the prestigious news agency, *Reuters*, was obliged to cable to England. By taking up the editorship of *Indian Opinion* in 1904 Gandhi entered the world of journalism. He never compromised with the standards of journalism that he set for himself and his staff during this time. Similarly, his un-ornamental style of writing and his restraint were emulated by the upcoming journalists of his times. *Green Pamphlet* and *Indian Opinion* focussed in the main on South African Indian's cause. *Hind Swaraj* was a veritable philosophic work—timeless and universal—though it dealt at its core with India at the start of the 20th century. It was a critique of civilization and in several respects, the quintessence of Gandhian philosophy. *Thus the three publications set the tone for how Gandhi would be using the print media in the future.*

About the impact of his writings during this period one can safely conclude that he was at least able to make the Indian community aware of its rights in the Colony. Gandhi is accused of not paying much attention to the plight of natives and nationals of other countries who were also important constituents of South Africa and that because of his not taking these people along, his victory proved static and once he left South Africa the movement he launched lost soul and most of its momentum.[63] This accusation is not wholly justified. Gandhi did write about the Chinese, the Arabs and the Malays, though he seldom advocated the rights of the native. He made up for this lapse later in life when he encouraged the natives of South Africa to fight for their rights when a delegation met him in 1928. Almost hundred years later South Africa was able to fight apartheid and wrest control over administration from the Whites. The Indian community empathized with the blacks in their fight against the White dominance. Gandhi's chosen lieutenant Thambi Naidu who passed away in late twenties passed on the mantle to his wife and daughters who were supporters of the Mandelas later[64] Nelson Mandela, the architect of modern South Africa, has acknowledged the contribution of Gandhi to the freedom of South Africa. B.R. Nanda in his book *Gandhi and his Critics,* notes that there is plenty of evidence to show that the emergent nations of Africa in their struggle for freedom received encouragement from the Gandhian methods.[65] Gandhi had foreseen it and written about it in *Young India* (January 12, 1928). The African National Council even endorsed passive action in its constitution.

This account of the South African years would be incomplete without trying to answer a vital question: Why did the South African government never really try to silence Gandhi, stop him from writing? Why—barring the *Hind Swaraj* episode (that too was done by the Bombay administration in India)—never a single attempt to censor his journals? True, he was ever the gentleman in his actions. True, his writings in content or style hardly ever had anything that could raise an establishmentarian eyebrow. But the movement he was leading had every element to make his detractors and the South African regime to see red, make them resort to highhanded methods to deal with him. Yet hardly any attempt was made to curb his freedom of expression. Why?

Probably because Gandhian strivings were essentially centered at a moral plane and a moral equivalent to face Gandhi's challenge was not available to them at that time could have been the reason.

Gandhi used very dignified language to put across his ideas which were in the nature of educating the Indians and others. His attitude as revealed in his writings, never had a tone of confron ation or challenge, rather Gandhi was developing a new technique and style of appealing to the fairness the British are known for.

REFERENCES

1. The incident was reported in the *Natal Mercury*, 26-5-1893 and 27-5-1893.
2. *The Natal Advisor*, 26-5-1893. This information is based on Gandhi's reference to the article in his letter to the paper, *The Collected Works of Mahatma Gandhi*, (*CWMG*) Vol. I., p. 57.
3. *Ibid.*, p. 58.
4. *Natal Mercury*, 7-7-1894, *CWMG*, Vol. I.
5. *The Natal Mercury*, 11-7-1894, *CWMG*, Vol. I, p. 145.
6. *The Times of Natal*, 26-10-1894, *CWMG*, Vol. I, p. 167.
7. 'Open Letter', and 'Letter to Europeans', *CWMG*, I, pp. 170-189.
8. As quoted by Joseph J Doke in *Gandhi-A Patriot in South Africa*, p. 52. Reuters sent the following message which caused all the misunderstanding: 'September 14. A pamphlet published in India declares that the Indians in Natal are robbed and assaulted and treated like beasts, and are unable to obtain redress. *The Times of India* advocates an inquiry into these allegations'.
9. M.K. Gandhi, *Satyagraha in South Africa*, (Navajivan Publishing House, Ahmedabad, India, 1972) p. 132.
10. The expression is borrowed from Krisnalal Sridharani, *War Without Violence*, (Bharatiya Vidya Bhawan, Bombay, 1962) pp. 299.
11. MK Gandhi, *Satyagraha in South Africa*, *op. cit.*, p. 131.
12. *IO*, 18-6-1903, *CWMG*, II, p. 16.
13. *The Immigration Restriction Act, Natal*, *IO*, 18-10-1903, *CWMG*, IV, pp. 1-2.
14. 'Mr. Wyberg and Asiatic Labour', *IO*, 18-10-1903, *CWMG*, IV, pp. 16-17.
15. 'What Constitutes Respect to the Court', *IO*, 29-10-1903, *CWMG*, IV, pp. 25-26.
16. 'The Proposed Site for Asiatic Bazar in Klerksdorp', *IO*, 12-11-1903, *CWMG*, IV, p. 4.
17. 'Appeal to Indian National Congress', *IO*, 26-11-1903, *CWMG*, IV, p. 62
18. 'The Plague Peg', *IO*, 16-7-1904, *CWMG*, IV, p. 224.
19. 'Does a Kaffir Feel', *IO*, 4-2-1905, *CWMG*, IV, p. 347.
20. As reported by James D Hunt, *Gandhi in London*, *op.cit.*, p. 46.
21. 'Criminal', *IO*, 8-9-1906, *CWMG*, V, pp. 411-12.
22. *Speech at Hamidiya Islamic Society*, *IO*, 22-9-1906, *CWMG*, V, p. 418.
23. **IO**, 20-10-1906, (From Gujarati), *CWMG*, V, pp. 473-475.
24. *CWMG*, VI, pp. 106, 160 and 206.
25. *IO*, 23-2-1907 {From Gujarati}, *CWMG*, VI, pp. 335-336.

26. 'Maxim Gorky', 1-7-1905, *CWMG*, V, p.5; 'Joseph Mazzini', 22-7-1905, *CWMG*, V, p. 27; 'Elizabeth Fry', 19-8-1905, *CWMG*, V, p. 45; 'Lord Curzon', 26-8-1905, *CWMG*, V, p. 47; 'Abraham Lincoln', 26-8-1905, *CWMG*, V, p. 50; 'Count Tolstoy', 2-9-1905, *CWMG*, V, p. 56; 'Florence Nightingale', 9-9-1905, *CWMG*, V, p. 61; 'Ishwarchandra Vidyasagar', 16-9-1905, *CWMG*, V, p. 65; 'George Washington', 30-9-1905, *CWMG*, V, p. 84; 'An Indian Poet', 7-10-1905, *CWMG*, V, p. 94; where Gandhi gave the life sketch of the Urdu poet Sayyid Altaf Hasan Hali and asked the readers to read his poetry ; 'Sir Henry Lawrence', 14-10-1905, *CWMG*, V, p. 101; 'Raja Sir T Madhav Rao', 21-10-1905, *CWMG*, V, p. 105; 'How England Won', 28-10-1905, *CWMG*, V, p. 116, which was the biography of Nelson; 'Sir Thomas Munro', 28-10-1905, *CWMG*, V, p. 119; 'Lord Melcalf : Liberator of the Indian Press', 4-11-1905, *CWMG*, V, p. 124; 'Sir T Muttuswami Aiyar, K.C.I.E', 11-11-1905, *CWMG*, V, p. 132; 'Badrauddin Tyabji', 25-11-1905, *CWMG*, V, p. 142; 'Tyler, Hampden and Bunyan', ***IO***, 20-10-1905, *CWMG*, V, p. 477.
27. For example, 'General Smuts Obdurate', *IO*, 20-7-1907, *CWMG*, VII, pp. 109-110.
28. *IO*, 28-4-1907, *CWMG*, VI, p. 448.
29. ES Reddy, *op.cit.*, p. 5.
30. *Johannesburg Letter, IO*, 21-9-1907, *CWMG*, VII, p. 246.
31. *Johannesburg Letter, IO*, 21-12-1907, *CWMG*, VII, p. 445.
32. 'Staggering Humanity', ***IO***, 27-7-1907, *CWMG*, VII, p. 118.
33. 'Trial of PK Naidoo and Others', ***IO***, 4-1-1908, *CWMG*, VII, p. 467.
34. Based on the account given in Richard Dawe, *Cornish Pioneers in South Africa*,Cornish Hillside Publications, ISBN 1-900147-10-6, pp. 128-47.
35. *Preface*, *CWMG*, IX, p. vi.
36. Joseph J Doke, *Gandhi-A Patriot in South Africa*, Publications Division, Government of India, New Delhi, p. 2.
37. *Speech at Farewell Meeting (London)*, *IO*, 11-12-1909, *CWMG*, X, pp. 539-543.
38. 'Last Note on Deputation', *IO*, 18-12-1909, ***CWMG***, X, p. 73.
39. *IO*, 5-2-1910, *CWMG*, X, p. 146.
40. *IO*, 5-2-1910, *CWMG*, X, pp. 147-8.
41. 'As One Sows One Reaps', *IO*, 23-4-1910, *CWMG*, X, pp. 228-9.
42. 'Hindus and Muslims', *IO*, 21-5-1910, [From Gujarati] *CWMG*, X, p. 256.
43. 'Calcutta Riot', *IO*, 17-12-1910, [From Gujarati] *CWMG*, X, pp. 387-88.
44. 'Education in Natal', *IO*, 26-2-1910, [From Gujarati] *CWMG*, X, p. 165.
45. 'Colour Prejudice', *IO*, 2-7-1910, [From Gujarati] *CWMG*, X, pp. 284-5.
46. *IO*, 11-6-1910, *CWMG*, X, p. 263.
47. *IO*, 27-5-1911, *CWMG*, XI, pp. 92-93.
48. *IO*, 3-6-1911, *CWMG*, XII, pp. 98-104.
49. *IO*, 23-12-1912, *CWMG*, XII, pp. 357-360.

50. ***IO,*** 4-1-1913, ***CWMG,*** XII, pp. 422-423.
51. MK Gandhi,*Satyagraha in South Africa, op.cit.,* p. 211.
52. Anthony Parel, *Hind Swaraj and other Writings* (Cambridge University Press, 1997) Introduction, p. xiv.
53. In a letter, *CWMG,* IX, pp. 478-81.
54. *Gandhi's reply to Wybergh,CWMG,* X, p. 296.
55. Rajmohan Gandhi, *Mohandas,* Penguin Viking, 2006, p. 151.
56. Dennis Dalton, *Gandhi's Power, op.cit.,* pp. 16-17.
57. *CWMG,* X, p. 210.
58. *CWMG,* X, p. 505.
59. *CWMG,* X, p. 507.
60. *CWMG,* LXVII, pp. 169-70.
61. *Speech at London Reception, IO,*1 3-91914, *CWMG,* XII, p. 525.
62. Joseph J Doke, *op.cit.,* p. 80.
63. Dennis Dalton, *op.cit.,* p 16.
64. Champa Limaye, 'he Birth of a Movement' *The Hindu,* 3-10-1999, Sunday, IV and 10-10-1999.
65. BR Nanda, *Gandhi and his Critics, op.cit.,* pp. 132-34, Gandhi had foreseen it and written about it in *Young India.*

2

A Discreet Pen

Case Studies of Champaran, Ahmedabad and Khera Satyagrahas

Gandhi's satyagraha fame preceded his return to India in 1915. He found he was already well known because of the success of his movement in South Africa. But on the advice of his political *guru,* Gopal Krishna Gokhale, he abstained from any political activity for the next three years. After all, he had been away for nearly a quarter of a century (three years in England and twenty-one in South Africa). So he spent the time to reacquaint and fully familiarize himself with the conditions then prevailing in India. Sensitive and perceptive, as he was, Gandhi learned fast. He travelled extensively throughout the length and breadth of India and closely observed the life of the common Indian. He felt drawn to the miserable plight of his fellow country-men. The reformer in him could easily identify areas of concern and the practical planner in him wasted no time in preparing an agenda for his future course of action.

Gandhi led three important local movements prior to the much publicized Non-Cooperation Movement of 1919. Two of these were concerned with peasants and one with mill workers. The first was the peasant movement related to the indigo planters in Champaran, Bihar the eastern province of India. In Champaran, Gandhi did not make use of the print media at all, but this movement is important as it assured Gandhi that he could use his methods even in Indian situations and in a wide variety of conditions with equal effect. In the mill-workers movement Gandhi depended more on leaflets as he needed to communicate mainly with the workers and mill-owners rather than public at large. The idea was not to publicize the problem but to help resolve it by educating the disputing parties. In the case of the Kheda satyagraha (of peasants) one of the parties was the administration. Hence Gandhi took the help of friendly dailies to put forward his views and show how unjust the administration was.

Champaran Satyagraha, 1917

As said earlier, Champaran provided Gandhi an opportunity to apply his method of Satyagraha to the Indian situation, although on a micro scale. Champaran is a district in the Tirhut division of North Bihar. It had been a scene of agrarian discontent for some time. The history of this discontent lay in certain policies of the colonial government in recent past. European planters had established indigo farms and factories in Champaran at the beginning of the nineteenth century. In 1916-17 a large part of Champaran was held by three proprietors, the Bettiah, Ramnagar and Madhuban estates. The villages falling under these estates were not managed by the landlords but were leased out to *thekedars* (temporary tenure holders), of whom the most influential group was that of the European indigo planters. The main issue of contention was the system of indirect cultivation. Peasants got on lease land from planters, binding themselves to grow indigo each year on specified land, in return for an advance payment at the beginning of the cultivation season. Further, a system called *tinkathia* was in vogue by which a tenant had to cultivate indigo on three-twentieths of his holdings, which usually was the best portion of his land. In addition, the planters forced the cultivators to sell their crops at a fixed and unprofitable price. At the time Gandhi's attention was drawn to this problem, the demand for indigo in the world market was declining due to the production of synthetic indigo in Germany. The planters tried to cut their losses by offering to release the cultivators form the indigo contract if the latter paid compensation or damages. Apart from this, the planters heavily inflated the rents and imposed many illegal levies on the peasants. As a result, poverty and shortage of food touched near famine conditions in the region.

Initially Gandhi showed no interest in the case of indigo cultivators when the issue was raised at the Lucknow session of the Congress in 1916.[1] An educated resident of the area persevered and finally managed to persuade Gandhi to come to Champaran for an on the spot assessment of the situation. Had it not been for him, Gandhi would have never gone to Champaran. After interacting with the peasants Gandhi realized that they were indeed the aggrieved party and sent communications to the Government to set things right. Knowing his reputation and smelling trouble the district administration ordered him to leave Champaran immediately. On his non-compliance, it was forced to commit the blunder of arresting Gandhi and presenting him in the district court. The judge found him guilty of disobeying the order to leave Champaran and asked him to comply immediately or pay a fine. Gandhi refused to do either. Making a statement in the court on April 18, 1917, Gandhi defined for the first time in India the moral basis of disobedience to the authority. He agreed to: 'submit without protest to the penalty of disobedience...not for want of respect for lawful authority, but in obedience to the higher law of being...the voice of conscience.'[2] Realizing its mistake, the Bihar Government ordered the Commissioner and District Magistrate to abandon the proceedings. Gandhi was set free to carry on his investigations. Thus in Champaran Gandhi achieved total success. His right to stay and investigate was vindicated and in due course, the peasants' grievances were fully redressed. The Government appointed Champaran Agrarian Committee with Gandhi as one of its members. The Committee unanimously recommended the abolition of *tinkathia* system and many illegal exactions. The enhanced rents were reduced. The Committee recommended 25 per cent refund of illegal recoveries. These recommendations were later included in the Champaran Agrarian Act of 1917.

In Champaran the chief supporters of Gandhi came from the educated middle class. Dr. Rajendra Prasad, Gorakh Prasad, and JB Kriplani worked closely with him. Local traders and village *mukhtars* (attorneys) also helped him. But it was peasantry that gave him the real mass support.

Champaran proved to be a landmark in demonstrating to the skeptics the efficacy of the weapon of Satyagraha. However, the power of this new weapon was to be tested fully before Gandhi could present it as an alternative to violence on a national scale. Two such opportunities presented themselves to Gandhi in form of Ahmedabad mill workers strike of February –March and the Kheda satyagraha of March-April 1918.

Gandhi had made little use of print media in Champaran, though some newspapers did report his activities,[3] especially when he defied the entry ban. Gandhi issued only one press statement published by *The Leader* on 23.4.1917.

Ahmedabad Mill Workers Strike (February to March 1918)

Gandhi got involved in the Ahmedabad mill workers strike under very curious circumstances. Anasuyabehn, who approached Gandhi on behalf of the workers, was the sister of his friend, Ambalal Sarabhai, the mill owner.

Ahmedabad was the leading industrial town of Gujarat. The mills depended wholly on the workforce which had to be given incentives from time to time so that they do not leave when circumstances were bad. Such situation occurred when plague spread in the city. In order to dissuade the workers from leaving the town, the mill owners decided to pay 'plague-bonus' which was sometimes as high as 75 per cent of the normal wages. After the epidemic was over, the mill owners decided to discontinue the bonus. But the workers opposed the move, claiming it was compensating the War-time rise in the cost of living. The mill owners were prepared to give 20 per cent increase but the workers were demanding 50 per cent. Both the workers and the mill owners agreed to refer the issue to a board of arbitration consisting of three representatives of the employers and three of the workers with the British Collector as the chairman. Gandhi appeared on behalf of the workers. Gandhi's presence made the mill owners decide to withdraw from the board. They were of the opinion that since Gandhi had no real authority or mandate from the workers, there was no guarantee that the workers would accept the arbitration award. They declared the lockout of the mills from February 22, 1918.

After studying the situation in detail Gandhi came to the conclusion that the workers' legitimate demand should be a 35 per cent increase. He urged the workers not to join work unless the mill owners agreed to a 35 per cent increase.

In this strike Gandhi introduced the system of leaflets to communicate with the workers, apart from having direct meetings with them. It was decided by Gandhi, Anasuyabehn and others to issue instructive leaflets everyday with a view to 'fixing firmly in the mind of the workers the principles and significance of the struggle, and supply them with simple but elevating literature which would conduce to their mental and intellectual progress'. The leaflets were issued in the name of Anasuyabehn but as stated by Mahadev Desai in *Ek Dharmayudha* (of which *A Righteous Struggle* was the English edition) they were in fact written by Gandhi.[4] These leaflets were read out at public meetings in the evenings. Seventeen such leaflets were issued.

A close reading of these leaflets reveals the stark difference between the trade union strikes of those days and today. Gandhi perhaps did not like to exploit the situation against the owners and close all doors of compromise. Therefore, reports of the speeches were deliberately withheld from the newspapers.

In *Leaflet No.1* the background of the strike was described. Under the heading, 'Worker's Pledge' two resolutions were listed: one said that the workers would not resume work until a 35 per cent increase on July wages was secured. The second resolution forbade the workers from indulging in any kind of violence or destructive activity.[5] The same evening Gandhi addressed the workers to assess their reaction to the content of the leaflet. *Leaflet No.2* considered what the workers should do to fulfill the pledge. Gandhi advised that they should be truthful, possess courage, have a sense of justice, should not bear any grudge against their employers, should be ready for suffering and finally, have firm faith in God.[6] Gandhi also addressed the workers the same day and warned the workers against following any advice, even though from a friend, which asked them to go back on their pledge.[7] Issued on February 28, 1918, *Leaflet No.3* discussed how the workers could keep themselves occupied during the lockout. Instead of wasting their time in gambling, gossiping or lazing around, they should take up the work of cleaning their surroundings. The literate among them should spend time in updating their knowledge. Those who knew any other skill should seek work for themselves or approach Gandhi and his associates for help. Gandhi also emphasized that no work should be considered too low by them.[8] In *Leaflet No.4* Gandhi sought to explain to the workers how he and his associates proposed to help the workers. At the outset Gandhi made it clear to the workers that they should not expect any help from the advisors Committee if they violated the principles of truth and non-violence. The Committee could help their cause by entreating to the employers to accept their demands and would also try to win public sympathy in case the employers did not oblige. The total involvement of the Committee could be seen from the statement that the Committee had resolved to enjoy food and good clothing only after ensuring that the workers could afford to do the same.[9] Meanwhile Gandhi wrote a letter to Ambalal Sarabhai imploring him to reconsider his decision in view of the miserable plight of workers. The Gandhian touch was very much evident in the closing sentence of the letter, 'Will you dine with me?'[10] In *Leaflet No.5* Gandhi dwelt on the theme of mutual benefit: if 'workers get an increase, they will be benefited and the employers will have earned credit'.[11]

Leaflet No.6 is different from the earlier leaflets in the sense that it aimed at educating not only the workers but also the employers. Gandhi argued that justice had to be inspired by fellow feeling and compassion: this was the form of justice followed by Indians throughout the ages. The type of justice generally prevalent in the West was the opposite of this, he said, adding that the employers seemed to be under the sway of the Western belief. Gandhi went on to appeal to the religious sentiments of the employers: 'We had confidently hoped that the Jain and the *Vaishnava* employers in the capital city of this worthy land of Gujarat would never consider it a victory to beat down the workers or deliberately to give them less than their due.' This sentence was followed by a mild warning on the consequences of not heeding to the workers' demands: 'At any rate we do not want to teach to the workers what they do in the West these days'.[12] *Leaflet No. 7* dealt with the virtues of *Satyagraha* as different from ordinary strike, citing examples from South Africa.[13] *Leaflet No.8* and *9* further dwelt on the topic of Satyagraha with Gandhi quoting examples ranging from the supreme sacrifices of Imam Hussein and Prahlad to the sacrifices by ordinary Indians in South Africa, regardless of their religion, caste, sex or age.[14]

Gandhi was a practical idealist. On examining the condition of workers he realized that it was not just the quality of life that was wanting, but also the style of living that was at fault. In *Leaflet No.10* he therefore concedes, 'Even if wages were to be doubled, in all likelihood abject poverty would remain unless other measures were also adopted.' To his dismay he had discovered that when short of money the workers borrowed money at a very high rate of interest. On the authority of the holy Koran and the Hindu scriptures he pointed out the ruinous effect of such a practice.[15] In *Leaflet No.11* Gandhi warned workers against falling prey to rumours. He also exhorted every individual worker to have faith in himself and his strengths because 'his hands and feet, the energy that enables him to work, constitute this inexhaustible capital of his and the wages constitute his dividends.'[16]

Around that time Gandhi had started receiving feelers from the mill-owners to persuade the workers to call off the strike by agreeing to the employers' proposal of only 15 to 20 per cent increase in their wages. Gandhi referred to this in *Leaflet No. 12* the day the lockout had been lifted (March 12, 1918). He asked the workers not to join work till their pledge of 35 per cent increase was met.[17] In *Leaflet No. 13* on the one hand he asked the workers to stick to their pledge and on the other not to use coercion against those who wished to join work.[18]

The prolonged strike was hurting the workers more and more. Their patience started to wane. Resentful murmurings that while Gandhi and Anusuyabehn were enjoying sumptuous meals at the Sarabhai residence, the workers were starving, were heard. When Gandhi decided to go on fast to show solidarity with the workers on March 15, 1918 [19] the workers felt that Gandhi had undertaken the fast in view of the criticism by a section of workers. They felt guilty. Gandhi had to explain to them that he had resorted to the fast to show to workers the value of keeping a pledge. *Leaflet No.15* further dealt with the issue of the fast. It stated that the fast was not intended to influence the employers because even if fifty persons were to fast on the employers' premises how the employers, for that reason could, give in to the workers' demand if it were unjustified. The fast was undertaken because Gandhi saw that the oath was losing its grip on the workers. He felt his fast could show how much he himself valued a pledge. Moreover, when the workers had talked of starvation Gandhi had asked them to rather starve than break their oath. He felt that it was in the fitness of things that action proved his words that he was prepared to die fasting.[20] This leaflet was followed by another issued by Shankarlal Parikh. The last leaflet, *Leaflet No.17* gave the details of the agreement and considered the settlement as a victory for both sides.[21]

Thus the strike which had continued for two months came to an end. Gandhi had used the final weapon in his moral armoury—fast—successfully. Ambalal gave in but Gandhi salvaged the former's prestige by scaling down his earlier demand. In this way the strike ended in a spirit of compromise, which was the hallmark of all the Satyagrahas resorted to by Gandhi. The settlement laid down that the workers on their first day would receive the pledged 35 per cent raise, on the second day 20 per cent (offered by the mill owners) and from third day until the day of the award by an arbitrator, they would split the difference and receive a 27.5 per cent increase. It so transpired that finally the arbitrator's award went in favour of the workers and 35 per cent raise was given to them.

Importance of Written Communication

Gandhi had decided to issue leaflets within a week of the strike. If Gandhi was to address the workers every evening, what was the necessity of issuing leaflets? The leaflets were issued in the name of Anusuyabehn. Why did Gandhi not sign them though on the authority of Mahadev Desai one knows today that he had authored them? A close examination reveals that the answer to both the questions raised above, lies in the fact that there was a definite, deliberate design behind the whole exercise. Gandhi knew well that anything put in black and white was more definitive in nature. Besides the words could be carefully chosen, opinions of others sought and if needed, suitable amendments to the text could be made. This is what was done. Moreover, a speech is confined only to the listeners. There was every danger of a speech being deliberately or innocently distorted while being reported. Also, printed matter could be widely disseminated. Even those who could not attend the meetings could get the message without the risk of distortion Another advantage was that printed matter could be gone through over and over again and thus digested and understood correctly. Besides, the other party, in this case the mill owners, could easily have access to what was going on in the workers' camp. Thus the printing of leaflets made the whole exercise very transparent. To put it succinctly, the leaflet served four purposes of communication admirably—wider spread of message; clarity and precision of the message for the reader; avoiding by word of mouth distortions and, of course, transparency.

As to Gandhi not signing the leaflets, the reason, perhaps was based on discretion and propriety. As far as the workers were concerned he was an outsider, there on the invitation of Anusuyabehn. Equally important was the fact that he had been asked by her to mediate between the workers represented by her and the mill owners represented by Ambalal Sarabhai, her brother. Gandhi, therefore, could not speak on behalf of only one party.

The content and tenor of the leaflets is another area worth commending. The issues involved in the strike were spelled out in the clearest of terms. There was no room for any doubt or misrepresentation. The do's and don'ts were clearly defined. The guiding spirit was nonviolence, both in words and action. The morale of the workers was held high by examples of real-life successes. Religion was used for uplifting the spirit and for reminding people of their duties, specifically, those of mill owners. Gandhi resorted to fasting but made it clear that his action was neither a pressure-tactic against the mill owners nor the result of the criticism by workers. It was for a higher cause. Finally, the end of the strike came about in the spirit of compromise and workers were encouraged to improve their lifestyle. Leaflets were used in the same way in which Gandhi had used his journal *Indian Opinion* in South Africa, though on a smaller scale. The following year, Gandhi used similar strategy during the Non-Cooperation Movement against the British Government involving the whole of India where leaflets would not have sufficed. He, therefore, used his journal and friendly dailies to publicize his cause and guide the course of the Movement.

Kheda Satyagraha (March-April 1918)

While Gandhi was still in the thick of Ahmedabad workers strike, he received reports of the plight of the peasants in the Kheda district of Gujarat who were ordered to pay their yearly revenue in spite of the failure of their crops. In 1917 the *kharif* (winter) crop was considerably damaged due to excessive rains. This coincided with the increase in the price of kerosene, iron, cloth and salt. This catapulted the cost of living for the peasantry and they demanded the remission of land revenue. The 'revenue code' provided for total remission if the crops were less than twenty percent of the normal production. Two Bombay-based barristers, VJ Patel and GK Parakh made enquiries and reached the conclusion that a major portion of crop had been damaged. But the government did not agree with their findings.

After another enquiry, the Collector of Kheda decided that there was no justification for the remission of land revenue. The official contention was that the agitation was not a spontaneous expression of the peasant discontent but was started by outsiders or the members of the Home League and Gujarat Sabha, of which Gandhi was the president at that time. One of the reasons for the official stand was the mistaken belief that a purely economic issue was being used as an opportunity for a political agitation to undermine the authority of the Government. The truth was that the initiative for the agitation came neither from Gandhi nor from the other Ahmedabad politicians; it was raised by local village leaders like Mohanlal Pandya of Kapadvanj *taluk* in Kheda.

Gandhi maintained that the officials had over-valued the crops and the cultivators were entitled to a suspension of revenue as a legal right and not as a concession by grace. Earlier on his arrival at Nadiad on February 16, Gandhi and his fellow workers had formed several groups, to investigate crop conditions in the villages. In a week's time reports from 425 out of 600 villages had been received; Gandhi had personally investigated in 30 villages. Thereafter he wrote a letter to the District Collector, Kheda to postpone the collection of land revenue. Gandhi then tried for a settlement through negotiation by asking the Commission, Northern Division, to announce that the collections of the second installment of the land assessment be postponed failing which he said he would be obliged to launch satyagraha. The Governor's reply was in the negative. The Kheda satyagraha was launched on March 22, 1918. Gandhi addressed a gathering of about 5000 people at Nadiad and gave them the details of the situation in Kheda. He apprised the people that the Government could penalize them if they did not pay their dues but asked them not to be afraid. They, he said, should take a pledge not to pay the land revenue that year. The pledge was put in writing and the people signed it (the pledge was later published in *Young India* on 12.6.1918). It read as follows:

> Our village has had crops under four annas. We therefore requested the Government to postpone collection the next year, but they did not do so. We the undersigned therefore solemnly declare that we shall not pay the assessment for the year whether it be whole or in part; we shall leave it to the Government to take any legal steps they choose to enforce recovery of the same and we shall undergo all the suffering that this may involve. We should also allow our lands to be confiscated should they do so. But we shall not by voluntary

> payment allow ourselves be regarded as liars and thus lose our self-respect. If the Government shall graciously postpone for all the remaining villages collection of the balance of the revenue, we, who can afford it, would be prepared to pay the revenue, whether in full or in part. The reason why the well-to–do amongst us would not pay is that, if they do, the needy ones would, out of fright, sell their chattels or incur debts and pay the revenue and thus suffer. We believe that it is the duty of the well-to-do to protect the needy against such a plight.[22]

The pledge drafted by Gandhi was a masterstroke of communication. The very use of the word 'pledge' had religious and spiritual connotation. The simple village folk valued this. The firmness of the peasants' resolve was very clear from the tone of the pledge. Yet scope for compromise was not ruled out. It was clear that the well-to-do were in a position to pay the revenue but they were making a common cause with their poor brethren and also making it clear to the Government that its order was in violation of its own declared 'revenue code' and hence unjust. A Satyagraha against injustice was the right of the people, the peasants in this case.

Gandhi's thorough going strategy was also in evidence in this case. He issued circulars asking farmers to communicate to him details of official coercive measures, if any. These circulars were first posted and then published in local dailies. The cause of the farmers was not a local issue. It acquired national importance when on March 28, 1918 Gandhi issued a statement to the press on the Kheda situation. *The Hindu,* from down south published it on April 1, 1918. In the press release Gandhi also invited the press and the public to come to the assistance of the peasants not only in terms of money but 'as the voice of a strong, unanimous and emphatic public opinion'.[23]

It is important to note that Gandhi himself gave out statements to the press for publication whereas in the Ahmedabad strike even the copies of his speeches which were addressed to the workers were not released to the press. In fact the press was discouraged from printing it. This was so because Gandhi treated the Ahmedabad strike as an internal problem between the mill-owners and the workers. It was an in-house dispute that neither needed nor desired publicity. The Kheda satyagraha was a fight for justice against oppressive administration. Hence it had to be highlighted to the fullest extent. Who else could have done the job but the press? Another problem was that of logistics. Unlike the mill-workers, the peasants could not be collected at one place. Gandhi, therefore, travelled to the affected villages and addressed the people, dispelling their doubts and fears and boosting their morale. Through his speeches Gandhi told the villagers the exploits or drawbacks of their fellow peasants, as the case may be, in other villages. The speeches to the peasants were not withheld from the Press as was the case in mill-workers strike. Dailies like *The Bombay Chronicle* and *The Gujarati* carried detailed account of his speeches, gave the number of people who attended and their response to the speeches. Gandhi was well aware of the impact of his tour. He wrote to a friend: 'Never mind that the voice does not reach the thousands, nay millions. They come not to hear but to see. And they see far more than what we can imagine.'[24]

When the peasants resolved not to pay revenue to the Government, the Kheda Commissioner addressed the workers threatening them of dire consequences. Reacting to this development, Gandhi released a letter to the Press (prominently displayed by *The Bombay Chronicle)* in which he wrote that the Kheda ryots were solving an imperial problem. 'They will show that it is impossible to govern men without their consent.' This eternal truth from then onwards became the hallmark of all the movements Gandhi led against the British Government.

Though Gandhi was leading a movement against the Government's wrong policies, he had not lost faith in British statesmanship. This was a characteristic feature of Gandhi's movements. In a speech at Nadiad, Gandhi stated:

> India cannot tolerate such punishments nor will the British statesmen ever uphold it. The British public would be horrified at it.... I have far greater faith in British statesmanship than the Commissioner has.[25]

Gandhi was also assisted in this struggle by Indulal Yajnik, Vallabhbhai Patel and Anasuyabehn Sarabhai. The satyagraha reached its peak by April 21, 1918 when 2337 persons pledged not to pay revenue. Most of the Patidars (rich peasant proprietors) took part in this Satyagraha. Some poorer peasants were coerced by the government into paying the revenue. Moreover, a good *Rabi* (summer) crop had weakened the case for remission. Gandhi began to realize that peasantry was on the verge of exhaustion. He decided to call off the agitation when the Government issued instructions that land revenue should be recovered from only those who had capacity to pay and no pressure would be exerted on genuinely poor peasants.

The Kheda agitation did not have uniform impact in the area. Only 70 villages out of 559 in Kheda were actually involved in it and it was called off after a token concession. But it certainly helped Gandhi in broadening his social base in rural Gujarat.

As the First World War started around this time, the Government thought it advantageous to make use of the services of Gandhi to recruit soldiers. This obliged them to consider favourably his demands regarding the Kheda satyagraha. The satyagraha ended on Gandhi's terms.

While Gandhi's involvement in Ahmedabad amounted to, in Gandhi's own words, 'meddling in your (Ambalal's) business and your family affairs',[26] the Kheda satyagraha involved the Government and affected a larger number of people and involved issues that challenged the power of the Government to tax the people. This movement, in a way was a curtain-raiser to the movements Gandhi was to lead later. As stated by Dennis Dalton Gandhi used his successes in this movement to enlist support for the War and later used the mobilization of the people during the Satyagraha with good effect, when in this same region, he led the Dandi March of 1930.[27] The distinguishing feature of all these movements was that they were all local in nature and were in fact the testing ground for Gandhi's ideals. They were also manageable in terms of space, time and issues. Later, when Gandhi launched his national level movements these areas gave good support to Gandhi. Further, during these movements Gandhi was also able to groom local level leaders who stood him in good stead. Indulal Yajnik, Sardar Patel and Anusuyabehn were his trusted leaders in Gujarat and Dr. Rajendra Prasad and Acharya Kriplani were his discoveries in Bihar. These leaders acted as important communication links with the people of their regions. Thus these movements acted as the stepping stones to national level politics.

REFERENCES

1. Gandhi was reluctant because he was preoccupied with the issue of abolition of indenture immigration from India in South Africa.
2. *The Leader*, 22.4.1917, *CWMG*, XIII, pp. 374-5.

3. For example, his speech at Champaran Enquiry Committee Meeting held on July 19, 1917 was reported by *The Hindu*, 20.7.1917 and the questions during evidence before the Champaran Committee were reported by the *Pioneer*, 28.7.1917.
4. F.n.1, *CWMG*, XIV, p. 214.
5. Ahmedabad Mill-Hands Strike, *Leaflet No. 1*, *CWMG*, XIV, pp. 214-15.
6. Ahmedabad Mill-Hands Strike, *Leaflet No. 2*, *CWMG*, XIV, pp. 219-20.
7. Speech at Ahmedabad Mill-Hands Strike, *CWMG*, XIV, pp. 222-23.
8. Ahmedabad Mill-Hands Strike, *Leaflet No. 3*, *CWMG*, XIV, pp. 224-25.
9. Ahmedabad Mill-Hands Strike, *Leaflet No. 4*, *CWMG*, XIV, pp. 227-8.
10. *Mahadevbhaini Diary Vol. IV*, *CWMG*, XIV, pp. 229-30.
11. Ahmedabad Mill-Hands Strike, *Leaflet No. 5*, *CWMG*, XIV, pp. 230-33.
12. Ahmedabad Mill-Hands Strike, *Leaflet No. 6*, *CWMG*, XIV, pp. 232-34.
13. Ahmedabad Mill-Hands Strike, *Leaflet No. 7*, *CWMG*, XIV, pp. 235-36.
14. Ahmedabad Mill-Hands Strike, *Leaflet No. 8-9*, *CWMG*, XIV, pp. 237-40.
15. Ahmedabad Mill-Hands Strike, *Leaflet No. 10*, *CWMG*, XIV, pp. 242-43.
16. Ahmedabad Mill-Hands Strike, *Leaflet No. 11*, *CWMG*, XIV, pp. 246-7.
17. Ahmedabad Mill-Hands Strike, *Leaflet No. 12*, *CWMG*, XIV, pp. 248-9.
18. Ahmedabad Mill-Hands Strike, *Leaflet No. 13*, *CWMG*, XIV, pp. 250-51.
19. Ahmedabad Mill-Hands Strike, *Leaflet No. 14*, *CWMG*, XIV, pp. 254-55.
20. Ahmedabad Mill-Hands Strike, *Leaflet No. 15*, *CWMG*, XIV, pp. 258-59.
21. Ahmedabad Mill-Hands Strike, *Leaflet No. 17*, *CWMG*, XIV, pp. 269-74.
22. *The Pledge*, *Young India*, 12.6.1918, *CWMG*, XIV, p. 279.
23. *Statement to the Press on the Kheda Situation*, *The Hindu*, 1-4-1918, *CWMG*, XIV, pp. 288-292.
24. *Letter to Patrick Geddes*, *CWMG*, XIV, p. 332.
25. *Message to Satyagrahi Agriculturalists*, *Mahadevbhani Diary Vol. IV*, *CWMG*, XIV, p. 349.
26. *Letter to Ambalal Sarabhai*, *CWMG*, XIV, p. 115.
27. Dennis Dalton, *Gandhi's Power: Non-Violance in Action*, (Oxford India Paperbacks) Preface.

3

Use of Print Media During the Non-Co-Operation Movement

One of the many uses Gandhi put print media to, was for imparting political education to the people for a well orchestrated defiance against the unjust actions of the Government. This was very much in evidence during the Non-Co-operation Movement he launched in 1920.

The Non-Co-operation Movement grew out of the agitation against the Rowlatt Bills which under the garb of curbing revolutionary violence, were, in fact, designed to curb the freedom of the common people. Gandhi urged the people to agitate against the Bills. When the Government retaliated by arresting the leaders of the agitation the general populace became restive. A peaceful, spontaneous meeting expressing resentment against the Government's actions was organized in the Jallianwala Bagh in Amritsar in defiance of the order of Section 144 imposed by the Government. The administration of Punjab decided to strike terror in the hearts of the protestors by ordering indiscriminate shooting at the assemblage. About 1000 died in the shooting and around 2000 were wounded as a result of the stampede.[1] The news of this incident was blacked out in the rest of the country as immediate curfew was imposed in the area. When the truth gradually came to light the British made a half-hearted attempt at assuaging the feelings of the people by appointing a commission to look into the matter. This commission could not shed its racist bias and failed to recommend exemplary punishment to General Dyer, the villain of the tragedy.

While, naturally, there was nation wide outrage over the Jallianwala Bagh incident, the Muslim community had another totally different reason for being outraged against the British. They considered the dismemberment of Turkey after the First World War, and the subsequent abolition of Caliphate as a breach of trust by the British. The Caliphate was considered by most Muslims as their highest religious head.

Gandhi combined the two issues and called upon the people to non-co-operate with the Government as long as it did not right the Punjab wrongs and reinstitute Khilafat (Caliphate) in Turkey. Clearly they were the burning issues of the time. The people were united in the opinion that these exemplified the high-handedness and insensitivity of the Government towards the Indians.

Non-co-operation with the Government meant boycotting Councils, law courts, educational institutions run by the Government. The constructive part of the programme included propagation of *swadeshi*, spinning, communal unity and giving up of the practice of untouchability and other social vices like drinking and gambling. Non-co-operation Movement, therefore, aimed at the destruction of the oppressive order and establishment of an equitable society based on moral values, in its place.

Hailed by historians and political analysts as 'unique' and 'pioneering' in terms of sheer mass participation and the strategies employed, the Movement opened up a new era in political emancipation and awareness creation. All of a sudden a slumbering nation found itself awake and searching for its identity. The methods employed were something unknown hitherto to the common man and the leadership alike. But it was a major step and, figuratively speaking, the Ganges was set on fire with the Himalayas keeping a close watch. There was expectation all round. And at the centre of all this, was Gandhi. Both the admirers and critics of Gandhi realized that things were moving faster than they had expected and the man who was calling the shots was Gandhi. How did he reach out to such a large number of people in so short a time? That was the wonder. Here again Gandhi was innovative. The strategies he employed in communicating with those around him, those outside his immediate circle and those who were looking at his initiatives critically, skeptically or sarcastically, all found themselves at the receiving end. Gandhi proved to be far ahead of them. He was emerging as an astute communicator who was conscious of every step that he was taking.

This chapter analyses how dexterously Gandhi made use of the print media to reach out to all sections of the people.

Agitation over Rowlatt Bills

Communication Through 'Extended Family' Network

In 1919 the atmosphere in India was charged over the Rowlatt Bills. Indians considered the Bills an attack on their self-respect. A public meeting was held by the Home Rule League on February 2, 1919 to protest against the introduction of the Criminal Law Amendment Bill and the Criminal Law Emergency Powers Bill, popularly known as the Rowlatt Bills, after the name of their author. Being indisposed, Gandhi could not personally attend the meeting. He sent a letter to Shankarlal Banker, the Secretary of the Home Rule League, which was read out at the meeting. The letter stated that it was their duty to 'educate public opinion to oppose the Bills with patience and firm determination.'[2]

Thus registering his opposition to the Bill before the Home Rule League, a prestigious organization of the period, Gandhi proceeded to write a letter to Madan Mohan Malaviya, who was then a member of the Viceroy's Council on February 8, 1919. Gandhi wrote: 'I read all speeches on the Rowlatt Bills today. I was much distressed ....Under the circumstances, I hope, at any rate, that all the members will leave the Select Committee, or, if necessary, even the Council, and launch a countrywide agitation.'[3] In similar vein, Gandhi wrote to VS Srinivas Sastri, another Indian member of the Viceroy's Council. The letter written only a day after the one written to Malaviya was clearer and more determined in tone. Gandhi wrote that the Bills and the Government's defence had stirred him to the very depths. When petitions and resolutions of 'gigantic' meetings fail the only course left for the people is to launch civil disobedience against such a Government. That was what he intended to do.[4] In view of his letters to the League, Malaviya and Sastri, it becomes clear that Gandhi deemed it necessary to 'educate public opinion' and 'launch a countrywide agitation' against the Government. He had approached them so that the opposition to the Bill would be more broad-based and started at the level of leadership rather than the masses. Probably he wanted to go to the people later with his agenda of action as they would have taken more time to understand the implications of the Bills as compared to the above mentioned knowledgeable leaders. Both Malaviya and Sastri disapproved of civil disobedience. Gandhi then decided upon approaching the people directly through the media.

The desire to convince the public that the Bill was an attack on their liberty was so intense that, despite his frail health, Gandhi launched an all out offensive against the passage of the Bills. As was the case with his earlier movements, Gandhi planned to tour the whole of the country and address public meetings but physically he was not strong enough to do so. He, therefore, took recourse to extensive use of the print media. Gandhi started with the 'Satyagraha Leaflets' and then used the journals edited by him like *Young India* and *Navajivan* to create the maximum impact. Gandhi also utilized the services of newspapers and journals friendly to his cause. *The Amrita Bazar Patrika,*[5] *The Bombay Chronicle,*[6] *The Hindu,*[7] in English, and *Gujarati* and *Prajabandhu* in Gujarati and Hindi respectively, extensively covered Gandhi's activities and speeches. Sometimes these newspapers also carried the schedules of agitations to be launched by Gandhi. Though the *The Times of India* and *The Statesman* were not supporting Gandhi's cause they cooperated in so far as they published Gandhi's letters addressed to them without fail. For some time Gandhi also enjoyed the hospitality of the columns of *New Age,* a journal edited by Annie Besant who later on parted company with Gandhi.

Launching Civil Disobedience Movement against Rowlatt Bills

The beginning of the civil disobedience movement against the Rowlatt Bills was made at a meeting held at the Sabarmati Ashram on February 24, 1919. A 'Pledge' drafted by Gandhi and signed by those present read as follows:

> Being conscientiously of the opinion that the Bills known as the Indian Criminal Law (Amendment) Bill No. 1 of 1919 and the Criminal Law (Emergency Powers) Bill No. 2 of 1919 are unjust, subversive of the principles of liberty and justice, and destructive of the elementary rights of individuals on which the safety of the community and the State itself is based, we solemnly affirm that in the event of these Bills becoming law and until they are withdrawn, we shall refuse civilly to obey these laws and such other laws as a Committee to be hereafter appointed may think fit and

> we further affirm that in this struggle we will faithfully follow truth and refrain from violence to life, person or property.[8]

The next step was to inform the Viceroy. A telegram to his private secretary was sent which read:

> EVER SINCE PUBLICATION ROWLATT BILLS HAVE BEEN CONSIDERING MY POSITION REGARDING THEM. HAVE BEEN CONFERRING WITH FRIENDS. IN MY OPINION BAD IN THEMSELVES BILLS ARE BUT SYMPTOM OF DEEP-SEATED DISEASE AMONG THE RULING CLASS, COMING AS THEY DO ON EVE REFORMS BILL AUGUR ILL FOR THEIR SUCCESS .THOSE WHO HAVE BEEN ASSOCIATED WITH ME IN PUBLIC WORK AND OTHER FRIENDS MET TODAY AND AFTER THE GREATEST DELIBERATION HAVE DECIDED TO OFFER SATYAGRAHA AND COMMIT DISOBEDIENCE OF SUCH LAWS AS COMMITTEE TO BE FORMED FROM OURSELVES MAY DECIDE .... [9]

The first step towards 'educating the public' was made in the form of publishing the summary of the Rowlatt Bills in a Gujarati paper which had a wide circulation in the State. The summary contained reference to the 'Satyagraha Pledge'. Gandhi highlighted the objectionable clauses in the Bills. Making full use of his legal training Gandhi exposed the danger inherent in the Bills. He concluded the exposition with the following words: 'It is the duty of every thinking Indian to save the people from this danger, a duty one can discharge only by offering satyagraha.'[10]

The next step was to make the participants and volunteers whom the people would approach aware of the rules and principles of the satyagraha. With this in mind, Gandhi issued 'Instructions to Volunteers' on behalf of the Committee of the Satyagraha Sabha These instructions were simultaneously published both in *The Bombay Chronicle* and *Young India* of March 12, 1919.[11]

Tours and Press Coverage

Despite his poor health Gandhi toured the country encouraging people to come forward and sign the 'Satyagraha Pledge.' In its issue of March 13, 1919 *The Amrita Bazar Patrika* carried a report of his speech in Delhi, quoting it in full.[12] *The Leader*, the same day carried the report of his speech of March 11 in Lucknow, but emphasized the low response of the public by adding 'altogether eleven people including the Chairman took the Pledge.'[13] The same issue of the paper also carried reports of Gandhi's speech at Allahabad.[14]

After touring the northern part of India Gandhi began his tour of the South. His first meeting in the South was held in Madras and was presided over by S. Kasturi Ranga Iyengar, the editor of *The Hindu*. In Madras Gandhi also addressed the Madras Labour Union and Madras Tramwaymen's meeting. On March 23, 1919 he issued a letter to the Press which was published both by *The Hindu* (4-3-1919) and *The Amrita Bazar Patrika* (25-3-1919).[15] This letter was released by the Associated Press of India. The letter's importance lies in the fact that Gandhi, for the first time, called for a day of protest involving the entire nation. He called upon the people to observe April 6 as the day of 'humiliation and prayer'; observe a twenty-four hour fast; to suspend, all work , except as may be essential in the public interest; to hold public meetings in all parts of India, not excluding villages, at which resolutions praying for the withdrawal of the two measures should be passed. The letter was published by the leading national dailies, leaving no doubt as to where their sympathies lay.

Gandhi continued his tour of the South covering Tanjore, Trichinopoly, Madura, Tuticorin, and Nagapatam. At every meeting in the South, Gandhi started his speech with an apology that he could not speak in Tamil though at one stage of his life he had started learning the language. He regretted the fact that he had to address them in English, a foreign language, because, sadly, the people were not conversant with Hindi. They should he said, learn it fast. Expounding on Satyagraha, he referred to Prahlad, the young boy in Indian mythology, who had defied the unjust orders of his father and who according to Gandhi was a satyagrahi of the first order. For those who believed that Prahlad was just a part of folk lore, he gave examples of Valliamma who died for the cause of Indians in South Africa. In every subsequent speech Gandhi added a new name to the list of satyagrahis. At Tuticorin, Gandhi added the name of Ahmed Mahomed Kachalia, his co-worker and satyagrahi in South Africa, to the list perhaps in view of the Muslim audience. Observing that the South was full of temples he acknowledged the religious spirit of the people and placed his faith in the belief that they would appreciate the role of religion in political life as much as he did. He allayed the fears that the non-cooperation movement might degenerate into Bolshevism eventually, with the argument that his movement was based on truth and non-violence, while Bolshevism thrived on violence.

Violence in Delhi

It was ironical that while Gandhi was emphasizing the difference between Bolshevism and his movement, underlining the non-violent nature of satyagraha, his attention was drawn to events of violence in Delhi. After conducting a thorough enquiry into the incident, Gandhi wrote a letter to *The Bombay Chronicle* which was published on 4-4-1919. While denying the Government's charges against the satyagrahis, Gandhi likened the Government's reaction to the whole episode as using the 'Namsmyth hammer to crush a fly.' He, however, did not spare the satyagrahis for what he thought was undisciplined behaviour on their part[16] Gandhi used the columns of the same newspaper to publish the schedule of the demonstration against the Rowlatt Bills to be held on 6-4-1919 along with detailed directions to the demonstrators so that the events like Delhi's were not repeated. B.G. Horniman who was the editor of the paper personally participated in the events of April 6 and was the only Englishman to do so.

Passage of Indian Press Act, 1919 and the Launching of Satyagrahi

The Government realized the gravity of the situation and passed the Indian Press Act curbing the freedom to publish anti-government articles. At a meeting held under the auspices of the Indian Press Association, with Sir Narayan Chandavarkar in the chair a resolution demanding the repeal of Press Act of 1910 was proposed by Gandhi and seconded by MR Jayakar. The meeting was one of the few occasions which found Nationalists, Liberals and Home Rule Leaguers on the same platform. In his speech Gandhi likened the Government's position to that of a meteorologist who had smashed his barometer and would yet claim to measure the atmospheric pressure.[17] Gandhi retaliated by issuing an unregistered newspaper *Satyagrahi* whose first issue appeared on April 7, 1919 With express request to 'read, copy and circulate among friends...' Gandhi declared that *Satyagrahi*[18] would exist only as long as the Rowlatt Legislation was not withdrawn. *The Bombay Chronicle* published the news that such a newspaper had come into existence along with the contents of the paper thereby making Gandhi's task all the more easy. It also published the leaflet containing instructions to satyagrahis,[19] and gave the list of laws the Satyagraha Sabha had chosen to disobey.[20] The editor, a close friend of Gandhi, saw to it that *The Bombay Chronicle* carried reports of all the activities of Gandhi, his letters as well as his notices regarding the meetings and directions to volunteers and the public in general. B.G. Horniman, the editor in question, had to pay the price for this association. Under the orders of the Government he was deported to England on 26 April, 1919. Gandhi treated Horniman's deportation as an attack on the freedom of the Press and waged a relentless propaganda war against the action and finally succeeded in getting Horniman back in 1926.

Swadeshi Vows

The declaration of Satyagraha was followed by the 'Swadeshi Vows' which initially included the pledge to use only Indian made cloth.[21] Gandhi held weaving as an occupation second only to agriculture. He held it as a key to the economic salvation of India. From then onwards 'swadeshi' was to become the main plank of his struggle against the British and his 'mantra' for the resurgence of India

Gandhi's Arrest

On April 9,1919 when he was in train from Bombay on his way to Punjab, Gandhi was served with an order not to enter either Delhi or Punjab and restrict his movements to Bombay alone. As he disobeyed the order he was arrested but not before leaving a message for the countrymen with his secretary, Mahadev Desai. The message was duly published by *The Hindu* on 10-4-1919. In the message Gandhi expressed his 'highest satisfaction' on being arrested as he had received what he was seeking i.e., 'either withdrawal of the Rowlatt legislation or imprisonment'. He asked the people to remain calm, maintain Hindu-Muslim unity and carry on the swadeshi program. He ended the message in his characteristic style with these words, 'it is my firm belief that we shall obtain salvation only through suffering and not by reforms dropping on us from England, no matter how unstintingly they may be granted.'[22] In their protest against their leader's arrest the crowds turned unruly at several places. On being discharged from custody the next day, his first act was to reprimand the Satyagrahis and the people in general through *Satyagraha Leaflet: No.3* for raising 'such a hue and cry' over his arrest.[23] Though still unaware of the details of tragic developments in Amritsar,[24] Gandhi suspended the civil disobedience movement on April 18, 1919 in view of disturbances and violence in Ahmedabad and Viramgaum. He did not hesitate to state that the call for civil disobedience was a 'Himalayan Blunder' on his part as he had overconfidence in the capacity of the people for non-violent action.[25]

Gandhi realized that lot of training in non-violent method was required before people could be called for group action like civil disobedience. The emphasis on educating the public became a mission with him from now onwards. He was, however, convinced that Satyagraha was not the cause of mob violence.[26] The publication of *Satyagrahi* was also suspended on 22-4-1919 [27] only to be resumed after six days.

After the suspension of satyagraha, Gandhi used the columns of *Satyagrahi* to educate the people on the meaning, significance and the philosophy behind satyagraha, and kept them abreast of the turn of events. Gandhi answered inquiries regarding as to when the satyagraha was to be resumed with patience. He also shared with his readers the information about the hartal against the deportation of B.G. Horniman (11-5-1919) but not before stating the dos and don'ts regarding the exercise.

As the Government started tightening its hold on the press in India, Gandhi's vocation included the preparation of informal, though well argued, defence in favour of the editors on whom the axe of the Government fell. Through the columns of *Young India* Gandhi addressed a memorial to the Viceroy of India requesting him to direct the release of Babu Kalinath Roy, the editor of *The Tribune*.[28] Gandhi also tried to enlist the support of papers like *The Times of India* that were not favourable to Gandhi by writing personal letters enclosing his arguments already published elsewhere for their perusal.[29] Later through the columns of his newspapers he fought for the freedom of Press in the case of the editor of *Pratap* and demanded his release (later for two Oriya papers as well.) Many more defenses were to follow in the course of the Non-Co-operation Movement.

Young India *Substitutes for* The Bombay Chronicle

After the deportation of B.G. Horniman *The Bombay Chronicle* had stopped publication. Thereupon the management of *Young India*, decided to convert their paper into a bi-weekly paper, so that it could, at least partly' fill the vacuum created by the stoppage of *The Bombay Chronicle*.[30] The management of *Young India* entrusted its editorship to Gandhi. After some time the *The Bombay Chronicle* resumed publication, though *Young India* continued to be bi-weekly.

Launching of Navajivan

Some friends suggested that Gandhi start a Gujarati paper so that more people could be made conversant with his ideas. This suggestion found favour with Gandhi. In the inaugural issue of *Navajivan ane Satya* (July, 1919) Gandhi wrote:

> I think I have a service to render to India by delivering a message to her ....I am convinced that I have no gift better than this [meaning satyagraha] for India. I have always been avid of placing before the people this priceless thing, and several others of which I have had ample experience. One powerful modern means for this purpose is the newspaper.[31]

This Gujarati paper played an important role in mobilizing Gujarat which was destined to play an important part in all the movements launched by Gandhi, especially the famous Dandi March.

Suspension of Civil Disobedience

Gandhi formally announced the suspension of Civil Disobedience in July 1919 so as to give Government a chance to mend its ways. In a letter to the Press, Gandhi described the act as 'a bitter pill' he had to swallow. He, however, warned the Government:

> I have been accused of throwing lighted matches. If my occasional Civil Resistance be a lighted match, Rowlatt legislation and persistence in retaining it on the Statute-book are a thousand matches scattered throughout India, the only way to avoid Civil Resistance altogether is to withdraw that legislation .... I have thus suspended Civil Resistance to hasten the end of that legislation. But satyagrahis will pay for its removal by their lives if it cannot be removed by lesser means.[32]

Disillusionment at Post-War Events and Knowledge of Punjab Atrocities

After War was over it was hoped by Gandhi and others that India would get something substantial by way of political reforms. Instead the Government declared that the Rowlatt Act, against which Indians had been agitating since April, would never be repealed. Around the same time the details of British atrocities on the people of the Punjab at Jallianwala Bagh in Amritsar and later, during the imposition of martial law in the state, started pouring in. Gandhi was deeply pained. Condemning the Government's actions in his newspapers he appealed for justice for the people of Punjab who he said, had been victims of arbitrary, unjust and disproportionate sentences pronounced on them without any regard for their age or sex, or the nature of crime they were supposed to have committed. Gandhi asked the Government to 'review, revise, and, if need be, reverse' the cruel sentences inflicted on innocent people. Gandhi wrote very convincingly, using his legal skills and proving beyond doubt that most of the cases were false. In a letter to a friend published in *Young India* (6-8-1919) Gandhi tersely observed: 'The Punjab sentences are inextricably mixed up with the Rowlatt agitation. It is therefore as imperatively necessary to have them revised as it is to have the Act removed.' [33]

Gandhi saw the Rowlatt Act as the root cause of the agitation in Punjab. Again in a public letter published in *Young India* (9-8-1919) Gandhi re-emphasized the connection between the Rowlatt Act and the Punjab repression. He averred:

> Had there been no Rowlatt legislation, there would have been no demonstration, and therefore no handle given to the mischievous elements. The wrong consisted not in the organizing of the demonstration or civil resistance, but in the Government so defying public opinion as to produce an agitation they had little anticipated.[34]

As mentioned earlier, parallel to the burning Rowlatt Bills issue a new development was causing deep resentment among the Muslims in India. The Muslims considered it a breach of faith on the part of the British Government to acquiesce in the dismemberment of Turkey after the War and agree to the end of Caliphate or Khilafat. Gandhi gave his full support to the Muslim through his journals.

He had firm belief that if Hindus supported the Muslims in their hour of trial the Hindu-Muslim bond would be strengthened.

Tour of Punjab Villages and Independent Inquiry into Punjab Atrocities

On the Government's request Gandhi had formally suspended the Civil Disobedience Movement in the middle of July 1919. He had also asked the people to co-operate with the Government to work the Reforms. For this purpose he toured the Punjab in November and December 1919 and again in February 1920. From Punjab he despatched a weekly series of newsletters for *Navajivan* in which he dealt chiefly with his experiences in Punjab. He won over the hearts of the people of the Punjab by convassing for money for building a memorial at Jallianwala Bagh. His interaction with the women of Punjab, who everywhere lavished the gift of home spun yarn to him, was very rewarding. Gandhi observed: 'It is my deep conviction that the women of the Punjab have understood my message.'[35]

It should be borne in mind that Gandhi was simultaneously addressing people in Punjab and sending his despatches to his Gujarati readers, via the *Navajivan,* whose readership included even the villagers in remote Gujarat He, therefore, acted as a link between the people of the Punjab and the people of Gujarat. The agony of the Punjabis was now shared by their Gujarati brethren. The evidence of this empathy came in the form of huge donations for the Jallianwala memorial and for the victims of Government atrocities in Punjab from the people of Gujarat.

Major Shift in Gandhi's Attitude Towards the Empire

Events were moving at a rapid pace in India. People were discontented over the Montague Chelmsford Reforms, introduced by the British Government to placate the Indians. The failure of the Allies to show sympathy for the cause of the Indian Muslims generated further anger towards the British Government. The Government had set up the Hunter Committee to probe into the Punjab incidents. Its highly biased report was published in May, 1920. It was in sharp contrast to the authenticity of the Congress Report, prepared after a thorough and painstaking investigation. It all proved to be the last straw for Gandhi. His faith in British justice badly shaken, he called upon the nation to withdraw its support to the Government. Till now, Gandhi had advised Indians to give the

Government a chance to mend its ways. No more. There was a sea change in his attitude to the Empire. Gandhi now wanted the country to generate sufficient moral strength 'to mend or end the Empire'. His patience was at an end.

Gandhi showed his sympathy and support for the Khilafat cause and won over the Muslims of India. The idea of non-cooperation was recommended to the Muslims by Maulana Abul Kalam Azad in his presidential address to the second Khilafat Congress at Calcutta held on February 29, 1920. The Muslim leaders accepted Gandhi's idea, but had some reservations regarding the non-violent nature of the movement. Using his persuasive power to the maximum Gandhi finally made them agree that the movement would remain non-violent for as long as it succeeded in achieving its objectives. After that they were free to use any method 'enjoined by the Holy Koran'.[36] On March 7, 1920 Gandhi issued a statement to the Press embodying his programme of non-co-operation with the British Government. Writing for *Young India* (14-7-1920) he aired his changed viewpoint: 'After all manners and method change with the times .What was good enough food for our babyhood cannot be good enough for manhood.'[37]

Steel in his Writings

At this juncture, around 1920 a new avatar of Gandhi was apparent in his writings. Commenting on this change, Bhabani Bhattacharya has observed: 'Anger was beyond his range of emotions; yet sometimes the words he used would spring into action a chastising whipchord'.[38] In an article on General Dyer, Gandhi's agony at the plight of the people of Punjab during the martial law is clearly evident. He believed that the oppression during the martial law was more condemnable than the Jallianwala massacre for while the former destroyed 'only a few bodies...the other tried to kill the soul of the nation.'[39] In fact, Gandhi was emboldened to say: 'I would risk violence a thousand times than risk the emasculation of the whole race'.[40]

Launching of the Non-Co-operation Movement

Gandhi went on a whirlwind tour of Jullundur, Amritsar, Lahore, Rawalpindi and Gujarkhan prior to the proposed *hartal* of August 1, 1920. His speeches were full of passion telling people to be prepared to die for their self-respect. But nowhere did he advocate violence.

During a speech in Lahore he went of the extent of praising the self-control and dignified stance of the British giving the example of the Viceroy, who showed no signs of grief in public after his son was killed in the War. Gandhi's unique message was clear: HATE THE DEED NOT THE MAN.

Gandhi believed that for self-respect and as a protest against the Punjab atrocities Indians should resign from the reformed Councils. The idea of obstructing from within would bring no substantial gain—only pittance. Yet he firmly believed that 'no European nation is more amenable to the pressure of moral force than the British.'[41]

Gandhi Counters Arguments Against Non-Co-operation

Non-violent non-co-operation being such a novel form of agitation, it was natural that misgivings continued to be aired regarding its efficacy, as also fears that the movement would degenerate into violence. The skeptics included the Government, well-meaning Indian leaders and a section of the public. Gandhi spared no effort in the gigantic task of educating the masses, intelligentsia and the rulers about the meaning of Satyagraha.

The most vocal criticism of non-co-operation came from none less than Rabindra Nath Tagore, the Nobel Laureate, Gandhi's close friend and admirer. Tagore thought of non-co-operation as a concept not dignified enough for India, a doctrine of negation, despair, separation, exclusiveness and narrowness.[42] Gandhi gave a brilliant and restrained reply to the poet's criticism and fears. The exchange between the two provides a contrast between the two contemporaries' styles of writing and the discourses today. There is an unmistakable dignity of language in the debate. Gandhi allayed the Poet's apprehension that 'non-co-operation is intended to erect a Chinese Wall between India and the West'. 'On the contrary', Gandhi asserted 'non-co-operation is intended to pave the way to real, honourable and voluntary co-operation based on mutual respect and trust.' With regard to the Poet's fear that the call to students to leave their schools and colleges could ruin their careers as they do not have alternative institutions to go to, Gandhi countered that the government schools and syllabi were so designed as to turn the students into clerks and interpreters. It is on the support of these classes that the British Government flourished. Gandhi also dealt with the criticism that the non-co-operation was the doctrine of negation and thus not advisable. Gandhi's response was 'rejection is as much an ideal as the acceptance of a thing. It is necessary to reject untruth to accept truth....We have lost the power to say 'no'.... This deliberate refusal to co-operate is like a weeding process that a cultivator has to resort to before he sows. Non-co-operation is the nation's notice that it is no longer satisfied to be in tutelage.... An India prostrate at the feet of Europe can give no hope to humanity. An India awakened and free has a message of peace and goodwill to the groaning world. Non-co-operation is designed to supply her with a platform from which she will preach the message.'[43]

Other critics pointed out the practical difficulties. They feared that violence and chaos would enter or follow the movement and called it a 'remedy worse than the disease'. This view was held especially by the members of the Parsi community. Gandhi, therefore, devoted a major part of his campaigning in 1921 to the Parsis and finally succeeded in winning them over.[44]

Some important leaders of the time, such as VS Srinivas Sastri, Dinshaw Edulji Wacha and Madan Mohan Malaviya, to name a few, did not see any merit in boycotting the reformed Councils for the creation of which they had agitated all these years.

A large number of lawyers and judges believed that if they non-co-operated, the plight of common man would be worse off with no one to defend his rights. The greatest difference of opinion was in evidence on the issue of students leaving their schools and colleges. Leaders of eminence like Madan Mohan Malaviya, Rabindra Nath Tagore (as already discussed) did not agree with Gandhi on this point. Motilal Ghose, the acerbic editor of *The Amrita Bazar Patrika* and Kasturi Ranga Iyengar the editor of *The Hindu* were notables who voiced their dissent in the severest of terms.

Gandhi answered all these criticisms through the columns of *Young India* and *Navajivan*. He generated public discussion on all these issues and presented the arguments put forward by both the parties so that the public could come to an independent judgment and freely follow the dictates of conscience. A selection from Gandhi's arguments in defence of his unconventional ideas in his journals is given below. In response to Sir Tej Bahadur Sapru advice to Muslims not to join the NCO Gandhi wrote:

> when ...Government does not represent the will of the people, when it supports dishonesty or terrorism, the judges and executive officials by retaining office become instruments of dishonesty and terrorism....I would submit to our distinguished countrymen who occupy high offices that their giving up their offices will bring the struggle to a speedy end and would probably obviate the danger attendant upon the masses being called upon to signify their disapproval by withdrawing cooperation.[45]

Gandhi believed that it was the duty of the people to non-co-operater because:

> Through the method of violence and bloodshed, the people can get nothing in a big country like India; likewise, *no power in the world can rule over such a vast country as ours if there is peaceful non-co-operation.*[46] (emphasis added).

He again and again beseeched that his method should at least be given a trial:

> I urge those who distrust me, not to disturb the even working of the struggle that has just commenced, by inciting to violence in the belief that I want violence. I detest secrecy as a sin. Let them give non-violent non-co-operation a trial and they will find that I had no mental reservation whatsoever.[47]

Not unmindful of the immense resources of British Government, he asked the people to use their untapped resource of non-co-operation:

> He is an indifferent soldier who ignores his opponent's strength. We must therefore know the strength of the Government with which we are engaged in a fierce struggle. The Government represents a corporation that is crafty in the main, godless, untruthful, but courageous, able, self-sacrificing and possessing great powers of organization. We must therefore meet its craftiness by simplicity and openness, godlessness by godliness, untruthfulness by truthfulness. We must match its courage with greater ability, sacrifice with greater self-sacrifice, and its organizing

> powers with greater organizing powers. It has almost matchless weapon of violence. We must meet them with non-violence. Unless we are able to satisfy the test, we must be content to occupy a status of servility. Non-co-operation affords the nation an opportunity of showing all the qualities required for sustaining its honour.[48]

He went on to emphasize his fears and faith by writing:

> My greatest anxiety about non-co-operation.... is that we have not come out of the mobocratic stage....Non-co-operation I am therefore now using in order to evolve democracy.[49]

Self-restraint and total non-violence was to be observed because Gandhi was confident that:

> The Government cannot shed blood no matter how free the views we express on swaraj. It will shed blood only when we ourselves first commit a murder, even if it be at the incitement of a Government agent.[50]

Gandhi Addresses Englishmen

Apart from addressing his fellow Indians Gandhi also drew the attention of the English subjects in India. In a letter addressed to 'Every Englishman in India', Gandhi complained about the exploitation of India's resources for the benefit of Great Britain, ever increasing military expenditure, extravagance in Government departments regardless of India's poverty and many other wrongs. Gandhi suggested that it was in the power of the English people to rectify the situation. He invited them to make common cause with the people of India whose 'salt' they were consuming, figuratively meaning to whom they owed their loyalty.[51] Predictably the letter received diametrically opposite responses. Some Englishmen were profuse in their praise while others were virulent in their criticism.[52]

Gandhi's Communication to the Youth of India, Particularly Students

Gandhi realized that if the youth could be mobilized, non-cooperation would become a potent force. In 1921 he addressed a large number of students throughout the length and breadth of India. As part of the non-cooperation programme Gandhi had asked the students to withdraw from their schools and colleges. As discussed earlier, leaders like Madan Mohan Malaviya, VS Srinivas Sastri and

Rabindra Nath Tagore did not agree with Gandhi on this point. Motilal Ghose, the editor of *The Amrita Bazar Patrika* and Kasturi Ranga Iyengar, the editor of *The Hindu*, were other notables who voiced their dissent in severest of terms. Motilal Ghose argued that since the schools were run with the taxes paid by the public, the public must make use of them. Finally, there was the question of parental consent. For those above sixteen years of age Gandhi's advice was that they should politely and firmly inform the parents of their decision. The Government also realized the seriousness of the situation and responded by issuing circular to educational institutions to take steps to counter disaffection against the Empire among the students.

Gandhi main objection against the schools was that they did not impart the correct values to the students and made them dependent on the unjust British system throughout their lives. But, for the moment he advised the students to leave the educational institutions because these were tainted by the money of the Government that had the blood of the people of the Punjab on their hands and was responsible for betraying the cause of the Muslims.

Students from all parts of India responded to Gandhi's call in large numbers. A chain of national schools and colleges with emphasis on character-building and constructive service came up. Tilak Mahavidyalaya, Allahabad, National Madrassa, Calcutta, National School, Nadiad, Tilak National School, Calcutta, National College, Calcutta, Kashi Vidyapith, Benares, National College, Bombay, Tilak Vidyalaya, Nellore and so on were the products of this period. While addressing the students in all these colleges, Gandhi laid emphasis on using Hindustani, a mixture of Urdu and Hindi as the medium of instruction; welcoming the so called untouchables as co-students; and, working for Hindu-Muslim unity.

This action shows how holistic all the programmes by Gandhi were and how well thought out his strategies were. He envisioned Hindustani as a uniting force not only for Hindus and Muslims but also for binding the whole of India. He was not much bothered about the script but pointed out that the Devanagari script was more scientific than the Arabic but if the Muslims felt otherwise both the scripts should be used.

Gandhi's addresses to the students were so full of passion that all sorts of charges were levelled against him. Responding to these Gandhi wrote in the *Navajivan*:

> It is being said these days that I am putting wild ideas into students' heads ....I am doing them injustice,... I have ...departed ...from truth...my language lacks the moderation to which I lay claim..... The fact is that the delusion under which I laboured in December last has vanished and so the language I speak today is different from what I spoke then.[53]

Gandhi, however, was aware of the impact of his speeches on the impressionable minds of the young. He did not want them to lose their reason in any kind of hero worship. He, therefore, urged the students to cultivate fearlessness, not to follow anyone blindly, however great, and to take decisions independently. 'Please don't ask me what I would do for you. I am not asking you to shake off Government's slavery to be slaves to me afterwards'.[54]

Burning of Foreign Cloth Criticized

The boycott of schools issue had not yet been put to rest when Gandhi's programme to boycott foreign goods and make a bonfire of foreign clothes came under fire. Interestingly, the closest friends of Gandhi joined issue with him on these points. CF Andrews, his confidante, found a 'subtle appeal to racial feeling' in the whole exercise. Gandhi's reply was: 'I am transferring the ill-will from men to things'.[55] It was more an outlet for the pent up anger of the common man, who was made to feel impotent by such a powerful and repressive regime.

Fear of Misuse of Gandhian Methods in Independent India

An interesting area of communication during the Non-Co-operation Movement pertained to doubts whether the people who participated in the acts of breaking laws or were disrespectful to laws, took part in boycotts and hartals would not employ the same methods when India attained swaraj.[56] This was a very valid fear. Gandhi was to see in his own life time how the people who he had mobilized for such activities later felt free to disobey even the essential orders of the Government.[57] Gandhi's standard reply at this time, however, was that a government under swaraj would not be repressive, therefore, there would be no need to oppose it.

Misleading Show of Communal and Caste Unity?

Some correspondents also asked Gandhi to shake off his complacency regarding Hindu-Muslim unity, saying it was not permanent in nature.[58] Similarly, he was warned that the indications of the uplift of the condition of untouchables were not reliable. Gandhi probably had too much faith in the goodness of human nature. He was convinced that these aberrations could be corrected in due course. Besides, in any case, a self government with warts was better than a foreign one without them, he believed. History has proved the doubts true and Gandhi wrong. Sensing that his ideas, however pure, may be compromised in practice, Gandhi wrote an article in the true meaning of swaraj in 14-8-1921 issue of the *Navajivan*.[59]

Gandhi was ever sensitive to the religious sentiments of the people. But at the same time he never surrendered easily before dogma and die-hard traditionalism or orthodoxy. Thus when some correspondents raised the question of the sanction of religion for some of the programmes followed in the Non-Co-operation Movement Gandhi saw the need for a satisfactory answer. To his call for equal treatment of untouchables the orthodox Hindus rose in revolt against Gandhi and sent in write-ups quoting scriptures to justify their stand. Gandhi was convinced that untouchability was a later day addition to the Hindu religion and, one need not follow the scriptures blindly. Similarly, some Muslims challenged the religiosity of non-violence. Gandhi had to quote the authority of all religions to bring home the point that there was nothing irreligious about any of the principles of the Non-Co-operation Movement launched by him.[60]

Communication with the Indian National Congress

Another area in which Gandhi had to face criticism was the charge brought by some Congress Party leaders against Gandhi for not taking the party into confidence before launching the Non-Co-operation Movement as Congress was considered to be premier party representing Indians. Gandhi was even asked to withdraw the movement and seek the prior concurrence of the Congress. Gandhi replied that such a move would be tantamount to betraying the cause of Muslims as non-co-operation had become inextricably linked with Khilafat. In matters of conscience, he said, partisan politics has no place. Sometimes such utterances by Gandhi are quoted as examples of his one up-manship. Gandhi, however, with his immense presence, later brought the Congress round to his viewpoint.

Building consensus for his views in the Congress was no easy task. Gandhi had made all efforts to convince Tilak of the virtues of satyagraha and about the expediency of allying with the Muslims over Khilafat. Tilak, however, was skeptical about the efficacy of non-violence as a political weapon and was not in favour of having an alliance with the Muslims over a religious issue. He was of the firm opinion that the basis of alliance between Hindus and Muslims should be secular one, like the Lucknow Pact of 1916 and not religious. A lot depended on Tilak's attitude, but unfortunately he passed away on August 1, 1920. Similarly, Lala Lajpat Rai and CR Das, the two other important Congress leaders, vehemently opposed Gandhi on the issue of boycotting Council elections.

Summing up the situation in the Congress during this period, Jawaharlal Nehru later wrote in *The Discovery of India* that almost the entire old Guard of the Congress opposed Gandhi's programme.[61] Therefore when the issue of non-co-operation and boycott was placed before the Provincial Congress Committee (PCC) the division over the issue was clearly discernible. The United Provinces, Bengal and Bombay Committees disagreed on the issue of Council boycott. The Madras PCC approved the policies of non-co-operation but rejected Gandhi's programme. Gujarat and Bihar fully backed Gandhi's programme. The Andhra and the Punjab PCCs approved of no-co-operation but deferred a decision on Gandhi's programme until the special Congress session. It was under these circumstances that a special session of All India Congress Committee was called at Calcutta in September, 1920. Lala Lajpat Rai was its President. A strong opposition to Gandhi's programme was expected at the session. But contrary to the intentions of most established political leaders, before the session began, Gandhi managed to get his proposals accepted at the open session of the Congress by the majority of 1000 votes. Among Gandhi's supporters were Motilal Nehru, Saifuddin Kitchlew, Jitendralal Bannerjee, Shaukat Ali, Yakub Hassan and Dr. Ansari; while his opponents included Madan Mohan Malaviya and Annie Besant. Gandhi succeeded mainly because of the support of the business groups and Muslims. The Congress supported Gandhi's plan for non-co-operation till the Punjab and Khilafat wrongs were righted and swaraj established. The final decision was left for the next session.

In the last week of December 1920 the Congress at its Nagpur session accepted a new objective for the national struggle which was the 'attainment of swaraj by the people by all legitimate means'. The Congress also reaffirmed the resolutions on non-violence and non-co-operation in stages passed in the September session. In the following year, in the month of March, the All India Congress Committee laid down a definite programme of action, to be completed before June 30, 1921.

It was not that Gandhi needed the Congress to legitimize his actions. Gandhi already had an impressive mass following. It was the way he worked to win support of as many sections of the people as possible. Winning the support of the Congress was definitely an additional advantage and made the movement all the more broad-based.

Encouraged by the Congress response, Gandhi moved on from his programme of boycott of schools and colleges run by the Government to the next phase of non-co-operation movement,. He suggested that India should concentrate its attention on reaching the following three goals by the end of June, 1921. These were:

- Collect one crore rupees for the Tilak Swaraj Fund;
- Put one crore members on the Congress register;
- Introduce the spinning wheel in 20 lakh households.

After this declaration Gandhi set out to realize these goals with his characteristic enthusiasm employing his time-tested and effective methods of educating the masses and those around him.

Handling the Radical Phase of the Non-Co-operation Movement

In its final phase, the Non-Co-operation Movement became radical in tone. Under the stewardship of Gandhi, the Congress volunteers rallied the people en-masse and the country was on the verge of revolt. Preparations were being made for a dynamic programme of action which would deliver the final blow and compel the Government to bow before public opinion. But his was also a testing time for Gandhi. There was an outbreak of violence in Malabar on the western coasts. The Moplahs, the descendants of Arab immigrants, who were generally poor cultivators declared a 'holy war' against their exploitative landlords, the Hindus and massacred them. With Ali brothers in jail Gandhi was left alone to deal with the problem. Gandhi could sense that the 'tender sapling' of bond between the Hindus and Muslims was at snapping point as a result of the violence. Attempting to make an objective evaluation, he said: 'there acts are not the acts of all the Muslims in India even, nor thank God, of all the Moplahs. Every Mussulman of note that I know has repudiated every one of their acts. Let our loyalty to Hindu-Muslim unity therefore remain firm and changeless.'[62]

This was followed by a series of articles on Hindu-Muslim unity. The emphasis was always on forgiving the misguided miscreants. Gandhi also blamed the British Government for remaining passive onlooker of the carnage of Hindus and not allowing non-co-operators to help the hapless victims.

Another incident of note in this phase was the rioting in Bombay on the occasion of the visit of the Prince of Wales. Gandhi had asked the people of India to boycott all the functions associated with the welcome of the Prince. The non-co-operators, in their enthusiasm, started attacking all those who did not follow this call. Parsis were especially the target of their attacks. Gandhi was shaken. He took the round of the city and testified to the hooliganism in his report in *Young India*. In the same issue he made a fervent appeal to the citizens of Bombay, especially those who had participated in the rioting, to seek forgiveness from their victims. This was not the swaraj he dreamed of. He wrote: 'The swaraj that I have witnessed during the last two days has stunk in my nostrils'.[63]

Radicalization of the movement brought about corresponding changes in the policies and methods of the Government. The Government made all efforts to break the unity of the movement. False propaganda was resorted to. A leaflet in Gujarati under the heading 'Message to the Dheds' was circulated stating that, if the Dheds were attacked for not joining the non-co-operators, the Government would protect them. The Government also organized the meeting of the *antyajas,* the untouchables, in the Town Hall of Bombay. Gandhi, writing in *Navajivan* considered it nothing but 'flattery or bribing'.[64] The Government stooped so low as to issue misleading leaflets in the name of Gandhi! Under the heading 'A Lying Placard' Gandhi printed the following message which was circulated by the Government or its sympathizers in Gandhi's name. The placard read as follows:

Stop Hartals!
Suspend all NCO activities O ye people of Delhi!
Come in hundreds!!
Come in thousands!!!
Welcome HRH the Prince of Wales.[65]

The 'jail bharo' movement was countered with bad treatment in jails. But Gandhi was optimistic about the success of Non-cooperation. He was of firm belief that every 'good movement passes through five stages: indifference, ridicule, abuse, repression and respect'.[66] The repression of the Government would be soon followed by respect, he held.

Gandhi knew that unless all sections of the population participated in his movement, success would be hard to come by. He therefore widened his support base. In 1921 Gandhi tried to solicit the support of the rulers of C.P. and Kathiawad to participate, at least in a limited way, in his programmes of spinning and temperance in view to better the economic and social condition of their subjects. Similarly merchants who dealt in foreign goods were implored to desist from doing so and join the swadeshi *yajna*. Similarly, the minuscule and obscure Khoja and Bohra communities of the Muslims were the object of Gandhi's attention in several of his writings. The Bhils of Central Provinces was targeted by one of the trusted lieutenants of Gandhi. Far-flung areas of Assam were approached by him.[67] Parsis and Christians,[68] women and children[69] were all inspired to join the yajna of swadeshi and swaraj.

To further popularize his views now among the Hindi speaking literates Gandhi started the Hindi edition of *Navajivan* called *Hindi Navajivan* which he dedicated to his Marwari readers.

It is said that Gandhi freed his writings from the written tradition and made it more of a conversation. At the peak of his movements, this characteristic became very much evident in the writings of Gandhi. He would rebuke the public with gentle sarcasm, cajole them into falling in line with him and confide in them his innermost thoughts thereby eliciting from them the same confidence in return. Especially in the *Navajivan* he would take up historical anecdotes familiar to the readers of the region. While addressing Hindus, the British rule became *Ravanarajya,* while for women his ideal was Sita. Sometimes such examples tended to obscure his progressive approach and presented him as a traditional leader.

Gandhi's Use of His Trial and Imprisonment

Gandhi had for long been spared imprisonment though most of the time he was publishing matter which the Government considered seditious. It was only when Gandhi suspended the movement that he was charged with seditious writings and imprisoned. Gandhi and Shankarlal Banker, publisher of *Young India* were tried and convicted in 1922 under Section 124-A of the Indian Penal Code for writing and publishing four inflammatory articles against the British. Commenting on the trial, BR Agarwala writes: 'This was the first trial of its kind where the legality and morality of the Indian no-cooperation movement was involved.'[70] That the non-cooperation movement has come to win respect can be well concluded from what the trial judge, Justice Broomfield had to say. He proceeded thus:

> Mr. Gandhiji, you have made my task easy in one way by pleading 'guilty' to the charge. Nevertheless, what remains viz, the determination of a just sentence, is, perhaps as difficult a proposition as a judge in this country could have to face. The law is no respecter of persons. Nevertheless, it would be impossible to ignore the fact that you are in a different category from any person I have ever tried or am likely to try.... It is my duty to 'judge' you as a man subject to law who has, by his own admission, broken the law and committed what to an ordinary man must appear to be grave offences against the State.[71]

After passing the sentence of simple imprisonment for six years the honourable judge concluded: 'And I should like to say in doing so that if the course of events in India should make it possible for the government to reduce the period and release you, no one would be better pleased than I.'[72] There could not have been a higher compliment for Gandhi and his movement, coming as it did from a judge of Justice Broomfield's calibre.

The trial, in the words of Bhikhu Parekh, as a remarkable episode in British colonial history, 'highlighted Gandhi's style of operation, the Raj's capacity for decency, and the gentlemanly manner in which the two sometimes conducted their politics.' Significantly, the colonial government never tried Gandhi again, though it did incarcerate him on several occasions.[73]

According to Justice Shelat, the importance of the trial lay in the importance of the issue involved: 'obedience of law against obedience to moral duty'.[74] Thus Gandhi could establish before the world that non-cooperation could be viewed as a breach of law, but on moral grounds it was unassailable. The withdrawal of non-cooperation may have, for the time-being cause bewilderment and confusion but in the long run established its moral and spiritual credentials.

About the trial and Gandhi's eloquent speech,[75] William Shirer, the American journalist writes thus:

> His moving speech to the court constituted the most devastating indictment of the British rule—or misrule -in India that had been heard in the land. It summed up with an inspired eloquence, which I believe will reverberate in India for centuries to come, the story of his life, why after first loyally accepting the Empire, he had turned against it and why he was devoting his life to freeing India from its grip. His trial, conviction and sentence was one of the crucial turning points on the road to revolution and Indian independence.[76]

Gandhi's communication skills were at their brilliant best during the Non-Cooperation Movement. Most of his important journals and newspapers were in existence during this period except the *Harijan, Harijanbandhu* and *Harijan Sewak*. Gandhi wrote every day about twenty to thirty printed pages. Instead of replying to letters personally he started the practice of publishing the replies in the columns of his papers except in case of very personal letters. Thus emerged the public Gandhi, whose life from now onwards was an open book. The advantage of this exercise was that all barriers to communication were now broken down and Gandhi was accessible to all and sundry. The Non-Cooperation Movement rested and thrived on the excellent communication skills of Gandhi especially on the extensive and the proper use of print-media.

The movement not only registered progress in the direction of political independence, but also showed remarkable results in the social sphere as well. The emphasis on removing evils like caste, communalism and untouchability bore fruit. In the processions, meetings and in jails people of all castes and communities worked together and ate together. This weakened the caste separated-ness and accelerated the pace of social mobility and reform. The so-called lower castes could raise their heads without fear. This movement brought about unprecedented unity between the Hindus and the Muslims. At places it was difficult to distinguish between a non-cooperation, Khilafat and a Kisan Sabha meeting.

In the economic field, the boycott of foreign cloth brought rich dividends. The decline in the import of cotton price goods created panic among the British capitalists. The Indian textile industry benefited. The popularization of *charkha* and *kargha,* the village reconstruction programme through self-help and through *panchayats* brought about economic revival, and handloom production went up.

In the political field, Gandhi was able to bring about unprecedented awareness in the remotest corners of India. Gandhi was able to rekindle a sense of dignity and self-respect among Indians, and instilling fearlessness in them.

REFERENCES

1. Home Political Deposit, September, 1920, No. 23, National Archives of India, New Delhi; Report of Commissioners, Vol. I, New Delhi.
2. *Summary of letter to Shankarlal Banker, The Bombay Chronicle,* 4-2-1919, *CWMG,* XV, p. 83.
3. *CWMG,* XV, p. 86.
4. *CWMG,* XV, p. 86.
5. The editor Motilal Ghose, an institution in himself considered Gandhi his 'younger brother' and gave him blessings for the success of Non-cooperation when the two met.
6. Friendliness with Gandhi cost the editor of this paper a lot. B.G. Horniman was deported to London. Gandhi launched a mass movement in protest against his deportation and finally succeeded in getting him back to India in 1926.
7. Kasturi Ranga Iyengar who was the editor of the paper initially did not approve of Gandhi's methods of mass-agitation. It was only after the findings of the Congress Committee on the excesses became public that he started wholeheartedly supporting Gandhi.
8. *New India,* 3-3-1919, *CWMG,* XV, p. 102.
9. *Telegram to Private Secretary of Viceroy, CWMG,* XV, p. 102.
10. 'Summary of Rowlatt Bills' *Gujarati,* 9-3-1919 *CWMG,* XV, pp. 110-19.

11. 'Instructions to Volunteers', *CWMG*, XV, pp. 118-20.
12. *Ibid*, pp. 126-127.
13. *Ibid.*, p. 128.
14. *Ibid.*, pp. 130-131.
15. *Ibid.*, pp. 145-6.
16. *The Bombay Chronicle*, *CWMG*, XV, pp. 174-6.
17. *CWMG*, XVII, p. 67.
18. The first issue was named *Satyagrahi*. Later the leaflets bore the title *Satyagraha*.
19. *CWMG*, XV, pp. 190-1.
20. *CWMG*, XV, pp. 192-4.
21. *The Bombay Chronicle*, *CWMG*, XV, pp. 195-8; 198-201.
22. *The Hindu*, 10-4-1919, *CWMG*, XV, pp. 207-9.
23. *CWMG*, XV, pp. 211-12.
24. In a letter to JL Maffey, Private Secretary to the Viceroy, on May 16, 1919, Gandhi wrote: ' I have said not a word about the events in Punjab, not because I have up to now not thought or felt over them, but I have not known what to believe and what not to believe. Even the official communiqués have not been over frank'. *CWMG*, XV, p. 311. This letter shows that because of the restrictions over Press, the events of Jallianwala Bagh in Amritsar were not known to people outside Amritsar.
25. M.K. Gandhi, *The Story of My Experiments with Truth*, Navajivan Publishing House, Ahmedabad, 1969, p. 367.
26. This statement was published in *The Hindu*, dated 21-4-1919, *CWMG*, XV, p. 245.
27 *The Bombay Chronicle* dated 22-4-1919 carried the news of the suspension. *CWMG*, XV, footnote 1, p. 216.
28 *Memorial to Viceroy*, this was presented on behalf of the citizens of Bombay, and was signed by Gandhi and others including Sir Narayan G Chandavarkar, Sir Dinshaw Wacha, GK Parekh and K Natrajan. *Young India*, 25-6-1919, *CWMG*, XV, pp. 360-61.
29. *Letter to ST Sheppard*, editor, *The Times of India*, enlisting his support in Kalinath Roy's case, *CWMG*, XV, pp. 365.
30. Writing in Gujarati in *Navajivan Ane Satya*, old name of *Navajivan*, in July 1919, Gandhi wrote that since *The Bombay Chronicle* had stopped publication the management of *Young India* has decided to make it bi-weekly, 'so that it may serve, partly, the purpose which the Chronicle had served'. *CWMG*, XV, p. 419.
31. *CWMG*, XV, pp. 419-21.
32. *Young India*, 23-7-1919, *CWMG*, XV, p. 470.
33. *CWMG*, XVI, p. 7.
34. *CWMG*, XVI, p. 15.
35. 'Punjab Letter', *Navajivan*, 22-1-1920, *CWMG*, XVII, p. 31.

36. 'Speech on Khilafat', Bombay, *Young India*, 24-3-1920, *CWMG*, XVII, p. 100.
37. 'Councils Boycott', *Young India*, 14-7-1920, *CWMG*, XVIII, p. 43.
38. Bhabani Bhattacharya, *Gandhi, the Writer*, National Book Trust, New Delhi, 1969, p. 105.
39. 'General Dyer', *Young India*, 14-7-1920, *CWMG*, XVIII, pp. 45-6.
40. *Young India*, 27-7-1920, *CWMG*, XVIII, p. 117.
41. 'Boycott of Council', *Navajivan*, 18-7-1920, *CWMG*, XVII, p. 57.
42. See Appendix-IV, *CWMG*, XX.
43. 'The Poet's Anxiety', *Young India*, 1-6-21, *CWMG*, XX, p. 161-64. For an excellent account of the debate between Gandhi and Tagore see Sabyasachi Bhattacharya, *The Mahatma and the Poet*, National Book Trust, New Delhi, 1999.
44. A series of speeches addressed to Parsis was published in the various issues of *Navajivan*, such as 'Speech at Meeting at Navasari,' *Navajivan* 5-5-1921, *CWMG*, XX, pp. 25-29; 'Some Doubts' *Navajivan*, 24-4-1921, *CWMG*, XX pp. 31-35, dealt with an open letter written by a well-known Parsi, GK Nariman against the non-cooperation movement which was published in many papers; *Navajivan* 8-5-1921, *CWMG*, XX. p. 74.
45. Gandhi's arguments appear in an article written by him in *Young India*, dated 21-7-1920 and were in response to Sir Tej Bahadur Sapru's advise to Muslims at Khilafat Conference at Allahabad not to join the Non-Co-operation Movement, *CWMG*, XVIII, pp. 68-70.
46. 'Our Duty', *Navajivan*, 1-8-1920, *CWMG*, XVIII, pp. 99-100.
47. *Young India*, 11-8-1920, *CWMG*, XVIII, p. 134.
48. 'Our Burden', *Young India*, 1-9-1920, *CWMG*, XVIII, p. 222.
49. 'Democracy 'Versus' Mobocracy', *Young India*, 8-9-1920, *CWMG*, XVIII, p. 242.
50. 'Some Difficulties', *Navajivan*, 7-1-1920, *CWMG*, XVIII, p. 446.
51. 'To Every Englishman in India', *Young India*, 27-10-1920, *CWMG*, XVIII,. pp. 373-75.
52. 'Rejoinder', *Young India*, 15-12-1920, *CWMG*, XIX. pp. 118-20, 'Moral Values' *Young India*, 5-1-1921, *CWMG*, XIX, pp. 200-202, 'Ungratefullest of Men', *Young India* 12-1-1921, *CWMG*, XIX, pp. 212-213, 'Did Jesus Cooperate', *Young India* 19-1-1921, *CWMG*, XIX, pp. 243-244.
53. *Speech at Students' Meeting, Benares, Young India*, 24-11-1920, *CWMG*, XIX, p. 24.
54. *Speech at Students' Meeting, Allahabad, Navajivan*, 19-12-1920, *CWMG*, XIX, p. 50.
55. 'Ethics of Destruction', *Young India*, 1-9-1921, *CWMG*, XXI, pp. 41-43.
56. *Navajivan*, 16-10-1921, *CWMG*, XXI, p. 304.
57. For instance when popular government was established in Bihar in 1937 many people refused to buy tickets in trains and buses and Gandhi

had to write a strongly worded article in *Young India* deploring this tendency.

58. 'Hindu-Muslim Unity a Camouflage', *The Modern Review,* quoted by Gandhi in *Young India,* 20-10-1921, ***CWMG,*** XXI, p. 320.
59. 'Definitions of Swaraj', *Navajivan,* 14-8-1921, *CWMG,* XX, p. 507.
60. 'What the Scriptures Say', *Navajivan,* 8-8-1920, *CWMG,* XVIII, p. 127.
61. Jawaharlal Nehru, *The Discovery of India,* (Asia Publishing House, New Delhi, 1947) pp. 164-5.
62. *The Hindu,* 22-9-1921, *CWMG,* XXI, p. 153.
63. *Young India,* 17-11-1921, *CWMG,* XXI, pp. 462-66, 466.
64. 'Message to the Dheds', *Navajivan,* 30-10-1921, *CWMG,* XXI, pp. 368-9.
65. *Young India,* 2-3-1922, *CWMG,* XXII, p. 508.
66. *Notes: Duties of Non-Co-operators Young India,* 9-3-1921, *CWMG,* XIX, p. 414.
67. Gandhi visited Assam in June 1921 and wrote a glowing account of its people in *Young India,* 1-9-1921, and apologized to the people for referring to them in derogatory terms in his book *Hind Swaraj.* "Notes: Lovely Assam", *Young India,* 1-9-1921, *CWMG,* XXI, p. 30.
68. "Christians and Non-Co-operation", *Young India,* 25-8-1921 *CWMG,* XXI, p. 14; and "Christian Non-Co-operators", *Young India,* 22-9-1921 *CWMG,* XXI, p. 174.
69. "Children's Blessing", *Navajivan,* 1-9-1921 *CWMG,* XXI, p. 95.
70. BR Agarwala, *Trials of Independence,* National Book Trust, New Delhi, 1991, p. 93.
71. *Ibid.,* p. 101.
72. *Ibid,* p. 102.
73. Bhikhu Parekh, *Gandhi,* Oxford University Press, 1997, p. 13.
74. BR Agarwala, *op cit.,* p. 104.
75. For the text of the speech see Appendix-I.
76. Willian L. Shirer, *Gandhi: A Memoir,* Rupa and Co., Calcutta, 1979, p. 69.

4

Expanding Role of Press

Preparation for Civil Disobedience Movement (1922-30)

The success in mobilizing the masses for the Rowlatt Bill agitation gave Gandhi the confidence to launch the nation-wide civil disobedience movement. This confidence ultimately spurred him on to strive for attaining swaraj in one year, albeit on the fulfillment of certain conditions. He firmly believed that swaraj alone could end the 'Satanic' rule of the British in India. He had set very high standards for the non-violent Non-Co-operation Movement (NCM) and had full faith in the capacity of the people to live up to his expectations. But just when the preparations were in its final feverish stage with the whole nation responding enthusiastically to his call, an ugly incident forced Gandhi to suspend the movement forthright. Twenty-one policemen had been killed in the incident involving a satyagrahi procession. The inviolable rule and spirit of non-violence had been broken—as Gandhi saw it—and he would have none of that.

A couple of years later, when Gandhi was asked whether he repented his decision (of calling off of the NCM) his reply was a firm no. 'That was the sanest act of my life', he said. 'Future historians will regard me as the saviour of India at the most critical period of her history. It I had not taken that step I would have been regarded by posterity as the greatest monster in the guise of a political leader, and India would have been doomed for many generations to come.'[1] In other words, he was convinced that had he not called off the movement at that juncture it would have turned violent, inviting repressive measures from the Government thereby leading to total disaster.

In the present chapter the developments in the interregnum between the Non-Co-operation Movement (1920-22) and the Civil Disobedience Movement (1930) and Gandhi's use of print media to create public awareness is examined. This was the period which, in Gandhi's own words, was meant to be utilized for the 'preparation for Civil Disobedience'—hence the title of the chapter. This interval is important for many reasons. It brought into focus the role and responsibility of the leader of a mass movement. During this period the principles of Gandhian creed were discussed threadbare. It was time for introspection by Gandhi as well. The situation demanded a firm leader in the greater interest of the country so that lumpen and misguided elements do not take matters into their own hands. It was also the time for consolidation of past successes and putting the experience gained by these to use. The events of the interregnum also give a foretaste of the atmosphere poisoned by suspicion and mistrust that would pervade the nation when freedom would be in sight twenty-five years later.

Some of the important issues raised during this period were:

- Questioning the leadership of Gandhi by a section of the people;
- Gandhi's own doubts about how far he would be able to carry people along with him;
- Division in the Congress over the issue of Council entry and the spinning franchise (whereby only those who spun a certain amount of yarn could be eligible for Congress membership);
- A rash of Hindu-Muslim riots throughout the country fanned by malicious propaganda by both the communities against each other in the press;
- The vicious turn untouchability had taken in Vycom in Travancore;
- The emergence of the revolutionary movement once again (earlier it was in 1905-09) in India; and
- A general feeling of despondency among the people.

Important Developments of the Period

Some very important developments in the history of the freedom movement also took place during this period. The Hindu-Muslim bonhomie, which was so much in evidence during the NCM days, received a rude shock with Gandhi and Shaukat Ali parting ways on what Gandhi called 'matter of principles'. It was the time when the Congress for the first time moved the Independence Resolution. The arrival of the Simon Commission to study the constitutional development and the boycott of the Commission by Indians was also the highlight of the period. The Nehru Committee Report that was the first attempt by Indians to venture into the area of constitution making was another important hallmark. The passing away of veterans like SN Bannerjee, CR Das, Hakim Ajmal Khan, Lala Lajpat Rai, Principal Sushil Rudra, Maganlal Gandhi, to name a few, was not only a personal loss to Gandhi but necessitated the coming forward of somewhat radical new leadership going by the standards of the time. The differences in the views held by Gandhi on the one hand, and Jawaharlal Nehru, Maulana Hasrat Mohani and Subhas Chandra Bose on the other, also found vocal expression during this period. The emergence of Sardar Patel as a pragmatic and worldly-wise leader of the people as was evident in his role in the successful Bardoli Satyagraha of 1928 is another event of note. In fact at the end of this period and just before the commencement of Civil Disobedience Movement Gandhi had the satisfaction of declaring that while the Nehru Report, which was endorsed at the All-Parties Conference at Lucknow at the end of August 1928, paved the way for 'constitutional' swaraj, the way to 'organic' swaraj, which was synonymous with Ramrajya, lay through Bardoli.[2]

Publication of Gandhi's Major Books and Writings

This period saw the serialization of two of Gandhi's monumental works *Satyagraha in South Africa*[3] and *Autobiography*[4] in Gujarati and English, almost simultaneously. Permissions were sought to translate the *Autobiography* into French, German, Swedish, Russian and Punjabi. Interest in the Gandhi phenomenon was growing worldwide. These publications were in addition to his routine articles in his journals besides his speeches which were either reported by the local press or published in his own papers. The content of *Satyagraha in South Africa* has already been dealt with in the first chapter. In the preface to the book Gandhi clearly stated that he was serializing his South African experiences in the belief that 'it may be helpful in our present struggle, and serve as a guide to any regular historian who may arise in the future'. He also recounted in the preface his various successes in applying the principle of non-violent satyagraha to varied situations in India such as Viramgaum peasants' movement, Champaran indigo farmers' movement, Ahmedabad mill workers' movement and Kheda peasants' movement expressing the hope that he would succeed in the present venture as well if his programmes were sincerely followed. His predictions turned out to be true when satyagraha succeeded in Bardoli in 1928-29. Bardoli served as a launching pad for the Civil Disobedience Movement of 1930. It seems that Gandhi serialized *Satyagraha in South Africa* to reassure himself and his countrymen that despite the temporary setback, his method was bound to succeed and that one should not lose hope.[5] Similarly, his *Autobiography* is a document of central importance in the study of his life-story. It carried the important message of the essential unity between personal and public morality. According to him if one defaulted at the personal level one may not achieve lasting success at the level of society as well. This explains Gandhi's calling off of the NCM after the incidents of violence. During the writing of his life-story Gandhi had suffered failures and defeats and had grown spiritually through them. This spirituality gave him strength to work in the political field and get voluntary obedience as a leader. The virtue of the *Autobiography* lay in the fact that one person was able to apply his spiritual power to infuse, though not permanently, a whole mass of people with immense moral strength, converting them into a force to reckon with in politics. It is difficult to present a concrete data on the direct impact of the two books on the Civil Disobedience Movement (CDM) but the success of Gandhi as a leader in the movements to follow is a good indicator. That the *Autobiography* was Gandhi's masterstroke as a communicator can be gauged by the nature of the contents of the letters Gandhi started receiving when his life-story was being serialized. People were aghast at the knowledge that their idol was like any other person given to temptations and weaknesses. A common bond was established, but it also inspired awe for the man who could stand up and lay bare all his weaknesses. There was a strange sincerity and purity in Gandhi's narrative that touched the conscience of the reader, establishing the final milestone in Gandhi's skill as a communicator. Gandhi was asked to respond to queries on highly personal and private matters. All these may not have a bearing on the CDM as such, but it was definitely an indication of the bond Gandhi had created with the common man.

On November 5, 1926, Gandhi wrote the Preface to *Srimad Rajchandra* which again was a timely publication. Gandhi was then serialising his *Autobiography* where he referred to the deep influence Rajchandra had on him. This Preface also helped Gandhi clarify his views on religion still further—a clarification that was badly needed in the period under review. Gandhi's bent of mind is also reflected in the talks on the *Gita* given at the Satyagraha Ashram during morning prayers over nine months (February 24 to November 27, 1926) which were later published in the form of a book in 1955. Another outstanding document of this period was his *Will* that he executed on October 10, 1926 which showed that his renunciation of world was complete and the service of the people had from then onwards become his only duty.[6]

It was the period of introspection both in the history of the nation and the life of Gandhi. It would, therefore, be an interesting exercise to study how Gandhi succeeded in tackling the problems to the extent of organizing the people once again for the most successful movements launched by him, i.e., the Civil Disobedience Movement in 1931. While the previous period was marked by exhorting the people to come forward to 'mend or end the Empire' the present interval was dedicated to the sober task of setting one's house in order before challenging the might of the Empire. At no point of time did Gandhi lose faith in the efficacy of this method of non-violent satyagraha. To characterize his state as that of despondency was 'libel'[7] according to him. For him politics had not taken an 'unfortunate turn' but was 'passing through a necessary stage'. The sea change in the consciousness of the poorer classes had naturally caused an imbalance, an upset in the socio-political scenario. His advice was to be patient, so that the evil that had come to the surface settles down at the bottom.[8] The NCM had been suspended, not abandoned, he said. Also, he added, as soon as the people are prepared for launching it, it would begin.

The turn of events showed that Gandhi's optimism was not misplaced, though there were moments when his optimism received a jolt and he worried about the affairs of the nation, particularly about the communal situation in the country and the poverty of his countrymen. In fact, his anxiety affected his health. Gandhi admitted in a letter to Dr. Ansari, 'My chief difficulty is how to control the mind and not let it think, unless I develop *dementia*...but I do not know how I can prevent the doings of Hindus and Mussalmans from making me think furiously. Nor do I know how to prevent the growing starvation of millions acting upon my mind.'[9]

Gandhi was unwell for a major part of the period between the years 1922-30. Speech making and addressing the public was, therefore, limited to only a few very important occasions. Gandhi had no choice other than to concentrate on his writing.

Gandhi Resumes Charge of the Movement

The decision to suspend the NCM was taken solely by Gandhi in his capacity as the leader of the movement. The Congress had acquiesced in the decision only reluctantly. The Congress leaders were neither happy with Gandhi's decision nor convinced by his arguments. Gandhi, a person not to easily give up, entered into long correspondence with most of these leaders and finally succeeded in convincing a majority of them.

Gandhi, well aware of the dissatisfaction gave vent to his feelings in the columns of *Navajivan*, 'The All India Congress Committee gave me a majority, but I could see that very few really liked the Bardoli resolutions. I got the votes because I was Gandhi and not because people were convinced ....When we are struggling to establish the rule of the people, of what avail is the victory of one individual? How far will the wagon go, having thus to be pushed all the time?...'[10] yet in the same article he also chalked out the programmes people should follow to secure the release of prisoners who had been arrested for non-cooperating with the government as the civil disobedience movement which was to be launched for securing swaraj in which these prisoners would have been released, had been suspended. In the programme people were asked to get enrolled with the Congress party; collect contributions for the swaraj fund; start and run national schools; visit homes of liquor addicts; persuade people to wear khadi and introduce spinning wheel in every home; help Antyajas; set up panchayats and nurse sick and injured people.[11] This intermixture of sentiments and directions shows how in his heart of hearts Gandhi was convinced that he was still the leader and believed that bringing a movement to its proper conclusion was his responsibility alone.

For a nation that had been gearing itself for something as dramatic as the achievement of *swaraj*, such a programme was certainly not viewed with enthusiasm. In a speech at Bombay on April 13, 1925 Gandhi is reported to have said that even Sardar Patel had asked him to place such a programme before the country as would 'enthuse the people'[12] The constructive part of the Non-Co-operation movement was generally considered to be of secondary importance in comparison to the achievement of swaraj by an energetic civil disobedience movement. Gandhi, however, held an altogether different view. For him the faithful carrying out of the constructive programme was the necessary, solid base for launching civil disobedience and finally achieving *swaraj*.[13]

The majority of the people in India, however, thought otherwise. They wanted some excitement and were impatient. Hence Gandhi met with opposition at every step and in all his programmes. Gandhi countered all the charges levelled against him with patience. Non-cooperation was a movement aimed not at exciting people but making them achieve the sober objective of swaraj he maintained. Satyagraha, Gandhi said, 'is not intoxication produced by *bhang*. It is not a passing fancy. Satyagraha is an urge from within. As time passes it does not slow down but grows more compelling.'[14]

Historians have recorded how the frustration of the people with Gandhi's leadership found expression in the revolutionary movements in India and encouraged the communists in their role in the freedom movement of India, though for a limited period. Some communist leaders even went to the extent of writing an open letter to Gandhi, inviting him to join their party and organize the peasant and workers movements instead of leading the national movement.[15] A section of Muslims also objected to Gandhi's decision to suspend the movement. They had all along been treating the Khilafat agitation as *jehad*, a holy war. It was no joke to start and stop *jehad* at will, they said. In reply, Gandhi requested to be deposed from the 'generalship' of the movement as he would never submit to the use of violence under any situation and for any cause, however noble it may be.

Along with criticism came appreciation as well. Gandhi received kudos for his generalship from no less a person than the elder brother of Rabindra Nath Tagore. Dwijendra Nath Tagore, in his characteristic poetic style, congratulated Gandhi for his foresight in the following words:

> A wise captain slackens the speed of his vessel whilst moving in the right direction, whenever it arrives at a spot

> abounding in dangerous rocks, and speeds his vessel as soon as he enters into the open sea which is free from all sorts of such impediments. But a foolish captain steers his vessel in the wrong direction for fear of rocks, where there is no such thing whatever under the sea, and proceeds towards an unknown region where hidden rocks are lying in wait to shatter his vessel into fragments the moment it approaches their dwelling place.
>
> Mahatma Gandhi is guiding his vessel in the former way, while his advisors want him to take the latter course.[16]

Gandhi put both the opposite views (one representing the objections raised by a Muslim correspondent and other the praise by Dwijendra Nath Tagore) in the same issue of *Young India* with clear inclination in favour of the latter view.[17] The same issue of *Young India* carried five more articles by Gandhi because Gandhi was expecting his arrest very soon and wanted to communicate all the important messages to the public before his incarceration. These articles covered various themes such as condemning the doubling of salt-tax by the Government, directions to the publishers and printers of his journal and the public in case he was arrested and also an article on the denial by authorities of reports regarding bad treatment of political prisoners.

Gandhi's Imprisonment and the Slackening of the Movement

On March 10, 1922 Gandhi was arrested and sentenced to six years simple imprisonment for seditious writings. He, however, was released before the end of his full term in 1924 and had to be operated for appendicitis. Gandhi had continued to write for his journals even from the prison but bad health forced him to give up editorship of *Young India* for some time.

Though Gandhi was glad that the country remained peaceful during his imprisonment it gradually dawned on him that some of the principles close to his heart were being questioned and a sort of rebellion was building against him. Gandhi was subjected to scathing criticism to the point that he even volunteered to give up his leadership of the movement.[18] On the other hand he was chary of too much dependence on him or people giving in to him just because he was Gandhi without actually being convinced of his stand. He remarked ruefully: 'I often think that it would have been better for the country and for me if I had served the full term of my imprisonment. The country would by that time have settled down to a programme which could be called its own.'[19]

Gandhi, however, firmly denied the reports that the political chapter of his life was over and that he wished to convert politics into social reform through the writings in his journals, especially the *Navajivan*.[20] To this charge Gandhi's emphatic reply was: 'I cannot agree to give the first place to caste reform. *Navajivan* is run to help the cause of swaraj. It exists entirely for this purpose. *The cause of social reform is dear to me, but it has no connection whatever with my present activities in the field of journalism*.'[21] [This remark shows that his phase of social journalism was yet to begin. It was only after the Dandi March of 1931 that Gandhi took up social journalism after a conscious decision to that effect.]

Not the one to give in to depression, Gandhi picked up the thread of civil disobedience movement where he had left off the unpopular constructive programme. He reiterated his stand that it was a necessary phase and preparation for final movement. He insisted in devoting full time to the programme, which consisted of popularization of spinning and the use of khadi, removal of untouchability and efforts at Hindu-Muslim unity. The programme of the boycott of foreign cloth, boycott of courts, government schools and Councils was also to be continued side by side.

Spinning

The most important item on Gandhi's constructive programme was spinning. He viewed it as a panacea for most of the economic, social and political ills of the Indian society. He wrote a large number of articles on a variety of issues, linking each one of them to the importance of spinning. Spinning was the one way to provide employment and life of dignity to the poor villager, who remained idle half the year round.[22] Spinning saved the Indian women from the lust of their employers or from flesh trade.[23] The music of the spinning wheel rose over the dissonance and cacophony of multiple political voices and ideologies.[24] For instance, Swarajists and No-changers both could agree to spin in spite of their different ideologies. Spinning struck at the roots of the Empire that had maintained itself all these years by selling British mill made cloth and stifled the indigenous cottage industry of India.[25] Khaddar, Gandhi believed, was a potent and effective answer to British repression.[26] For Gandhi symbolically, this rough cloth made the best flag of defiance against the Empire. Gandhi had put forward all these advantages of spinning in his writings with encouraging response from the public.

Counters Criticism of Spinning and Khadi

Gandhi's emphasis on spinning and khadi was, at times, scoffed at. Some people genuinely believed that it was not good for the health of the Indian economy. One such write-up poetically presented was brought to Gandhi's notice by a correspondent. The writer of the letter reported that in the *Chaitra* issue of the *Vasant* magazine the editor had tried to show how Gandhi's emphasis on Khadi was going to ruin the mills in India and warned the people not to be taken in by Gandhi's advise however attractive it may seem. The article created quite a furore and was discussed in various fora. Gandhi put things in the correct perspective through the columns of his journal. Without entering into any argument with the editor, Gandhi's brief reply was 'let work speak for itself.' He also made it clear that he had no 'particular love or dislike for the mill cloth' and it was not khadi, but foreign cloth, that was a 'threat to the textile mills in India.'[27]

There were people who considered spinning as a demeaning exercise. Some caste Hindus believed that if was an occupation of Muslim weaver classes, the *julahas,* and therefore not to talk of spinning they were not prepared to even wear such cloth.[28] Others considered it a woman's chore.[29] Some even considered it an effort by Gandhi to 'decasteise' them by bringing all to the level of *vaishyas,* or even worse, *sudras.* Gandhi's considered reply to this was:

> In my view a Sudra is one who earns his living by doing service or wage labour for others. Thus considered all who do service are Sudras. How can one who pursues an independent occupation be treated as a Sudra? I do not see this does any harm to *varnashrama.*[30]

The economics of spinning was disputed by some. They argued that if a person had the capacity to earn more by other means, there was no need to spin and weave. This question had been put to Gandhi several times. In one of his articles Gandhi finally chose to respond. He stated:

> My conviction tells me that God gave us the intellect for knowing ourselves A living should be got out of agriculture,

> etc. The chief cause of all the wickedness there is in the world is the misuse of the intellect. It is through the misuse of the intellect that there is so much inequality in the world. Tens or millions go about begging while a hundred or two become millionaires. *The true economics is that by which every man or woman gets a living by physical labour.*[31] (emphasis added).

People who had at one time enthusiastically participated in Gandhi's movement for popularizing spinning now argued that they were disillusioned by the results and found the whole exercise impractical. The exchange of views on this topic would be instructive to those who considered or consider Gandhi muddle-headed. Gandhi quoted a letter by 'a friend' and gave a fitting reply to it. The letter and Gandhi's reply run thus:

> Your activity [meaning hand spinning] is useless. Why are you wasting your body and mind in dishing up old stuff in the pages of *Young India* and *Navajivan*? I can no longer read them with profit. I have found by experience that spinning wheel is no use... Substitute hand-spinning with machine-spinning. Erect a spinning mill in every Taluka.
>
> ***Gandhi's Reply:*** As the argument is specious and comes from one who in his own way tried the charkha, I propose to examine for the sake of those who may hold the views that the friend does....
>
> The friend has forgotten the central truth that the wheel furnishes occupation and a small income to the millions who must have an additional income if they are not to starve .It is not possible to put up a handloom in every home. *A loom in every village and a charkha in every home is the formula.* If a spinning mill is put up in every Taluka, it will result in nationalizing the exploitation of many by the few. All cannot be employed in the Taluka mill. Moreover, we must import the machinery needed for over 2,000 Talukas And the experts for managing and working the mills will have to be trained....The failure of charkha is felt by nobody, the failure of the Taluka mill will mean consternation among the people of the Taluka concerned.[32] (emphasis added)

A section of people attacked khadi on aesthetic grounds and pointed out that it was coarse and unmanageable.[33] Gandhi countered with the argument that once one appreciated the fact that khadi was sacred, stood for national dignity, and gave people self-reliance and was a cloth for all seasons, the coarseness of khadi would be worth tolerating.[34]

It was not that Gandhi's spinning programmes were a total failure. At many places they had been carried out by enthusiastic and devoted Congressmen and had achieved wonderful results. Dr. P.C. Ray a renowned scientist and a social worker from Bengal, who Gandhi jestingly described as 'khadi-crazy', did commendable work in popularizing khadi and spinning wheel in remote areas of Bengal and Assam and kept Gandhi, posted about his successes. Ray and his associates also made improvements in the spinning wheel. His communications to Gandhi were frequently referred to by the latter in his journals.[35]

With a 'simple calculation' on khadi Gandhi dissuaded people from wasting time coming to the station for his *darshan*. He wrote:

> The average annual per capita requirement of cloth comes to 13 yards. Let us assume that this quantity of cloth weighs three seers. So much can be easily produced by one person if he spins no more than half an hour daily. That is to say, if half the population spins only for one hour a day it can supply the yarn needs of the entire country. May I hope that instead of taking the trouble to come to the station, my brothers and sisters will restrain their eagerness and give that time to spinning?[36]

In the article, 'Mill-hands and Khadi', Gandhi brought the economics of khadi with the most telling effect by quoting from *Majoor Sandesh* a periodical published by Majoor Mahajan, the textile workers union of Ahmedabad.

> If you buy a pound of khadi;
> Ten annas will go to one of our peasants.
> One-and-a-half to two annas will go to one of our poor carders.
> Four to six annas will go to some poor women who spun the yarn.
> Eight to nine annas will go to some weaver who wove the yarn spun by those sisters.
> Three quarters of anna will go to one of our washerman.

> If you wear khadi, all this money will remain in our country and will go to some of our brothers and sisters.[37]

Gandhi' economics could not be faulted. It goes to the credit of Gandhi that he gave extensive and detailed coverage to the success stories and the experiments in khadi through the columns of his journals.

Gandhi's zeal for spinning, however, crossed all limits when he made spinning a compulsory condition for the membership of the Congress Party. This led to the deepening of the crisis within the Party which had already experienced a division in the form of two groups euphemistically called, the Swarajists, who defied the Gandhian plan of boycott of Councils and the other group known as No-changers, who stuck to the earlier programme. Gandhi later managed to bring the two together with great difficulty in 1925.

Like a typical school-teacher Gandhi also got the yarn spun by the Congress workers examined by a team of experts and declared the results province wise in his papers. Medals and awards were also given away and reported in his papers.[38] When a municipal address described Gandhi as 'khaddar king' in view of his services, with characteristic humility and sense of humour he replied, 'What a poor khaddar king I must be'.[39] Gandhi's Khaddar contagion caught on. Even Motilal Nehru—of the silk handkerchiefs and chauffeur driven cars— walked the streets of Allahabad hawking the rough tough cloth. Aghast, *The Times of India* turned almost abusive. 'Pt. Nehru,' it said 'was making an ass of himself.' Gandhi was quick with a fitting reply, though his tone was of gentle irony— nonetheless effective. He wrote, 'It is to be wished that many leaders will follow Panditji and earn the title that has been so courteously bestowed upon Panditji by *The Times of India*. It is generally time to rejoice when one receives curse from opponents'. He reminded the paper that during the War the British irrespective of their class had taken up sewing clothes for soldiers and this was not considered a demeaning activity but thought of as a proof of patriotism. The Indians are also engaged in similar activity.[40] Gandhi pointed out that the paper did not represent the views of all the Europeans and as a proof quoted at length a letter from Poland wherein the writer had offered to hawk khadi in his country to make his countrymen aware of the great struggle that was going on in India.[41]

Khadi became a symbol of the defiance of the British repressive regime. The sheer numbers that wore khadi gave an ocular demonstration of their desire for freedom. The British could also read the message and at several places Governmental employees were not allowed to wear khadi.

Gandhi encouraged the practice of leaders being honoured with garlands not of flowers but with yarn garlands which could later be used to weave khadi. Gandhi also started the practice of auctioning the best khadi cloth that was presented to him. The rich paid exorbitant price for the auctioned cloth.[42] This small act shows his ingenuity as a motivator.

Soon even the British started recognizing the potency of khadi as a political, social and economic weapon. Gandhi quoted with pride the 'reluctant testimony' of Harcourt Robinson, an Englishman, who had spent many years in British India and who claimed to have intimate knowledge of Indian market-psychology. Gandhi wrote:

> He (Mr. Robinson) ascribes the heavy drop in the mount of British cotton fabrics purchased by India not to post-war economic dislocation and economic stress, nor to the poverty of the masses.... nor to the famines... but to the competition of Indian and Japanese mills and most of all to khaddar....He regards khaddar as the real enemy.... He says: 'Khaddar is a native-made cloth, woven on a primitive loom from hand-spun yarn by unskilled, amateurish workers. It is coarse, stiff, full of knots and faults, and always looks dirty—yet there is a positive vogue about it, even wealthy natives taking a pride in garments made from it. For khaddar represents in its concrete form the slogan of a rapidly growing Nationalist party: 'India for Indians'. Not a penny spent on it leaves the country. He who wears it helps to feed India's millions, proclaims his country's independence and shows himself a patriot of the first water.... Khaddar is one of the weapons used by, and indeed invented by, Mahatma Gandhi in his fight against foreign rule in India. Half-saint, half fanatic, and wholly patriot, Mahatma Gandhi now speaks, in his person and through native Press, to the very hearts of India's educated classes. *Non-Co-operation is not dead in India because it is no longer talked. It has now reached the stage of silent and*

> *dangerous activity*.... Let Mr. Gandhi's missionaries once rope in the masses, and India will no longer be a poor buyer, she will be no buyer at all.... The blow is not aimed only at cotton. It is a definite attempt to ruin the market for all British goods.[43]

This outpouring of a British gentleman was a salutary acknowledgement of the power of khadi Gandhi had been speaking about all these years. In February 1929 Foreign Cloth Boycott Committee was created by the Congress with Gandhi as its chairman. This Committee worked so efficiently under Gandhi that by May 1929 there were reports that one third of textile mills in Great Britain had to be closed down because demand from India fell to zero point, making it impossible for the Indian buyer to carry forward contracts.[44]

Hindu-Muslim Unity

The communal problem had for long been a thorn in Gandhi's side. Convinced that swaraj could not be achieved unless Hindus and Muslims learned to live in peace with each other; he strained every nerve in his body to bring about this unity. He wrote a lengthy article in the *Navajivan* which was later translated for *Young India* and also distributed in the form of a pamphlet. In this article Gandhi effectively countered the charge that by arousing the Muslims and giving importance to the Khilafat issue Gandhi had fired up the religious consciousness among them, resulting in their converting this consciousness into a *jehad* against the Hindus. Gandhi also criticized the *shuddhi* movement started by the Arya samajists as ill conceived and liable to be misunderstood by the Muslims. In the same vein he criticized the *tabligh* movement started by the Muslims which was a counterpart of the *shuddhi* movement and aimed at reconverting the non-Muslims to Islam. In this article he also sought to clear the charges of being communal made by both the Hindu and Muslim camps against each others' leaders. The sensitive issues of cow slaughter and playing of music in front of mosques was also deftly handled by him. Finally, an appeal for peace was made.[45] Elsewhere in defence of his stand that Pt. Madan Mohan Malaviya was not anti-Muslim, Gandhi gives a translation of a personal letter written by Panditji to Gandhi in *Young India*. It runs as follows:

> I agree with every word of what you have written about helping Moplah women and children.

> 'Where is the merit in a man who returns good for good?
> The wise call him only good who does good to evil doer.
>
> They alone are good who do good to those that do harm to them and these good souls adorn the earth; for it is the better for their birth.'
>
> Please do not infer from the verse quoted above by me that in my opinion all Moplahs have injured Hindus. But even assuming that all the Moplahs have done us an injury, even then must we serve them in the hour of their need. In such conduct lies the beauty of our religion.[46]

Similarly, Gandhi also published another letter by Pt. Malaviya wherein he had appealed to the people of India to contribute more liberally to the Moplah relief fund. By publishing these two letters Gandhi sought to remove the charge of being communal from the name of Pt. Malaviya by showing to the readers the true nature of the great man.

For all the pains he took, he received more brick-bats than bouquets. The Arya Samajists were furious at Gandhi's description of their sect as exclusivist and especially with regard to his views on *Satyarth Prakash* (first published in 1875),[47] the book written by Swami Dayanand Saraswati, the founder of Arya Samaj. Gandhi refused to take back his criticism though he said that he meant no disrespect to either Swami Dayanand Saraswati, the founder of the movement or its contemporary leader, Swami Shraddhanand, the founder of Gurukul Kangri, an educational institution based on Vedic principles, in Haridwar.Though Arya Samaj organizations from Punjab and Gujarat had sent him letters taking exception to his views Gandhi finally chose to publish the well argued letter from Principal Ram Deva, the head of the premier Arya Samaj educational institution, Gurukul Kangri of Haridwar. Defending his (Gandhi's) stand on the plea that his opinion was formed only after reading *Satyarth Prakash* Gandhi puts the question to the writer of the letter: 'Will he forget that a man's moral teaching may be of a high order and yet his vision may be narrow?'[48]

Apart from the Arya Samajists the orthodox Hindus charged him of being partial to the Muslims and thus weakening the Hindu cause. A sample of one such out-bursts is as follows:

> You are already in a mood to flatter the Mohammedans and it seems as though you think, by exonerating them from

> their high-handedness, you can keep them in close touch with the Hindus. You must now learn to distribute blame among the parties involved , as justice requires it , as this policy of seeking to blame the weak and meek members of the nation and flattering the strong and highhanded element is by no means a wise policy.[49]

Under the heading 'A Homily' Gandhi's only advice to the correspondent was to have a 'large heart'.

Gandhi's co-religionists questioned his Hindu credentials by characterizing his non-violence as Christian in concept. To this Gandhi's reply was that it was a matter only between him and his Maker.[50] This was the period when Gandhi for the first time was being accused of being pro-Muslim at the cost of his co-religionists. He was even given a Muslim name in 'consideration' of his services![51] But all this did not deter Gandhi. He, in fact, gave full publicity to these sentiments giving reasons for his actions. And most of the time it turned out that the critics had been misinformed about the incident on which their arguments rested.[52]

The Muslim outbursts were no less vituperative. They charged Gandhi for contributing to the backwardness of the Muslims by propagating the boycott of schools and colleges thus bringing to naught the lifelong efforts of Sir Syed Ahmad the founder of Aligarh School. Under the heading the 'Mussalman indictment' Gandhi quoted a letter by a Muslim correspondent who had levelled the above mentioned charge against him in his (Gandhi's) famous pamphlet on Hindu-Muslim tension. Gandhi's reply to this is worth quoting. He says:

> Had I been a prophet and foreseen all that has happened, I should have still thrown myself into the Khilafat agitation. In spite of the strained relations between the two communities, both have gained. *The awakening among the masses was a necessary part of the training.* [53] (emphasis added)

A study of the letters received by Gandhi from both the communities shows that he was generally seen as an impartial judge for both the communities. These letters also show that he was trusted by both Hindus and Muslims and was recognized as a person who could not be easily ruffled. Copies of pamphlets showing each others' religion in lurid colours were sent to Gandhi, who acknowledged their receipt but never made them public. He was ever keen to highlight the stories of mutual trust between both the communities.[54] This shows the maturity and foresight of Gandhi both as a leader and a journalist.

Gandhi had taken upon himself the role of a relentless crusader against the evil of communalism. When reports of incidents of desecration of temples in Moradabad and Gulbarga reached him, he wrote a strongly worded article addressing both the Hindus and Muslims. He wrote:

> I must feel, more keenly than most Hindus can, these desecrations. I am both an idolater and an iconoclast in what I conceive to be the true sense of the terms. *I value the spirit behind idol worship.* It plays the most important part in the uplift of the human race. And I would like to possess the ability to defend with my life the thousands of holy temples which this land of ours has. My alliance with the Mussalmans presupposed their perfect tolerance for my idols and my temples. *I am an iconoclast in the sense that I break down the subtle form of idolatry in the shape of fanaticism that refused to see any virtue in any other form of worshipping the Deity save one's own .This form of idolatry is more deadly for being more fine and evasive than the tangible and gross form of worship that identifies the Deity with a little bit of a stone or a golden image.*[55] (emphasis supplied)

Communal tension took an ugly turn when on September 9 and 10 1924 a mass attack on the Hindus forced the entire Hindu population of Kohat (North West Frontier Province) to leave their homes and flee to Rawalpindi. Unable to stop the recurrence of communal riots, Gandhi, after a good deal of deliberation, decided to go on fast. In a letter to C.F. Andrews he wrote:

> Don't you fret my decision. It has been taken after deep prayer and clearest indication. This fast of 21 days is the least I can do. Oh the agony of it all! Every day has been a day of torture. But I shall soon be at peace....The light has come like a flash. *Can a man do more than give his life?*[56] (emphasis supplied)

The same day in a letter to Motilal Nehru informing him of his decision Gandhi confided: 'That is how I have learnt to understand religion.'[57] Gandhi issued a brief communication to the Associated Press of India which was later published in his journal *Young India*. The statement is a powerful appeal to sanity to both the communities. It runs as follows:

> The recent events have proved unbearable. *My helplessness is still more unbearable.* My religion teaches me that whenever there is distress which one cannot remove, one must fast and pray. *I have done so in connection with my dearest ones. Nothing evidently that I say or write can bring the two communities together.* I am therefore imposing on myself a fast of 21 days.... As a penance I need not take the public into confidence, but I publish the fast as (let me hope) an effective prayer both to Hindus and Mussalmans, who have hitherto worked in unison, not to commit suicide. I respectfully invite the heads of all communities, including Englishmen, to meet and end this quarrel which is a disgrace to religion and to humanity. *It seems as if God has been dethroned. Let us reinstate him in our hearts.*[58] (emphasis added)

The above mentioned statement is a brilliant example of Gandhi's communication skills. Here is a leader who by showing his utter helplessness wins the sympathy of the public. This helplessness makes him take the extreme step of putting his life at stake for one's 'own dearest ones'. Though insisting that fasting is a private affair he is publicizing it in the hope that it would stir the conscience of the guilty and the misguided. In was in fact a personal appeal to one and all. Publicity was crucial to the whole act of fasting as was the element of self-suffering. Bhikhu Parekh has maintained that in a Nazi set-up Gandhi would have faced difficulties because there he would have been eliminated before he could publicize his cause.[59] This is a conjecture and brings us back to the question: Was the gentlemanliness of the British a factor in the success of the Gandhian method? The larger and deeper truth, the universality of human nature and human behaviour, gets a beating when different nations and races are shown to have certain peculiar characteristics, overriding basic humanism.

Gandhi's fast had a sobering effect. Unity conferences were organized, but communalism had taken too deep a root to be pulled out so easily.

Gandhi's zeal for truth and transparency pushed him into two sticky situations which did not better the communal situation. Maulana Shaukat Ali and Gandhi had jointly undertaken to investigate into the causes of the Kohat riots that had taken place in 1924 and effect reconciliation between the two communities. The local Muslim leaders had refused to assist them in the inquiry and, on the basis of the evidence available, Gandhi and Maulana came to divergent conclusions. Public admission of their differences ran the serious risk of being misrepresented and exploited by communal elements. Since the beginning of the Khilafat movement in 1920-21 they had worked together. The difference between the two leaders on a communal issue might or might not affect their personal relations, but it was certain to have unhappy repercussions on the general atmosphere in the country. Gandhi, therefore, took utmost care to present the matter in proper light to the Maulana and to the general public. Finally the statement was issued in *Young India*, (26-3-1925) Preceding the text of the statement was an address directed to the readers. Gandhi acknowledged that:

> There are material differences between us on the inferences we have drawn from the same facts. There are differences too in the degree of reliance we have placed upon the evidence given by witnesses....We also examined the suggestion made by Hakim Saheb and supported to an extent by Pandit Motilalji not to publish the statements. But we, *at least I*, came to the conclusion that the public which had hitherto known the Ali Brothers and me to be always in agreement about so many public things should know that we too might differ on some matters, but without suspecting each other of conscious bias or willful perversion of facts and without mutual affection being in any way affected. *Our open acknowledgement of our differences will be an object-lesson in mutual toleration.*[60] (emphasis added)

The difference between the two leaders was over the fact that whereas Gandhi apportioned the blame on both the communities but objected to the conversions taking place in Kohat and also to the behaviour of the members of the Khilafat committee of the region, Shaukat Ali considered the issue of conversions, if not forced, of not much consequence and thought the provocation for the riots was caused by the poem written by Jivandass with unedifying references to the Prophet and Islam. Over who fired the first shot, Shaukat Ali was of the firm opinion that the Sardar whose son was guilty of relations with a Muslim woman was the culprit whereas Gandhi had absolved him because of the lack of evidence and absence of eye witnesses.

The second issue on which Gandhi's position led to controversy was an equally sensitive one. Commenting in *Young India* to a report that two members of the Ahmadiya sect had been stoned to death in Afghanistan as penalty for apostasy, Gandhi had said: 'I understand that the stoning method is enjoined in the Koran only in certain circumstances which do not cover the cases under observation. But as a human being living in the fear of God I should question the morality of the method under any circumstance whatsoever...Every formula of every religion has in this age of reason, to submit to the acid test of reason. Error can claim no exemption even if it can be supported by the scriptures of the world.'[61] This was too radical an attitude for the orthodox and led to some angry protests. The President of the Punjab Khilafat Committee wrote: 'You have shaken the belief of the millions of your Muslim admirers in your capacity to lead them'.[62] In response to this Gandhi suggested: 'intolerance of criticism even of what one may prize as dear as life itself is not conducive to the growth of corporate life. Surely Islam had nothing to fear from criticism even if it be unreasonable. I therefore suggest to the Maulana the advisability in the light of my criticism of applying himself to an elucidation of the tremendous issues involved in the incidents reported from Kabul.'[63] He clarified his position further:

> In my writing about Islam I take the same care of its prestige as I do of Hinduism. I apply the same method of interpretation to it that I apply to Hinduism I no more defend on the mere ground of authority a single text in the Hindu scriptures that I can defend one from the Koran. Every thing has to submit to the test of reason. Islam appeals to people as it appeals to reason.[64]

Gandhi's advocacy of submitting everything to the test of reason seemed to contradict his stand as the votary of 'the inner voice'. The crux of the matter is what Gandhi's definition of religion was. Basically religion for him meant *karuna, ie.* compassion. The acid test of all religions was whether they promoted compassion or not.

Gandhi's emphasis on the relationship between religion and politics did not appeal to many rationalists. His condition that only 'god-fearing' people could become good non-co-operators was objected to. At this Gandhi gave the assurance that a man need not declare his religion to participate in national programme.[65] This controversy again cropped up with the inclusion of the word God in the Congress pledge. Gandhi promptly removed the word God from the pledge for those who had conscientious objection to it. He went on to say that the existence of God in the form of truth or some principle was recognized even by atheists.[66]

Limited Success on the Communal Front

Gandhi's fast did not stop rioting. It is estimated that there were 112 cases of communal riots in different parts of India between the years 1922-27.[67] At one point Gandhi gave up all efforts at arbitration and waited for the parties to come to their senses on their own. 'Parties are just now better organized for quarrels than for a settlement. No doubt they will finally meet. But it seems they will do so only after they have finished with the arbitration of the sword.'[68] When Gandhi gave up mediation in the Hindu-Muslim affairs Maulana Abul Kalam Azad tried to use the forum of the Congress Party to bring about communal harmony. Gandhi's telling comment on this initiative was: 'I despair of the Congress discovering or enforcing a solution. *Let us not conceal from ourselves the truth that the Congress does not represent the fighters in either camp.*'[69]

Gandhi also did not approve of governmental mediation. His opinion was: 'To stop anti-Muslim writings like *Rangila Rasul*[70] is the work of the Hindus, as to stop anti-Hindu writings us the work of Mussalmans. The leaders have either lost control over mudflingers or are in sympathy with them. In any case Government protection will not make us tolerant to one another.'[71]

In another comment on the Hindu-Muslim question, Gandhi's words carry a strong smell of fatalistic premonition. In a letter to a friend he wrote:

> I look upon the Hindu-Muslim riots as a kind of surgical operation. It would have been excellent if could have avoided it, but evidently we had been suffering from inflammation of this particular limb and the condition was no longer curable by bandaging the part. When this rioting is over,

one day we will certainly become united. And if this society much decayed to last, let it perish. In any case the present condition is worse that the profound darkness in which it was slumbering.[72]

Gandhi had adopted a policy of remaining silent about communal matters for some time. There came situations, however, when Gandhi had to break his self-imposed silence in religious matters, more appropriately, communal matters. One such situation came in 1927 when Swami Shraddhananda, the leader of the Arya Samajists was murdered at his residence by a Muslim. Gandhi realized the grimness of the situation. He rightly surmised that the murder may well lead to retaliatory murders of Hindus. He called for sanity saying 'the atmosphere that prevails today holds out no hope that we shall escape with only one murder'. It would be better, he said if both the communities realized that the present situation is not an isolated one but had risen due to the misunderstanding between the two communities. Therefore, he urged, it was necessary to make efforts to resolve the differences and to bear in mind that all religions say the same thing.[73] This message was given through the *Hindi Navajivan,* which shows that Gandhi was aware of the sections that should be addressed.

Gandhi's words, however, did not go well with the Hindu community, which felt it was the aggrieved party and also believed, rightly or wrongly, that Gandhi was not condemning the act in the strongest of terms. In an article entitled 'A Candid Critic', published in *Young India* on 21-1-1927, Gandhi quoted at length a letter in which there was criticism of his defence of the man who murdered Swami Shraddhanand. The letter and Gandhi's reply are worthy of being quoted in full. The letter says:

> I have perused your article 'Swamiji the Martyr' with care and reverence it deserves. I have read it five times before attempting to criticize it....
>
> The article is undoubtedly written in a fascinating language. I envy your style. It attracts, but to me it appears, that is rather dangerously attractive.
>
> My estimation is based on my estimation of your character. I have often debated with some friends on this subject. They hold that you are a statesman in the garb of a saint—ready

to forgo truth in the cause of your country. I have on the contrary maintained that you are a saint— who has entered politics in fulfillment of your mission, to practise truth in the face of the most trying and perplexing circumstances. I shall be very obliged to know if my estimation is correct. For if it is not, the criticism that follows has little value. I am of the opinion that a man of policy is within his rights to write in the manner you have done.

You will agree with me that to suppress truth is a form of falsehood; to refuse to call a spade a spade when you feel like is cowardice; and that fearlessness and truth go together.

Do you see, Mahatmaji, that the murder of Swamiji was inhuman, barbarous and cruel act of a Muslim ruffian and that the entire Muslim community should be ashamed of it?.... Instead of condemning the deed and the doer, and those who are responsible for this act (those who describe Hindu leaders as Kafirs—the hot Muslim propagandist and the mad priests) you have begun to defend the murderer and hold an apology for the community....

You say further, Islam means peace. Is this truth? Islam as taught by the Koran and practised by Muslims ever since its birth never meant peace. What makes you write a thing so patently wrong?....

You never minced matters when condemning the writings of Government, you never minced when you condemned Arya Samaj, why fear to condemn Muslims for even proved wrongs?....

I am sure if such a black act had been committed by a Hindu against a Muslim leader (which Heaven forbid!), you would have condemned the murderer and the community in unsparing terms.... Why do you accord preferential treatment to your 'blood brothers' the Muslims?....

To this Gandhi replied:

The writer is frank and obviously in earnest and *reflects the prevalent mood.*

To clothe me with sainthood is too early even if it is possible I myself do not feel a saint in any shape or form. But I do feel

> I am a votary of Truth in spite of my errors of omission and commission ....I have no policy in me save the policy of truth and ahimsa. *I will not sacrifice truth and ahimsa even for the deliverance of my country or religion. This is as much as to say that neither can be so delivered.*
>
> I feel... the assassin ... is himself a victim of foul irreligious propaganda in the name of religion.... I do hold the maulvis and all those who have indulged in exciting hatred against the Swamiji to be responsible... I have given my opinion that the followers of Islam are too free with the sword. But that is not due to the teachings of the Koran. That is due in my opinion to the environment in which Islam was born....[74]

This interaction between his critic and Gandhi brings to light a few interesting facts of his communication skill. The critic acknowledges the fact that Gandhi's style of writing is 'dangerously attractive' but still goes on to question the validity of the views put forward by Gandhi. It is a dialogue between one 'adult' and another. Gandhi in his turn reciprocates the respectful love shown by the 'critic' and admires his candour and earnestness. Without being either condescending or pontifical he puts forward his views in the most straightforward manner. In fact, Gandhi rarely shied away from criticism. He preferred to walk half way to meet his critics and published the severest of the criticism along with his defence. Transparency was the hallmark of his communication strategy.

The above example is one of the many similar interactions between Gandhi and his critics.

It was a bad time for Hindu-Muslim relations. Soon Gandhi and Shaukat Ali, the two figures that symbolized the friendship between the communities parted ways. The relations had become strained since the two gave different versions of the Kohat case. Soon Mohammad Ali was found defaulting on the spinning clause and his membership of the All India Spinners Association was terminated. But the last straw seems to have come in the form of Shaukat Ali's speech at Kanpur where he had criticized Hindus as a community. This speech appeared in the 18-11-1928 issue of Hasrat Mohani's paper *Khilafat*. Gandhi's pain was evident in the personal letter he wrote to Shaukat Ali which runs as follows:

> No, the speaker at Cawnpore is not Maulana with whom I

> had been so long familiar and with whom I have passed many happy days as with a blood-brother and a bosom friend....I would go all the way with you in accusing the Hindu of his many misdeeds; but I am unable to hold with you that he was ever the aggressor, ever the tyrant and his Mussalman brother always the injured victim....[75]

The story of Gandhi versus communalism is in three stages—hope, withdrawal and despair. He began with a confident, proactive stance, but when faced with an ugly, worsening situation beyond his control he withdrew into himself, making silence his mode of communication. And finally, in torment over his sheer helplessness, his health broke down. He had had his premonitions, as noted earlier. Somewhere in his mind he must have realized that communalism was one battle he may not win.

Untouchability

Gandhi's inborn quality—a necessity for his head and heart—to question and test tradition and authority is best reflected in his ceaseless campaign against the evil of untouchability. In this area too he ruffled many an orthodox feather.

A social worker had informed Gandhi that untouchables in Kerala had launched Vaikom satyagraha, a non-violent movement to win the right of temple entry. He was able to convince Gandhi that the people were prepared and that the movement was expected to get the support of some enlightened sections of high caste Hindus. The leader of the *tiya* community, Narayan Guru had also given his blessings. The satyagrahis had to suffer a lot as the priests employed bad elements to sabotage the satyagraha. They appealed for Gandhi's help asking him to get their movement endorsed by the Congress. Gandhi followed the policy of local movements being managed at local level and did not press the Congress to endorse the Vaikom satyagraha.[76] A Vaikom deputation consisting of K. Madhavan Nair and Kurur Nilakantan Nambudripad interviewed Gandhi on Vaikom Satyagraha and this interview was reported in *The Hindu*. Gandhi's views can be clearly gauged from the following extract of the said interview.

> Q. Is not the removal of untouchability and unapproachability an all-India question, and Vaikom being the first pitched battle in the war against these two evils, will not a

defeat these speak a disaster to the movement in general, and if it will, is it not the duty of all Indians to help in the fight? What is the significance of the word 'local as applied to Vaikom? If help from outside is pressure and overawing repugnant to the principles of satyagraha, can Vaikom non-caste Hindus seek aid in the form of money or volunteers from any place outside Vaikom? Can even Travancorians belonging to places other than Vaikom participate in the struggle? If they can seek help from people of Travancore and even from the people of the Madras Presidency, why can't they receive help from Hindus throughout India? Why should satyagrahis refuse help from the Hindu Sabha and similar bodies?

A. The question is partly answered in the answer given before. In the sense that the prohibition of the use of every well, tank, roads, etc. in every part of the country is the result of a common evil affecting the Hindus, the Vaikom struggle may also be regarded as an all-India question, but every such matter arising locally must be fought locally and it is neither desirable nor practicable that the whole [of] or the central organization should fight out such questions. It will lead to chaos and confusion. The consequence can be better understood if there are a number of such fights going on at the same time. The central organization will be considerably weakened by the frittering of its energies in such a way. The local area will not develop the necessary strength to tackle such questions unaided. Self-reliance and self sufficiency of each local area will make the whole of India strong and enable it to take the great fight that is in store. The solution of the problem at Vaikom will not solve the question of untouchability for the whole of India. India may share the victory it gains, but will not be responsible for the defeat it sustains.[77]

As events would later prove this kind of 'decentralization' proved to be a wise and a farsighted one as it strengthened the local units of satyagrahis. On his part despite appearing literally to having washed his hands off the Vaikom struggle, Gandhi, wrote a number of articles in his papers discussing the issues involved in the movement and making the developments known throughout India.[78]

Fight against untouchability however remained with Gandhi the main area of Satyagraha till the end of his life. Elsewhere he wrote: 'Untouchability is a terrible reality. If they had a tongue, we should not be able to sleep for the noise the untouchables would make about the treatment meted out to them in the name of religion."[79] Later, when the ruler of Travancore was succeeded by Maharani and on whose order the satyagrahis were released from prison, Gandhi congratulated the Maharani for this gesture and wrote, 'The best service that a Hindu state can render to Hinduism is to rid it of the curse and set an example in liberalism to the Hindus of British India.'[80]

To provide a frontal attack on untouchability, the Congress Working Committee set up a Committee for the removal of untouchability with Madan Mohan Malaviya as its President and Jamnalal Bajaj as its secretary. The Committee did commendable work. Temples were opened to untouchables in Bombay by an orthodox Telegu community after the persuasion by the Committee Secretary and the decision was arrived at unanimously. Similarly eight important temples were thrown open to untouchables in Jabalpur by the year 1929.

The Congress Party Position

Congress unity was threatened by the establishment of the Swarajist Party which aimed at entering the Councils, defying the Non-Co-operation Movement's decision to boycott Government institutions. This hurt Gandhi. He realized that his ideas of non-violence, his emphasis on spinning by Congress members were not being taken seriously. In an issue of *Young India* he framed some resolutions to be presented before the coming Congress session. He laid down that if these were not accepted he would relinquish his leadership.[81] Gandhi's resolutions were accepted by the majority but a perceptive person like him could sense the casualness about the whole exercise. This pained him. On the thoughts that crossed his mind at that time Gandhi wrote:

> Up to the point of the poll, I was enjoying the whole thing as a huge joke, though I knew all the while that it was as serious as it was huge .I now see that my enjoyment was superficial. It concealed the laceration that was going on within.
>
> .... It takes much to make me weep. I suppress tears even

> when there is occasion for them. But in spite of all my efforts to be brave, I broke down utterly....I turned round to look for Maulana Abul Kalam Azad. He had stolen away from me and was standing at the farthest end opposite to me. I told him I would now like to go. He said, 'Not yet, for a while. For we must speak too.' And he invited the audience to speak. Those who spoke did so with a sob....All begged pardon and assured me of their unwavering support. Mahomed Ali broke down twice. I tried to sooth him.[82]

Out of regard for him the Congress once again gave in to the unusual 'tyrant'. But the issue of the position of the Swarajists within the Congress was yet to be resolved. After the meeting of the All India Congress Committee in June, both the No-changers and the Swarajists had started fighting for the control of the Congress. While Gandhi was busy persuading Motilal Nehru to see his point of view, the Government resorted to severe repression in Bengal, thereby heightening the need for unity within the Congress. An agreement was arrived at between Gandhi and the Swarajists in Calcutta on 6 November, 1924 whereby the latter agreed to support the constructive programme and the introduction of daily spinning as a qualification for the membership of the Congress Party and in return was permitted its Council's programme in the name of the Congress. It was now the turn of No-changers to question Gandhi.

As a follow-up of the Calcutta Agreement, an All Parties Conference was called in Bombay so as to put to naught the Government's attempt of dividing the leadership in India. Gandhi promised not to 'stand in the way of any honourable means that may be desired by the committee for bringing all the parties together'.[83] Meanwhile negotiations were on between the Swarajists and Gandhi over further areas of cooperation. Gandhi openly called the pact between the Swarajists as a 'splendid defeat' for himself and on the occasion of the death of the Swarajist leader C.R. Das on June 16, 1925, whose hospitality he had recently enjoyed while on his tour of Bengal, talked of how the views of the two had come closer recently. In deference to the wishes of the late leader and after consulting Motilal Nehru, Gandhi, at last, gave up his insistence on the spinning franchise. He declared that he had given the 'power of attorney' over political matters to the Swarajists and wanted to devote his time to the constructive programme. With the rehabilitation of the Swaraj Party at the AICC meeting in Patna on September 22, 1925, politics occupied the centre-stage in Congress once again. Gandhi's formula to regulate the relations between the two wings was: 'Wherever the two parties are evenly balanced, Non-co-operators or No-changers should surrender full control to the Swarajists and voluntarily give up office if they hold any. Where the No-changers are in an overwhelming majority, they should not hamper the Swarajists, and should help them wherever they conscientiously can.'[84] Gandhi retired from the Presidentship of the Congress on December, 24, 1925 but not before warning his successor Mrs. Sarojini Naidu against being over generous, as he believed women generally are, regarding Congress funds which at the moment were not much. Mrs. Naidu was quick to respond that she would leave financial matters to 'such distinguished misers as Mahatmaji.'[85] On January 3, 1926, Gandhi announced his decision to voluntarily to retire for one year from public work and rest in his Ashram. He, however, watched from distance, though not with full agreement, the efforts of different parties and groups in India to unitedly oppose the appointment and then the visit of the Simon Commission which was in utter disregard of the sentiments of the people of India. His major concern, however, during this period was the peasants movement in Bardoli, which was reaching its successful culmination under the able leadership of his trusted lieutenant, Vallabhbhai Patel.

National Schools

National schools were the next target at the hands of critics. A general impression had been created throughout the country that with the suspension of civil disobedience all the other programmers of the non-co-operation movement had also been suspended or abandoned.[86] The national schools that had come up with so much fanfare during the heydays of the movement saw the number of students dwindling alarmingly.[87] Several letters highlighting the pathetic plight of these schools reached Gandhi for his comments and for seeking directions from him. Gandhi asked the concerned parties to hold on to their posts and be prepared for further sacrifices.[88] He also addressed conferences on the issue of national education and suggested various measures to improve the working of these institutions.

Peoples Movements in Princely States

Another area of attention for Gandhi during this period was the peoples' movements in some of the Princely states. The Congress

Party was sympathetic to the movements but Gandhi advised against non-co-operation in these states.[89] His argument was that people should devote attention to the constructive part of non-co-operation in these states instead of non-cooperating with their rulers. If the people had any grievances they should get these redressed by persuading the government and bringing about a change in their attitude.[90] This was the advice he gave to the people of his own state of Kathiawad:

> In the past they must have been able to do what they liked, but today their decadence is sustained only under the wing of the Sovereign. When the master is there we need not enumerate the faults of the slave.... Indian Princes will not reform themselves if we criticize them. The more we scratch the greater will be the itching. So they will go to their Sovereign and seek ointment.[91]

Dialogue with Revolutionaries

This period also saw the revival of the debate whether the Gandhian method of non-violent struggle could gain swaraj for India or violent method of the revolutionaries. Though Gandhi had made his views clear on the militancy issue in his book *Hind Swaraj* published in 1909, (for details refer to Chapter-I) the issue was raked up again. Gandhi was asked, since he could not bring swaraj in one year as promised by him, would he not give chance to the revolutionaries to redeem this pledge with the people. It is interesting to note that Gandhi never fought shy of entering into a dialogue with the revolutionaries. In fact, he gave full coverage to their point of view in his journals appending elaborate answers to their queries. This state of affairs was natural in the circumstances, where even mature statesmen like Patel were asking Gandhi to place before the country a programme that would 'enthuse' the people. Some revolutionaries suggested that Gandhi's days were over and that he should retire from politics. Gandhi gave a rather stern reply to this suggestion. He averred:

> I am afraid your advice to me to retire from public life is not so easy to follow as it is to give. I claim to be servant of India and there through of humanity. I cannot always have it my own way. If I have had my share of fair weather I must face the foul too. I must not abandon the field of battle so long as I feel that I am wanted When my work is done and I have become a disabled or worn out soldier, I shall be put away.

Till then I must continue to do my work and endeavour to neutralize in all ways accessible to me the poison of the revolutionary activity.... India is not Calcutta or Bombay. India lives in her seven hundred thousand villages. If the revolutionaries are as many let them spread out into these villages and try to bring sunshine into the dark dungeons of the millions of their countrymen. That would be worthier of their ambition and love of the land than the exciting and unquenchable thirst for the blood of English officials and those who are assisting them.[92]

This answer led to further correspondence between the revolutionaries and Gandhi. He was accused of intolerance in so far as the revolutionaries were concerned and of underplaying their sacrifices. Gandhi stuck to his arguments. He contended that the sacrifice, nobility and love of the revolutionaries were a waste of effort. He went to the extent of holding the revolutionaries responsible for 'retarding the progress of the country' and inviting repression.[93] Gandhi also refused to accept the analogy of a surgeon to describe revolutionaries and defending his method of non-violence wrote, 'I could not fight my wife with violence, I could not fight my brothers with violence, I refuse to fight the Mussalmans with violence and I dare not fight the Hindus, some of whom are opposing men on the issue of untouchability, with violence. I therefore, deduce from that fund of experience that I cannot fight Englishmen with violence.'[94]

Thus in this period Gandhi had to take on challenge from a source which had a large following of the youth, the revolutionaries. The arguments put forward by both the parties is worth recalling since this is the dialogue which continues even after five decades of Gandhi's martyrdom.

Communication with People from Outside India

The nature and novelty of the Indian struggle also caught world-wide attention. Gandhi received and responded to numerous letters from countries such as Russia, Sweden, Poland, Germany, Switzerland, the United States of America, besides Britain. Most of these letters reflected a genuine attempt to understand what was going on in India. There were also suggestions and advice to make the movement more effective. Both financial and moral help, in the form of publicizing the Indian cause, were offered. Gandhi was also invited to tour China, America and Finland which Gandhi turned down as he felt that if there was any power in his message it would be felt without the physical contact.[95] In response to a letter received from Sweden wherein the writer had deplored the misrepresentation of the non-cooperation movement in the Swedish press that the movement had failed, Gandhi explained that the West was unable to comprehend the movement because 'it has nothing in common with the historical struggles for freedom in the West. It is not based on brute force or hatred. It does not aim at destroying the tyrant. It may fail because India may not be ready for mass – non-violence. But it would be wrong to judge the movement by false standards. *My own opinion is that the movement has no wise failed. Non-violence has found an abiding place in India's struggle for freedom*'.[96] Gandhi believed that time had not come for India's voice to be heard all over the world. In a personal letter to the French writer and philosopher, Romain Rolland, he wrote. 'India must suffer much more than she has suffered till now, and on a larger scale than before, to he heard in Europe or in the West. Today its voice will be a voice in wilderness.'[97]

Bardoli Satyagraha

The grand finale of the period under review came in the shape of the successful Bardoli Satyagraha in which the peasants of the Bardoli taluka of Gujarat refused to pay the enhanced revenue and, despite all kinds of repressive measures adopted by the administration, held their ground. The movement organized under the leadership of Sardar Patel was closely monitored by Gandhi, who for some inexplicable reasons did not want his name to be associated with it. Encouraged by the success of the movement some leaders suggested that the satyagraha should be extended to the national level. Gandhi firmly said no, for he thought that it was not ethical to expand the terms and conditions of a movement in view of its success. The satyagraha, however, gave a boost to Gandhi's morale as he believed that it had proved to some extent that he was able to prepare the people for the long promised Civil Disobedience Movement which was planned to begin from Gujarat in 1922. The Congress which had, during the period under review shared an uneasy relationship with Gandhi, moved closer and Gandhi gave his assent to the resolution of *Purna Swaraj*, complete independence, and launched the Civil Disobedience Movement on March 12, 1930.

Summation

Between the years 1922 to 1930 Gandhi left no stone unturned in 'preparing the country for Civil Disobedience' through his intensive and extensive writing. By the end of 1929 his efforts had started showing results in the form of successful completion of the Bardoli satyagraha and the presentation of the Nehru Report which was the first blueprint of the polity Indians hoped to create for themselves. After a long period of self-imposed *sannyas* from political affairs Gandhi now showed an inclination to participate in political matters, taking his own path of social and political reforms to reach the goal of political action. In fact, it was difficult to put in separate compartments Gandhi's political programmes and his programmes of social and economic reforms.

Till date he believed that Indians still needed some more preparation. However, while condemning the act of throwing bombs in the Assembly by Bhagat Singh and Batukeshwar Dutt, Gandhi laid the blame squarely on the Government's repressive policies for generating the 'philosophy of mad revenge and impotent rage.'[98] But he warned the Congress from being associated with any act of violence, as that would hurt their movement based on non-violence.[99]

In spite of all these developments Gandhi quietly pursued with single-minded determination his programme of foreign cloth boycott and propagation of khadi. Gandhi toured Burma, which was then an Indian province, and also conducted the longest and the most successful tour of Andhra. Gandhi always gave a detailed account of his tours, thereby making people of other regions of India aware of what was happening in the regions Gandhi visited. The tours were also intelligent mass contact programmes because Gandhi insisted that the addresses presented to him by the local organizers should furnish him with data regarding the number of spinning wheels, plight of women and untouchables, and similar other details. He educated the people on the economic and social issues. Political issues, however, came up only when the people showed a desire to have a discussion on them. If he commended the Andhra people for their work in the area of khadi, he appreciated the students of United Provinces for their enthusiasm for the cause of independence and readiness for sacrifice.

Gandhi's silence on purely political matters, however, did not mislead the people into thinking who their leader was and what was he aiming at. An interesting letter quoted by Gandhi in ***Young India*** shows where he stood in the estimation of the people. Babu Hardayal Nag, an octogenarian leader of Bengal gave words to the sentiments of the people in India in general. He wrote:

> .... I understand you are making preparations for India's fight for freedom. I know that my life is not worth much. I also know that I must pay my quota of the price for India's independence. In the Russo-Japanese war, a Japanese commander had to cross an unbridged ditch. He asked his soldiers to throw themselves in it and to make a bridge of human bodies so that his troops might pass over it. I know in the coming struggle you will also have to cross certain unbridgeable ditches. Please enlist my name as one of those who will voluntarily fill up those ditches with their bodies for your troops to cross them, if for no other purpose.[100]

Gandhi welcomed the letter and commended it to the youth of the country. He invited them to prepare as the Bengali octogenarian was preparing but cautioned them that for him preparation meant 'fulfilling the conditions laid down in the constructive resolution'. This caution is understandable because there was a growing yearning in the hot-blooded youth for something more exciting, like the revolutionary activities or the secretive methods of the communists.

Gandhi's life mission had been to remove the fear of the British rulers from the minds of the common people of India. Instances that showed that Gandhi had started getting results of his training in this direction came to light. The Gujarati paper *Prajabandhu* reported a speech by Gandhi at the unveiling ceremony of Tilak's statue in Ahmedabad. Gandhi congratulated the Municipality for being courageous enough to display the statue of Lokmanya Tilak.[101] Yet Gandhi was more cautious than during the days of the NCM. While on tour to Burma, in response to a question regarding the political condition in India he replied that it still was 'in the melting pot'.[102]

Gandhi Resumes Command

In 1929, the Congress Party passed a resolution declaring the aim of the Congress to attain *Purna Swaraj* and to start civil disobedience to give effect to it. Gandhi did not have faith in all the Congressmen being converted to his doctrine of non-violence, which he considered to be the first condition for launching of the movement. Eventually he was able to secure from the Congress the sole authority for launching and conduct of the movement.

In view of the impending struggle, the authorities started on a course of gagging the press and frequent persecutions for sedition under Section 124-A of the Indian Penal Code were resorted to. Gandhi favoured a public agitation for the repeal of the Section which, according to him, required a force equivalent to the force required for the attainment of swaraj.[103] While lashing out at the Government in this matter, Gandhi did not discriminate between a communist or a non-violent satyagrahi. He advocated equal right of expression for all.

Sensing that Gandhi still had not lost his 'magic touch' over the people and impressed by his remarkable organizing capacity as the Chairman of FCB (Foreign Cloth Boycott) Committee, a large majority of Congressmen wanted Gandhi to accept the Presidentship of the organization for 1930. In an article entitled 'Who Should Wear the Crown', while strongly recommending Jawaharlal Nehru's name, Gandhi enumerated the reasons for declining the offer. He wrote:

> I feel I have become almost unfit for attending to details of office work which I must do, as is my nature, if I accepted the office. *I know too that I am not keeping pace with the march of events. There is, therefore, a hiatus between the rising generation and me. I look a back number in their company....* So long as I retain the affection and the confidence of our people, there is not the slightest danger of my not being able without holding office to make full use of such powers as I may possess. *God has enabled me to affect life of the country since 1920 without the necessity of holding office....*those who know the relations that subsist between Jawaharlal and me know that *his being in the chair is as good as my being in it. We may have intellectual differences but our hearts are one.*[104]

When Jawaharlal Nehru showed his inability to accept the office in view of his other engagements, Gandhi asked Motilal Nehru to persuade him. And finally, when Jawaharlal Nehru accepted office, Gandhi wrote a detailed article in *Young India* describing his qualities of head and heart, 'if he has the dash and rashness of a warrior, he has also the prudence of a statesman', Gandhi wrote. 'A lover of discipline, he has shown himself to be capable of rigidly submitting to it even where it has seemed irksome.... He is pure as a crystal, he is truthful beyond suspicion. He is a knight *sans peur sans reproche. The nation is safe in his hands.*'[105] Further he gave full coverage to Nehru's maiden speech in his columns and praised the restraint shown in it. Gandhi continued with the praise of his protégé by writing, 'Pandit Jawaharlal Nehru more than justified the choice of the people. His address brief and to the point was bold, extreme in conception but moderate in expression. It bore evidence of a man capable of viewing things with complete detachment'.[106] Writing for *Hindi Navajivan* Gandhi reiterated, 'Jawaharlal Nehru has proved to be the jewel of India. In his address lofty thoughts are couched in sweet and courteous language. Several topics have been dealt with thoroughly and yet the address is short. The splendour of the soul shines in every sentence.... As was the address so was his deportment.'[107]

In this way Gandhi prepared the people in general and the Congress in particular, for accepting his choice. The British were also told in no uncertain terms that Gandhi was always there in the background and there would not be any radical departure from the Gandhian path as Gandhi and Nehru's hearts were one! The youth who were clamouring for new leadership were also silenced. In one stroke Gandhi was able to demolish all his opponents and critics while assuring for himself that his methods would be followed. This was a major tactical decision and was to a large extent responsible for the success of the Civil Disobedience Movement to be launched shortly.

REFERENCES

1. *Interview at Dinajpur, Amrita Bazar Patrika*, 23-5-1925, *CWMG*, XXVII, p. 141.
2. Gandhi wrote this as a message to *The Indian National Herald*, 28-8-1928, *CWMG*, XXXVII, p. 212.
3. Gandhi started writing in Gujarati the history of satyagraha in South Africa on 26-11-1923, when he was in Yerwada Central Jail. By the time he was released on 5-2-1924, he had completed 30 chapters. The Gujarati edition appeared in the *Navajivan* between 13-4-1924 – 22-11-1925. The English translation by Valji. G. Desai which was seen and approved by Gandhi , was published by S. Ganeshan, Madras, in 1928.
4. The Gujarati original of *Autobiography* appeared in weekly instalments

in *Navajivan*, from 29-11-1925 to 3-2-1929. The English translation by Mahadev Desai and in part by Pyarelal Nayar, Gandhi's secretaries, appeared in *Young India* from 3-12-1925 to 7-2-1929.

5. In a letter to Pt. Jawaharlal Nehru written on 10-1-1930 Gandhi wrote: 'civil disobedience ...should be offered by me alone or jointly with a few companions even as I did in South Africa if you have studied the History of Satyagraha. If you have not, you should.' *CWMG*, XLII, pp. 382-3.
6. The *Will* reads as follows: ' I do not possess any property of my own. If, after my death, if any article is found of my ownership, I bequeath the same to the trustees of the Satyagraha Ashram,.... I also bequeath to the...Trustees all my rights in whatever books or whatever articles I have written or may write hereafter, and also appoint them to administer my affairs after my death if and when necessary'. ***CWMG***, XXXI, p. 491.
7. In Letter to C. Rajagopalachari, *CWMG*, XXV, p. 36.
8. 'Conundrums', *Young India*, 2-4-1925, *CWMG*, XXVI, p. 443.
9. *Letter to Dr. MA Ansari*, *CWMG*, XXXIII, p. 274.
10. *Navajivan*, 5-3-1922, *CWMG*, XXXIII, pp. 4-5.
11. *Ibid.*, p. 8.
12. *The Bombay Chronicle*, 14-4-1925, *CWMG*, XXVI, p. 505.
13. In a letter to T. Prakasam, the editor of *Swarajya*, Gandhi wrote: 'Whether we are few or whether we are many, so long as we believe in the programme of non-violence, there is no absolution from the full constructive programme. Enforce it today and the whole country is ready for mass civil disobedience tomorrow.' *CWMG*, XXXIII, p. 21.
14. 'Impatient Kathiawad', *Navajivan*, 11-5-1924, *CWMG*, XXIV, p. 24.
15. 'No and Yes', *Young India*, 17-3-1927,*CWMG*, XXXIII, pp. 163-67.
16. *Young India*, 9-3-1922, *CWMG*, XXIII, p. 44.
17. *Notes, Young India*, 9-3-1922, *CWMG*, XXIII, p. 44.
18. In an article entitled 'Defeated and Humbled', Gandhi gave vent to his feelings after the Congress session in which his resolutions regarding the conditions for Congress membership and future programmes were voted out. Seeing the state of affairs in the organization, Gandhi wrote: 'I seemed to be hopelessly out of place. My grief consisted in the doubt about my own ability to lead those who would not follow.... My innermost wish was and still is to retire from the Congress and confine my activity merely to Hindu-Muslim unity, khaddar and untouchability.' *Young India*, *CWMG*, XXIV, p. 338.
19. 'A Heart-searcher', *Young India*, 8-5-1924, *CWMG*, XXIV, p. 338.
20. On the basis of some letters received by him Gandhi came to know about these thoughts and wrote about them in 'My Notes', *Navajivan*, 11-5-1924, *CWMG*, XXIV, p. 33.
21. *Ibid.*
22. As reported in *The Searchlight*, 8-5-1925, *CWMG*, XXVII, p. 33, and *The*

Englishman, which reported Gandhi on the topic of 'Charkha', addressed to Rotarians, *CWMG*, XXVIII, p. 81.

23. 'Fallen Sisters Spinning', *Young India*, 28-5-1925, *CWMG*, XXVII, p. 165.
24. *Speech to Students, Dinajpur, Navajivan*, 31-1-1925, and as reported in an interview to the *Amrita Bazar Patrika*, 23-5-1925, *CWMG*, XXVII, p. 141.
25. Interview to the Free Press of India, as reported in *The Bombay Chronicle*, 9-3-1925, *CWMG*, XXVI, p. 239.
26. *Ibid.*
27. 'Triumph of Spring', *Navajivan* 25-5-1924, *CWMG*, XXIV, pp. 126-129.
28. 'Not Man's Work', *Young India*, *CWMG*, XXVII, pp. 219-221.
29. *Ibid.*
30. 'Three Questions', *Hindi Navajivan*, *CWMG*, XXIV, 282.
31. *Ibid.*
32. 'Machine Spinning *v.* Hand-Spinning', *Young India*, 26-6-1924, *CWMG*, XXIV, p. 303.
33. *Notes:* 'Luxury and Laziness', *Young India*, 5-6-1924, *CWMG*, XXIV, pp. 185-6.
34. 'False Notion', *Navajivan*, 15-6-1924, *CWMG*, XXIV, pp. 255-256.
35. See *Notes Young India*, 15-5-1924, *CWMG*, p. 45. Gandhi published the letter sent by Dr. Ray wherein he had described how an engineer in Chittagong had taken to the life of bread labour and how he was motivating others to do the same.
36. 'My Request', *Navajivan*, 25-5-1924, *CWMG*, XXIV, pp. 115-116.
37. *Navajivan*, 25-5-1924, *CWMG*, XXIV, p. 120.
38. 'Under the Test', *Young India*, 4-9-1924, *CWMG*, XXV, 79-82.
39. As reported in *The Hindu*, 20-3-1925, *CWMG*, XXVI, 347.
40. 'Pandit Nehru and Khaddar', *Young India*, 15-4-1926, *CWMG*, XXX, 287-289.
41. *Ibid.*
42. As reported in *The Hindu*, 26-9-1927, *CWMG*, XXXV, p. 32.
43. 'To No-Changers', *Young India*, 19-1-1928, *CWMG*, XXXV, pp. 477-78.
44. 'Progress of F.C.B', *Young India*, 30-5-1929, *CWMG*, XL, p. 430.
45. 'Hindu-Muslim Tension: its Cause and Cure', *Young India*, 29-5-1924, *CWMG*, XXIV, pp. 136-154.
46. *Notes, Young India*, 22-5-1924, *CWMG*, XXIV, 103.
47. In his article on Hindu-Muslim Tension (mentioned vide footnote 21) Gandhi while defending Swami Shraddhanand, the Arya Samaj'sleader's secular credentials, has this to write about him:
    His speeches, I know, are often irritating. But even he wants Hindu-Muslim unity. Unfortunately, he believes into possibility of bringing every Muslim into the Aryan fold, just as perhaps most Mussalmans think that every non-Muslim will some day become a convert to Islam.. ..I have read the *Satyarth Prakash*, the Arya Samaj Bible....I have not read

a more disappointing book from a reformer so great. He has claimed to stand for truth and nothing else. But he has unconsciously misrepresented Jainism, Islam, Christianity and Hinduism itself.... He has tried to make narrow one of the most tolerant and liberal faiths on the face of the earth. And the iconoclast though he was, he has succeeded in enthroning idolatry in the subtlest form. For he has idolized the letter of the Vedas, and tried to prove the existence in Vedas everything known to science.

48. 'Arya Samajists Again', *Young India,* 19-6-1924, *CWMG,* XXIV, 264-266.
49. *Notes, Young India,*7-8-1924, *CWMG,* XXIV, 326.
50. In his article on Hindu-Muslim Tension (refer to f.n. 267.) Gandhi writes; My claim to Hinduism has been *rejected* by some, because I believe and advocate non-violence in its extreme form. They say I am a Christian in disguise. I have been even seriously told that I am distorting the meaning of the *Gita* when I ascribe to that great poem the teaching of unadulterated non-violence....I must be dismissed out of consideration. My religion is a matter solely between my Maker and myself. p. 140.
51. 'A Plea for Truth', *Young India,*16-7-1925, *CWMG,* XXVII, 374.
52. *Ibid.* It was alleged by a correspondent that when the Hindus ask for help as they did when they were assaulted by the Muslims in Lucknow, or Delhi Gandhi pleaded helplessness but when it came to condemning Hindus he was very prompt thus encouraging the Muslims. Gandhi made it clear that when there was communal rioting in Kidderpore in Calcutta he was invited by a Hindu to intervene who accompanied him to the areas of tension and agreed with him that the Hindus were at fault.
53. 'Hindu-Muslim Tension:its Cause and Cure', *op.cit.,* 137.
54. For instance Gandhi quoted in full the report sent by some K. Rajagopalachari from Tirupati wherein the writer had described how the leaders of both the communities in their wisdom avoided the communal riot which was clearly predicted. For details see. *Young India,* 3-7-1924, *CWMG,* XXIV, 349.
55. 'Gulbarga Gone Mad', *Young India,* 28-8-1924, *CWMG,* XXV, 46.
56. *CWMG,* XXV, 157.
57. *Ibid.,* dated 17-9-1924.
58. *Young India,* 25-9-1924, *CWMG,* XXV, 171-172.
59. Bhikhu Parekh, *Gandhi,* OUP, 1997, p. 111.
60. 'Kohat', *Young India,* 23-3-1925, *CWMG,* XXVI, 336-337.
61. Notes, *Young India,* 26-2-1925, *CWMG,* XXVI, 202.
62. 'My Crime', *Young India,* 5-3-1925, *CWMG,* XXVI, 226.
63. *Ibid.,* 227.
64. 'Stoning to Death', *Young India,* 26-3-1925, *CWMG,* XXVI, 415.
65. 'String of Questions', *Young India,* 4-5-1921, CWMG, XX, p. 58.

66. See 'God and Congress', *Young India*, 5-3-1925, CWMG, XXVI, 222-225.
67. M.M. Kothari, *Critique of Gandhi*, Critique Publications, Jodhpur, 1996, p. 147.
68. 'National Arbitration?' *Young India*, 24-9-1925, *CWMG*, XXVIII, 222. 69 'Maulana Azad' Appeal', *Young India*, 24-9-1925, *CWMG*, XXVIII, 222.
70. A pamphlet bearing this title was written and circulated by an Arya Samajist. It carried derogatory remarks about Prophet Mohammad
71. ' Ragila Rasul', *Young India*, 22-9-1927, *CWMG*, XXXV, p. 16.
72. *Letter to Najuklal N Choksi*, *CWMG*, XXXI, p. 178.
73. *Hindi Navajivan*, 6-1-1927, *CWMG*, XXXII, p. 454.
74. 'A Candid Critic', *Young India*, 20-1-1927, *CWMG*, XXXII, pp. 586-88.
75. *Letter to Shaukat Al*, *CWMG*, XXXVIII, pp. 129-32.
76. Notes, *Young India*, 3-7-1924, *CWMG*, XXIV, p. 36.
77. *The Hindu*, 26-5-1924, *CWMG*, XXIV, 92-93.
78. See, for instance, 'Notes: Vycom Satyagraha', *Young India*, 8-5-1924, *CWMG*, XXIV, pp. 7-8; 'Notes: Religious Spinning', *Young India*, 15-5-1924, *CWMG*, XXIV, p. 50; 'Interview to the Hindu', *The Hindu*, 19-5-1924, *CWMG*, XXIV, pp. 66-69; 'Notes: Vycom Satyagraha', *Young India*, 19-6-1924, *CWMG*, XXIV, pp. 259-60; 'Notes: A Repudiation', *Young India*, 10-7-1924, *CWMG*, XXIV, pp. 363-65; 'Notes: Vycom Satyagraha'. *Young India*, 18-9-1924, *CWMG*, XXV, pp. 163-4; 'Notes: From Vycom'. *Young India*, 5-2-1925, *CWMG*, XXVI, pp. 72-73; 'Vycom Satyagraha', *Young India*, 2-4-1925, *CWMG*, XXVI, pp. 437-439 (In this article Gandhi congratulated the satyagrahis on the successful conclusion of their movement).
79. 'Difficulties in the Way', *Young India*, *21-8*-1924, *CWMG*, XXV, 25.
80. *Notes*, *Young India*, 11-9-1924, *CWMG*, XXV, 115.
81. 'The Acid Test', *Young India*, 19-6-1924, *CWMG*, XXIV, 267-270. One of the resolutions made it compulsory for Congress office-bearers to spin for half an hour daily and produce at least ten tolas of yarn and wholeheartedly believed in non-cooperation programme.
82. 'Defeated and Humbled', *Young India*, 3-7-1924, *CWMG*, XXIV, 334-340.
83. M.K Gandhi, *The Story of My Life*, Vol. II, 485-9.
84. 'The All-India Congress Committee', *Young India*, 1-10-1923, *CWMG*, XXVIII. 261-262.
85. *CWMG*, XXXIX, 351.
86. 'Suspend or Abandon?' *Young India*, 1-12-1924, *CWMG*, XXV, pp. 392-3.
87. According to a report published in *Young India*, 24-7-1924, *CWMG*, XXIV. 421-423, only fifty per cent of such schools continued to function and in these too only one-fourth of the student strength had remained.
88. *Ibid.*

89. Gandhi maintained: 'there can be not satyagraha in the princely states in order to win swaraj for India. It can be in respect to local problems.' 'Satyagraha in Princely States' *Navajivan*, 15-6-1925, *CWMG*, XXIV, p. 246.
90. 'Kathiawad Political Conference', *Young India*, 15-1-1924, *CWMG*, XXV, p. 574.
91. "The Suzerain and the Vassals", *Navajivan*, 28-4-1929, *CWMG*, XL, p. 300.
92. *Notes, Young India*, 12-3-1925, *CWMG*, XXVI, 286.
93. "My Friend the Revolutionary", *Young India*, 9-4-1925, *CWMG*, XXVI, 486-492.
94. As reported in *Amrita Bazar Patrika*, 15-5-1925, *CWMG*, XXVII, 91.
95. Letter to K.T. Paul, *CWMG*, XXX, 542.
96. 'From Sweden', *Young India*, 11-2-1926.
97. *Letter to Romain Rolland*, *CWMG*, XL, p. 327.
98. 'The Bomb and the Knife', *Young India*, 18-4-1929, *CWMG*, XL, p. 259.
99. *Ibid.*
100. 'Notes: A Young Octogenarian's Offer', *Young India*, 28-2-1929, *CWMG*, XL, p. 47.
101. *Prajabandhu*, 28-2-1929, *CWMG*, XL, p. 53.
102. 'Answers to Questions', *Young India*, 28-3-1929, and *The Tribune*, 9-4-1929, *CWMG*, XL, p. 122.
103. 'Sword of Damocles', *Young India*, 18-7-1929, *CWMG*, XLI, p. 196.
104. 'Who Should Wear the Crown', *Young India*, 1-9-1929, *CWMG*, XLI, pp. 239-41.
105. 'The Congress', *Young India*, 9-1-1930, *CWMG*, XLII, p. 374.
106. *Ibid.*
107. 'Jawaharlal Nehru', *Hindi Navajivan*, 9-1-1930, *CWMG*, XLII, p. 380.

5

Strategy During the Salt-Satyagraha and Round Table Conference

The Indian National Congress in its Lahore session in December 1929 passed as resolution proclaiming complete independence, *Purna Swaraj*, as the country's immediate goal and authorized the launching of the civil disobedience movement to achieve it. Explaining to a correspondent as to why the prefix *'purna'* was used with *'swaraj'*, Gandhi wrote: 'Swaraj' in the Congress constitution was given a double meaning; it could be within the Empire if possible, without, if necessary. A word or an expression had therefore to be found in order to connote the last meaning only. We could not do without the term *'swaraj'*. Hence, the expedience of *'purna* swaraj'.[1]

Congress Working Committee Authorizes Gandhi to Launch Civil Disobedience Movement

For a long time, Gandhi was not clear about the form of campaign to adopt for the proposed Civil Disobedience Movement. He was trying hard to discover a formula which would enable him to avoid suspending the campaign on the ground of wide-spread violence. One way of ensuring this was to have a committed group of satyagrahis to start the campaign. The question was whether Congress would authorize him to do so. The solution was finally provided by a resolution passed by the Congress Working Committee on February 15, 1930 authorizing Gandhi and his co-workers who believed in non-violence as *an article of faith* to start civil disobedience, and called upon all Congressmen to extend full co-operation to civil-resisters. With this resolution in hand, which Gandhi called his 'charter of freedom'[2] he set about the task of looking for volunteers from among his ashram inmates who, he believed, had been trained for non-violent and selfless service. The countdown to the Civil Disobedience Movement (CDM) had now begun.

Preparations: Gandhi's Strategy

Directions Regarding Independence Day Celebrations

In an article entitled 'Independence Day', Gandhi gave a detailed account of how the day i.e., 26th January, ought to be celebrated making sure that the occasion was marked by sobriety and non-violence. He prohibited making of speeches and taking out of processions. Recounting for his readers the nature of celebrations on the occasion of the National Week since 1919, he asked the whole cities and whole villages to observe the day. It would be well, he wrote, if all meetings were held exactly at the same time, to the minute, at all places. At these meetings Congress functionaries were to read out the Congress resolution for independence before the people and perform flag-hoisting ceremony. For ensuring attendance in big numbers, Gandhi advised house to house visit by volunteers and the circulation of leaflets. The villages were asked to follow the customary method of advertising by the drumbeat. People who were religious minded were instructed to begin their day with prayer and keep themselves busy in constructive work. Finally, Gandhi appealed to the Congress to engage whole time workers to organize the event efficiently. The directions were published in *Young India* so that the information reached every corner of the country.[3]

Communication with Critics: Liberals, Revolutionaries and Englishmen

Gandhi always made it a point to communicate with those who disagreed with him before he put his plans into action. There was a section of Indian leaders, known as Liberals, who advocated negotiated settlement with the British Government, and were in favour of the Congress attending the first Round Table Conference (RTC) held in London in September 1930. In an article addressed to them Gandhi wrote: 'The days of being satisfied with costly toys is over. It is the substance that India wants.'[4] The 'substance', according to him, was 'complete independence'.

On the opposite side of the spectrum were the militants who were impatient for violent revolutionary action to gain independence. Gandhi was convinced that the CDM was sufficiently revolutionary to inspire these militants. He expressed in one of his articles that the militants would 'listen to no argument however reasonable it may be, unless they are convinced that there is a programme before the country which requires at least as much sacrifice as the tallest among them is prepared to make. They will not be allured by our speeches, resolutions or even conferences. Action alone has any appeal to them. This appeal can only come from non-violent action which is no other than civil resistance.'[5]

Liberals and revolutionaries aside, there was another group – the Englishmen. These English friends questioned the very rationale of the demand for independence. Gandhi gave a fitting reply to these 'friends'. In an article published in his newspaper, Gandhi put before them the case for India. He explained to them how the Congress had at Calcutta promised to achieve Dominion Status for India by December 1929 and had also resolved that if it was not achieved, demand for independence would be made. 'Organisations like men, if they are to command respect and grow, must have a sense of honour and must fulfil their promises', he stated. Further, he put the question, 'what is there intrinsically wrong in wanting independence?' To the argument that India was not yet fit for independence, Gandhi had this to say, 'We shall never be fit by being taught to feel helpless and being made to rely upon the British bayonet to keep us from fighting among ourselves or from being devoured by our neighbours.'[6]

Gandhi Addresses the Common Man

While the communications to the liberals, the militants and the English friends were in the nature of reactions or responses, Gandhi adopted a paternalistic mode in addressing the people of India. He gave them a list of 'Things to Remember on the 26th'.[7] Along with the list was published the text of the declaration of independence[8] that was to be read out at every meeting. A reading of the text would throw light on the India that Gandhi dreamt of and the goal the people would be inspired to lay their lives for. The restraint shown in the language and content could move the most hardened souls without inciting them to any violent action.

Briefing the Opponent

Gandhi made it a rule that the opponent be informed in advance regarding the steps to be taken by the satyagrahis so as to allow for the possibility of a negotiated settlement. Gandhi's 'ultimatum' to the Government was in the shape of eleven innocuous looking points[9] which Gandhi himself described as 'childish' and which, inter alia, included demands for prohibition, abolition of salt-tax, reduction in military expenditure and salary of government officials etc.

Dealing with Reaction

For a nation excited and in suspense over the coming country-wide movement the charter of demands must have seemed a tame affair, an anti-climax. Even Nehru thought so. People felt let down by Gandhi. To a letter expressing such sentiment, Gandhi replied explaining that the eleven point demand was in the nature of 'relief preparatory to independence'.[10] The struggle for independence was not to cease with the acceptance of the eleven points, but the Congress would lift the ban on participating in the RTC after its acceptance, Gandhi assured. In a rare show of self-affirmation, Gandhi declared in no uncertain terms that he was the leader of the movement leading to *Purna Swaraj*. 'As for my leadership, if I have it, it has not come for my seeking, it is a fruit of faithful service. A man can little discard such leadership as he can the colour of his skin. And since I have become an integral part of the nation it has to keep me with all my faults and shortcomings....'[11] This declaration was enough to clear all the controversy regarding leadership and consequently the nature of struggle.

Pondering over and Deciding Immediate Strategy

Until February 27, 1930 it seems that Gandhi had no idea that he would start his CDM on the issue of breaking the salt law. In an article in *Young India*, Gandhi referred to a letter from an Englishman wherein the writer had argued that salt-tax was a blessing in disguise. He claimed that medical research had shown a link between salt and cancer and, on this premise, he advised Gandhi not to make an issue out of salt tax. Gandhi told the 'good intentioned' gentleman, not to mix issues.[12] In another article on the same day, Gandhi referred to a 'canard' spread by the Press that he would advise the non-payment of salt-tax to begin the CDM.[13] It is therefore not very clear when Gandhi decided to start his movement on this issue.

ROUTE OF SALT MARCH

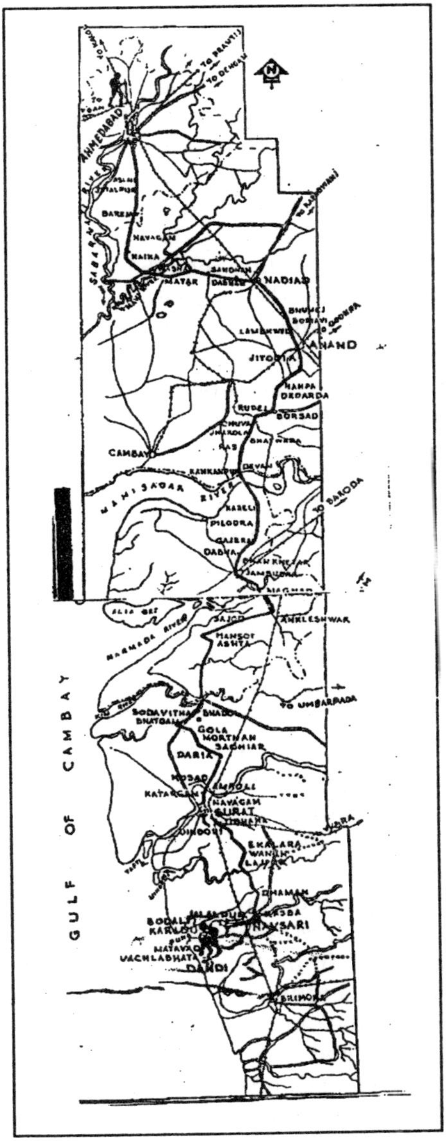

(*Source*: Collected Works of Mahatma Gandhi, Vol. XLIII)

Ultimatum to the Opponent

The Mode

Gandhi advanced patiently step by step towards civil disobedience. As referred to earlier, he first informed the Viceroy about his plan. Gandhi wrote a letter to the Viceroy regarding his decision to break the Salt Law and start the Movement if the demands were not met. This time Gandhi introduced an element of drama by asking an Englishman to carry the letter to the Viceroy thus emphasizing that he bore no ill will against the English people. His grievance was only against the Government's policies. Reginald Reynolds, the carrier of the letter, was made to read the letter beforehand because Gandhi did not wish him to be associated with anything with which he was not in full agreement. Significantly, Gandhi re-christened Reynolds as 'Angad' alluding to the character in the epic Ramayana where Angad acted as the messenger between Rama, representing the forces of good, and Ravana, the forces of evil.

The Idiom

Gandhi addressed Lord Irwin as 'Dear Friend', instead of 'Your Excellency', making the letter sound personal. After this form of address, Gandhi made it clear at the outset that while he considered the British rule to be a curse, he did not consider the Englishmen, in general, to be worse than any people on the earth. He then went on to enumerate why he considered the British rule a curse. The British rule had impoverished India by foisting an expensive civil administration on the Indian people. Politically, Indians were reduced to serfdom. He invited the Viceroy to 'make way for immediate removal' of evils such as the iniquitous land revenue system and the incurring of huge expenditure in the name of the administration and defence of the country. Should the Viceroy be unable to see his way to deal with the above mentioned evils, Gandhi announced the intention to start the civil disobedience movement by breaking the provisions of the Salt Law which he considered the 'most iniquitous of all from the poor man's standpoint'. Towards the end of the letter Gandhi wrote that he would publish the letter only on the receipt of the reply from the Viceroy. True to his promise, the letter was published only after the Viceroy sent a telegram expressing his regret that Gandhi should be 'contemplating a course of action which is clearly bound to involve violation of the law and danger to public peace.' [14]

Action Subsequent to the Breakdown of Negotiations

In a strongly worded article, 'Begging the Question', Gandhi gave full vent to his feelings on receipt of the Viceroy's reply. His now famous expression, 'On bended knees I asked for bread and I received stone instead' was part of this article. He further went on to write:

> The reply says that I contemplate a course of action which is clearly bound to involve violation of the law and danger to public peace. In spite of the forest of books containing rules and regulations, the only law the nation knows is the will of the British administrators, the only public peace that the nation knows is the peace of public prison. India is one vast prison house. I repudiate this law and regard it as my sacred duty to break the mournful monotony of the compulsory peace that is choking the heart of the nation for the want of free vent.[15]

People Informed in Advance about the Itinerary of the March, Arrangements and the Information Expected from the Villagers

Gandhi announced his decision to march from Sabarmati Ashram to Dandi[16] along with seventy-eight volunteers chosen by him and 'manufacture' salt, thus breaking the Salt Law. The march on foot undertaken by Gandhi and seventy-eight Congress volunteers was the most significant event in the history of the breach of salt law in our country. It commenced in accordance with a fixed schedule to be carried on by them during the long journey ending at Dandi .On 12 March 1930 at 6.10 A.M. Gandhi came out of his room, calm and composed, accompanied by Prabhashankar Patani, Mahadev Desai and Pyarelal, his secretary. He offered prayers, looked at his watch and exactly at 6.30 A.M. commenced his march with seventy-eight volunteers. All the relevant details of the March had been published in the *Navajivan* and *Young India*. The villagers were asked to provide food or provisions for preparing food, to the volunteers. Gandhi was very strict about the simplicity of the food. He put in black and white the items that should be given. Once, when some satyagrahis indulged in rich food, Gandhi sternly reprimanded them.[17]

Gandhi made the march an on the spot information-gathering exercise. He asked the villagers to give him information about: the demographic composition of the village; number of untouchables in the village; whether there was a school in the village or not and the number of boys and girls attending these schools; number of spinning wheels; data regarding monthly sale of khadi and the number of people who wore nothing but khadi.; salt consun ed per head and salt used for cattle; number of cows and buffalos in the village; amount of land revenue paid and at what rate per acre; the area of common grazing ground, if any; drinking habits of the people and the location of liquor shops; and educational and other facilities, if any, for the untouchables 'It would be good if this information was written on a sheet of paper neatly, and handed over to me immediately on my arrival', was the direction from Gandhi.[18] These directions were willingly followed by the villagers, as we shall see.

In a speech at a prayer meeting at Sabarmati Ashram on the eve of his departure Gandhi explained to the gathering how the Salt Law could be considered violated in legal terms. He explained that by manufacturing or possessing such manufactured salt or by selling the salt one would be held guilty of violating the Salt Law. The lawyer in Gandhi considered this clarification important so that people do not resort to all sorts of activities and waste their resources without attracting the provisions of law which they had resolved to break. Clarity in communication was the strong point of Gandhi's skill as a communicator.

Gandhi followed a clearly decided path for his march. He would stop at one place in the morning and address its residents, have meal and then proceed. By evening the marchers would reach the next village where they would have their meal and halt for the night. The scenario was that of a national festival were crowds lined up the path of the marchers to cheer them. Marching as a form of communication proved to be far superior to all the methods employed earlier by Gandhi. His army was also exceptionally disciplined and non-violent. It commanded respect and awe wherever it went. It generated an enthusiasm similar to the march in South Africa among the participants and viewers, as well as readers of the account. In an interview to Haridas T Majumdar, a journalist who was one of the volunteers for the march, Gandhi had said that whereas in South Africa the marchers were surrounded by hostile environment, in India it was otherwise. The march in South Africa was attended by greater hardships than the present one.[19]

At every stop Gandhi would analyze data submitted to him. A sample of what Gandhi said at his second stop at Aslali village illustrates how wisely and astutely Gandhi communicated with the common man, simplifying hard data to make even the dullest of them understand how the Government was exploiting them. 'Take the case of your own village ...for a population of 1,700 [and] ....200 bullocks .... a total of 1,150 maunds of salt will be required. The Government levies a tax of Rs. 1-4 on one pukka maund of salt .... you pay a tax of Rs. 720...can your village afford to pay this amount in taxes every year?.... the poor destitute villagers do not have the strength to get this tax repealed. We want to develop this strength,' Gandhi is reported to have said.[20] Extolling the gathering for attending in such big numbers, he said that it was 'good omen' and a 'sight for gods to see' – thus giving the whole exercise a spiritual dimension.

It was, however, not praise alone that he showered on the villagers. At his second stop at Bareja, Gandhi confessed that he was pained to see that the village did not have a single habitual khadi-wearer. 'We do not disown our mother because she is fat or ugly to look at and adopt other woman, more beautiful to fill her place. Foreign cloth will never bring us freedom.'[21] The question of the prestige of mother or sister always touches an Indian to the quick, more so in case of rustic folks – and Gandhi was aware of the impact of his words.

Gandhi's presence impacted the villagers in a big way and emboldened them. At the next stop at Navagam it was reported that all the Matadars had told Gandhi that they would not accept the Headman's office, with the result that the then incumbent resigned.[22] The news travelled fast. Resignations became the rule in each village Gandhi touched. It can be said that the Dandi March had, in its wake, left the villagers electrified with a new consciousness.

Gandhi for the first time employed what later became popular as 'embedded journalists' in his team of marchers. Press representatives were accepted by Gandhi as part of the entourage on the condition that, before asking the villagers for anything, they would seek Gandhi's permission as Gandhi and his volunteers were 'living on alms' given by villagers. Explaining the inclusion of press representatives, Gandhi told his volunteers as well as the villagers that in the last analysis, the press representatives had come for public service.[23] Public service in this context meant publicising the cause of the people. In a speech at Vasana, Gandhi wanted to know if he had been lodged outside the village because his convoy consisted of

Muslims and Antyajas.[24] This was important for Gandhi who treated any trace of communalism or untouchability as against the principles of satyagraha and did not want the hospitality of those who practised them. At Borsad, he appealed to students and teachers to come out in large numbers for the movement because theirs was a prominent role, as witnessed by history all over the world.[25]

Wiping out fear of an unjust and repressive government was one of the aims of the CDM. Hence, at Buva, Gandhi exhorted the people with these words: 'Although I make strong speeches and have set out to violate the law, the Government dare not arrest me. Why are you afraid of such a Government?'[26] Through this speech Gandhi also tried to convey to the Government that they should take cognizance of his breaking the law. In similar vein he again dared the British Government when he remarked, 'I am surprised that a person like me who cannot wield even a tiny stick can make such a mighty Empire tremble.'[27] Erik Erikson, the famous American psychologist, in an article written in the commemorative volume on Gandhi, has referred to Gandhi's habit of gentle, humorous teasing—the above remark is one such example. The Government was, no doubt provoked by such quips and finding itself helpless *vis-à-vis* Gandhi, took out their anger against lesser leaders.

Gandhi's speeches daring Government to arrest him, forced the British Government to show some activity on this front. It was hesitant to lay hands on Gandhi for the fear of igniting public ire. It, therefore, started prosecuting local leaders and journalists on minor charges. Gandhi was anticipating this and was fully prepared. In spite of his busy schedule he took out time to write about these prosecutions and comment on their unjust nature. Gandhi very well realized the predicament of the Government for the situation in which they were caught. There was no violence yet laws were being broken. Gandhi commented:

> Let no one think that lighter punishments are being awarded or I am being left alone because the Government is afraid of anything. The real reason is deeper and perhaps creditable to the Government. They are ashamed of punishing people for holding opinions and publicly expressing them. They are sensitive to the world opinion rising against them for their conduct... Section 124-A is really concerned with violence. The authors of the section probably never

> conceived the possibility of anybody harbouring sedition and yet having no trace of violence in him.[28]

The claims of the Muslim leaders that the march was essentially of the Hindus were proved false when, showing their affection for and proprietary right over Gandhi, some villages, where the population was predominantly Muslim, complained that Gandhi did not pass through their villages. Replying that he never visited any village uninvited, he explained, 'In Dandi, a Muslim had invited me and I will be putting up in his bungalow. Satyagraha will commence from a Muslim friend's house. My Muslim friends should not, therefore, feel aggrieved.'[29] Gandhi again took up the question in his speech at Broach. He reiterated that he needed the help of all communities in India to make his struggle a success. Though the Ali brothers were not with him at the moment he hoped their resistance was only short-lived. The question as to how many seats would go to Muslims in the Viceroy's Council, Gandhi said that if he were the Viceroy he would let the Muslims and other minority communities take all they like. The Hindus will be content with the rest. This was the approach Gandhi advocated throughout his life but there were few takers for this policy. Whether there were any reactions to this statement at that time is not known to the author/ researcher but it is assumed that no serious note was taken of this speech by Congress or the Hindu organizations at this time. This statement also shows the efforts made by Gandhi to allay the fear of Muslims of being outnumbered and overpowered by Hindus in public offices. Gandhi also clarified that the Congress had promised not to accept any communal award that did not satisfy the parties concerned.[30]

Putting things in the right perspective Gandhi firmly denied the charge that the movement was for Hindu raj, as made by Maulana Shaukat Ali. Coming straight to the point that the Hindu-Muslim question revolved round the issue of sharing the spoils of office he thought that the Congress Party's decision not to enter office should put the issue to rest. He invited the Muslims to shed their fears and suspicion because the cause he was fighting for was universal in nature. Salt tax did not discriminate between communities; it was applicable to all alike. No doubt the Hindus were in majority in the movement but by asking the Muslims to boycott the movement, Maulana was not helping matters.[31]

Gandhi's success as a communicator can be gauged from the fact that his speeches varied with the audience. For a total Hindu gathering his speeches contained Hindu mythological references or references to the religious books and scriptures like the *Ramacharitamanas* or the *Gita*. For a rustic audience the facts of economics and self-respect were of paramount importance. For a mixed (in terms of religion) urban audience he would find out points of law and practical affairs and also appeal to their sense of right and wrong. Gandhi began his speech in Surat thus: 'I have gone through the holy books of Islam, Hinduism, Christianity and Zoroastrianism. All these state that women and poor should at no time be taxed. If I go through the rules of war, we shall find that they lay down that old persons, children and women should be left untouched in war. The same is applicable to this tax.'[32] This statement also underlies the fact that Gandhi was waging a unique 'war' against the British where rules applicable to war as framed by the civilized world were expected to be followed. At every step the British were being sent subtle messages that their actions were immoral by their own standards of morality as well.

To drill the message home of 'might versus right' Gandhi continued writing articles for his journals which were read not only by his supporters but by his critics and the Government officials as well. In these articles Gandhi focussed on the evil effects of the British rule. An Englishman took exception to this argument and wrote to Gandhi that the moral influence of British rule far outweighed the material loss. Gandhi acknowledged this letter and in his ingenious way made a fine distinction between 'the British rule' and the 'British contact' and accepted that the latter exercised whatever moral influence we may feel. To the question as to why Gandhi spared the Princely states and criticized the British alone for the misery of the Indians, in a reply that was directed towards the Englishman as well as the Princely States, Gandhi wrote: 'Remove the dead weight of the British rule which 'stunts' them and us, and they and we as independent parts of the same ancient land will grow as if by magic. But if they hug the golden chains that bind them to the British footstool, they are at liberty to hold on to their chains. India outside the States zone is awake and will bear the yoke no longer, even if it has to break in the attempt.' This was both a response to the Englishman's query as well as a message to the Princely States. Continuing his reply Gandhi conceded that he had stressed the economic ruination of India in his letter to the Viceroy. The hard truth was that the 'moral and spiritual wrong which is the direct result of the foreign rule is probably greater even than the economic wrong. Those who are engaged in the war of independence are not, it is obvious, moved by the economic wrong, *They* do not *feel* it. *They* are moved solely by the moral and spiritual wrong which they feel in every fibre of their being.'[33]

Second Phase: Expansion into Mass Civil Disobedience

On Gandhi's directions mass civil disobedience was started on April 6, 1930. Gandhi had generated sufficient atmosphere of non-violence in the country by his Dandi March to feel confident that the common people would join in the struggle. Following his call, innumerable headmen quit office. Significantly, Pandit Madan Mohan Malaviya, who had refused to resign during the NCM, resigned from the Legislative Assembly, followed by six others. To ensure that his efforts in creating the right atmosphere did not go waste, Gandhi, in an article in *Young India* laid down the rules for the new phase of the movement.[34]

On the 5th of April, 1930 Gandhi reached Dandi. The speech he delivered at Dandi was the essence of all the experiences he had had on the way and the sum total of his philosophy of civil disobedience. Gandhi also did not fail to educate the simple folk of the hamlet about the intricacies of the law, so that nobody exploited them because of their legal ignorance. Gandhi communicated to them his rationale for making civil disobedience a mass based movement. 'This is the struggle of not one man,' he emphasized, 'but of millions of us. If three or four men can fight or win swaraj, they will rule the country afterwards. Hence in this struggle for swaraj millions should offer themselves for sacrifice and win such swaraj as will benefit the vast masses of the country.'[35] This statement is of profound importance when we know today how freedom struggles led by only small groups have later led to the installation of that group only and the subsequent discontent of the masses on that score. Gandhi made all efforts to rule out such a possibility.

Taking a dig at the Government's predicament, Gandhi exhorted the people to follow him in breaking the infamous Salt Law. He said:

> The Government's plight is that of the serpent which has swallowed a rat. It would find it hard to resort to either

> course of action—allowing me to remain out or putting me behind the bars. I point out this ordinary duty to you. Everyone, whether a Hindu, a Muslim, or a Parsi, should follow it. When all of us do so, it is beyond the power of any Government to arrest us.

Women came out in large numbers to volunteer for civil disobedience. Gandhi, however, did not favour their courting arrest because he felt that the chivalrous English would not like to lathi charge or use force against women. He did not want to put this disadvantage of the opponent to use. But he asked the women folk to be active in picketing of foreign cloth shops and liquour booths. This only shows that even at the height of success Gandhi never let go of his principles or compromise on them.

So much was the value attached to Gandhi's words and leadership that the police force that went to Dandi to stop the breach of the Salt Law went unarmed. In spite of the unprecedented restraint shown by the British administration, in one instance, the police tried to snatch salt from one resister who refused to part with it. In the scuffle that ensued the man was wounded and his wrist started bleeding. Seeing blood coming out, the onlookers descended on the area and started digging the earth for salt, as an act of defiance. All this activity was totally peaceful and non-violent. Gandhi recounted this incident with pride for the readers of *Young India*.[36] Later, in a speech before the villagers of Aat, he said, 'That incident will remain indelible in the history of India.'[37] He was right. Even in the film on Gandhi directed by Richard Attenborough the event is recounted. Erik Erikson gives his analysis of the event subscribing to the 'teasing' or 'testing' theory of his, referred to earlier. He writes:

> If one watches a moving picture of Gandhi's *satyagrahis* marching to the sea, it is, as it were, physiognomically obvious that they express a certain "teasing" attitude toward the British authorities, implying that, surely, the English could not make a bloody issue out of a people's determination to scoop up the salt out of their own sea. That the British (and the Indian constabulary) eventually did react with a brutality multiplied by a sense of being taunted and of "not being able to take it" cost them much of their inner authority in Indian eyes as well as their own.[38]

This was a moral victory for Gandhi!

The CDM was also a movement for educating the people on political matters and creating awareness among them. Thus when Pt. Jawaharlal Nehru was arrested and Gandhi wanted to share this important piece of information with simple Gujarati women of Umber who had not even heard of Pt. Nehru, he explained, 'He was to all India what Sardar Vallabhbhai Patel was to us in Gujarat.'[39] This simple statement, simply put, shows how the movement which was active in Gujarat was actually taking on the shape of a all-India movement with people taking interest in or being informed about what was happening outside Gujarat and vice-versa.

The whole country was brimming with optimism. The common man and the leaders shared this confidence alike. Recounting a dialogue between himself and Motilal Nehru in the funeral speech in honour of the great leader, Gandhi said when he assured Motilal Nehru that when he recovered from his illness he would see a free India, Nehru had prompltly replied that swaraj had already been won![40] Earlier Jawaharlal Nehru had also expressed similar sentiment. In a letter to Gandhi written from prison he wrote:

> May I congratulate you on a new India that you have created by your magic touch! What the future will bring I know not, but the past has made life worth living and our prosaic existence has developed something of an epic greatness in it. Sitting here in Naini Jail I have pondered on the wonderful efficacy of non-violence as a weapon and have become a greater convert with the response of a convert to it than ever before.[41]

Such effusive responses must have gladdened Gandhi's heart. Freedom seemed so near and imminent that Gandhi was asked what would he do after India gained freedom? Would he retire from active politics or participate in its reconstruction? Gandhi was cautious in reply. He said, 'I should like to take an active part in the reconstruction of my country provided I retain my health and vigour and my people's confidence in me and my methods. That, indeed, would be a labour of love.'[42]

Not only was the movement felt in India, the world had come to know of it thanks to the publicity it got through foreign correspondents covering it. Gandhi's 'Message to America' was prophetic. He had said: 'I have no manner of doubt that after the sacrifice that has already been made since April 6, the spirit of the people will be sustained throughout till India has become independent and free to make her contribution to the progress of humanity.'[43] By now Gandhi had clearly acquired the status of an international political figure. He was aware of this and cashing on it sent an appeal from Dandi, 'I want world sympathy in this battle of Right against Might.'

Women participated actively in the Salt March as this picture taken on the occasion of Gandhi picking up salt on the conclusion of the Salt satyagraha shows.

The more glorious chapters of the struggle were yet to be written when Gandhi and his satyagrahis would become immortalized in public memory. The success of the movement made the government take harsher steps. The Government passed the Press Act Ordinance giving itself sweeping powers. In a fitting reply Gandhi asked the press not to be cowed down, arguing:

> They may confiscate type and machinery, they will not confiscate pen and still less speech, but I recognize that they can succeed in confiscating even these last two. But what they will never succeed in suppressing and what is after all the thing that matters is the thought of the nation and at the present moment there is hardly a man or woman breathing in India who with every breath does not breathe of disaffection, sedition, disloyalty and whatever other term one may use to describe the mentality of the nation which has set its mind on destroying the existing system Governement.[44]

The Congress Working Committee and other organisations affiliated to the Party were also banned. The Legislative Assembly which had some Indian members as well was bypassed and the Government decided to rule by ordinances. Party leaders, other than Gandhi were arrested in large numbers. The British authorities also removed salt from expected sites of attack in order to frustrate the satyagrahis. In response to Government's action Gandhi changed his strategy. He announced the raid of Government salt depots, and announced that the satyagrahis would raid Dharasana Salt Depot. Finally on May 5, 1930 Gandhi was arrested in the darkness of night and lodged in Yerwada Prison, Pune. Gandhi's grandson, Rajmohan Gandhi, has captured the drama of his arrest in his book on Gandhi. His description is as follows:

> 'Do you want me?' Gandhi asked, even though he knew the answer. In response to another question he was informed that his arrest was occurring under Regulation 25 of 1827, which authorized arrest without a trial. A new speech from him from the dock was not what the Raj wanted.[45]

Gandhi's mouthpieces, *Young India* and *Navajivan* were banned. However, even during Gandhi's incarceration the two newspapers continued 'publication' in a cyclostyled form and seven thousand copies of the *Young India* came out regularly whereas 10,000 of *Navajivan* also saw light of the day. With his arrest the true worth of his training of satyagrahis shone forth with the world watching.

The remarkable spirit of non-violence shown during the raid of Dharasana Salt Works became well-known throughout the world when it was reported live by an American reporter. Webb Miller of the United Press sent a moving account of the takeover attempt of the satyagrahis facing up to brutal police action. The British Government by sheer violence managed to save the Depot. Miller's graphic account was published in more than a thousand papers at home and abroad. The brutality of the British-led police aroused wide-spread revulsion even in England. The very need of the British to fall to the level of such brutality itself spelt victory for non-violence. Instead of being discouraged by such oppression the feeling among Indians was that of pride and optimism—optimism that independence was just a matter of time.

Gandhi's arrest temporarily put to halt the phase of communicating with the masses of India. Now Gandhi was to mainly deal with the leaders, administrators and the intelligentsia. Quite some time later, Gandhi got a brief opportunity to interact with the masses while on his visit to England, where he addressed the mill workers of Lancashire. He won them over with his simple arguments and sincerity. In the decision-making, however, he was not a great success as the Government had already made up its mind and was only pretending to negotiate.

Gandhi Persuaded to Attend the Round Table Conference

After the arrest of Gandhi, some Liberal leaders tried to persuade the Congress to participate in the second Round Table Conference (RTC). Gandhi was in favour of the Congress attending the RTC only on the condition that the British Government accepted self-government for Indians and would meet only to discuss the details during the transitional period. He also reserved for himself the liberty of 'testing every swaraj scheme by its ability to satisfy the object underlying 11 points' listed in his letter to the Viceroy. He also laid down that the minimum condition for the suspension of civil disobedience would be non-enforcement of the penal clauses of the Salt Act and the restoration of the normal rule of law.

Gandhi-Irwin Talks

The Gandhi-Irwin talks form a landmark in the history of British rule in India. For the first time since its establishment the British Government agreed to deal with a representative of the country—a person who had always challenged and defied their authority— on an equal footing and with due courtesy. The negotiations did not prove very gainful for the nationalist cause. The Viceroy turned out to be a hard bargainer and managed to secure all the immediate advantages. The truce terms were bitterly criticized by the radical nationalists. The only gain that seemed to accrue from the negotiations was that it legitimized satyagraha as a weapon of political warfare and demonstrated the power of the common people based on moral strength. At the personal level the talks were significant as a reflection of personalities of the two men. Both of them believed in the 'higher power' and the 'moral governance of the universe'. Both of them believed that they were destined to be 'doing something big for India and humanity.'[46] It has been aptly remarked believably, that Gandhi yielded 'much to the Viceroy because of his regard for the man.'[47] The talks seem to establish equality between India and Great Britain, a fact which did not escape Winston Churchill's discerning eye. Fuming, he spoke in the British House of Commons of the 'nauseating and humiliating spectacle of this one time Inner Temple lawyer, now a seditious fakir, striding half-naked up the steps of the Viceroy's palace there to negotiate and to parley on equal terms with the representative of the King-Emperor.'[48]

Gandhi-Irwin Truce

As a result of the negotiation between Gandhi and Irwin, a truce was reached between the Government and the Congress, paving way for the Congress participation in the RTC. The Congress appointed Gandhi as its role representative at the RTC. He was released from jail.

Gandhi's communication skills were put to severe test in the period immediately following the truce. The death of Motilal Nehru in 1930 had left Gandhi without a confidante. Gandhi's inability in stopping the death sentence to the revolutionary youths Bhagat Singh, Rajguru and Sukhdev made his situation difficult *vis-à-vis* the youth of the country. At this stage since freedom seemed so near at hand, some of the minorities, especially the Muslims and the Sikhs, started voicing their concern that they might get swamped by the majority community when the British were no longer the rulers of India. They demanded that they be assured of a sizeable number of seats in future legislature so that their interest be safeguarded.

The Revolutionaries

The issue of the execution of Bhagat Singh proved to be a real test for Gandhi. Even to this day Gandhi has not been able to clear his name of the charge that he did not make sufficient efforts to save the much loved patriot's life. Great expectations from Gandhi were based on the assumption that he had become so powerful that he was in a position to get whatever he wanted from the British authorities. He was accused of not trying hard enough. Gandhi had pleaded with the Viceroy for the commutation of Bhagat Singh and his associates' sentences. Gandhi's letter to the Viceroy written on 23-3-1931 shows that Gandhi and others were not aware that the three patriots had already been executed in the early hours of the morning and the reply of the Viceroy could not have been other than what he gave later. In this letter Gandhi had written:

> Though you were frank enough to tell me that there was little hope of your commuting the sentences....you said you would consider my submission on Saturday [i.e., 23-3-1931]....popular opinion rightly or wrongly demands commutation. Where there is no principle at stake, it is often a duty to respect it. In the present case the chances are that, if commutation is granted, internal peace is most likely to be promoted. In the event of the execution, peace is undoubtedly in danger. Seeing that I am able to inform you that the revolutionary party has assured me that, in the event of these lives being spared, that party will stay its hands, suspension of sentence pending cessation of revolutionary murders becomes in my opinion a peremptory duty. Political murders have been condoned before now. It is worth while saving these lives, if thereby many other innocent lives are likely to be saved and maybe even revolutionary crime almost stamped. Since you value my influence such as it is in favour of peace, do not please unnecessarily make my position, difficult as it is, almost too difficult for future work.... "Charity never faileth."[49]

Through this letter Gandhi had tried to convince Irwin how commutation would be a politically wise step while at the same time being legally defensible and morally appropriate.

Gandhi is accused of not trying hard enough because he refused to make commutation a condition for Congress participation at the RTC, since it was not there in the original demands. The radical nationalists had expected him to do so. So, when he went to attend the Karachi session of the Congress in 1931, for the first time in India he was greeted with the slogans of 'Gandhi Go Back' and 'Down with Gandhism' and presented with black flowers by the youths of the Naujawan Bharat Sabha as a token of the ashes of the martyred patriots. The speech that Gandhi delivered after this incident should be read with care by all who doubt the sincerity of Gandhi. Later the tribute he paid to Bhagat Singh and his comrades at the session speaks volumes about the practical idealism of Gandhi. He said:

> I wish to tell you these young men with all the authority with which a father can speak to his children that the use of violence can only lead to perdition....Do you think that all the women and children who covered themselves with glory during the last campaign would have done so if we had pursued the path of violence? Would they have been here today? Would our women, known as the meekest on earth, would women like Gangabehn, who stood the lathi-blows till her white sari was drenched in blood, have done the unique service they did if we had violence in us? ....And our children .... Who renounced their toys, their kites and their crackers, and joined as soldiers of swaraj—how could you have enlisted them in a violent struggle?[50]

The answer to this could only have been in the negative. Continuing with his tribute to Bhagat Singh, Gandhi warned the youth against following his example, for he believed that the country 'must not be liberated through bloodshed.' Though he was strongly against the use of violence by these men, he refrained from using strong words against them. His criticism was reserved for the Government that 'missed the golden opportunity, to win over the rebels to its side..... The Government by its own act dealt a severe blow to the settlement and had shown its capacity to disregard public opinion once again and to exhibit the great brute force it possesses.'[51] In an interview to the Press, Gandhi described the raising of black flags and slogans against him as 'the legitimate expression' of the anger of the members of the Naujawan Bharat Sabha. Paying rich tributes to the martyrs he said:

> One's head bends before Bhagat Singh's bravery and sacrifice. But I want the greater bravery, if I might say so without offending my young friends, of the meek, the gentle

and the non-violent, the bravery that will mount them gallows without injuring, or harbouring the thought of injury to a single soul.[52]

Later, Gandhi also held a meeting with the members of the Naujawan Bharat Sabha and had a candid exchange of views, with respect shown by both the parties to each-other's points of view. This openness on the part of Gandhi was misconstrued by some as leniency, if not sympathy for the cult of violence. When a Sikh youth was canonised for murdering the district magistrate of Midnapore, Gandhi was compelled to express his views in unequivocal terms:

> The praising of Sajjan Singh as a hero raises a doubt in my mind about the wisdom of my having been the author of the Congress resolution about Bhagat Singh. My motive was plain enough. The *deed* was condemned. The *spirit of bravery and sacrifice was praised.* The hope behind was that was we would thereby be able to distinguish between the deed and the motive and ultimately learn to detest deeds such as political murders, no matter how high the motive might be. But the effect of the Congress resolution has been quite the contrary. It seems to have given a passport for extolling murder itself.[53]

Gandhi also published a letter written by the martyred Bhagat Singh's comrade, Sukhdev. After giving due recognition to the courage and sacrifice of the writer, Gandhi went on to enumerate eleven 'hard facts' against the use of violence. Gandhi's contention was that revolutionary activities involving violence took India farther from the goal of independence; increased military expenditure; led to Government reprisals and demoralisation of the people; did not contribute to mass awakening and was against Indian tradition of and history. Given the state of the country, he said the stream of violence would take too long to percolate to the masses and thus delay freedom, adding that such violence may well boomerang on Indians. He also pointed out that the revolutionaries had seen for themselves the success of the non-violent struggles. Their violent activities had, in fact, caused damage to the Movement. (for independence).[54]

Though Gandhi's arguments in favour of non-violence were based on the understanding of the reality of Indian conditions in which violence could not have been allowed for mass participation as was witnessed during the CDM, his insistence on it rested on a deeper philosophy. He believed that anything that was acquired by force would need force or violence for its sustenance as well. Violence would not allow the future Indian society to be built on a just foundation. His ambition went beyond just attaining freedom from the British. He wanted to establish a just society where the richest and the poorest enjoyed equal rights.[55] An essential ingredient in the building of the society of his dreams was education and awakening of the Indian consciousness which he believed the people were already getting through satyagraha.[56]

Efforts to Remove Misgivings on Truce

The success of the CDM had enthused the nation with confidence, with people and leaders alike sure that freedom was just a matter of time. At such a juncture of hype in the national psyche, Gandhi's suspension of the movement, and his apparently fruitless dialogue with Lord Irwin proved unwelcome indeed. People felt betrayed, leaders let down. Gandhi–Irwin Pact was severely criticized not just by the public but some of his closest confidantes. What Gandhi needed now was effective communication with disillusioned leaders who were demanding answers. Why did Gandhi, who was in a position of strength, agree to any kind of compromise? What substantial change had taken place to warrant Gandhi's viewing the RTC as beneficial to Indian interests? Subhas Chandra Bose criticized Gandhi's stance at the Congress session, whereas Nehru personally conveyed his displeasure to Gandhi through a letter.[57] Reginald Reynolds the English Quaker who had acted as an emissary wanted to know what new development had taken place to warrant the change and need to cooperate with the Government.[58] Gandhi assured Reynolds that he was neither deserting the cause not giving it up.[59]

The common people also joined in the criticism of Gandhi's truce. A particularly angry letter to Gandhi accused him of sacrificing the interests of the country for his 'Truth'. It read as follows:

> How can you explain away your inconsistency involved in your making fond and easy advances to the RTC after the Congress deciding not to participate in it and Jawaharlal ironically calling them only a few months ago 'old women'?

> Are you always going to sacrifice your country for Truth and treat us like test-tubes in your experiment of non-violence and Truth? Do you realize that you are staking the whole nation for your individual self-evolution?
>
> Many of us feel that you have become a National Habit which is useful for the capitalist but tragic for the exploited.[60]

Gandhi's considered reply to this angry outburst was that the decision to participate in the RTC was that of the Congress. It had not participated earlier because the RTC had not agreed to its terms. It was participating now as the RTC has agreed to its terms. The Congress, even under the present circumstances, retained the freedom to revive the Movement if the other party did not honour its commitment. There was, therefore, no question of sacrificing the interests of the country. Further, he remarked, 'I do not realize that I am 'staking a whole nation for self-evolution.' A nation cannot advance without the units of which it is composed and, conversely, no individual can advance without the nation of which he is a part also advancing.'[61] There were also suggestions to 'wade through blood' while 'pursuing the creed of non-violence' and attain the goal of independence. Gandhi agreed that the Government's actions were far below expectations but insisted: 'I will not lose hope till I know that nothing is to be gained from negotiation.'[62]

The Round Table Conference and Gandhi's Predicament

All said and done, Gandhi himself was not sure whether he would be participating in the RTC till the moment of his departure to England. He was not happy with the tardy pace of the Government's efforts to implement its part of the bargain. There were gross violations of the agreement regarding the release of prisoners and return of farmers who had boycotted revenue payment. After a long time silence and thorough investigation of complaint, Gandhi submitted a 'Charge-sheet' enumerating the instances of the breach of truce by the Government to HW Emerson, Home Secretary, on July 21, 1931. The Government's reply to the charge sheet and the Congress rejoinder appeared in *Young India* on September 24, October 1 and October 8, 1931. At this point it appeared as if the truce had broken down and Gandhi was in no mood to participate in the RTC.

While a sizeable section of Indians believed that Gandhi was betraying their trust in attending RTC, an admirer and long time friend of Gandhi felt that Gandhi was making excuses for not attending the RTC. He wrote what Gandhi called an 'elegant censure' and in order that Gandhi did not 'miss his wrath through any mishap' sent it through registered post. The letter runs thus:

> No one has for some time told you quite bluntly and in good English, that you are making an unmitigated fool of yourself, and out of personal vanity and the desire to act as a dictator, are descending to lies and subterfuges which even ordinary men, who lay no claim to special sanctity, do not indulge in.
>
> You know full well, that the main reason for your not attending the Round Table Conference is due to your inability to solve the Hindu-Muslim question....
>
> You, who prate of worshipping at the altar of truth the same altar that I worship at, are by half-truths, cunning words and deliberate deception are trying to force the blame of your deliberate pre-arranged determination not to go to the Round Table Conference on the Government.[63]

The letter was written when there was news that Gandhi may not after all attend the RTC. The writer was, with a frankness allowed in friendship clearly warning Gandhi that, by standing on his prestige and not entering into negotiations with the Government he was forcing it to take recourse to bloodshed. This was a false notion the Government had put into the minds of those who genuinely wished for a settlement between the British Government and Congress. Hence the writer of the letter was not to be blamed. What is interesting here, however, is that how such stringent criticism was not only received by Gandhi in the right spirit and also highlighted by him. Highlighting the objection of his friend in his paper, Gandhi clarified his stand to the Englishmen who had been misled by Government propaganda. The Hindu-Muslim question disturbed him and he was indeed reluctant to go to attend the RTC unless the communal tension was resolved, yet his reasons for not attending the RTC were breach of agreement on the part of Government.

Under the pressure of public opinion, the British Government reopened negotiations with Gandhi in August 1931 and after consultations with Congress Gandhi agreed to go to England as the sole representative of the Party, which he claimed represented India.

He was not very hopeful of any progress but being a born optimist he decided to take the chance.

Gandhi Publicizes India's Cause En-Route England

Gandhi set sail for England in September 1931. He used his voyage to England to communicate with the peoples of countries the ship touched. In a speech at his reception at Aden, Gandhi said; 'It is my conviction that India, numbering one-fifth of human race, becoming free through non-violence and truth can be a great force and service to the whole of mankind.'[64] On board the ship he continued with his prayer meetings where invariably the issue of Indian independence would come up. He also sent messages to the different political groups and parties in Egypt where struggle for independence was on. The theme continued in his address to students at Marseilles where he described the non-violent struggle as a 'process of purification' for Indians for their weaknesses.[65]

The real test however was to come when Gandhi was to face the workers of Lancashire who believed that his programme of boycott of British textiles was responsible for their plight. CF Andrews had forewarned Gandhi about their anger against him. He had told Andrews that the mill workers need to be apprised of the actual state of things and he was optimistic that they would understand him. He clearly wrote to Andrews that the 'proper course is to show the labourers how they have been unconsciously assisting in wrong done by Lancashire to India and therefore how necessary it is to retrace the step'[66] This he managed to do with remarkable ease. The speech he gave at the meeting of the workers was a masterpiece of communication where Gandhi employed all the tools of rhetoric with good effect. The speech goes as follows:

> I would be untrue to you, I would be a false friend, if I were not frank with you....I strove with Lord Irwin last March for the liberty to boycott liquor and foreign cloth. He suggested that I might give up the boycott for three months as a gesture and then resume it. I said I could not give it up for three minutes. You have three million unemployed, but we have three hundred million unemployed for half the year. Your average unemployment dole is seventy shillings. Our average income is seven shillings and sixpence a month.....I do believe that it is a debasing thing for a human being to

> remain idle and live on doles.....imagine, therefore, what it must be to have three hundred million unemployed, several millions becoming degraded each day for want of employment, devoid of self-respect, devoid of faith in God.
>
> I dare not take before them the message of God. I may as well place before the dog over there the message of God as before those hungry millions who have no lustre in their eyes....To them God can only appear as bread and butter. Well, the peasants of India are getting their bread from their soil; I offered them the spinning wheel in order that they may get butter, and if I appear before the British public in my loincloth, it is because I have come as the sole representative of those half-starved, half-naked dumb millions.
>
> Even in your misery your are comparatively happy. I do not grudge you your happiness. I wish well to you. But do not think of prospering on the tombs of poor millions of India....Do not attribute your misery to India. Think of the world forces that are powerfully working against you. See things in the daylight of reason.[67]

Mark Lindley, an American scholar has analyzed this speech carefully for its impact and rhetorical value. Lindley states, Gandhi by not making the assertion of friendship with statement like ' I am your friend' nonetheless substantiates his friendship. Gandhi in his earnest desire to make the British workers see the miserable plight of their Indian counterparts employs rhetorical devices like alliteration to make his speech effective. Lindley points out at the 'charming sequence of numbers 3, 3,3, 300, 70, 7, 6 as well as alliterations like hundred millions, hungry millions, half-starved naked millions' and so on. Finally Gandhi concludes that the British workers were better off than their counterparts in India both economically as well as spiritually since they were in a position to listen to reason whereas the stark poverty of Indians had made them insensitive to both God and reason.[68]

Apart from what Mark Lindley has pointed out, it must be borne in mind that the ideas expressed in his speech had been expressed by Gandhi earlier as well in several of his articles. They had the impact in this speech because here they were put together before an audience who was not used to such frank talk by a person who appeared ascetic and thus devoted to truth. There was no question of doubting his words and also his logic showed that world forces were the culprits and not the Indians who were boycotting their cloth. And these Indians were objects of sympathy rather than hatred. In this manner Gandhi won over the workers through the power of truth. He stayed in the mill-hands quarters and participated in the functions organized by them with great enthusiasm.

Gandhi Received by Women Workers at Darwen (England) 1931

Equally at ease was Gandhi with the intellectuals of Britain and the world. Albert Einstein, the great scientist of the century, wrote a letter of praise to Gandhi for his non-violent activism.[69] The famous British playwright, Bernard Shaw, confessed to Gandhi, 'I knew something about you and felt something in you of a kindred spirit. We belong to a very small community on earth.'[70] Charlie Chaplin met Gandhi and was to recount later in his autobiography the deep impression Gandhi made on him. Maria Montessori, the educationist exchanged notes with Gandhi on the philosophy of education.[71] HN Brailsford, the painter, met Gandhi and discussed the philosophy of art with him. But the meeting that Gandhi was looking forward to personally was the meeting with Evelyn Wrench, the editor of *The Spectator,* because of the role that paper had played in enlightening the people of Britain about India's problems.[72]

Gandhi's fame had reached England before he had set his foot on the soil of England. It is without a parallel in history for a man to receive such warm welcome from the people of country against whom he had been waging a relentless war. 'Perhaps it is not for the man but for the cause I am espousing that people shower their affection on me,' Gandhi stated in all humility. The heart-warming welcome the people of England accorded him, is best revealed in a Reuters report to this effect. When Gandhi arrived in London, the rush of people was so great that police precautions became necessary. The member of the reception committee summed up brilliantly the impression that Gandhi had on the common people, '....Mahatma Gandhi, if I may say so, you are a strange man—to the people of your country and more so to my people. You are so sincere that you make some of us suspicious. You are so simple that you bewilder some of us....'[73] Another example of the enormous impact of Gandhi's personality on the people of England can be gauged from the report in *The Post,* an English daily (2-10-1931). The interviewer concluded his interview with the following words, 'Despite his smallness and frailness, he is imposing; and such personal magnetism has hitherto been outside my experience. The humble man is impregnable; that I have repeated; but only now do I realize the truth of the remark. *Gandhi's humility is a thing for tears.*'[74] (emphasis added)

British 'Divide and Rule' Defeats Gandhi at Round Table Conference

Gandhi's trip to England was not a triumphal march. Historians record how miserably he failed in his attempts at reaching a settlement at the RTC. On the basis of this they conclude that Gandhi's trip was a failure. The RTC turned out to be a consummate fraud played on the people of India by the British Government. Gandhi saw through the sham. He repeatedly said that he was going through the whole exercise because he had promised Irwin that he would explore all possibilities of coming to an honourable agreement with the British. Otherwise, he saw the RTC was only a 'debating society' and the members who claimed to represent the various sections of the Indian society were actually not representative of anyone except their own sectarian interests. He could clearly see through the game the British were playing by pitting one community against another, one caste against another, and then claiming that Indians could not come to any decisions because of their own differences. In short, they all but said that the Indians were not fit to rule themselves. The Congress Party that had been instrumental in shaking the foundations of the British Empire was deliberately shown to represent only Hindu interests. Nationalist Muslims like MA Ansari, whose inclusion Gandhi had suggested, were mysteriously dropped from the delegation without assigning any reason. In an interview to the Press Gandhi succinctly summed up the situation:

> I maintain that the failure to discover a solution for the communal question is largely due to want of knowledge about the new constitution and also to the *unrepresentative character of delegates.* The Government know only too well that the Congress is the only body which can deliver the goods. What then is the use of their pretending that the Congress is one among different groups, namely, Hindus, Muslims, Depressed Classes, Christians, landlords, zamindars? When the struggle was in progress, the Hindu Sabha was not different from the Congress. I am certain that if a referendum is held tody, the Hindus and Depressed Classes will by overwhelming majority be found to be in sympathy with the Congress. I am certain that the Nationalist Muslims will render a good account of themselves. If I had my way, I certainly would surrender to the Muslims, *but it will be of no use for the Government to exaggerate the differences which are largely due to the composition of the delegation which is their own action.*[75] (emphasis added)

The farce of the whole situation was exposed when Gandhi was arrested on his return to India and the Communal Award including reservation of seats for the Depressed Classes was declared by the Government the following year.

Summation

Thus Gandhi returned to India with a baggage full of English people's goodwill, but empty handed where any success at the RTC was concerned. One is reminded of an observation of Will Durant, the author of *The Story of Civilization.* Asked to define civilization, he had said, 'Civilization is a stream with banks. The stream is sometimes filled with blood from people killing, stealing, shooting, and doing things that historians usually record, while on the banks, unnoticed, people build homes, make love, raise children, sing songs, write poetry and even whittle statues. The story of civilization is what happened on the banks. Historians are pessimistic because they ignore banks for the river.'[76]

This is precisely how historians have dealt with Gandhi. Highlighting his temporary failure to tame the river pirates, they have ignored his real, constructive work on the banks. They have failed to see the bridge of goodwill he had built not only with the common people and intellectuals of England but of the world—a lasting bridge, as history, if not historians, has shown. Constitutional matters could very well wait till India was ready. Gandhi understood this. The pity is that very few others did.

REFERENCES

1. 'Why 'Purna Swaraj?', *Young India,* 6-2-1930, *CWMG,* XLII, p. 455.
2. 'Never Faileth', *Young India,* 20-2-1930, *CWMG,* XLII, p. 480.
3. 'Independence Day', *Young India,* 6-1-1930, *CWMG,* XLII, pp. 398-400.
4. 'To the Indian Critics', *Young India,* 23-1-1930, *CWMG,* XLII, p. 422.
5. *Ibid.*
6. 'To English Friends', *Young India,* 6-2-1930, *CWMG,* XLII, pp. 424-6.
7. *Young India,* 6-2-1930, *CWMG,* XLII, p. 426-7.
8. For text see Appendix-II
9. For text see Appendix-III
10. *Speech at Prayer Meeting, Sabarmati Ashram, Young India,* 12-3-1930, *CWMG,* XLIII, p. 59.
11. 'My Inconsistencies', *Young India,* 13-2-1930, *CWMG,* XLII, p. 470.
12. 'Salt and Cancer', *Young India,* 27-2-1930, *CWMG,* XLII, p. 498.
13. 'Salt Tax', *Young India,* 27-2-1930, *CWMG,* XLII, p. 499.
14. *Letter to Lord Irwin, Young India,* 2-3-1930, *CWMG,* XLIII, pp. 2-8.
15. 'Begging the Question', *Young India,* 23-3-1930, *CWMG,* XLIII, pp. 51-52.
16. For route of the march see map.
17. *Speech at Bhatgam, Young India,* 29-3-1930, *CWMG,* XLIII, pp. 146-149.
18. 'The Final Test', *Navajivan,* 9-3-1930, *CWMG,* XLIII, pp. 31-33.
19. *Interview to Haridas T. Majumdar, The Bombay Chronicle,* 18-3-1930, *CWMG,* p. 61.
20. *Speech at Aslali, Navajivan,* 16-3-1930, *CWMG,* XLIII, p. 62.
21. *Ibid.,* p. 63.
22. *Talk to Press Representatives, Prajabandhu,* 16-3-1930, *CWMG,* XLIII, p. 73.

23. *Talk to Press Representatives, Prajabandhu*, 16-3-1930, *CWMG*, XLIII, p. 73.
24. *Speech at Vasana, Prajabandhu*, 16-3-1930, *CWMG*, XLIII, p. 75.
25. *Speech at Borsad,, Prajabandhu*, 16-3-1930, *CWMG*, XLIII, p. 73.
26. *Speech at Buva, Gujarati*, 30-3-1930, *CWMG*, XLIII, p. 120.
27. *Speech at Surat, Prajabandhu*, 6-4-1930, *CWMG*, XLIII, pp. 162.
28. 'Mountain in Labour', *Young India*, 27-3-1930, *CWMG*, XLIII, p. 130.
29. *Speech at a Public Meeting, Tralsa, The Bombay Chronicle*, 26-3-1930, *CWMG*, XLIII, p. 123.
30. *Speech at Broach, Young India*, 3-4-1930, *CWMG*, XLIII, pp. 125-6.
31. 'What it is Not', *Young India*, 12-4-1930, *CWMG*, XLIII, pp. 55-7.
32. *Speech at Surat, Prajabandhu*, 6-4-1930, *CWMG*, XLIII, pp. 162.
33. 'The Fourfold Curse', *Young India*, 12-3-1930, *CWMG*, XLIII, p. 54.
34. 'Remember 6th April', *Young India*, 12-3-1930, *CWMG*, XLIII, p. 171.
35. *Speech at Dandi, Navajivan*, 13-4-1930, *CWMG*, XLIII, p. 184.
36. 'Barbarous', *Young India*, 10-4-1930, *CWMG*, XLIII, pp. 203-5.
37. *Speech at Aat, Prajabandhu*, 13-4-1930, *CWMG*, XLIII, p. 213.
38. Erik H Erikson, *op. cit.*, p. 186.
39. *The Hindu*, 16-4-1930, *CWMG*, XLIII, p. 263.
40. *Speech at Motilal Nehru's Funeral, Allahabad, CWMG*, XLV, pp.157-8.
41. *CWMG*, XLIV, p. 469.
42. *The Bombay Chronicle*, 28-3-1931, *CWMG*, XLV, p. 332.
43. *The Sunday Times*, 27-4-1930, *CWMG*, XLIII, p. 336.
44. 'Veiled Martial Law,' *Young India*, 8-5-1930, *CWMG*, XLIII, pp. 352-3.
45. Rajmohan Gandhi, *Mohandas*, Penguin Viking, 2006, p. 337.
46. Private letter from Lord Irwin to Gandhi quoted in the footnote, **CWMG**, XLV, pp. 134-5.
47. Preface to *CWMG*, XLV, p. vii.
48. Speech at Epping, February 23, 1931, R. James (ed), *Winston S Churchill: His Complete Speeches*, (New York, 1974), Vol.V, p. 4985.
49. *Letter to Viceroy, CWMG*, XLV, pp. 333-4.
50. *Speech at Karachi Congress, Young India*, 2-4-1931, *CWMG*, XLV, p. 349.
51. *Statement on the Execution of Bhagat Singh and Comrades, Gujarati*, 29-3-1931, *CWMG*, XLV, p. 336.
52. *Young India*, 2-4-1931, *CWMG*, XLV, p. 344.
53. 'The Cult of Violence', *Young India*, 16-4-1931, *CWMG*, XLVI, p. 1.
54. 'One of the Many (?)', *Young India*, 23-4-1931, *CWMG*, XLVI, pp. 27-28.
55. 'Of Princes and Paupers', *Navajivan*, 22-3-1931, *CWMG*, XLV, p. 328.
56. *The Bombay Chronicle*, 28-3-1931, *CWMG*, XLV, p. 332.
57. See Nehru's note on Provisional Settlement, AICC File No. 329, 1931.
58. *Letter to Reginald Reynolds, CWMG*, XLV, p. 221.
59. *Letter to Reginald Reynolds, CWMG*, XLVI, p. 16.
60. 'Questions and Answers', *Young India*, 26-3-1931, *CWMG*, XLVI, p. 341.

61. *Ibid.*
62. 'An Honest Doubt?' *Young India*, 4-6-1931, *CWMG*, XLVI, p. 313.
63. 'A Fickle Friend' *Young India*, 17-9-1931, *CWMG*, XLVII, p. 408.
64. *Young India*, 24-9-1931, *CWMG*, XLVII, p. 390.
65. *Young India*, 1-10-1931, *CWMG*, XLVII, p. 421.
66. *Letter to CF Andrews*, *CWMG*, XLVII, p. 40.
67. Mark Lindley, 'Gandhi's Rhetoric' in *Gandhi and the World Today (1998) – An American View*, Centre for Gandhian Studies, University of Kerala, Trivandrum, 1999, pp. 76-81.
68. *Ibid.*
69. As reported in *The Manchester Guardian*, 28-9-1931, *Young India*, 15-10-1931, *CWMG*, XLVIII, p. 66.
70. For text see, *CWMG*, XLVIII, fn.1, p. 82.
71. *Interview with Maria Montessori*, *Young India*, 22-10-1931, *CWMG*, XLVIII, p. 128.
72. *The Spectator*, 24-10-1931, *CWMG*, XLVIII, p. 175.
73. Footnote 2, *CWMG*, XLVIII, p. 45.
74. Footnote 1. *CWMG*, XLVIII, p. 45.
75. *Amrita Bazar Patrika*, 15-10-1931, *CWMG*, XLVIII, p. 144.
76. Norman Cousins in his introduction to Will Durant, *Profiles of Gandhi*, India Book Co., Delhi, 1970, p. 10.

6

Social Journalism

The Apolitical Phase (1932-37)

Between 1932 and 1937 Gandhi focussed his communication skills solely for educating the people on apolitical—social and economic—matters of relevance to the country. He knew that such an awareness of the situation among the people was an essential prerequisite for any freedom movement and subsequent nation-building.

The period under review was an important phase of the freedom struggle, of which Gandhi had been at the forefront since 1919 and was generally recognized as its leader. Yet Gandhi opted out of the political scene because for the most part of this period either he was unwell or in jail where he was allowed communication only on matters related to the 'untouchables.' His jail term which was to expire in August 1935 was cut short and he was prematurely released on May 8, 1933. He was rearrested on August 4, 1933, when he announced his programme of marching to Ras, a village in Gujarat, as part of civil disobedience. He was finally released on August 23, 1933 when he declared his intention to go on a twenty-one day purificatory fast and his condition deteriorated. Conscientious as he was, Gandhi refused to take advantage of the Government's generosity and kept away from political matters till the original date of his release from prison. In October 1934 Gandhi voluntarily resigned from the Congress Party to devote all his time and energy to the cause of untouchables and village uplift. The important political events of the time, like the Congress sessions, the resolutions passed by the Congress Working Committee and even the Government of India Act of 1935, failed to elicit any comments from Gandhi. He finally broke his silence on political matters in

1937, on the eve of elections to the Provincial Assemblies envisaged under the Act. He encouraged the Congress to fight the election, wrote articles in his journals and newspapers justifying the Congress stand and later, also provided the guidelines along which the Congress governments should function.

From January 1932 to August 1934 Gandhi's major concern was untouchablity. In the latter half to the period under review, Gandhi was totally involved in village uplift programmes. The cause of the untouchables was still alive, but it no longer seemed to be the only concern of Gandhi.

In light of this the present chapter is divided into two parts. The first part deals with the period when the cause of untouchables was the *exclusive* concern of Gandhi. The second part deals with the period when the village uplift programmes took up all his time and attention and Harijan uplift became its byproduct

Part-I
A Stigma of Hinduism

Gandhi was to a large extent instrumental in bringing the issue of untouchability on to the centre-stage of the Indian national movement by extensive writing on the subject supplemented by tours and personal contact programmes. Never before in history had untouchability in India been exposed to such a systematic and organized attack and on such a large scale. Before him, there had been sporadic movements against untouchability in different parts of India, for instance, in Bengal by the Brahmo Samajists and reformers like Ishwar Chandra Vidyasagar; in Maharashtra by Jyotiba Phule; in far south, by Narayan Guru and his followers—to name a few. Gandhi's efforts, however, were more effective because he launched a multi-pronged attack against the evil. He attempted to tackle it from the religious angle, by entering into learned discussions with religious leaders. He attacked it at the social level by urging the so-called 'untouchables' not to keep lying defeated under the age-old yoke of ignominy that made them live lives of outcasts, but rise and fight against it. He attacked it from the legal angle by encouraging passage of laws that would remove the traditional taboos. He appealed to the conscience of the caste-Hindus by exhorting them to do penance for the wrong they had been doing for ages, by refusing to practice untouchability and by helping to alleviate the sufferings of the down-cast communities. Through his speeches, writings and actions, Gandhi tried to bring home the fact that untouchability was a crime against humanity and that both the exploiters and the exploited needed to introspect and reform themselves. On the method Gandhi employed, Pt. Nehru's observation is noteworthy:

> In our own period numerous movements to break the tyranny of the caste have risen among the middle classes and they have made a difference, but not a vital one, so far as masses are concerned. Their movement was usually of direct attack. Then Gandhi came and tackled the problem after the immemorial Indian fashion, in an indirect way, and his eyes were on the masses. He had been direct enough, aggressive enough, persistent enough, but without challenging the original basic functional theory underlying the four main castes. He has attacked the rank undergrowth and over growth, knowing well that he was undermining the whole caste structure thereby.[1]

The Epic Fast

From 1930 onwards, eradication of untouchability became a mission with Gandhi. His confrontation with Dr. Ambedkar at the Second Round Table Conference in London in 1931 made him see through the British game of dividing the nation once again by projecting Dr. Ambedkar as the sole representative of the Depressed Classes[2] and agreeing to award separate electorate to the Depressed Classes. This made him aware of the urgency to address the issue. Therefore, at the Conference itself he declared that he would put his life at stake and oppose the award of separate electorate to the Depressed Classes as contemplated by the British. When the British declared the Ramsay McDonald Award in 1932 in which Separate Electorate was provided for the Depressed Classes, Gandhi then in jail, went into fast unto death for the withdrawal of the Award. He had reasoned against this move at the RTC saying that while the Muslims were justified in having a separate electorate as they were bound to remain Muslims for times to come, such was not the case with the Depressed Classes. In a letter written in anguish to the British Prime Minister he wrote that a movement for reform was already afoot. The evil of untouchability was bound to go. A separate electorate would put to naught the sincere efforts of the reformers to give them equal status and make them one with the rest of the Hindus. Instead, a separate electorate would permanently separate them from the rest of the Hindus giving them a distinct identity, just like the Muslims.[3]

Gandhi was willing to stake his life for what he considered to be the welfare of the 'untouchables' and made up his mind to resist the proposed separate electorate even when discussion was going on at the RTC in London. He had also planned to educate the Indian public on its damaging effect on the untouchables in particular and the Hindu community in general. Therefore, when he was arrested on his arrival in India he wrote to the Secretary of State, Sir Samuel Hoare on March 11, 1932, reminding him that his statement that he would resist with his life the award of separate electorate was 'not said in the heat of the moment, nor by way of rhetoric'.[4]

Gandhi usually went on fast as a last resort. Why was it that in the present context it was the first step? The reason could be that Gandhi wanted to honour his word given at the RTC of opposing the move for separate electorate with his life. Secondly, Gandhi could not in person educate the public on the damaging results of the already declared Award from the jail, nor could he have waited to come out of the jail and start a movement against it. The only immediate course of action left for Gandhi was to go on fast.

In a statement to the Press issued on September 16, 1932 Gandhi said that his fast was 'intended to sting the Hindu conscience into right religious action' and that if the Hindu mind 'is not prepared to banish untouchability root and branch, it must sacrifice me without the slightest hesitation.' The fast was against 'a statutory separate electorate' for the Depressed Classes since they were intimately interwoven into the Hindu society. Any attempt to separate them would harm the organic growth of the society. Seeing this danger to their society the high caste Hindus should take pledge to remove all kinds of untouchability from their midst and do penance for their past acts.

Reactions on Gandhi's Decision to Fast

Many people in India and abroad could not comprehend the significance of Gandhi's fast. The Prime Minister of England sent a longish telegram to Gandhi making fun of his sincerity regarding the uplift of the Depressed Classes as he was coming in the way of their enjoyment of political power by obstructing the acceptance of the separate electorate for them. Gandhi wrote: 'I have claimed to speak on behalf of the very class to sacrifice whose interest you impute to me a desire to fast myself to death. I had hoped the extreme step itself would effectively prevent any such selfish interpretation.'[5] Others called Gandhi's fast 'a political stunt' and refused to be influenced by it. Dr. Bhimrao Ambedkar, the leader of the Depressed Classes, later to become the Chairman of the Drafting Committee of the Constitution, wrote thus:

> There was nothing heroic about it. It was the opposite of heroic. It was an adventure. It was launched by Mr. Gandhi because he believed that both the Untouchables and the British Government would quake before his threat of fast unto death, and surrender to his demand. Both were prepared to call off his bluff and as a matter of fact did call it off. All this heroism vanished the moment Mr. Gandhi found that he had overdone the trick. The man who had started by saying that he would fast unto death unless the safeguards to the Untouchables were completely withdrawn and the Untouchables reduced to the conditions of utter helplessness without rights and without recognition was plaintively pleading , 'My life is in your hands, will you save me?' [6]

Any person who reads about the life of Gandhi, can easily discern how prejudiced were the minds of the people mentioned above on this matter and how they failed to understand Gandhi's motive or perhaps deliberately distorted the whole thing to serve their immediate purpose. For one thing, one does not put one's life at stake for mere 'adventure'. Secondly, as we shall shortly see, Gandhi was in the habit of clearly laying down the terms and conditions and in this case too had enunciated the condition on which he would break the fast and despite his being on the verge of death did not compromise on these principles. Thirdly, a man who refused to make up with his own brother over the issue of untouchables for full twelve years cannot be accused of being insincere about their uplift. The above line of thinking unfortunately continues among a section of people even today. Gandhi on his part, forgave Ambedkar for his outpourings which he said were due to the bitterness in his heart as the result of maltreatment at the hands of upper castes, both of him and members of the Depressed Classes. Gandhi went to the extent of offering himself to be spitted upon by the Doctor for the atonement of the sins of the upper castes!

With the publication of the writings of Dr. Ambedkar by the Maharashtra Government [7] the differences in the views of the two leaders regarding what was good for the Harijans has come to light. While Ambedkar believed that political rights in the form of separate electorate would put the Harijans on the road to progress, Gandhi viewed the Harijan question first in the social and religious context and later in the political and still later in the electoral context. This divergence of views was to be later the reason behind Gandhi compromising on the issue of reservations for members of the Depressed Classes in the legislatures, an issue which still remains a debatable point with regard to its impact on actual Harijan uplift. While Gandhi helped raise the consciousness of the so-called untouchables for their rights, Ambedkar fired them with political ambition.

There was, however, a vertical division in the ranks of the Depressed Classes on reservation and Gandhi's fast. Leaders of the Depressed Classes other than Ambedkar denounced the Award unequivocally. Speaking in the Central Legislative Assembly on 13 September, 1932 MC Rajah declared:

> Never in the annals of history of India had the issue of the Depressed Classes assumed importance as it has today, and for this we of the Depressed Classes must forever be grateful to Mahatma Gandhi. He has told the world, in words which cannot be mistaken, that our regeneration is the fundamental aim of his life....[8]

People who visited Gandhi immediately after the fast vouched for the religious and pure atmosphere that surrounded Gandhi at that time. A correspondent from an English daily wrote thus: 'No journalist could see Mahatma Gandhi today and discuss the position with him five hours after he had commenced 'a fast unto death' without being immensely impressed.'[9] Referring to a later day fast the Press Attaché of Lord Mountbatten, Alan Campbell-Johnson had similarly observed: 'You have to live in the vicinity of Gandhi fast to understand its pulling power. The whole of [his] life is a study in the art of influencing the masses, and judging by the success he has achieved...he must be accounted one of the greatest artists in leadership of all time.' [10]

Touching letters from loved ones and friends did not shake Gandhi's resolve to fast, which, for him, was a decree from God. Friends from across the Continent implored him to rethink but Gandhi turned down their request with a gentle reference to command from God, or with the help of his sparkling wit. William Shirer, the famous American journalist cabled from Vienna, that the American opinion was 'profoundly befuddled' by Gandhi's fast and he could not understand his willfully throwing away his 'undisputed political leadership of Indian nationalism by starving to death.'[11] More understanding was the response from Egypt from where the widow of Egyptian nationalist leader Zaghloul Pasha wrote:

> Egyptian people, men and women, who have been following with brotherly sympathy the heroic struggle of India and its great chief Mahatma Gandhi for liberty are now watching with beating hearts Mahatma's sublime act of self –sacrifice for sake of India's unity and freedom.... I express my sincere hope that India' s people inspired by Gandhi's sublime act of self-abrogation would unite in one great mass of brothers and patriots to save India's liberation and save life of her great son whose life and work are patrimony of East and humanity at large.[12]

Similar appeal was made by Rabindranath Tagore to the people of India. In response to a letter Gandhi wrote to him on the eve of his fast, Tagore wrote back with great feeling:

> It is worth sacrificing precious life for the sake of India's unity and her social integrity. Though we cannot anticipate what effect it may have upon our rulers who may not understand its immense importance for our people we feel certain that the supreme appeal of such self-offering will not be in vain. I fervently hope that we will not callously allow such a national tragedy to reach its extreme length. Our sorrowing hearts will follow your sublime penance with reverence and love.[13]

Srinivas Sastri, an otherwise critic of Gandhi's methods wrote in appreciation, 'Millions of homes rejoice and bless your superb service performed in your superb style. I confess, I trembled in doubt but the result vindicates and establishes you as indisputably the foremost untouchable and 'unapproachable'.[14]

Vinoba Bhave, on the other hand implored Gandhi to give up his fast. Gandhi responded to his concern in a lighter vein:

> You seem to have mastered the art of holding out false assurances to the poor! When a poor man like me was pining for a letter from you, you did not write at all; and now I am getting ready to lie down on my death-bed, you write to say, "Now that I have started writing I will write regularly." But maybe I am destined to survive this ordeal, since the vows of *Krityugis* are not known to remain unfulfilled.[15]

Yervada Pact

Gandhi's aim seemed to have been realized by the instantaneous countrywide awakening which followed the commencement of the fast and which later led to the agreement, known as the Poona or Yervada Pact, between leaders of orthodox Hindus and the representatives of the Depressed Classes on constitutional provisions for Harijans. The Pact gave 148 seats to Harijans in the legislatures as against 78 under the Government Award. The important change was in the manner of election. The election was to be in two stages. In the first round, Harijans in the reserved constituency were to elect a panel of four candidates; in the second round all voters of the constituency, irrespective of their caste, were to elect the candidates of their choice. Thus the electorate which elected the representatives was a common one. This vindicated Gandhi's stand of not dividing the Hindu community.

The Pact was, however, a compromise on the part of Gandhi. He was compelled to agree to what he had opposed, i.e., reservation of seats even in joint electorates. He had opposed any kind of reservation at the RTC as well. He continued to be opposed to them even during his fast. But with leaders like Ambedkar insisting Gandhi had no alternative but to agree to the lesser evil.

The most important gain of the Pact, as Arun Shourie rightly notes, was that it was arrived at by Indians without the interference of the British Government.[16] Gandhi had always wanted that Indians resolve their differences without help from outside. In the present case, he saw the cause of untouchables as a purely religious cause of Hindus and discouraged even Indians belonging to different faiths from participating in the discussions.

The agreement was accompanied by a pledge by the Hindu leaders at a public conference in Bombay, chaired by Pt. Madan Mohan Malaviya on 25 September, 1932 to secure for Harijans complete political and social equality and to work for removal of all disabilities and hardships suffered by them. The Resolution was of far-reaching importance as some of its features later formed the spirit behind Article 15 and Article 17 of the Constitution of independent India. The Resolution read as follows:

> This Conference resolves that henceforth, amongst Hindu, no one shall be regarded as an untouchable by reason of his birth and those who have been so regarded hitherto will have the same rights as the other Hindu in regard to the use of public wells, public roads and other public institutions. This right shall have statutory recognition at the first opportunity and shall be one of the earliest acts of the Swaraj Parliament; if it shall not have received such recognition before that time.
>
> It is further agreed that it shall be the duty of all Hindu leaders to secure, by every legitimate and peaceful means, an early removal of all social disabilities now imposed by custom upon the so-called untouchable classes including the bar in respect of admission to temples.[17]

Not only did Gandhi draft this resolution himself he published it at least three times in the *Harijan* so that the resolving parties remember it. This was an example of communication through repetition.

But for the deft use of Press, Gandhi's fast would not have had the impact it had. Gandhi's practice of issuing Press statements was helpful in disseminating the relevant and correct information to all concerned regarding the issues he was trying to highlight. It would be pertinent to note here that Gandhi was well-aware of mis-reporting or exaggerated reporting by the Press and therefore issued a well-drafted and clear statement about the terms and conditions of his fast. He even encouraged his Secretary, Pyarelal, to document the day to day account of the fast which was published in the form of a book in 1932 itself. In this manner, Gandhi made an effective use of print media for furthering his cause. Once his credentials as the foremost champion of the untouchables, who would stake even his life for their uplift, was established, Gandhi approached the untouchability question with a new vigour.

Gandhi's other Strategies to Tackle the Evil of Untouchability

Gandhi adopted a multi-pronged strategy to tackle the evil of untouchability. He issued Statements on Untouchability from jail; entered into discussions with Shastris on the religious justification of the evil, if any; organized activities for alleviating the sufferings of untouchables through organizations founded by him such as the Harijan Sewak Sangh, which was supported by the communication and education through his journals devoted to the cause of untouchables published in English, Hindi and Gujarati, namely the *Harijan, Harijan Sewak* and the *Harijan Bandhu;* and, conducted tours by train and on foot to create awareness regarding the injustice done to the untouchables.

Statements on Untouchability

Following the lifting of restriction by the Government on Gandhi's interviews and his carrying on propaganda in connection with anti-untouchability work, Gandhi issued 13 'Statements on Untouchability' from prison (November 4, 1932 to December 30, 1932) that touched upon various issues related to the practice.

Gandhi addressed the doubts, fears and anxieties of people, both belonging to the so-called upper castes and the so-called untouchables in the statements issued to the Press. The general belief was that since untouchability was sanctioned by religion, Gandhi was violating it in advocating that people should give up untouchability and that he was himself a renegade for doing so. Gandhi reiterated that he has been a practicing Hindu for the last forty years and a firm believer in the teachings of the Gita that contained the essence of the Vedas. Nowhere had he come across any reference purporting to the religious sanction behind the practice of untouchability. He has accepted the meaning of Shastras as given in the Gita, according to which it means 'right conduct embodied in living authority'.[18] However, he said, there was no use of all this sterile discussion. The evidence of age-long injustice meted out to Harijans was right in front of us for all to see.[19] While the Harijans should improve their lot by giving up their bad habits,[20] those interested in their welfare should help them in their efforts by making arrangement for education and public facilities for them.[21] To the charge that Harijans are unfit for association because of their 'dirty work' Gandhi stated that such 'dirty work' is performed by mothers for their children and by doctors while studying medicine, and they are not ostracized for doing so.[22]

Sometimes in their misguided zeal for reforms, the volunteers doing Harijan work resorted to coercion. When this was reported to Gandhi he admonished those who were guilty and alluded to the spiritual nature of the whole exercise of Harijan uplift by referring to his fast unto death.[23] There was a predictable reaction to this statement when some people wrote to Gandhi that his fast was itself a kind of coercion and that the Poona Pact was signed under such coercion for the concern for Gandhi's life. When this charge was repeated Gandhi responded by saying that his fast was 'intended to strengthen the weak, to energize the sluggards and to give faith to the skeptics.'[24]

The issue of the coercive nature of Gandhi's fast again cropped up when Gandhi declared his decision to go on fast for allowing the opening of Guruvayur temple to Harijans. A correspondent stated that he had no respect for Gandhi's religious or social reforms, but was supporting him on his fast as he wanted to save him for political movements of future where he felt Gandhi was very effective. Gandhi was quick to retort that one should not give up one's convictions for any thing or anyone, however important that cause or person may be.[25]

The temple entry issue became an important point of discussion between Gandhi and his correspondents. Some said that Gandhi was acting as a Hindu communalist by espousing a religious cause while he should be focusing on national issues,[26] others counseled him to give up the issue of Harijan entry to temples as they were not interested in visiting temples [27] and may even pollute them because of their dirty habits, and nature of work.[28] Interestingly another point of view was that there was no point in making the temple entry an issue as temples themselves were polluted enough to be unworthy of the whole exercise.[29]

As was his wont, Gandhi conducted a referendum to ascertain the wishes of the temple goers with respect to allowing entry to the Harijans as declared by him before undertaking his fast. Fear was expressed that people may vote against Gandhi or may vote against their wishes just to save Gandhi's life. In the first case Gandhi said he would respect the wishes of the people while for the second, Gandhi strongly implored them not to do so.[30]

In the final Statement Gandhi published the result of the referendum.[31] Of the 27,465 men and women approached by the volunteers, 55 per cent voted in favour of Harijans being allowed to enter the temple, 9 per cent against, 27 per cent stayed neutral, not deciding either way. Democratically, the clear majority meant nothing could now stop Harijans entry. But Gandhi, respecting the wishes of those against the entry, offered a compromise. It was thus agreed that, at certain fixed hours, Harijans would worship in the temple along with those who had no objection to their presence. The rest of the hours were reserved for those who were opposed to the entry of 'untouchables'.

The purpose of dealing in some detail with the above 13 statements is to illustrate the communicational efficacy of Gandhi's dialogues with the people. Almost all the valid doubts about the movement were aired and Gandhi's stand fully publicized. That the statements appeared almost every alternate day indicates how preoccupied Gandhi was with this social evil. Considering the prevalent orthodoxy of the times, abolition of untouchability was a revolutionary move in itself. The malaise was, and to some extent in certain quarters still is, so deeply ingrained in the Hindu psyche that it is almost impossible to root it out. The arguments put forward by Gandhi appealed to the hearts of the people, but when it came to conduct i.e., putting it into practice, most of them shied away. It required great courage of conviction to stand up and defy traditions which had been followed for time immemorial. Gandhi too was painfully aware of this dichotomy but plodded on.

It goes to Gandhi's credit that within a short span of less than a month he was able to generate sufficient interest in the condition of the Harijans throughout the length and breath of India. The Statements on Untouchability were essentially in the nature of dialogue between Gandhi and the general public. Newspapers too joined in the debate and published letters written by Gandhi on important matters to general public and vice-versa, on matters that were not covered by the Statements. No question or doubt was of less importance to Gandhi. No letter went unanswered because it raised inconvenient issues. His earnestness was reflected in the Statements in good measure. The Statements, in a way, performed the function of 'curtain-raiser' for what was to be enacted later on the stage of Harijan uplift.

It was clear to Gandhi that being rightly or wrongly associated with religion, the untouchability question had to be handled delicately and patiently. The social division of labour also made it difficult for high caste men to do away with the services performed by the so-called untouchables. It was as humungous problem for Gandhi as was the communal question. Besides, being an issue that concerned Hindus alone, Gandhi persistently discouraged any help from other communities. Gandhi also took care that the movement did not degenerate into a fight between the high and low castes amongst Hindus, because that would have divided India further. He tried his best to arrive at mutually agreed consensus and clearly spelled out that both sections should reform themselves—the high castes by doing penance for the sin of maltreating their co-religionists and the 'untouchables 'by keeping themselves and their surroundings clean and by keeping away from vices like drinking, carrion eating etc. He also made it clear that for him social and political issues were not separate from each other[32] and once the evil of untouchability was banished from Hindu society, Muslim and Christian untouchability would also go in due course.[33] He also made it clear that Harijan cause though occupying most of the time, was not the only issue he had in mind. He was aware of the communal problem acutely.

Discussion with Shastris

As noted earlier, the biggest hurdle in the way of banishing untouchability was the belief that it had the weight of religious sanction behind it. Gandhi, therefore, approached the so-called custodians of Hinduism, the Shastris, asking them to shed some light on the issue. For his part, he refused to believe that such an inhuman system could ever have religious sanction of the ancients. He was in correspondence with the well-known Sanskrit scholar SD Satavlekar over a number of issues related to Hindu religious texts. Gandhi enlisted the support of Satavlekar on untouchability work and sought his opinion in the matter.[34] On the basis of the information supplied to him by Satavlekar and some other scholars, he wrote to Anandashakar Dhruva, the well-known Marathi writer and Sanskrit scholar, with following instructions:

> Now about the correct interpretations of the Shastras. I send with this some of the literature on the subject given to me. Go through it carefully and draft a well-reasoned reply as soon as you can and obtain on it the signatures of all the pundits whom you can persuade to join with you.... It should be addressed to four types of readers: to the honest sanatanists, to impartial students who wish to know the truth, to persons who are working for the removal of untouchability and to whom your statement can be of great help in meeting the arguments of the sanatanists and, last to non-Hindus who should know that the true sanatana dharma does not consider anybody as untouchable from birth and that, if in certain circumstances, a person is considered untouchable, he or she soon becomes touchable again.[35]

These actions point out to a clear strategy employed by Gandhi in fighting the evil of untouchability. The biggest hurdle, that is the presumed religious basis of untouchability, was to be tackled first. The truth about the Shastras should emerge from people known and respected for their knowledge of the Shastras. That would carry more weight. It would help clear the misunderstanding in the minds of the sanatanists some of whom genuinely believed that untouchability had basis in religion. It would help the uninitiated understand the true nature of their religion and get for it the respect it deserved. It would help those who were tirelessly working for the removal of untouchability by providing them solid ground to fight their case in the court of the public. Even non-Hindus would now know the truth about Hindu religion. This was indeed a clever strategy employed by Gandhi!

Gandhi posted the Shastris a set of 10 questions to think over and then fixed a meeting with them on December 12, 1932. The questions that he sent for their response are listed below[36] :

1. Define untouchability according to the Shastras.
2. Can the definition of untouchables given in the Shastras be applied to the so-called untouchables of the present day?
3. What are the restrictions imposed by the Shastras on the untouchables?
4. Can an individual be free from untouchability in his own life-time?

5. What are the injunctions of Shastras regarding behaviour of the touchables with the untouchables?
6. Under what circumstances will the Shastras permit temple-entry by the untouchables?
7. What are Shastras?
8. How is the authoritativeness of the Shastras proved?
9. How will the differences arising over the definitions or interpretations of Shastras be decided?
10. What are your conclusions?

Gandhi seemed to enjoy his meeting with the Shastris. Writing about it to Jawaharlal Nehru, who was following the movement with keen interest, Gandhi stated, 'I am having a glorious time with the *Shastris*. My knowledge of the letter of the Shastras is better, but of true religion they are able to give me little.[37] This letter shows how the issue of untouchability was important for the future leaders of India and how they were following Gandhi's efforts closely. The letter also hints at Gandhi's understanding of religion and sharing that with Nehru, an atheist, must have been an attempt to share a common ground with him because Nehru, for the most part, did not approve of the use of religious symbols by Gandhi.

As a consummate strategist Gandhi not only gave full publicity to the Statement issued jointly by the Shastris after the meeting but also asked them to affix their signatures to the Statement. He had been able to involve the most well-known Shastris of the time and get consensus on the issue that untouchability in its present form has no sanction of religion behind it! This was indeed a great achievement.

The statement bearing the signatures of the eminent Shastris of the time such as Swami Kevalananda, Narayan Shastri Marathe, Laxman Shastri Joshi, Bhagwandas, Anandshankar B Dhruva, Indiraraman Shastri, Keshav Laxman Daftari and PH Purandhare ran as follows:

> Three kinds of untouchables are mentioned in the Hindu Shastras: (1) Persons classed as untouchables by birth, i.e., progeny of the union of a Shudra with a Brahmin woman. (2) Persons guilty of any of the five heinous sins or of certain practices, condemned in Hinduism. (3) Persons whilst they are in polluted state.

> There is nothing to show that any of the communities now classed as untouchables come under the first category. Therefore, the rules governing untouchability and ex-communication under the first head are inapplicable to them. Assuming that any of these communities can be brought under the first head, they can be free from their untouchability with all the privileges enjoyed in common by the four varnas by clean living, initiation into the Shaiva or the Vaishnava worship, and the like.
>
> The second kind of untouchability obviously cannot attach exclusively to any class or community as a whole. It may apply to individuals in any and every community....
>
> The third kind of untouchability, due to one's being in a polluted state, obtains among all classes whether regarded as untouchables or not. There is no warrant in the Shastras for considering tanners, Bhangis and others as permanent untouchables, merely by reason of their occupations. Their untouchability is due to the external uncleanness caused by the nature of their work. All untouchability under the third head is cured by a bath and a change of clean clothes at the due time.
>
> Thus it is necessary that the rights common to all varnas, e.g., of entry into temples, educational institutions, of use of public wells, ghats, tanks, rivers, etc., should equally accrue to the untouchables so called, and that it is wrong to deprive them of such common rights. This is probable from the texts, the fundamental principles and the spirit of the Dharmashastras.[38]

The thoroughness with which Gandhi addressed the issue of untouchability should have put to rest the doubts of the sanatanists,[39] but that did not happen. So deeply ingrained was the belief in the Hindu psyche that all amount of appeal was useless. Neither logic nor emotional appeal could cut much ice with the orthodox elements who continued to heckle Gandhi on the issue. An evidence of this mindset was a joint letter written by some correspondents from Ratlam to Gandhi. This letter and Gandhi's response are found in his secretary Mahadeva Desai's notings.[40] The letter inquired whether it was right for the people to give up the practice of untouchability out of regard for Gandhi. Gandhi replied that in so far as the actions of these people did not violate dharma, they were morally sound. The questioner also wanted to know Gandhi's views on the question of the weapon of fasting being used for establishing adharma. Gandhi responded that this was very unlikely to happen because suffering is borne only by those who are convinced of the rightness of their cause.

After the above mentioned meeting with the sanatanists, Gandhi avoided any future discussions with them. Later, seeing the immense impact of his tours, attempts were made during the tour to draw Gandhi into discussions with sanatanists. He declined, saying: 'I have no desire to engage in a public debate on the origin of untouchability, I do not believe in such debates, nor do I lay any claim to Sanskrit scholarship. But I am ready, nay eager, to hold friendly conversations with any sanatanist for the sake solely of arriving at a mutual understanding, discovering points of contact, and generally, elucidating truth."[41]

Legislation for Harijans[42]

Gandhi was not averse to taking the help of law if it helped free the reformers from the shackles of law. Inspired by the intensive propaganda taking place throughout India against untouchability some enlightened legislators with reformist bent of mind introduced Bills aimed at removing the disabilities placed on Harijans from entering temples by some Provincial Governments and in some provisions of law. During this period two Bills were awaiting the Viceroy's sanction, one for the introduction in the Central Assembly by Ranga Iyer and the other for introduction in the Madras Council by Dr. Subbaroyan. On January 23, 1933, the Viceroy gave his sanction to the introduction of Untouchability Abolition Bill by Ranga Iyer in the Assembly, subject to the condition that the fullest opportunity would be given to every section of the Hindu community to express its opinion on the provision. Sanction to Dr. Subbaroyan Temple Entry Bill in the Madras Council was refused on the ground that it was too far-reaching in implication to be taken up by a Provincial legislature. Afterwards, Ranga Iyer drafted a second Bill based on Dr. Subbaroyan's which the Viceroy permitted to be introduced in the Central Assembly, subject to the same qualification as in the case of his former Bill. Gandhi gave wide publicity to these Bills in his journals imploring with legislators to give their full-hearted support.

Opposition and Doubts about Gandhi's Support to Temple Entry

Gandhi supported the Bill by Ranga Iyer for doing away with the provisions denying Harijans access to temples. He was of the opinion that the authors or signatories of the Bombay resolution would automatically support the Bills. MM Malaviya who had chaired the session refused to accept this point of view. Malaviya considered temple entry as a totally religious issue and was against any legal interference in the matter. Besides, he was of the opinion that the Bombay resolution did not cover temple entry.[43] Gandhi was disappointed but not deterred. He wrote an article in the *Harijan* stating why it was important to remove legal disabilities. Gandhi argued: 'Let me repeat for the hundredth time that there is a legal bar against temple entry which cannot be removed by any agreement on the part of the Hindus. A legal bar can only be removed by a legislative act.'[44]

Opposition to Gandhi's efforts also came from an unlikely quarter — from an industrialist of eminence. Chimanlal Giridhardas Parekh, Chairman, Ahmedabad Mill-Owners' Association, who was reported to have urged the Viceroy not to sanction the introduction of Temple Entry Bills, as it would lead to a religious civil war. Gandhi, when questioned, shrugged off any such possibility. 'War would take place if there are two parties to fight one-another. Self-styled sanatanists would be simply beating the air if they staged a war,' he said.[45]

Gandhi was also opposed by Ambedkar, who saw himself as the champion of the rights of the untouchables by virtue of being one. He was against the Bills on two counts. One, it was too optimistic to imagine that the caste Hindus would by majority allow Harijans to enter temples and, two, because as long as Harijans continued in the Hindu fold the stigma of lowliness would stick to them.[46]

Gandhi was also taken to task for abandoning the creed of non-cooperation by seeking the help of the Government on the issue of Harijan reform. ST Ramanuja Iyerngar wrote: 'he has given up his creed of non-co-operation with the Government so far as untouchability is concerned by accepting special favours, and is actively blessing legislative efforts, once taboo, to facilitate the removal of untouchability….'[47]

In the light of the above discussion it seems that Gandhi was not able to cut much ice with the sanatanists over the issue of legislative help regarding temple entry during this period, but he was able to generate enough awareness regarding the problem. This awareness bore fruit later when the Princely states took the lead in declaring the abolition of untouchability and the opening of temples within their territories to 'untouchables'.

Role of Harijan Sewak Sangh

An all India body known as the Harijan Sewak Sangh, with GD Birla as President and with branches in all provinces, was established by Gandhi for organizing Harijan work. Gandhi kept up a regular correspondence with its dedicated secretary, AV Thakkar, making detailed suggestions for the economic and efficient working of the Sangh. Gandhi also finalized the draft constitution of the Sangh prepared by Mahadev Desai. The constitution was adopted on January 3, 1935. The Sangh devoted its resources and energies to Harijan uplift. It opened schools for Harijans, dug wells for them, persuaded private owners of temples to open temples for them and also opened dispensaries and public utility services for their benefit. Gandhi contributed by conducting tours for collecting funds for the Sangh besides creating awareness among the upper castes about the wrongs done to Harijans and among Harijans to improve their condition with self-confidence.

After Gandhi's arrest in January 1932 his newspaper *Young India* had been discontinued. As the movement against untouchability grew stronger, Gandhi decided to bring out a newspaper dedicated to the cause of Harijans. Thus was born *Harijan* in English on February 11, 1933 under the editorship of RV Shastri. The Hindi edition, *Harijan Sewak,* followed in the same month with the Gujarati edition, *Harijan Bandhu,* coming out in March. For a short while even a Bengali edition made its appearance.

With the launching of these journals Gandhi was in his element. He took upon himself the work of getting all points of view expressed and debated in his newspapers. Therefore while the first issue of *Harijan* carried a portrait of a scavenger by Rabindranath Tagore, it also carried a message from Dr. Ambedkar who openly challenged Gandhi's support to the *varanshram* system, which he rightly believed, was the source of caste discrimination.[48] The *Harijan* also published a personal letter written by MM Malaviya to Gandhi charging him with 'spiritual arrogance' for fasting in the cause of

Harijan entry to Guruvayur temple. Gandhi published the letter as a reminder to those who were planning fasts emulating him, and wrote in support of Malaviya's arguments.

Apart from well-known personalities, the common public, the sanatanists – the students and the rulers of Princely states, also joined in the debate on Harijan issues through the columns of the journals. Articles and suggestions on better methods of scavenging, tanning and hygienic working conditions[49] poured in. Announcements of loans for deserving Harijan students and opening of schools where Harijans could study without discrimination, also were frequently made in these journals. Some readers showed alarm at this focus on Harijans alone and warned Gandhi that it would lead to separation of Hindus from Harijans. The author of one such letter proved to be prophetic in his warning when he wrote: 'They will not be absorbed in Hinduism, but there will be cries of 'Long live untouchables', 'Long live Harijans.'[50]

Very soon Gandhi realized that it was a difficult task for him to keep alive the interest of the people on an issue that was short on excitement. The enthusiasm of the general public waned; Harijans became impatient with the slow pace of reforms and sanatanists rallied strength. A resolution against the Poona Pact was passed in the Bengal Legislative Assembly. Gandhi tried to inject some vigour in the movement by declaring his decision to go on fast.

In spite of the drawbacks, the movement did register results. The Gaikwad of Baroda withdrew state recognition to untoucahbilty. The Chief of Bhor abolished untouchabiltiy in his territory. In Madurai where members of Sri Meeankshi Devastanam Committee were elected, out of 1887 valid votes polled, 1498 voted for candidates who supported Harijan entry.

Totally engrossed in Harijan uplift work, which he found very satisfying and rewarding, Gandhi chose to ignore criticism for his neglecting the main course of the freedom movement by leaders and public in general. Some thought that a leader like him was acting irresponsibly by ignoring the main objective of his movement by focusing only on Harijan uplift. The Swarajists misconstrued it as deliberate move on the part of Gandhi so that they get an opportunity to try their method of constitutional reform. Those who believed that he was hurting the Civil Disobedience Movement itself by providing a confused leadership also accused him of surreptitiously helping the Liberals, and threatened to go ahead with the movement without his lead.[51] A reason for Gandhi not taking active interest in politics was that he had been released before the end of his term from jail on account of his bad health. Gandhi, being a man of principles, did not like to use this gesture of the Government to his own advantage. However, it goes without saying that Gandhi's heart and soul were totally immersed in the cause of Harijans.

Soon Gandhi was to intensify his efforts further by adopting a strategy of direct communication with the people of India through his Harijan tours, first by train, and, in the most intense phase, on foot.

Harijan Tours

Gandhi had a knack of communicating more effectively with the masses by addressing them directly. His dialogues with the village folk, euphemistically called his 'speeches', were capable of bringing about a metamorphosis in their lives. Comparing his written word to his spoken word, Nehru is reported to have rightly observed that while his writings were grim, while talking Gandhi was capable of light-hearted banter and was most of the time in full control of himself.[52] This quality was very much in evidence when he was meeting people. In India where *darshan* that is, seeing a great man in person, is a long standing and established tradition, Gandhi's decision to tour far and wide to educate the people on the evil of untouchability was a great strategy. It was famously said that wherever Gandhi went became the capital of India. While one region of India had the good fortune of Gandhi's presence in flesh and blood, the rest of the country was kept in touch by an account of his tour. The Harijan Sewak Sangh organized the country-wide tour and the Sangh Secretary gave a detailed programme of the proposed tour to the press well in advance. A look at the meticulous detail with which the programme was made, shows the earnestness and effort of those involved in it.[53] This was not like the luxury tour of present day politicians but a tour in third class compartment in trains or on foot with the barest of necessities. It was more in the nature of a pilgrimage than a tour! In the course of his travels the content of the speeches delivered by Gandhi were very much same as his writings, but here Gandhi had the advantage of addressing the people in accordance with the composition of the audience and also of indulging in impromptu repartees—a spontaneity the written word was incapable of.

Gandhi's tour began on an auspicious note from Wardha, the geographical centre of India, with the opening of temple for Harijans by Gandhi's 'fifth son', Jamnalal Bajaj. The symbolic significance of the move was reiterated by Gandhi when he expressed the hope that 'the spirit with which Jamnalalji has opened his temple to the Harijans and with which Vinoba and his companions have cast in their lot with Harijans will prove infectious and spread through the whole of the country'.[54] And it did prove so.

His presence and the sincerity of his words won over people from different sections- rich as well as poor, Hindus and Muslims, Congressmen and non-Congress leaders alike[55] to his cause. Brahmin women gave their gold for the cause of Harijans with the husbands looking on with eyes moist with emotion.[56] Not only did the rich part with their money but also the poor gave away their meager savings. 'For me the money you give is a token of your identification with the cause,'[57] said Gandhi and people willingly believed him and contributed to the cause.

Initially the Muslims had reservations regarding Gandhi, a national leader identifying with a religious cause. Gandhi explained to them the implications and the spirit behind his movement and won them over to his side. 'Once the bar sinister against the Harijans is removed, the way will be opened for a wider unity among Hindus, Mussalmans and other sister communities', he told them.[58] Later, he further elaborated on the issue and said:

> 'I may, in answer, give this assurance not only to these Mussalman friends, but through them to all whom it may concern, that in the evening of my life I am not likely to take up a sectional cause to the detriment of a public issue. And if at present moment I appear to be advocating a sectional cause, you may depend upon it that behind that sectional cause lies deep down the desire that the whole of the public may benefit by it.'[59]

Gandhi saw the movement for Harijan uplift as a penance by caste Hindus for their ill-treatement of the 'untouchables' over so many centuries. He, therefore, asked them to man the Harijan Sewak Sangh. Some Harijan groups protested against this practice. One such Harijan deputation suggested that the Sangh Board should appoint advisory committee of Harijans, Gandhi pointed that the suggestion was dangerous as there may be factions and divisions among Harijans and therefore it would be better that they select members of the advisory committee themselves.[60] This discussion reveals how well acquainted Gandhi was with the situation among Harijans—a precious asset for a good communicator.

Gandhi devised a variety of arguments to convince the caste Hindus to change their mind-set in favour of the 'untouchables'. He would appeal to their sense of religion, to humanity, to realistic approach and sometimes even say things appearing to be downright superstitious. In an appeal to the religious faith of the *savarnas,* to so-called upper castes, Gandhi stated 'whatever little a *savarna* Hindu does for Harijans, he does to uplift himself or herself and Hinduism.'[61] If a mother did not discriminate against her progeny how could God do so, he lamented.[62] Gandhi sometimes thought aloud in his speeches. On seeing the sad plight of Nayadis, an 'unseeable' caste, Gandhi was so moved that he could not help saying, 'show me the authority in support of this inhuman conduct'.[63] He even went to the extent of characterizing the devastating earthquake that shook Bihar as a chastisement from God for practising untouchability! For this unscientific explanation Tagore took him to task[64] but Gandhi continued to stand by his statement saying that it sprang from faith and was not a superstition.[65]

In South India Gandhi also encountered other movements for the uplift of the Harijans. One such movement was the one started by the great social reformer Shri Narayan Guru. He had asked the 'untouchables' to come out of the Hindu fold and had also opened separate temples for them. In an address submitted to Gandhi by Narayan Guru's organization Gandhi was asked not to conduct his movement in the name of Hindu religion to which Gandhi disagreed saying that a penance only purifies and does not harm anyone and that he was not doing anything to consolidate himself.[66] Another important movement that was active in the south was the Self Respect Movement under the leadership of EV Ramaswamy. The Self Respect Party approached Gandhi presumably with the object of opening a common front with him. They wanted that Gandhi should include Christians and Muslims as well and also should give up the issue of temple-entry and concentrate only on the economic and educational uplift of Harijans. Gandhi again did not agree with this reform movement as well. He said that he preferred to take one issue at a time and would concentrate on the problems of Christians and

Muslims later. He also did not agree that temple entry was not an issue with the lower castes. He stated emphatically that one may not visit temple by choice but should at least not be debarred from going there.[67]

Gandhi was able to bring about major changes in the lives of people, especially those who had similar inclinations. One such incident recorded by Gandhi was of a 16 year old girl whom he met during his tour of the South. This girl, Kaumudi gave away all the ornaments she was wearing for the cause of Harijan uplift and continued to follow the path shown by Gandhi all her life. She was seen giving free Hindi lessons from her sick-bed by reporter of a national daily as late as in the year 2000.[68]

The impact of Gandhi's tour could be seen in some concrete results. The Travancore Government declared public tanks and wells open to all castes.[69] A library was opened for Harijans at Devacottah.[70] Industrialist, JK Birla on condition of anonymity donated a sum of Rs. 25000 to be paid in installments of Rs. 2000 per month for constructing wells for Harijans throughout the country.[71]

Though Gandhi succeeded in convincing the people to his point of view most of the time it would be wrong to conclude that his tours were triumphal marches. Gandhi was attacked violently during his tours through Bihar. Shaken but undeterred by the experience Gandhi introspected that perhaps more sacrifice was expected of him; and more intensive communication was required.

Gandhi Converts his Tours into 'Walking Tours'

After his experience in Deoghar where, in order to pacify a crowd, Gandhi decided to go on foot to the meeting, he decided to conduct the rest of his tour walking in order to emphasize 'the religious character of the mission'.[72] This decision was put in force at Jagannath Puri on May 8, 1934.Walking tours were not physically possible over long distances thus Gandhi was obliged to cut short his visit to Bengal. The Bengali leaders, not to be outwitted, planned pilgrimages on foot themselves, supplementing in their own way, Gandhi's efforts.

The walking tours had amazing impact. Gandhi was seen as a pilgrim setting forth on a spiritual journey.[73] This form of communication was qualitatively more effective than his tours by train or in motor cars.

The 'Harijan tours' were finally concluded in Benares on August 2, 1934, after covering 12000 miles, of which 156 miles were on foot. Gandhi managed to collect about ten lakhs of rupees du: ing the tours. End of the tour also coincided with the end of his self-imposed abstention from politics.

Part-II
Village Uplift Programme

The village uplift programme adopted by Gandhi after the conclusion of his 'Harijan Tours' was to a large extent the result of his experiences in the villages of Orissa during the walking tour of the province. The 156 miles of walk had brought Gandhi into close contact with the villagers. He saw the misery of their daily lives. It was a 'revelation' that pained Gandhi[74] to the core of his soul. He concluded that though the majority of the Indian population lived in villages, the villagers were treated not different from the 'untouchables' by the city-dwellers.[75] The welfare of these 'untouchables' became, from then onwards the sole concern of Gandhi. His involvement with the village reconstruction was so total that in a letter to a journalist friend who had asked Gandhi to write an article for his paper, Gandhi wrote, 'This village work is so taxing and so baffling that if I could help it I could stop all writing and simply bury myself in a village and their work away for all I am worth and that I should love to do [in] perfect silence.'[76] Gandhi chose Segaon, a village near Wardha, in present Maharashtra as the head quarter for his village work. He even persuaded the Congress Party to host its annual conference for the first time in a village, Faizpur, where Gandhi had gone to inaugurate an exhibition on village industries. He began with the sole concern of villagers' betterment, but gradually broadened the meaning and scope of his programme.

Meaning and Scope of Village Uplift

The village reconstruction programme of Gandhi's conception did not merely aim at the improvement in the living conditions of the people who lived in villages. It stood for a total change of outlook on life, emphasizing the importance of being close to, and in harmony with, nature. Thus if on the one hand Gandhi chose to discuss issues of the nutritional value of unpolished rice, jaggery, honey, green vegetables, soya beans and balanced diet, on the other, he held discussions on controlling population through self-control rather than artificial contraceptives. Village uplift included the economic development of villages but that development was to come not through the establishment of modern industries but by supporting and developing cottage industries like spinning, weaving, dairy-farming, etc.

The common thread running through most of his writings during this period was the protection of the people in the villages, cities and countries from the evil effects of modern civilization that had sounded a death-knell to morality, human values and virtues of simple living. Gandhi was of the opinion that at the local and national level untouchability and communalism hampered social harmony, as the persecution of Jews by the Nazis and the infringement of the rights of the Palestinians and Czechs at the international level disturbed international harmony and peace. Thus we see the central concerns of Gandhi did not change but the issues of economic, social and moral exploitation became the main themes during that period. Politics was put on the backburner. Untouchability was absorbed in the larger canvass of 'village development', the term being defined in the broadest sense possible. It would be important to note here that the strain found in the village development programme was the one outlined by Gandhi in his seminal work, *Hind Swaraj*. Gandhi has himself acknowledged this fact.

Issues that Gandhi had to Contend with During this Period

Before going into a detailed discussion on Gandhi's village development programme it would be worthwhile to give a brief account of the various developments that provided an environment for Gandhi's actions and reactions and from which he could not possibly keep aloof. During the period under discussion the problem of the so-called untouchables was again brought on centre-stage by the bombshell thrown by Dr. Ambedkar in his speech at Yeoli on October 4,1935 where he is reported to have said that since the untouchables could see no future for themselves while remaining in the Hindu fold they should convert to any religion that promised them equality of social status.

This development compelled Gandhi to take up the issue of the propriety or otherwise, of conversion, from one religion to another. Since the Christian missionaries were involved in a large way in converting the so-called untouchables to Christianity, Gandhi held long, scholarly discussions with Christian missionaries explaining to them where the majority of them had gone wrong. The Muslims were also drawn into discussion when Gandhi's eldest son, Harilal, converted to Islam. This was great personal embarrassment and a public shock. The reconversion of Harilal to the Hindu faith brought in another controversial issue, the issue of *shuddhi,* the practice of which had created bad blood between the Arya Samajists and Muslims. Before the controversy could be put to rest another controversy of equally volatile nature emerged: should the Hindustani language be written in the Devanagari or the Arabic script? Gandhi was at pains to explain the purpose behind his insistence on a common language and script for India. The language and the script controversy further expanded when the provincial languages clamoured for attention and a section of regional leaders expressed the fear of their being washed away in the onslaught of a relatively new language like Hindustani. Gandhi felt so helpless in the matter that he advised Nehru to write an article on the issue and publish it. The emergence of Jinnah on the national scene at this juncture further deteriorated the communal situation. Amidst all this turmoil Gandhi stayed put at Segaon, a village near Wardha, now in Maharashtra, assuming an apolitical leadership of the country yet not withdrawing like Aurobindo from worldly affairs. How he went about it and what were the main features of his programme shall be discussed below.

Gandhi decided to resign from the active membership of the Congress Party in September, 1934. At the Congress Session held in October, he submitted his resignation, along with some amendments to the Constitution of the Congress Party, one of which was the establishment of the All India Village Industries Association (AIVIA). The Congress accepted both his resignation and amendments including the one providing for the establishment of AIVIA; Gandhi was left free to follow his programme.

The AIVIA was the brainchild of Gandhi conceived during his Malabar tours[77] He shared his idea with his readers in a series of articles before formally presenting the idea at the Congress session in October 1934. He drafted the Constitution of AIVIA and published the bye-laws for its working in the *Harijan.*[78] The members of the AIVIA were to take a pledge to use the best part of their energy and talents to the furtherance of the object of AIVIA which was all round welfare of the villagers of India. Thus an impression was created in the minds of both the workers and the readers of the pledge, (the common people) that village development was a serious matter and had the backing of conscience or religion behind it. Gandhi's thoroughness was reflected in the fact that he planned to open a school for training AIVIA workers. In an article in his journal he published the prospectus and syllabi of the training course and invited applications for the school.[79] From August 1937 the AIVIA started issuing regular bulletins, thus making the Association a more organized and professional body. Gandhi's village development programme was noticed by the Government which announced an outlay of rupees one crore for the economic development of rural areas.[80]

A review of the articles written by Gandhi in his journals and other newspapers during September 1934 to August 1937, when Gandhi broke the self-imposed moratorium on political matters clearly indicates Gandhi's priorities during this period (See Chart-IV). Out of the forty-six articles written by Gandhi, in the period from September 1934 to November 1934, twenty were concerning Harijans but fifteen were on matters of nutrition and economic development of village industries. The articles that could come under the definition of politics included his statements and interviews as to why he wanted to resign from the Congress. Only one Statement to the Press referred to Government's promise regarding the repeal of Salt Tax. In December 1934 the Constitution of the All India Village Industries Association was ready and consequently most of Gandhi's writing skill was used in discussing the various aspects of its organization and work. Simultaneously Gandhi announced his intention to expand the *Harijan*.[81] Thus in the period between December 1934 to February 1935 out of the total number of 56 articles written by Gandhi 15 dealt with Harijan issues and 29 dealt with village matters. In October, 1935 came the famous appeal by Ambedkar to the members of the Depressed Classes. Henceforward, discussion with leaders of Depressed Classes and the utility or otherwise of converting to another faith also became the subject matter of Gandhi's writings. This trend continued till November 1936. In January 1937 Gandhi toured Travancore whose ruler had issued a proclamation regarding opening of temples to Harijans. Thus in the trimester from December 1936 to February 1937 one finds a sudden spurt in articles on Harijans and temple entry. In the rest of the period again we find that Gandhi reverted to village related issues. In March 1937 Gandhi started taking interest in political matters especially those that related to the Congress Party. He drafted the All India Congress Committee resolution on the issue of acceptance of office by Congress Ministries under the Government of India Act of 1935, subject to certain assurances by the Governors. Finally in August 1937 Gandhi wrote in the *Harijan*, 'I need offer no apology for crossing the self-imposed limit in the conduct of *Harijan*. The reason is obvious. The Government of India Act is universally regarded as being wholly unsatisfactory for achieving India's freedom. But it is possible to construe it as an attempt, however limited and feeble, to replace the rule of the sword by the rule of the majority.' [82]

Thus Gandhi announced his decision to enter politics.

Main Concerns of the Village Development Programme

In a statement to the Press Gandhi made it clear that the objectives of All India Village Industries Association would be the 'economic, moral and hygienic uplift of the villages of India'.[83]

Economic Welfare

Gandhi's emphasis on economic welfare of villages had sound theoretical foundations. He was very right in concluding that the poverty in the villages was largely due to their neglect by planners who focussed their attention on cities alone. He rightly pointed out that 'Whilst the Government has perhaps the largest share in pauperizing the villages, cities that have developed out of ruin to villages, cannot escape their responsibility for the growing pauperism of the dumb millions and it is not yet too late to resuscitate villages by organizing their industries as far as possible.'[84] Gandhi may be called a forerunner of Paul Sweezy, Andre Gunder Frank and a host of other theorists of underdevelopment in the national context when he laid down the theory that cities flourish at the expense of villages.[85]

Gandhi's reservations about modern machinery were quite well-known. Therefore when he suggested the increased use of village implements for village industries, he was met with strong opposition. 'Rejuvenation of villages in the face of the current fashion of highly developed mechanization and centralization is no easy job', Gandhi believed.[86] The idea of village development with emphasis on traditional tools of economic life was considered a retrograde and quixotic step even by many of the closest friends of Gandhi. When

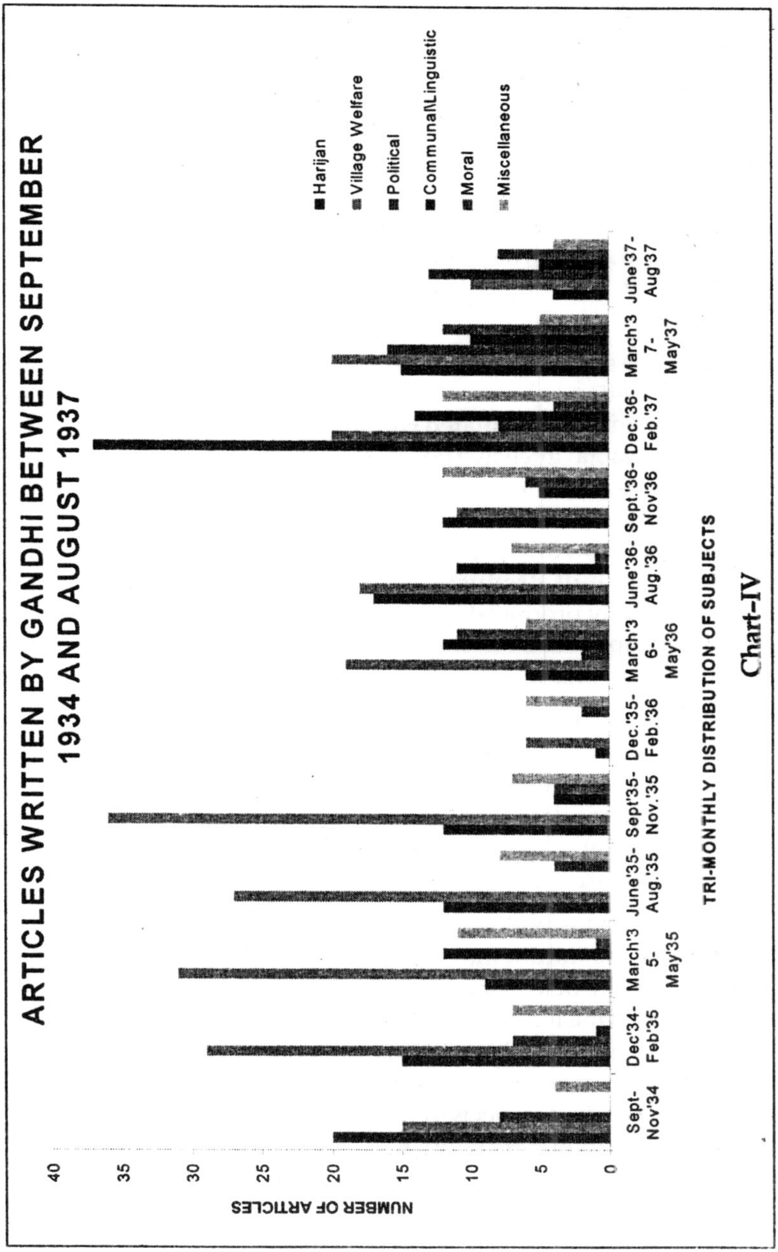
ARTICLES WRITTEN BY GANDHI BETWEEN SEPTEMBER 1934 AND AUGUST 1937
Harijan
Village Welfare
Political
Communal/Linguistic
Moral
Miscellaneous
NUMBER OF ARTICLES
0
5
10
15
20
25
30
35
40
Sept-Nov'34
Dec'34-Feb'35
March'35-May'35
June'35-Aug.'35
Sept'35-Nov.'35
Dec.'35-Feb.'36
March'36-May'36
June'36-Aug.'36
Sept.'36-Nov'36
Dec.'36-Feb.'37
March'37-May'37
June'37-Aug'37
TRI-MONTHLY DISTRIBUTION OF SUBJECTS

Chart-IV

Gandhi wrote to Srinivas Sastri[87] seeking approval for his scheme of village industries Sastri wrote back,

> I have sent copies of your letter to a few intimate associates. If their replies indicate any more hopeful ones of co-operation than are now perceptible I shall address you again. *To my unaided mind, you appear to be opening the first campaign of an endless and quixotic war against modern civilization.* Long ago you proclaimed yourself its sleepless enemy, and now you would, if you could, turn it back on the course it has pursued for several millennia. (emphasis added)[88]

Time has proved that Gandhi's insistence on village industries was an indication of his economic genius. He was right in pointing out that for an over populated country like India, labour-intensive rather than capital intensive development plans were more suitable. He went a step further and pointed out the moral relation of the individual to his economic activity. He asserted, 'Benevolence which is inherent in human nature is the very foundation of the economics of khadi....A mill product does not have that personal touch ....Mechanically produced goods can merely please the eye, but the art of khadi appeals to our human feelings.'[89] This idea is very close to the Marxian idea of the alienation of labour.[90]

Gandhi recounted some encouraging results as a result of the workers involvement with their work. An all–round development was witnessed in the lives of the artisans. They started taking interest in other related industries as well instead of whiling away their time. Better hygiene was observed at the workplace. At some places co-operative stores were also opened by workers.[91]

Apart from the philosophy behind the programme, Gandhi saw to it that the maximum interest of the people was generated in his programmes He held discussions on swadeshi with his co-workers and published the report.[92] Differentiating between the old and the new concept of swadeshi, Gandhi elaborated: 'The old emphasized the indigenous nature of the products, irrespective of the method or the produce or the prospects of the product....According to the new orientation...I would certainly have our swadeshi organization to seek out all village industries and find how they are faring.'[93]

Articles on khadi were frequently published in his journals. In one article Gandhi would appeal to emotions by arguing that if one does not wear and purchase khadi 'it is a crime against semi-starved humanity';[94] in the next he would give an account of how the money earned on khadi was split up among the workers that is, those engaged in manufacture and distribution of khadi.[95] Gandhi's speeches, delivered at the opening of various khadi stores and exhibitions, were published.[96] Detailed reports on the 'pilgrimages' (tours) made by AIVIA workers for the sale of khadi and other swadeshi articles were given wide publicity by Gandhi in his journals.[97] Gandhi also emphasized the idea of self-sustained khadi which meant 'khadi spun and woven in the first instance by villagers for themselves and whenever possible, out of cotton grown, ginned and carded in their respective villages'[98] and further published an encouraging report of such self-sustaining khadi available.[99]

Many devoted workers were working on improving the spinning wheel and Gandhi made it a point to report about them so that others who were interested would benefit from the information.[100] Gandhi also took stock of the situation from time to time and discussed the reasons for the fall, if any, in the sales.[101]

The economic soundness of khadi was questioned many a time. Gandhi gave reply to this question with reference to village employment. He said: 'Khadi is the true economic proposition in terms of the millions of villagers until such time, if ever, when a better system of supplying work and adequate wages for every able-bodied person above the age of sixteen, male or female, is found for his field, cottage or even factory in every one of the villages of India; or till sufficient cities are built up to displace the villages so as to give the villagers necessary comforts and amenities that a well-regulated life demands and is entitled to.'[102] He backed his claim by pointing out that it could be verified from the records of the All India Spinners Association that khadi industry was the largest of all the other single industries and that the AISA was the largest distributor of wages among the largest number of rural wage earners with minimum overhead charges and practically every pice circulating among people.

Gandhi, for the first time, took up and discussed threadbare the issue of spinners' wages and its repercussions on the price of khadi. Unlike the economists of today Gandhi thought it wise to increase the price of the product so that the spinners get a decent wage.[103] He wrote articles advocating humane environment for the khadi workers and a market for their products.[104]

Gandhi at times had to contend with the problem of spurious and substandard khadi flooded in the market by unscrupulous traders. He made repeated appeals to their conscience while asking the purchasers to be vigilant[105] and also sought legal opinion of no less a person than the ex-Advocate General of Madras, T.R. Venkatarama Sastriar in the matter[106]

Gandhi and Nehru did not share identical views on the importance of khadi's role in the removal of poverty. Sometimes newspapers exaggerated this difference conveying, however, the meaning that Nehru opposed Gandhi's khadi programme. Gandhi checked out with Nehru and then published a correct report in his journal.[107] This was considered necessary by Gandhi as Nehru was an important leader of the youth, and his views carried weight with them.

Gandhi was so involved in the khadi work that he wanted to develop a 'science of khadi' a science which would be capable of satisfying the 'the hunger of body mind and soul'. For this purpose he published a set of questions asking for data regarding production of cotton, the quantity of yarn produced and imported by India, the number of spinning wheels available in different provinces and similar questions having bearing on the production of khadi and the employment it generated.[108] The same issue carried another article on the proper management of khadi organizations.[109] If khadi was to be treated as 'science', the khadi workers were expected to know the rules or laws of it. Gandhi gave a list of 13 questions, the answers to which he expected every khadi worker to know.[110] This article prompted a series of articles by Gandhi wherein he replied to the queries of khadi workers.[111] This practice continued in the subsequent articles as well.[112]

In 1920 too, he had taken up the khadi cause with equal enthusiasm. The difference was that later, this industry became the heart that pumped blood into his village uplift programme. With AISA already working on the development of khadi for more than a decade now, its activities were co-ordinated with the AIVIA leading to better results. The AIVIA being central to the village uplift programme, Gandhi kept a close watch over its activities and gave it overall supervision. Meeting with the members of the Association was not logistically possible so Gandhi used his journals to pass on instructions or information to them.[113] Through his journals Gandhi could coordinate the activities of the various units of the organization.

An important offshoot of Gandhi's village industries programme was his *theory of Trusteeship*. When Gandhi talked about the economic development of villages the socialists were quick to point out that one of the hurdles in his way was the *zamindari* system prevalent in the villages of India. As long as the *zamindars* continued to exist, the exploitation of village folk would continue. Only the state could do away this iniquitous system by removing it by force. Gandhi was totally against this suggestion of the use of force by the state. He said, 'The state represents violence in a concentrated and organized form. The individual has a soul, but as the State is a soul-less machine, it can never be weaned from violence to which it owes its very existence. Hence I prefer the doctrine of trusteeship'.[114] According to the well-known historian, Bipan Chandra, Gandhi's conception of trusteeship also had a radical potential which is usually missed. Bipan Chandra quotes Kriplani to prove his point who had pointed out that Gandhi's concept of trusteeship did not make the industrialist/ zamindar the owner but only a trustee, the ownership remained with the worker whose interests the trustee was called upon to safeguard.[115]

Interestingly Gandhi sought the origin of this theory in his conception of *varna vyavastha*. According to him every person possessed a specific temperament. Those inclined to knowledge were *Brahmins*, those inclined to valour, *Kshatriyas* and those inclined to economic activities and accumulation of wealth were the *Vaishyas*, and those inclined to other pursuits were *Sudras*. These divisions were horizontal and not hierarchical. A society flourishes best if each individual is allowed to follow his or her own nature. Therefore, one could neither punish someone for being rich, nor could the state forcibly take away their wealth. The rich should voluntarily give away a portion of their wealth for the good of the society because they are not the owners but trustees of that wealth in the accumulation of which the society has also contributed.

Gandhi was of the opinion that one should devote a good part of the day to some kind of physical labour. He suggested that one should put in at least eight hours to work employing physical labour, e.g., spinning, weaving, grinding corn husking rice etc. Was the danger of one being intellectually dull in the process? Gandhi was asked. He ruled out any such possibility but emphasized on the other hand that it would give the man satisfaction of earning something by the sweat of his brow.[116] This argument was especially directed towards those for whom physical labour was not a necessity for earning money or livelihood.

Health and Hygiene in villages and elsewhere was another big concern for Gandhi. Gandhi sent questionnaires to doctors, *vaids* and *hakims* seeking their opinion on the nutritive value of various articles of food and wrote on the authority of the feedback on the nutritive value of rice,[117] tamarind and lemon,[118] and soybeans[119] in particular. Gandhi also conducted a campaign on cow's milk versus buffalo's milk. He quoted verbatim the findings of medical men in his journal pointing out that cow' s milk was more digestible and hence good for children, invalids and old people. Buffalo's milk being rich in fat content formed soap in the intestines which required extra mineral salts for digestion which were then taken from the bones by the body leading to weak bones.[120] Gandhi had a somewhat religious preference *vis-à-vis* the cow and thus overlooked the fact that in the tropical zone it is the buffalo which is the native animal, more affordable and economically viable.

Gandhi was a stickler for cleanliness. The first thing that would catch the eye of Gandhi wherever he went was whether the place was clean or not. If it was not so, Gandhi would not hesitate in taking up the work of cleaning himself. The first condition for anyone who wished to stay with Gandhi was to undertake to clean his own latrine, and, if asked by Gandhi, to do the same job for others. Articles on cleaner surroundings and disposal of nightsoil in a hygienic manner[121] formed the core of his writings on hygiene. Gandhi asked his co-workers to personally see to it that the rules regarding proper disposal of nightsoil was observed strictly.[122] How Gandhi managed to take work from his high caste co-workers in areas reserved only for the so-called untouchables was something to marvel about. Paramhansa Yogananda recounts in his book, *Autobiography of a Yogi*, the following anecdote during his visit to Wardha in 1935,

> The afternoon brought an opportunity for a chat with Gandhi's noted disciple, daughter of an English admiral,

Madeleine Slade, now called Mirabai. Her strong, calm face lit with enthusiasm as she told me, in flawless Hindi, of her daily activities.

'Rural reconstruction work is rewarding! A group of us go every morning at five o'clock to serve the near-by villagers and teach them simple hygiene. We make it a point to clean their latrines and their mud thatched huts. The villagers are illiterate; they cannot be educated except by example!' She laughed gaily.[123]

It is not difficult to imagine what effect these examples would have had on the villagers! Thus in his emphasis on cleanliness Gandhi proved himself worthy of the title he had conferred on himself i.e., of a 'scavenger'.

As a natural corollary to his concern for hygiene was his concern for health, prevention and cure of diseases and the care of the sick and invalid. He wrote with knowledge of first hand experience on the prevention and cure of epidemics.[124] He had a special concern for the plight of lepers in India and on the basis of his personal experience of caring for lepers, wrote sensitively about how they should be cared for.[125] Similar method of seeking medical expertise on common first aid in cases of snake and scorpion bites was sought by Gandhi and made available to his readers who did not have the means to get such expert information.[126] While in Segaon, Gandhi would get hold of snakes dead or alive, in order to teach the people to differentiate between poisonous and harmless snakes.

Moral development was a major concern for Gandhi. He strongly wrote against the evils of drinking, gambling, bribery, unscrupulous and obscene advertising, but *brahmacharya* – broadly meaning, control of the senses – was one of the abiding concerns of Gandhi. During this period Gandhi entered into lengthy discussions with the champions of artificial birth control, rejecting it on the ground that it led to moral degradation of the people. Gandhi made himself clear in his discussions with Margaret Sanger, the well-known advocate of artificial birth control,[127] that since his philosophy of life envisaged 'self-realization through self-control,' artificial birth control had no place in it. Gandhi did not endorse Ms. Sanger's contention that 'sex-expression without desire for children was the need of the soul'. He was firmly of the opinion that the union between man and woman should only be for the purpose of procreation and, indulgence other than that was lust and, therefore, condemnable. When Ms. Sanger drew his attention to how desperately women in Bombay *chawls* wanted to put an end to this almost endless cycle of childbirths, Gandhi was of the opinion that the only way out was for the women to resist their husbands. Ms. Sanger was quick to counter that such a move would lead to nothing but a family squabble and strife and putting the hapless women in an even more untenable plight, considering that the vast majority of women in the country were economically dependent on their husbands. Quite naturally, they would not dare displease their spouses. To all this, Gandhi's suggestion was that ways to amend divorce laws and making the state take over the care of such women would be devised.[128] The thought that sex could be the final consummation of love, perhaps, never occurred to Gandhi.[129] In a letter to a friend, Gandhi confessed, 'after good deal of experience I have come to feel that in the matter of marriage boys and girls will behave in strange ways.'[130] In his later articles on the issue he took to advocating the virtues of *brahmacharya* in married life.[131]

Gandhi was more forthright in his condemnation of the advocates of contraceptives when in an article addressed to the youth he wrote:

> I have no doubt that those learned men and women who are carrying on propaganda with missionary zeal in favour of the use of contraceptives are doing irreparable harm to the youth of the country under the false belief that they will be saving thereby the poor women who may be obliged to bear children against their will ...Sex urge is a fine and a noble thing. There is nothing to be ashamed of in it. But it is meant only for creation. Any other use of it is a sin against God and humanity[132]

The debate on brahmacharya v. contraceptives generated a lot of discussion during this period. Intellectuals, common folk, and even *sannyasis* joined in arguing with Gandhi from their respective points of view. A correspondent wrote to Gandhi that in his discussion with Margaret Sanger Gandhi forgot the point that man was after all also an artist and that he was not satisfied with bare necessity, but must have beauty, colour and charm as well. The correspondent went on to say,

> I do not mean to underrate the value of the discipline of self-control or what is technically known as *brahmacharya*. I would always admire it as the art of the control of the sex-instinct carried to perfection. But just as other arts do not interfere with the *science* of life, with the whole life...,with the proper scheme of all the values of life, so also I will not allow the value of the ideal of *brahmacharya dominate* other values, far less use it as an *instrument* of solving problems, such as over population.[133]

Gandhi agreed with the correspondent that man is undoubtedly an artist and a creator and that he must have beauty and thus colour, but held that man's artistic and creative nature at its best 'taught him to see art in self-restraint and ugliness in uncreative union'.[134]

The matter did not rest here. Gandhi was flooded with letters from young people who encountered difficulties in practising self-control according to his advice. A number of letters written to Gandhi and published by the latter in his journals, rejected his ideas on *brahmacharya* as impracticable in so far as the common man was concerned. It is not a well-known fact that Gandhi also entered into a discussion with Swami Paramhansa Yoganand in this connection. The Swami, while on a visit to Wardha, pointed out that the West found it strange that why in spite of its spiritual image India had a very high child mortality rate and a low average life span? He further inquired if Gandhi had any *working method* to teach self-control to the masses? Gandhi answered that he did not think that Indians were any more spiritually minded than the Westerners. It also did not mean that since the average life span in the West is higher than that in India it is more spiritually minded. 'Whoever is spiritually minded must show a better, not necessarily a longer, life', Gandhi concluded. As to the 'working method' that he had in mind, Gandhi said that the only way was to set personal example in self-control.[135]

Women in particular tried to argue with Gandhi on the merits of birth-control through contraceptives. Mrs. C. Kuttan Nair, a social worker from Cochin, interviewed Gandhi specifically on the matter of contraceptives and their effect on women. While her interview covered most of the ground already covered by Ms. Sanger, she posed a pertinent question to Gandhi: would he permit the use of contraceptives in cases where a woman was too weak for child-bearing and where one of the parents was diseased? Gandhi replied in the negative, because, in his opinion one exception could lead to another. He, however, allowed voluntary sterilization, which was 'a sort of contraceptive', for man 'since he is the aggressor.' [36] From all this it appears as if Gandhi thought that sex was the privilege/ compulsion of man while woman's role was only passive, providing male libido an outlet.

Women social workers did not give up their efforts at converting Gandhi, realizing that if Gandhi championed their cause it would give a big boost to popularizing contraceptives. Mrs. Edith Howe Martin, a birth-control crusader from England, pleaded with Gandhi to reconsider the case of birth–control for the sake of the 'poor woman'. Gandhi retorted, 'There is no *poor* woman. Poor woman is mightier than man, and I am quite prepared to demonstrate it to you if you come to the villages of India. Any woman there would tell you that, if she did not want it, there was no man born of woman who could compel her. I can say this from my own experience in relation to my wife, and mine is no solitary instance.'[137] Gandhi's statement to Ms. Howe about his relation to his wife however does not conform to the revelations in his *Autobiography*.[138] In the matter of woman's role in birth control his advice to women on over-desirous husbands is rather dramatic: 'It is pure lechery to stand in the way of a woman when she desires to abstain. If he forces himself on her, it is her duty to make him desist even by slapping him. She should close her door to the lustful husband. She must refuse to be the wife of a sinful husband. We must inculcate such courage in women,'[139] so said Gandhi.

If Gandhi was not prepared to give up his stand, the advocates of artificial birth-control were equally determined not to give up theirs. The sharpest taunt, however, came from a lady advocate of contraceptives who wrote thus:

> We the advocates of contraceptives, have come on the scene only recently. You self-controllers had the field all to yourselves all these long generations maybe thousands of years. What have you to show to your credit? Has the world learnt the lesson of self-control? What have you done to stop the misery of over-burdened families? Have you heard the cry of wounded motherhood? Come, the field is even now open to you. We do not mind your advocacy of self-control. We may even wish you success, if perchance you

save wives from the unwanted approaches of their husbands.[140]

Gandhi appreciated the force of the argument but insisted that though his method may be difficult, one should least have a correct ideal to pursue. In this particular case Gandhi may appear somewhat tolerant, but when it came to what he presumed to be 'moral lapses' of his friends he was very strict, at times to the point of cruelty. For instance, when one of the associates of Gandhi, Anand Hingorani asked for blessings on the birth of his son, his third issue, Gandhi reprimanded him for his 'moral lapse'. Later when the infant died Gandhi wrote: 'I am sorry for Vijay's death yet not quite so. He came to punish man and discharge his debt...My blessing was not available for the act. And if it means anything let it be a shield against the repetition of the blunder.'[141] These ideas of Gandhi created a feeling of guilt among his relatives and friends who could not be as strict in following *brahamacharya* as Gandhi did.[142] His second son hid from Gandhi the fact that his wife was expecting a child and was nonetheless reprimanded for the lapse on the two counts, one for resorting to the untruth by hiding the fact and secondly for his 'moral lapse'. An Ashram inmate, almost had a breakdown when she got married and was unable to follow strict self-control. Gandhi had to write an article in the *Harijan*[143] besides reassuring her through a letter[144] that she should not consider herself as 'fallen'. Gandhi's ideas regarding union only for procreation was also shown to be impractical on the ground that a union may not always lead to off-spring. This dilemma was presented by an ardent follower of Gandhi's idea of *brahmacharya*. Gandhi did not have any satisfactory answer to this. Gandhi could only say that a real *brahmachari* does not fail.

In the course of these discussions emerged the most controversial views of Gandhi on sex, marriage and self-control. Gandhi himself had doubts about the validity of his views. He candidly confessed: 'I am myself eager to know why a thing which is claimed to be scientific and beneficial and which has very distinguished supporters[145] repels me the most not withstanding my effort to see the bright side of it.'[146] In the period under discussion one finds articles on these topics in unusually large number along with a personal piece on what Gandhi considered his greatest failure.[147] The crux of the matter is that Gandhi failed to see population growth as an economic issue which threatened to set to naught all the village development programmes in the long run. He treated it as a moral issue. His interpretation was shared by very few of his associates. Perhaps his unconventional views damaged his image as one among the 'commonest of common man' and put him on the pedestal of saints, thus alienating him from lesser mortals. In later years when Gandhi stretched the concept of *brahmacharya* even further to conduct his 'body-experiments'(which shall be dealt with in the following chapter) his associates refused to publish his account in his own journal, *Harijan*, apprehensive of the effect it may have on the public mind. The major part of the charge that Gandhi was impracticable stems from his views expressed above, which put a question mark even on the most useful of his ideas on village development, education and the moral responsibility of public men. The common man is used to seeing a person in the totality of his views and not in parts.

Social Harmony and Justice

Gandhi recognized the issues of untouchability, communalism, conversions and language disputes as major hurdles in the way of social harmony and justice. This was the period of mixed results for Gandhi on the Harijan reform front. On the one hand was his triumph that the Travancore Government had thrown open the temples to Harijans, on the other, it was a bolt from the blue when Dr. Ambedkar exhorted his fellow Harijans to convert to other faiths if necessary. He clearly pointed out that 'Secession of stalwarts like Dr. Ambedker can but weaken the defences of Harijans. We know that non-Hindu Harijans, no matter how eminent they may be, are not able to help Hindu Harijans. Indeed they are a class apart even in their adopted faiths. Such is the hold untouchability of the Indian type has on the people of India.'[148]

Gandhi had throughout held the view that converting from one faith to another was not morally justified unless a real change of heart had taken place.[149] He rubbished the claims of Christian missionaries that people were converting to Christianity out of their regard for the religion.[150] He took them to task for presenting the Hindu religion as a religion of heathens. He criticized them for bribing the people with promises of better health care, education and employment for converting them to their faith.[151] He pointed out that if the Christian missionaries were motivated purely by human concerns, their purpose should not be conversion but helping people understand their own religion better. He plainly said that he did not consider Christianity in any way superior to his own faith. He respected Christ and valued his teachings, but never thought that if he did not believe in Him he would be damned.

Gandhi had stopped commenting on Hindu-Muslim issues for some time. When his son Harilal converted to Islam, he was compelled to give his opinion in the matter. He reiterated that if the conversion of his 'wayward' son to Islam was after a genuine change of heart he would have welcomed the conversion as he considered Islam to be as good as Hinduism. He, however, doubted that such a change of heart had actually taken place. In that case he called upon his Muslim friends to condemn such conversions.[152]

Gandhi was proved right in the reading of his son's character, for Harilal soon reconverted to Hinduism (November 1, 1936). Though the Arya Samajists generally hold out that Gandhi requested them to perform *shuddhi* ceremony on their son, the fact is quite the contrary. Gandhi clearly wrote that there was no question of *shuddhi* as no 'pollution' had taken place as the result of Harilal's conversion to Islam.[153] Thus he prevented a situation that could have blown up into Hindu-Muslim hostility. Harilal did go for the *shuddhi* ceremony but without his father's consent or concurrence. In fact, so concerned was Gandhi on the issue of Hindu-Muslim unity that when Dr. Ansari died on May 10, 1936, he wrote a touching letter to Dr. Zakir Hussain to take up the mantle of Hindu–Muslim unity so that communal relations do not suffer.[154]

Gandhi had always visualized a special role for Hindustani as the lingua franca of India. The question of the script of the language took communal tones during this period when Gandhi opined that the *Devanagari* script was more scientific. He, however, made it clear that if the Muslims objected to the adoption of *Devanagari* script, he would prefer Hindustani to be written in both the scripts, *Devanagari* as well as the Arabic.[155] The controversy however, refused to die with both sides adopting rigid positions. The situation became all the more critical when the champions of Gujarati, Marathi, Tamil, Telegu and Bengali languages expressed their fear that adopting of Hindustani would lead to their respective languages withering away and consequently their culture. Gandhi sought to ease the situation by suggesting a common script for most of the languages[156] which, however, was not accepted.

Summation

The apolitical phase of Gandhi's leadership is generally dismissed as unimportant by the scholars on Gandhi. The focus is more on his political activities and views. The purpose behind dealing with this part of Gandhi's leadership separately is to emphasize the fact that his intensive work among villagers and Harijans was largely responsible for his hold over the masses which was put to good use in political movements though Gandhi never consciously planned it as such. Yet he knew that constructive programme was the basis of swaraj, its very foundation. Gandhi's efforts at mobilizing the villagers and the common people, is largely responsible for the existence of participatory democracy that we have in India today. One can understand this achievement better with reference to Pakistan, where neither Jinnah nor any other leader immediately succeeding him, had any mass base. Pakistan paid for it in terms of unstable governments and military dictatorships.

REFERENCES

1. Jawaharlal Nehru, *The Discovery of India*, New Delhi, 1960, p. 110.
2. The term 'Depressed Classes' was used in the early thirties to denote the untouchables and was in use during the period of petitions The term ' Dalit' is a self given term of recent origin. Baburao Bagul include among Dalits, adivasis, toiling classes and women. Ghanshyam Shah expanded the term to include converted untouchable Muslims. Ambedkar used it infrequently (Marathi word).
   The 1935 Act used the term Scheduled Castes to denote the Dalits. Being a purely legal term it did not have any emotional content. According to some dalit writers the term 'Harijan' denoted a passive identity and they are of the opinion that Harijan uplift was used by Congress both for patronage and vote bank.
3. *Letter to Ramsay MacDonald*, September 9, 1932, *CWMG*, LI, pp. 31-32.
4. *Letter to Sir Samuel Hoare*, *CWMG*, XLIX, p. 190.
5. *Letter to Ramsay MacDonald*, September 9, 1932, ***CWMG***, LI, p. 32.
6. Footnote 1, *CWMG*, LI, p. 128.
7. B.R. Ambedkar, *Dr. Babasaheb Ambedkar, Writings and Speeches*, Volumes 1-14, Education Department, Government of Maharashtra, Bombay, 1979-95.
8. Pyarelal, *The Epic Fast*, Navajivan, Ahmedabad, 1932, p. 248.
9. *The Times of India*, 21-9-1932, *CWMG*, LI, p. 116.
10. Quoted in Pamela Mountbatten, *India Remembered: A Personal Account of the Mountbatten During the Transfer of Power*, Roli Books, London, 2007, p. 187.

11. Footnote 1, *CWMG*, LI, p. 128.
12. *CWMG*, LI, p. 133.
13. Footnote 2, *CWMG*, LI, 109.
14. Footnote 2, *CWMG*, LII, p. 137.
15. Letter to Vinoba Bhave, *CWMG*, LI, pp. 88-9.
16. Arun Shourie, *Worshipping False Gods*, ASA Publications, New Delhi, 1997, p. 307.
17. Resolution at the Hindu Leaders Conference, Bombay, September 25,1932, drafted by Gandhi. ***CWMG***, LI, p. 139.
18. Statement on Untouchability-I, 4-11-1932, *CWMG*, LI, pp. 341-45.
19. Statement on Untouchability-VIII, 17-11-1932, *CWMG*, LII, p. 9.
20. Statement on Untouchability-V, 14-11-1932, *CWMG*, LI, pp. 427-30.
21. Statement on Untouchability-VI,15-11-1932, *CWMG*, LI, pp. 434-36.
22. Statement on Untouchability-II, 5-11-1932, *CWMG*, LI, pp. 346-49.
23. Statement on Untouchability-III, 7-11-1932, *CWMG*, LI, pp. 366-68.
24. Statement on Untouchability-VII, 16-11-1932, *CWMG*, LII, p. 1.
25. Statement on Untouchability-IX, 29-11-1932, *CWMG*, LII, pp. 71-2.
26. Statement on Untouchability-IX, 29-11-1932, *CWMG*, LII, pp. 71-2.
27. Statement on Untouchability-X, 10-12-1932, *CWMG*, LII, pp. 151-55.
28. Statement on Untouchability-X, 10-12-1932, *CWMG*, LII, pp. 151-55.
29. Statement on Untouchability-X, 10-12-1932, *CWMG*, LII, pp. 151-55.
30. Statement on Untouchability-XI, 15-12-1932, *CWMG*, LII, pp. 185-86.
31. Statement on Untouchability-XIII, 31-12-1932, *CWMG*, LII, pp. 304-8. This statement was simultaneously published in *The Bombay Chronicle* and *The Hindu*.
32. *The Bombay Chronicle*, 17-11-1932, *CWMG*, LII, pp. 1-2.
33. Gandhi said in response to the letter of Manmatha Roy published in *Amrita Bazar Patrika*, 30-11-1932, *CWMG*, LII, p. 87.
34. *Letter to SD Satavlekar*, 17-11-1932, *CWMG*, LII, p. 16.
35. *Letter to Anandshankar B Dhruva*, 19-11-1932, *CWMG*, LII, p. 22.
36. QUESTIONS FOR SHASTRI PARISHAD, *The Hindustan Times*, 27-12-1932, *CWMG*, LII, p. 265.
37. *Letter to Jawaharlal Nehru*, *CWMG*, LII, p. 312.
38. *Statement on Untouchability in Hindu Shastras to the Press*, *The Hindu*, 4-1-1933, *CWMG*, LII, pp. 347-50.
39. A sect of Hinduism, particularly believing in the principle of 'avatars' i.e., God taking birth in various forms such as Rama, Krishna etc. to save humanity and also believing in the theory that man's actions determines his life and sufferings or joys therein.
40. *Mahadevabhaini Diary*, Vol. II, *CWMG*, LII, pp. 62-64.
41. 'For Sanatanists', 2-2-1934, *CWMG*, LVII, pp. 91-2.
42. Gandhi is criticized by some for adopting a patronizing attitude towards the so-called untouchables by giving them the name 'harijan'. The word

was not coined by Gandhi. It was proposed in 1931 by an 'untouchable' reader of *Navajivan,* who referred to its use by Gujarati poet Narsi Mehta, the author of Gandhi's favourite bhajan 'Vaishnava jana'.

43. For the text of the telegram to this effect see, with instructions to Gandhi to publish it in the *Harijan,* see Appendix XII, *CWMG,* LIII, pp. 501-2.
44. 'Agreeing to Differ,' *Harijan,* 18-2-1933, *CWMG,* LIII, p. 334.
45. Interview to Associated Press, *The Bombay Chronicle,* 17-1-1933, *CWMG,* LIII, pp. 68-9.
46. *Mahadevabhaini Diary,* Vol. III, 117-22, Appendix X, *CWMG,* LIII, p. 500.
47. Quoted by Gandhi in his article 'The Ideal Harijan Teacher', 25-3-1933, *CWMG,* LIV, pp. 187-90.
48. 'Dr. Ambedkar and Caste', *Harijan, CWMG,* LIII, p. 260.
49. 'An Overdue Civic Reform', *Harijan,* 11-2-1933, *CWMG,* LIII, p. 268. 'Disposal of Carcasses', *Harijan,* 18-3-1933, *CWMG,* LIV, pp. 65-66. "A Worthwhile Scheme", *Harijanbandhu,* 19-3-1933, *CWMG,* LIV, p. 124.
50. 'A Friend's Warning', *Harijan,* 22-4-1933, *CWMG,* LIV, pp. 490-92.
51. Sampurnanda, a prominent Congress leader from Bihar was reported by the newspaper *The Statesman* to say that. See Footnote 2, *CWMG,* LVII, p. 408.
52. JL Nehru, 'The Spirit of India' in BK Ahluwalia, *Facets of Gandhi,* Lakshmi Book Store, New Delhi, 1968, pp. 19-20.
53. Tour Programme Province-wise:

Province	*Days*	*Dates*	*Working Days*
CP	31	8th Nov—8th Dec	23
Delhi	5	10th—14thDec	3
Andhra	14	16th—29thDec	10
Madras	5	30thDec—3rd Jan	3
Mysore	10	4th—13th Jan	8
Cochin	7	14th—20th Jan	8
Tamil Nadu	20	21st Jan—9th Feb	10 (including 6 days full rest)
Orissa	7	11th—17th Feb	5
Bengal	28	18thFeb-17th Mar	20
Assam	7	18th—24th Mar	5
Bihar	14	25th Mar—7th Apr	10
UP	35	8th Apr—12th May	20 (including 7 dayscomplete rest)
Punjab	14	13th—26th May	10
Sind	7	27th May—2nd June	5
Rajputana	7	3rd—9th June	5
Ahmedabad	7	10th—16th June	0 (Rest)
Guj-Kathiawad	14	17th—30th June	10

Bombay City Maharashtra	7	1st–7th July	5
Hyderabad	17	8th–24th July	11
Karnataka	7	25th–31st July	5

Issued by A.V. Thakkar, General Secretary, Servants of the untouchable society, November 7, 1933, Appendix I, *CWMG*, LVI, pp. 501-504.

54. *Harijan*, 17-11-1933, *CWMG*, LVI, p. 194.
55. Speech at a Public Meeting Amraoti, *Harijan*, 1-12-1933, *CWMG*, LVI, p. 240.
56. Speech at Sweepers' Meeting, *Harijan*, 17-11-1933, *CWMG*, LVI, p. 194.
57. Extract from Speeches, *Harijan*, 17-11-1933, *CWMG*, LVI, pp. 206-7.
58. Speech at Bilaspur, *Harijan*, 8-12-1933, *CWMG*, LVI, p. 282.
59. Speech at Public Meeting, Trichnapoly, *Harijan*, 16-2-1934, *CWMG*, LVII, pp. 146-7.
60. *Harijan*, 5-1-1934, *CWMG*, LVI, pp. 393-5.
61. Speech at Gollapalem, *The Bombay Chronicle*, 27-12-1933, *CWMG*, LVI, p. 391.
62. Speech at a Women's Meeting, Mangalore, *Harijan*, 9-3-1934, *CWMG*, LVII, p. 210.
63. *Harijan*, 2-3-1934, *CWMG*, LVII, p. 198.
64. The poet expressed his hurt in a letter written to Gandhi showing how dangerous it would be for India if leaders who had large following like him propagated such unscientific ideas. 'What is truly tragic about it is the fact that the kind of argument that Mahatmaji used by exploiting an event of cosmic disturbance far better suits the psychology of his opponents than his own, and it would not have surprised me at all if they had taken this opportunity of holding him and his followers responsible for the visitation of the Divine anger', wrote the poet. Appendix-I, *CWMG*, LVII, p. 503.
65. 'Superstition vs. Faith, *Harijan*, 16-2-1934, *CWMG*, LVII, p. 155.
66. *Harijan*, 2-2-1934, *CWMG*, LVII, pp. 10-13.
67. Interview with the members of the Self Respect Party, *Harijan*, 9-2-1934, *CWMG*, LVII, pp. 42-44
68. 'Bapu's Kaumudi Shuns Publicity',*The Hindustan Times*, 20-11-2000.
69. *The Hindu*, 22-1-1934, *CWMG*, LVII, pp. 21-22.
70. *The Hindu*, 30-1-1934, *CWMG*, LVII, p. 63.
71. 'The JK Well Fund', *Harijan*, 15-6-1934, *CWMG*, LVIII, p. 79.
72. 'Message to the People of Ganjam', *The Hindu*, 14-5-1934, *CWMG*, LVII, pp. 485-86.
73. 'In Praise of Walking', *Harijan*, 20-7-1934, *CWMG*, LVIII, pp. 212-13.
74. In an interview to *The Manchester Guardian*, as reported in *The Hindu*, 25-11-34 Gandhi is said to have remarked that his recent walking tours through the villages in connection with the anti-untouchability campaign was a revelation to him. The village people seemed to him 'inert and

despondent'. Their poverty-stricken conditions have been making 'a more and more forcible appeal', *CWMG*, LIX, p. 353.

75. Writing in *Harijan*, 30-11-34, under the heading 'What is It?', Gandhi wrote: 'To me, the campaign against untouchability has begun to imply ever so much more than the eradication of the ceremonial untouchability of those who are labeled as untouchables. For city-dwellers, the villages have become untouchable. He does not know them, he will not live in them, and if he finds himself in a village, he will want to reproduce city-life there.' *CWMG*, LIX, p. 414.
76. Letter to C.R. Srinivasan, editor of *Swadeshmitran*, Madras, *CWMG*, LXI, p. 369.
77. In one of his articles written for *Harijan* Gandhi wrote: 'The idea of forming the Association took definite shape during the Harijan tour as early as when I entered Malabar. A casual talk with a khadi worker showed to me how necessary it was to have a body that would make an honest attempt to return to the villagers what has been cruelly and thoughtlessly snatched away from them by the city-dwellers.' 'Village Industries', *Harijan*, 16-11-34.
78. *Bye-Laws of the All–India Village Industries Association*, 28-11-34, *CWMG*, LIX, pp. 10-13.
79. 'AIVIA Training School', *Harijan*, 17-4-37, *CWMG*, LX, pp. 92-3.
80. The Government had proposed allotment of one crore of rupees to the provinces for the economic development and improvement of rural areas in order to forestall Congress activities in the villages and had issued a confidential circular in this connection. F.n.1. *CWMG*, LX, p. 72.
81. 'Expansion of 'Harijan', *Harijan*, 21-12-34, *CWMG*, LX, p. 16.
82. 'Congress Ministries', *Harijan*, 17-7-37, *CWMG*, LXV, p. 406.
83. *The Bombay Chronicle*, 10-11-34, *CWMG*, LIX, p. 304.
84. Statement to the Press, *The Hindu*, 16-10-34, *CWMG*, LIX, p. 179.
85. These Latin American writers had sought to explain the underdevelopment of third world countries with reference to the fact that the colonial masters of these countries had for ages used them as sources of raw material and as markets for their surplus finished products thereby contributing nothing to their economic development and being thus responsible for their impoverishment.
86. 'In the Throes of Birth', *Harijan*, 23-11-34, *CWMG*, LIX, p. 386.
87. Letter to V.N. Srinivas Sastri, *CWMG*, LIX, pp. 362-63.
88. F.n.1, *CWMG*, LIX, p. 363.
89. 'New Life to Khadi', *Harijanbandhu*, 21-10-34, *CWMG*, LIX, pp. 205-208.
90. See the following statement by Marx: 'Let us suppose that we had carried out production as human beings. Each of us would have in two ways affirmed himself and the other person. (1) In my production I would have objectified my individuality, its specific character, and therefore enjoyed not only an individual manifestation of my life during

the activity, but also when looking at the object I would have the individual pleasure of knowing my personality to be objective, visible to the senses and hence a power beyond all doubt. (2) In your enjoyment or use of my product I would have the direct enjoyment both of being conscious of having satisfied a human need by my work, that is, of having objectified man's essential nature, and of having thus created an object corresponding to the need of another man's essential nature. ... Our products would be so many mirrors in which we saw reflected our essential nature.'" (*Comment on James Mill*)

91. 'Its Deeper Meaning', *Harijan*, 7-8-37, *CWMG*, LXVI, p. 14.
92. 'Discussion on Swadeshi', *Harijan*, 28-9-34, *CWMG*, LIX, p. 87.
93. *Ibid.*
94. 'Need for Exactness', *Harijan*, 5-10-34, *CWMG*, LIX, p. 128.
95. 'Instructive Figures', *Harijan*, 12-10-34, *CWMG*, LIX, p. 167.
96. *Speech at Itwari Khadi Bhandar, Nagpur, Hitvada*, 24-2-35, *CWMG*, LX, p. 253. 'The Bombay Khadi Bhandar', *Harijan*, 10-8-35, *CWMG*, LXI, pp. 322-324; *Speech at Khadi and Village Industries Exhibition, Lucknow, Harijan*, 4-4-36, *CWMG*, LXII, pp. 297-300.
97. *Notes, Harijan*, 22-3-35, *CWMG*, LX, p. 328.
98. 'Self-sustained Khadi,' *Harijan*, 29-3-35, *CWMG*, LX, p. 353; 'Mission of Khadi', *Harijan*, 6-7-35, *CWMG*, LXI, p. 232; 'Self-Sufficient Khadi', *Harijan*, 3-8-35, *CWMG*, LXI, pp. 305-6.
99. "Self-sustained Khadi," *Harijan*, 20-4-35, *CWMG*, LX, p. 443. Example of a village in Bihar, 'Self-sufficing Khadi', *Harijan*, 24-8-35, *CWMG*, LXI, pp. 359-60.
100. 'Improvement in Spinning', *Harijan*, 29-6-35, *CWMG*, LXI, p. 213.
101. 'Discussion on Reorganizing Khadi Production', *Harijan*, 10-8-35, *CWMG*, LXI, pp. 320-322.
102. 'Is Khadi Economically Sound?', *Harijan*, 20-6-36, *CWMG*, LXIII, pp. 77-79.
103. 'A Knotty Question', *Harijan*, 5-10-35, *CWMG*, LXII, pp. 11-12; 'New Khadi Scheme', *Harijan*, 26-10-35, *CWMG*, LXII, pp. 66-67.
104. 'Need for Humane Custom', *Harijan*, 2-11-35, *CWMG*, LXII, pp. 85-86
105. 'Uncertified Khadi', *Harijan*, 11-4-36, *CWMG*, LXII, pp. 320-1.
106. 'For Uncertified Khadi Dealers', *Harijan*, 6-6-36, *CWMG*, LXIII, p. 19
107. 'A False Alarm', *Harijan*, 6-6-36, *CWMG*, LXIII, pp. 15-17
108. 'What is Khadi Science?', *Harijan*, 16-1-37, *CWMG*, LXIV, pp. 248-251.
109. *Notes, Harijan*, 16-1-37, *CWMG*, LXIV, pp. 251-52.
110. 'What Khadi Workers Should Know?', *Harijan*, 13-2-37, *CWMG*, LXIV, pp. 365-367.
111. 'How to Begin?', 10-4-37, *CWMG*, LXI, pp. 429-431.
112. 'Long Live Khadi', *Harijan*, 28-3-37, *CWMG*, LXV, p. 29; 'Khadi in Swadeshi Exhibitions', *Harijan*, 10-4-37, *CWMG*, LXV, p. 68; "Spinners Wages", *Harijan*, 17-4-37, *CWMG*, LXV, pp. 90-91.

113. See 'How to Begin' series published in the *Harijan* on 25-1-35, *CWMG*, LX1, p. 10; 1-2-35, LX1, pp. 50-51; 8-2-35, LX1, pp. 90-2; and speech and discussion with members of AIVIA, *Harijan*, 22-3-35, *CWMG*, LX, pp. 310-312; *Speech at AIVIA Meeting*, reported in *Harijan*, 16-5-36, and *The Bombay Chronicle*, 11-5-36, *CWMG*, LXII, pp. 378-80.
114. Interview to Nirmal Kumar Bose, *The Hindustan Times*, 17-10-35, *CWMG*, LIX, p. 318.
115. Bipan Chandra, *India's Struggle for Independence*, p. 218.
116. 'Questions and Answers', *Harijan*, 8-3-35, *CWMG*, LX, p. 267.
117. 'Polished vs Unpolished', *Harijan*, 26-10-34, *CWMG*, LIX, p. 226; 'Villagers' Hands'," *Harijan*, 28-12-34, *CWMG*, LX, p. 33. In this article Gandhi gave Dr. Ansari's opinion on the nutritive value of unpolished rice, *chakki* ground whole wheatmeal and molasses. 'All About Rice', *Harijan*, 15-2-35, LX, pp. 229-30. In this article Gandhi referred to the experiment conducted by Shankarlal Banker, a well-known AIVIA worker who had proved that unpolished rice was not difficult to digest if cooked properly.
118. 'Neem Leaves and Tamarind', *Harijan*, 16-11-35, *CWMG*, LXII, pp. 119-20. On the authority of Dr. Akroyd, Director of Nutrition Research, Gandhi advised the village folk to use tamarind in their food because it was good for digestion and rich in vitamin C though less in comparison to lemon. He also pointed out that there was no evidence to prove the popular belief that it induced fever and rheumatism.
119. Gandhi reproduced a pamphlet published by the Bombay Presidency Baby and Health Week Association in favour of the nutritive value of soyabeans, *Harijan*, 28-9-35, *CWMG*, LXI, p. 458, to begin with and followed it up with two more articles on the nutritive potential of soya beans. He pointed out how the beans have benefited diebetic patients like Vinoba Bhave's father *Harijan*, 19-10-35, *CWMG*, LXII, p. 42, and in the following article on soya beans gave a detailed account of the varieties and farming of beans quoting the authority of Bombay Health Association. *Harijan*, 9-11-35, *CWMG*, LXII, pp. 104-5.
120. 'Cow's Milk v.Buffalo's', *Harijan*, 22-2-35, *CWMG*, LX, pp. 248-50.
121. 'Manure Pits', *Harijan*, 1-3-35, *CWMG*, LX, pp. 269-70; 'Advice to Villagers', *Harijan*, 15-3-35, *CWMG*, LX, pp. 299-300; "Scavengers All", *Harijan*, 15-3-35, *CWMG*, LX, pp. 302-3.
122. Mirabehn the daughter of an Admiral was entrusted the work of teaching hygiene to the inhabitants of a village name Sindi where the people were in the habit of using the sides of roads for easing themselves. When the people refused to listen Gandhi told her to take bucket and shovel, and any other volunteers and daily go to clean. F.n.2. *CWMG*, LX, p. 104.
123. 'With Mahatma Gandhi at Wardha', Paramhansa Yogananda, *Autobiography of a Yogi* (The Philosophical Library, New York, 1946) pp. 436-7.

124. *Speeches at Borsad, Harijan,* 8-6-35, *CWMG,* LXI, p. 95. Gandhi addressed at least ten meetings in these villages asking the people to rat proof their houses and distributed leaflets on disease proofing their bodies as their was the danger of the spread of plague in their villages.
125. 'Leprosy and Prevention,' *Harijan,* 7-9-35, *CWMG,* LXI, p. 397. It is common knowledge that Gandhi kept in his Ashram Parachure Shastri, a leper, and personally massaged and nursed him till the latter's death in 1945. Gandhi also conducted a discussion through his journals whether lepers should marry and produce children quoting views of experts in the matter.
126. 'About Snake-bites', *Harijanbandhu,* 20-10-35.
127. Margaret Sanger a public health nurse of the United States of America was a revolutionary figure in the area of birth control by artificial means. After initial resistance in her own country over her organizing birth control clinics which were regarded as obscene, Mrs. Sanger's viewpoint came to be accepted throughout the world. She came to India in 1935 to discuss with India's leaders the problem of overpopulation. She spent ten weeks in India speaking on birth control to large audiences throughout the country. During her stay in India she held more than forty public meetings, established about fifty centers of birth-control information, secured the endorsements of the All India Women's Conference, the All India Medical Conference and Bombay Municipality and spent two days with Gandhi. She wrote to her husband in late November, 'Gandhi has invited me to stay with him in his simple place and I think that this is the *greatest honour* that India can pay me or anyone.
128. 'Interview to Margaret Sanger,' *Harijan,* 25-1-36, *CWMG,* LXII, pp. 156-160.
129. Margaret Sanger was to write later, '.... I am convinced his personal experience at the time of his father's death was so shocking and self-blamed that he can never accept sex as anything good, clean or wholesome' 'A Summit Meeting on Birth Control', in Norman Cousins (ed) *Profiles of Gandhi* (Indian Book Company, 1969) p. 36.
130. *Letter to Bhagwandas, CWMG,* LXVI, p. 180.
131. 'Birth-Control-I', *Harijan,* 14-3-36, *CWMG,* LXII, pp. 261-3. Gandhi had been slightly liberal in his views regarding the role of sex in married life and had suggested that married couple could indulge in the same during 'safe period' that is when there was no risk of child birth. Vinoba Bhave took objection to this view and wrote a strong letter to Gandhi. Gandhi therefore, 'corrected' his 'error' in the light of Vinoba's views and wrote the above mentioned article wherein he has given the background for the change of his views.
132. 'For the Young', 28-3-36, *CWMG,* LXII, p. 295-7.
133. 'For Contraceptives', *Harijan,* 4-4-36, *CWMG,* LXII, pp. 309-12.

134. *Ibid.*
135. Discussion with Swami Yogananda, *Harijan*, 7-9-35, *CWMG*, LXI, pp. 392-4. It is relevant here to note that during this period Gandhi had on the insistence of his fellow workers given up his practice of using young girls as walking sticks as some unscrupulous men also started following the practice. He agreed, 'Every act of mine is scrutinized by thousands of men and women, as I am conducting an experiment requiring ceaseless vigilance. I must avoid doing things which may require reasoned defence.' vide 'A Renunciation', *Harijan*, 21-9-35, *CWMG*, LXI, p. 437 Later, however he resumed the practice when he found that his 'renunciation' hurt the feelings of the women in question.
136. Interview to Mrs. C. Kuttan Nair, *The Hindustan Times*, 11-1-35, *CWMG*, LX, p. 69.
137. Discussion with Edith Howe Martin, *Harijan*, 1-2-35, *CWMG*, LX, pp. 95-97.
138. Mahadev Desai who was himself a confirmed opponent of artificial contraceptives wrote the details of the interview between Mrs. Howe and Mrs. Sanger for the *Harijan* and his bias clearly showed when he concluded with the remarks that Mrs. Howe look 'puzzled' and that Mrs. Sanger was 'so impatient to prove that Gandhiji is a visionary that she forgets the practical ways and means that Gandhiji suggested to her'. It seemed to delight Mahadev Desai that his idol always scored a point over these ladies!
139. *Speech At Gandhi Seva Sangh Meeting*-IV, *CWMG*, LXII, p. 233.
140. 'Self-Control Again', *Harijan*, 30-5-36, *CWMG*, LXII, p. 458.
141. *Letter to Anand T. Hingorani*, *CWMG*, LXIV, p. 126. Gandhi was later proved right in his reprimand when Hingorani's wife died in 1944 because of frail health.
142. Margaret Sanger had raised this point with Gandhi in the course of her discussions with him on birth control. Gandhi had then dismissed it as a problem of 'imbeciles.' *op cit*; f.n. 51.
143. 'The Married Estate,' *Harijan*, 22-3-42, *CWMG*, LXXV, pp. 380-81.
144. *Letter to Annapurna, March 2, 1942*, *CWMG*, LXXV, p. 379, Gandhi wrote, 'You have not at all fallen by marrying....But you could surely be said to have fallen if you led a life of luxury and forgot your duty'.
145. Rabindranath Tagore and Sarojini Naidu had publicly expressed their support for Mrs. Sanger's mission.
146. 'For Contraceptives', *Harijan*, 4-4-36, *CWMG*, LXII, p. 310.
147. 'Nothing Without Grace', *Harijan*, 29-2-36, *CWMG*, LXII, pp. 210-12. In this article Gandhi shared with his readers his experience of the failure of his experiments in self-control and confessed of what he called his 'fall'.
148. 'On its Last Legs', *Harijan*, 26-10-35, *CWMG*, LXII, p. 65.
149. Notes: 'Deploring Conversions', *Harijan*, 22-3-35, *CWMG*, LX, p. 327.

Commenting on the conversion of Harijans to Christianity, Gandhi wrote: 'Conversion under the stress of physical discomfort is no conversion.'

150. Gandhi referred to the claims made at a meeting of Christians reported in the *Church Times*, where it was claimed that in the Telegu area 900,000 had converted to Christian faith and 'speak of a sense of mystical union with God'. Gandhi first of all challenged the figures quoted on the basis of his experience in these villages and secondly, stated that in his talks with Christians he found that they the evil of untouchability exists among them as well. 'What is a Miracle', *Harijan*, 19-12-36, *CWMG*, LXIV, p. 151.
151. 'Discussion with Pierre Ceresole and Christian Missionaries', *Harijan*, 18-7-36, *CWMG*, LXIII, pp. 90-1.
152. *Statement to the Press, Harijan*, 6-6-36, *CWMG*, LXIII, p. 5.
153. *Speech at Harijan Workers Conference, Kengeri, Harijan*, 4-7-36, *CWMG*, LXIII, p. 50.
154. *Letter to Zakir Hussain, CWMG*, LXII, p. 441-2.
155. 'Hindi v. Urdu,' *Harijan*, 3-7-37, LXV, 362-65.
156. 'The Question of Languages', *Harijan*, 21-8-37, *CWMG*, LXVI, pp. 460-62.

7

Countdown to Freedom: Gandhi's Successive Roles as Advisor, Mobilizer, Negotiator and Pacifier

'If all the Hindus and Muslims who come to see me or write to me do not deceive me, then it is clear that no one is happy with the division of India. They all accept it against their will.'

– *Mahatma Gandhi*

Speech at Prayer Meeting, New Delhi, July 7, 1947, *CWMG, Vol. LXXXVIII, p. 297.*

As India moved towards freedom, rapidly changing circumstances made Gandhi play different roles. In 1937 when on the persuasion of Gandhi, the Congress Party fought and won elections and later assumed office, Gandhi saw it as an opportunity to put into practice his well thought-out ideas of governance. He used his journals to write weekly letters to the Congress Governments covering the whole gamut of administration. Here Gandhi assumed the role of a self-appointed advisor to the governments.

When the Second World War broke out in September 1939, Gandhi was initially sympathetic to the cause of the British seeing them as the aggrieved party. When he saw that the majority in the Congress thought otherwise, with good reasons to distrust the Government's conciliatory declaration, he fell in line with the Congress viewpoint. As British intentions became clearer day by day, Gandhi was convinced that the good of India lay in the British leaving India. He mobilized people for the Quit India Movement dealing a fatal blow to the Empire. Though Gandhi was imprisoned before he could launch the movement, his earlier mobilization through press was enough for people to carry the movement through.

He had already conveyed through his journals the do's and don'ts of the movement and issued directions to his volunteers throughout the length and breadth of the country.

When the War ended in August 1945, and the British elections saw the victory of the pro-India Labour Party, Gandhi was released from prison. Now he had to don the mantle of a negotiator for independence. He entered into negotiations with the British officials, Princely States, Muslim League and other important groups. At this stage, Gandhi made minimal use of the Press.

Finally, when Partition of the subcontinent became a distinct possibility, and the whole country was consumed by communal fire, Gandhi took on the most tragic role of his life—that of the pacifier. At this stage Gandhi used the last weapons in his non-violent armoury, of touring the riot affected areas, addressing people through his prayer meetings and finally resorting to the *brahmastra,* the ultimate weapon, of fasting unto death for achieving communal amity. In the final years Gandhi was busy squashing rumours which could have led to further communal flare ups. He laid stress on the responsibility of the Press in such situations and was instrumental in getting a screening committee to see what should or should not be published and how communal riots should be reported. Gandhi thus did not make deliberate use of Press. His speeches were reproduced in all the important dailies and read throughout the country. Recognizing the importance of Gandhi's role the Government directly broadcast of his prayer speeches on the All India Radio. Thus at the fag end of his life Gandhi was using another important agent of mass-media, the radio.

The bright dawn of freedom was eclipsed by the flames of communal riots. Gandhi's once powerful clarion call, 'Do or die', acquired a heavy tragic tone. Thousands of men, women and children fell prey to communal riots on both sides of the communal divide. The cost of freedom proved crushingly heavy, and yet history demanded of India a last payment in blood—the assassination of Mahatma Gandhi. His voice, eternally silenced, poignantly continued to communicate what he had tried to convey all through his life. Communal cacophony was silenced, killings stopped and rioters—some shamefaced and others not - withdrew.

Perhaps no country that had been under colonial rule had the privilege of the kind of preparation for freedom that Gandhi had initiated in India, especially the open dialogue on all subjects via the print media. That is why, despite the holocaust of Partition, the country was born healthy and could survive challenges to its integrity and democratic functioning all these years. In the Foreword to the ninetieth volume of the *Collected Works of Mahatma Gandhi* which was published in 1983, Mrs. Indira Gandhi, the then Prime Minister wrote: '...he was the one of those who spoke as he thought and acted as he spoke, one of those few in whom no shadow fell between word and deed. His words were deeds, and they built a movement and a nation and changed the lives of countless individuals.' This miracle was much in evidence in the period under review, when Gandhi had the opportunity thrust upon him both to build a movement and a nation—a movement for a democratic and secular nation and a nation characterized by diversity in unity. And for this Gandhi made full use of his communication skills largely through the columns of his journals.

Gandhi as an Advisor

Instruments of Instructions or Humble Notes[1]

The Government of India Act, 1935, ushered in Provincial Autonomy. Elections were held in the British governed provinces. Gandhi's persuasive skills were in demand as soon as the Congress won overwhelmingly in the general elections. The Congress leaders were divided over the issue of accepting office in the Provinces where they had won elections. Nehru was against the acceptance of office. He wanted the 'slave constitution' (the Government of India Act of 1935) to 'go, lock, stock and barrel and leave the field clear for our Constituent Assembly'. A large section of Congressmen were in favour of accepting office and so were many English friends of India. Gandhi was also inclined to the latter viewpoint. He brought Nehru round to his point of view through meetings and personal correspondence. Gandhi himself drafted the office acceptance clause of the Congress resolution and in a statement to the Press acknowledged his role.[2]

In July 1937, Congress Ministries assumed office in the Central Provinces, Madras, Bihar, Bombay, United Provinces and Orissa, to be followed later by North West Frontier Province and Assam. This instilled a great degree of confidence among the Congressmen and frustrated the Muslim League. It started raising the cry of the fear of dominance by the 'Hindu' Congress and separated itself from mainstream Congress-led politics.

Gandhi's writings during this period reflect the dominant mood of the times. On the one hand, he advised Congressmen not to lose their heads over their popularity and power, and, on the other, he wrote article after article assuring the readers that the Congress was not a communal organization and the Muslims of India need not fear its assumption to office. The articles in this period carry both a sense of achievement and an undercurrent of worry – that though something precious had been won, it could be destroyed by brash actions based on wrong notions.

Political Education of the New Rulers

No sooner had the Congress Ministries assumed office than Gandhi threw open the columns of *Harijan* for the 'political education' of the new rulers and started a series of articles on their duties and responsibilities. For this he sought prior permission of Jawaharlal Nehru in a personal letter.[3] It was written on July 15, 1937 and the first article on 'Congress Ministries' appeared in the *Harijan* dated July 17, 1937.[4] The very first article in the series begins with the statement:

> Since the Working Committee and other Congressmen have allowed themselves to be influenced by my opinion on the office issue, it is perhaps due to the public for me to explain my conception of office acceptance and what is possible to do in terms of the Congress election manifesto.

Following this statement was the list of things that the new Ministries were 'immediately' supposed to take up. They were to enforce prohibition by making education self-supporting instead of paying for it from liquor revenue. The jails were to be turned into reformatories and workshops. Salt was to be made free for the common man. All purchases of cloth were to be in khadi. The Congress Governments were asked by Gandhi to pay more attention to the villages and the peasantry rather than the cities. After listing the tasks, Gandhi went on to say that this was the first random list.

In the same article Gandhi elaborated upon how the Ministers should conduct themselves on their personal behaviour. They should travel third class, wear khadi dhoti, kurta and waistcoat and follow a disciplined and simple life both in personal and public matters. Finally Gandhi warned the Ministers that they should take care of all the communities living in their provinces so that the mischievous and false propaganda of dubbing the Congress Ministries as 'Hindu' Ministries were proved wrong.

The above mentioned article was important as it set the tone for the issues Gandhi would be taking up later.

Responsive Government and Alert Citizens

In the article entitled 'The Fundamental Difference', Gandhi pointed out that since the Ministers represented the votes of the public, from the Governor downwards, they should respect peoples' authority. He asked the people to co-operate with the Government but if 'the latter go wrong or neglect their duty, it is open to any person to complain to the Secretary of the AICC and seek redress. The two points show that how Gandhi envisaged the totally 'Indian' Government to perform![5] These articles were in addition to the numerous letters he wrote to Congress leaders.

Continuing Public Dialogue on Prohibition

Being the leading figure in the national movement, Gandhi's articles always attracted attention. Gandhi welcomed it. He enjoyed entering into dialogue with the informed public. Thus when his very first article was criticized for advocating prohibition, he sought to elaborate upon the point in another of his articles, showing how the drink evil ruined lives especially of the peasants.[6] Another letter questioned Gandhi's stand in exempting the Europeans from Prohibition on the grounds that they could not do without drinks on the ground that it was 'against the spirit of truth and non-violence as also against good logic'. Gandhi replied, 'I am unable to lay down a universal law for all human beings and for all climes that drink is an evil'. It may be a necessity in cold climates. In India prohibition was necessary in view of its being a social evil.[7] Gandhi was ever against education being funded by revenue from this social evil. This was a constant refrain in his writings. He was determined to bring about the desired reform.[8] These articles by Gandhi did have an impact and the Congress Working Committee, at its meeting in Wardha from August 14-17, 1937 passed the following resolution:

> Inasmuch as prohibition has been one of the chief planks of the Congress since the inauguration of the non-co-operation movement in the 1920, and thousands of men and women have had to suffer imprisonment and physical injury in the

furtherance of this cause, the Working Committee is of opinion that it is incumbent upon the Congress Ministries to work for this end.

Welcoming this resolution, Gandhi gave a twelve-point programme for the implementation of the resolution[9]. The Government of Bombay Presidency followed suit and introduced total prohibition from the first of August, 1938.

Gandhi was not one to let go of an issue unless he touched upon the various dimensions of it. When he came to know that a number of Christians objected to prohibition, Gandhi quoted two well-known Christians in support of his viewpoint.[10]

When it was pointed out to Gandhi that prohibition would be impracticable in India because those addicted to drinking may resort to illicit distillation or bootlegging, Gandhi retorted, 'Thieving will abide till doomsday. Must it therefore be licensed?'[11]

Since most of the liquor trade was in the hands of the Parsis they were the worst affected in Bombay Presidency with effect from August1, 1938. Gandhi met a deputation of Parsis, and published the details of their discussion in his journal. The Parsis were Gandhi's friends and he was at his persuasive best in dealing with them. Sir Cowasji, an old friend, was the most vehement in his attack on prohibition. He contended that drunkenness was bad, not drink. Why the entire community be penalized for the sake of the few who drink? Gandhi disarmed him by reminding him how he had helped Gandhi in the past at various junctures, and how he expected him to stand by him at this particular juncture! Another Parsi gentleman angrily asked as to what right the government had to regulate his life. He said, 'I tell you, although I do not drink, if someone came and told me that I might not drink, he would make my blood boil'. Gandhi replied with a smile, 'Even so you do not steal, and yet there is a law against thieving. Would you therefore steal to defy to the law?' Mr Khareghat, the veteran temperance reformer, pointed out that according to their religion, Parsis were duty bound to offer their guests good bread and good wine. Gandhi argued that in such a case it must have been unfermented wine. Whatever it may be, one wonders how this could be a religious duty at all! What would a poor man do? Gandhi argued with Khareghat. Obviously Gandhi was able to convince a section of the deputation because the Parsis abstained from any agitation.[12]

In another article on prohibition, Gandhi dealt with a letter from the Archbishop of Bombay. The letter in question was published separately in the same issue of *Harijan.*

Gandhi's legal mind first of all sought to clarify the meaning and scope of the policy of prohibition. He started by pointing out that the word prohibition was a misnomer for what the Bombay and the other Provincial Governments were doing. Nowhere, he said, were the Governments prohibiting people from drinking. They were just closing liquor shops which were absolutely under Government control. The shop-owners had no statutory protection save what they got from year to year. Every owner of a liquor shop knew that his licenses may not be renewed the next year. He could also be outbid if he possessed a country liquor or toddy license as these were auctioned every year. Therefore the licensees had no vested interest in their licenses beyond the year for which they were held and then too subject to the observance of the stringent conditions laid down for them. Therefore, Gandhi claimed, the law for the abolition of liquor licenses was an 'ordinance of reason for the common good made and promulgated for the community by the competent authority. All that the State was doing was to remove from the drinker the temptation or the facility which the State considered harmful to him except for medicinal purposes. As regards the charge whether the law was *just* as per the yardstick of the conscience of the millions of India, Gandhi replied with authority that it was so.[13] Gandhi, however, was pained when Subhas Chandra Bose gave a communal dimension to the issue of prohibition stating that it affected the minorities like Muslims and, especially Parsis, adversely.[14]

Gandhi was accused by some that he was partial only to the drink evil whereas other kinds of intoxicants were more injurious to health and had a worse effect on social life. Gandhi replied, 'I claim to be a practical reformer. I know almost instinctively what vices are ripe for being publicly dealt with.'[15] The removal of drink evil was urgently required. The problem of other intoxicants could be taken up later. Gandhi assured the correspondent that for him all intoxicants were equally bad.

Corruption

With power came the problem of the power hungry — the scramble for offices and corruption. Gandhi was flooded with letters asking for one or the other person to be included in Ministries, sometimes with the warning that his non-intervention may lead to communal riots. Writing on the menace of self-seekers, Gandhi expressed his inability and disinclination to help them and made it plain that the 'offices have to be held lightly, not tightly.'[16] In an article entitled 'My Meaning of Office Acceptance', he made it clear that acceptance of office was meant for serving the masses and consolidating the Congress position through the constructive programme so as to reach the goal of swaraj.[17]

During this period Gandhi also addressed the fundamental questions regarding the practicability of non-violence in the day to day affairs of the government. Responding to the question whether the State could carry on strictly, on the principle of non-violence, Gandhi replied, 'A Government cannot succeed in becoming entirely non-violent, because it represents all the people. I do not today conceive of such a golden age. But I do believe in the possibility of a predominantly non-violent society. And I am working for it. A Government representing such society will use least amount of force. But no Government worth its name can suffer anarchy to prevail. Hence I have said that even under a Government based primarily on non-violence a small police force will be necessary.'[18]

Discipline in the Party

When it came to right conduct in politics, Gandhi did not spare even his closest friends and associates. When K.F. Nariman, a Congress member from Bombay, accused Sardar Patel of being responsible for his defeat in Bombay Presidency elections, Gandhi in his statement to the Press made it clear: 'I can give this assurance that in the event of the Sardar being found guilty of such conduct I should cut off the intimate contact I enjoy with him.'[19] Knowing the nature of his relationship with Sardar this was a very strong statement. It showed two things, one that he was confident of the non-complicity of the Sardar in the matter and second, he was against cultivating any friendship at the cost of uprightness in political or public matters. Similarly he castigated the people sitting in the Assembly's visitors-gallery for their unseemly demonstration against the ex-Premier of Central Provinces. Gandhi wrote in unequivocal terms,

> I suppose there will be parties even after we have Complete Independence of our make. It will go hard with us if the parties will not tolerate one another or show towards one

> another ordinary courtesy. And the Congress which claims to represent the whole nation can ill afford to be intolerant towards its political opponents or others. If it is, and it is, the only all-India body, it represents all interests. It represents even Shri Raghavendra Rao who was at one time a respected member of the Congress organization. It may be that the votes in the constituency for which he stood were tampered with. If they were, the law would look after it. But he must be presumed to be honest till he is proved guilty. And even if he is proved guilty, the guilt would be no warrant for unseemly demonstration against him.
>
> Intolerance, discourtesy, harshness are not only against Congress discipline and code of honour, they are a taboo in all good society and are surely contrary to the spirit of democracy...Unseemliness is Indiscipline.[20]

These words are not from *any* editor of a daily newspaper but from one whose opinion carried weight and who was widely respected. These words also show what kind of governance Gandhi dreamt of for independent India. No wonder as long as Gandhi's immediate successors ruled India the Congress Party was a generally disciplined and well-organized Party with no match.

Gandhi did not hesitate in highlighting the correspondence received by him regarding corruption in Congress organization through the practice of bogus voting and bogus membership and called upon the AICC to deal with the issue.[21]

When floods struck Orissa, appealing for funds and relief materials for victims Gandhi advised the Ministers thus: one, they should adopt means and measures to make people who may be affected, learn the art of helping themselves by engaging in any productive occupation and, two, they should make a proper effort to harness engineering skill so as to guide into healthy channels the course of the rushing waters during the monsoons.[22] This simple and practical foresight is a lesson the Governments even today have not learned. They still go through the motion of doling out relief material instead of going deep in to the cause of the malaise and take corrective steps or rehabilitate people on a long term basis.

A stickler for rules, Gandhi was against wasting time on unnecessary rules and regulations which delayed matters and were the breeding grounds of corruption. When he was asked as to what the governments should do about the loads of files lying in the offices, his cryptic reply was 'burn them'.[23]

Relation between the Ministries and the Congress Organization

Gandhi also clearly enunciated the relationship the Congress Ministries should have with the mother organization, that is, the AICC. He very rightly pointed out that the Congress Ministries enjoyed fourfold responsibility. As an individual, a Minister was responsible to his constituents. Collectively the Ministers were responsible to the majority of the legislators who, by a no-confidence vote or similar means, could remove them from office. But a Minister as a Congress member owed his position and responsibility to his Provincial Congress Committee and the AICC. This was a clear signal for Party unity against insubordination by local ministers or indiscipline. Gandhi was firmly of the opinion that without discipline no organization could last for long. There was a place and forum for criticism, but such criticism should be based on facts and aimed at improving the organization and not motivated by personal jealousies or ill-informed facts.[24]

While Gandhi was all for discipline in an organization he was not averse to democratic functioning or to voicing difference of opinion. He chose to reply to one such question put to him after the Quit India Movement. The question referred to the psychological change brought about after 1942 whereby the Congress members stopped looking at the High Command for observance of days etc. Gandhi replied that if Congressmen had really learnt to act for themselves since August 1942, it was a great thing and it did not matter whether in doing so they made mistakes—'A child often stumbles before it begins to walk.' But he was afraid that this was not a fact. If it were true all Congressmen would have followed non-violence in their actions.[25] In other words, though he encouraged initiative and independent thinking he was in favour of submitting to party discipline.

Ideological Issues Tackled

The Congress Party had a sizable section of Socialists among its ranks. In a discussion on the Zamindari system Gandhi is reported to have remarked, 'The difference between your view and mine is based on the question whether the Zemindari system is to be mended or ended. I say it should be mended and if it cannot be mended, it would end itself.' When it was pointed out to him that the zamindars were the instruments of bureaucracy, Gandhi agreed but maintained that they were just 'helpless tools'. On the question that the land belonged to the tiller Gandhi gave his trademark answer, 'The man who supplies brains and metal is as much a tiller as the one who labours with his hands. What we aim at, or should, is to remove the present inequalities between them.'[26] Later Gandhi wrote in strong words about the involvement of Congress workers in the anti-zamindari violence in Andhra.[27] In an interview to Louis Fischer Gandhi clarified his definition of socialism. 'My socialism means 'even unto this last'. I do not want to rise on the ashes of the blind, the deaf and the dumb. In their socialism probably these have no place. Their one aim is material progress.... I want freedom for full expression of my personality ....Under the other socialism, there is no individual freedom. You own nothing not even your body.'[28]

The socialists had secured a victory in the Congress when Subhas Chandra Bose was elected the President of the Congress at Haripura in 1939. The members were divided on the issue of the direction of the Congress policy and most of them feared that it could be a break from the policy hitherto followed under the guidance of Gandhi. Bose had insisted that six months ultimatum should be given to the British Government after which mass action should be resorted to. Gandhi, however, felt that the country was as yet not prepared for civil disobedience. G.B. Pant moved a resolution expressing confidence in the old Working Committee and calling on the President to form a new Working Committee 'in accordance with Gandhiji's wishes'. But the differences between Bose faction and Gandhi supporters were so wide that Gandhi saw no possibility of bridging them. He, therefore, advised Bose to form his own Working Committee and seek the approval of the AICC for his programmes, and, if it was not accepted, to resign. Gandhi was advised by Tagore to handle the case with utmost care and Gandhi's letters to Subhas bear out how he valued Gurudev's request.[29] Bose resigned at the AICC meeting at Calcutta on April 29, 1939, and on May 3, 1939 formed a new group called the Forward Bloc. Gandhi later on drafted the resolution charging Subhas Chandra Bose with indiscipline and disqualifying him as the president of the Bengal Provincial Congress Committee.[30]

Education: Curriculum and Source of Funding

Gandhi fully realized the importance of education in moulding the character of individuals and contributing to the social and political development of the country. 'Having spoken strongly in 1920 against the present system of education, and having now got the opportunity of influencing, however little it may be, Ministers in seven Provinces, who have been fellow-workers and fellow-sufferers in the glorious struggle for freedom of the country, I have felt an irresistible call to make good the charge that the present mode of education is radically wrong from bottom to top."[31] His scheme of education was based on two propositions: (1) Primary education extending over a period of at least 7 years, covering all the subjects up to matriculation standard, except English. A vocation used as a vehicle for drawing out the minds of boys and girls in all departments of knowledge, should replace what passes today as Primary, Middle or High School Education and, (2) such education, taken as a whole, can and must be self-supporting; in fact self-support was to be the acid test of its reality.[32] Gandhi's formula elicited encouraging responses from the readers, especially from the teaching community.

Some found Gandhi's ideal of self-supporting schools flawed, unbalanced. Concentrating totally on vocational studies and neglecting humanist subjects, the critics felt, would tantamount to legalizing child labour. Gandhi countered by saying that the prejudice against self-supporting schools stemmed from not understanding the details of the scheme and basing ones judgment on wrong facts. 'It is very like a man refusing to read the description of a human being and calling him a monkey, because he has seen no other animal but a monkey, and because the description in some particulars, but only in some answers that of monkeys.'[33] Gandhi repeated his suggestions at the Conference held on the occasion of the Silver Jubilee of Marwari Shiksha Mandal, where educationists of eminence like Dr. Zakir Hussain, Abdul Huq, Saudamini Mehta, K.T. Shah, Tijare, Vinoba Bhave, P.C. Ray, D.B. Kalelkar and others were present.[34]

While the British were wary of touching upon social evils prevalent in the Indian society lest it should be taken as interference by foreigners, with memories of 1857, the Congress Governments did not have that fear of revolt. The Congress Governments in different provinces in fact vied with each other in putting an end to social evils. When a social worker from Madras, Dr. Muthulakshmi Reddi issued a public appeal to the Madras ministry to pass her bill which put a stop to the immoral custom of dedicating *devadasis* to a life of shame, Gandhi immediately recommended the adoption of such legislation through the columns of his journal.[35]

Gandhi had come to perform the role of one-man Ombudsman where the general public went with its grievances against the Congress Ministries. This was a delicate role, for the policies under criticism were the ones which, though unpopular, were in the nature of social reform—such as, the imposition of Hindustani in Madras Province. Gandhi took pains to make it clear that Hindustani was not going to interfere with the growth of the regional languages, besides 'it was unpatriotic to harp on provincialism at the cost of nationalism.'[36]

Issue of Cow Slaughter

Cow slaughter was a communally sensitive issue. Gandhi had dealt with it in *Hind Swaraj* and had written several articles thereafter. But on the eve of independence it acquired a new significance. There was a campaign launched by Hindus to ban cow slaughter through the provisions of the Constitution and leaders like Rajendra Prasad were amenable to this request. Gandhi's secular stand on the subject was unequivocal. He spoke on the matter in one of his prayer speeches:

> People send me wires expecting me to persuade Jawaharlal and the Sardar to enact laws to protect the cow. But I will not do so. I will ask these devotees of the cow not to waste their money on the telegrams. Let them spend that money on the cow....After all, most cows are owned by the Hindus. Why do they sell them to slaughter houses?[37]

Again, he wrote:

> In India no law can be made to ban cow-slaughter....I have been long pledged to serve the cow but how can my religion also be the religion of the rest of Indians? It will mean coercion against those Indians who are not Hindus....I shall therefore suggest that the matter should not be pressed in the Constituent Assembly.[38]

These views are important because they come from one who was instrumental in the establishment of institutions for the protection and service of cow and her progeny. Even today the provisions against cow slaughter mentioned in the Directive Principles of State Policy are referred to as 'Gandhian provisions' which is patently wrong.

Ram Rajya/Khudai Rajya

Amidst the turmoil all around, Gandhi continued to dream of his Ram Rajya or Khudai Rajya. This was the blue-print of the society he wanted future India to strive for. It would be a society based on truth and non-violence. He wrote:

> Independence must begin at the bottom. Thus every village will be a republic or *panchayat* having full powers....In this structure composed of innumerable villages, there will ever-widening, never-ending circles. Life will not be a pyramid with the apex sustained by the bottom. But it will be an oceanic circle whose center will be the individual always ready to perish for the village, the latter ready to perish for the circle of villages, till at last the whole becomes the one life composed of individuals, never aggressive in their arrogance but ever humble, sharing the majesty of the oceanic circle of which they are integral units.
>
> Therefore the outermost circumference will not wield power to crush the inner circle but will give strength to all within and derive its own strength from it ...Let India live for this true picture, though never realizable in its completeness...In this picture every religion has its full and equal place...In this [picture] there is no room for machines that would displace human labour and that would concentrate power in a few hands.[39]

In such a society there would be no hierarchical division based on castes. The so-called untouchables would enjoy a life of prosperity and dignity. Gandhi wrote: 'The place of untouchables in the swaraj of my conception will be the same in every respect as that of caste Hindus'.[40] When it was brought to his notice that the reality was at variance with his statements and the Congress showed more solicitude for the Muslim demands than for the just rights of the Harijans, Gandhi replied, 'The Congress being a political organization is likely to be more susceptible to political pressure, which the Muslims are in a far stronger position to exert than the Harijans. If it succumbs to that pressure, it will pay price for it. The Harijan Sewak Sangh, however, being a non-political organization, should never put expediency before its primary duty towards Harijans.'[41]

'If India becomes free in my lifetime and I have still energy left in me, of course I would take my due share, though outside the official world, in building up the nation on a strictly non-violent basis.,' Gandhi fondly hoped.[42]

Gandhi also touched upon the issues of standardization of the national tri-colour,[43] universal adult franchise,[44] meaning of civil liberty in a democratic setup[45] and a whole lot of other issues that had a bearing on the future polity.

The most remarkable aspect of these communications is that Gandhi spoke with a natural authority free of any arrogance. People accept such authority if it is born of love and caring and Gandhi, if anything was a storehouse of such feelings.

Princely States: Gandhi's Shares his Vision of a United Indian Nation

Events seemed to have justified the wisdom of the Congress Ministries resolution of non-intervention in the affairs of the States. Gandhi conceded that the constitution, however unjust, arbitrary and illogical it may be, was such that, legally and politically, every State, small or big, was an independent entity in its relation to the other States and that part of India which is called British India, in contradistinction from the Princely states, was geographically and ethnically one and indivisible with the rest of India. He further took pride in the fact that by its resolution of noninterference the Congress put the State people on their mettle and set in motion the natural forces, i.e., the powers latent in the people themselves.[46] Despite this idealism the fact remained that Mysore, Travancore and Hyderabad resented Congress popularity in their states. In the later half of 1938 the struggle for States' people for responsible government was intensified. Attributing this awakening to the spirit of the times, rather than the influence of the Congress, Gandhi invited the Princes and their advisors to recognize the people's demands as legitimate and added : 'There is no half-way house between the total extinction of the States and the Princes making their people responsible for the administration of their States and themselves becoming trustees for the people, taking an earned commission for their labours…And if the Princes believe that the good of the people is also their good, they would gratefully seek and accept the Congress assistance.'[47] In another article, he reminded the Princes that 'if they are straight and if they have their people really at their back, they have nothing to fear from the Residents. Indeed they should realize that the Paramount Power resides not in Simla, not in Whitehall, but in their people.'[48]

The peoples' movement was particularly active in Travancore, Rajkot, Jaipur, Hyderabad and certain States in Orissa. Most of the rulers sought to crush the peoples' movements and were at times supported by the Paramount Power. This resulted in the severe repression exercised by these Governments. Gandhi criticized this policy in Ranpur (Orissa),[49] Limbdi, Rajkot and Dhenkanal.[50] The State of Rajkot was the subject of personal attention for Gandhi for several reasons. Gandhi's father Karamchand Gandhi had once served as the *dewan* of Rajkot. Ba and Manibehn Patel participated in the civil disobedience movement there and Gandhi undertook a fast for the redressal of grievances.

Though suppression of the people was the general rule, a few enlightened Princes did sympathize with and met some of the legitimate demands of the people. In Ramdurg, Jamkhandi, Miraj and Aundh, the Rulers granted liberal concessions to the people and in such cases Gandhi impressed upon the States Peoples' organization to be restrained in their demands.[51]

Gandhi was consistently against any move to pressurize the States for acceding to India. He visited Kashmir in order to mediate between Sheikh Abdullah and the Maharaja of Kashmir and advocated transfer of power to the people under the leadership of the Sheikh. He also admired the Sheikh for his secular and bold policy in Kashmir *vis-à-vis* the Hindus and Sikhs.

Correspondence with International Leaders on World Situation

Gandhi had by this time had come to acquire an international status. The Prime Minister of Czechoslovakia wrote a personal letter to him appealing for intervention on behalf of his country. Later Gandhi wrote a letter to Hitler which was however not sent to the dictator by the British authorities. Written on July 23, 1939 the letter states, 'It is quite clear that you are today the one person in the world who can prevent a war which may reduce humanity to the savage state. Must you pay that price for an object however worthy it may appear to you to be?'[52] Gandhi wrote another letter to Hitler dated December

24, 1940, in which, with great insight, he warned him that if 'not the British, some other power will certainly improve upon your method and beat you with your own weapon. You are leaving no legacy to your people of which they would feel proud. They cannot take pride in a recital of a cruel deed, however skillfully planned.'[53] He wrote a special article in the *Harijan* on the plight of Czechoslovakia, advising the Czechs to resort to satyagraha against the Nazis.[54] Gandhi's moral influence on international affairs can be well seen from a cable from Morges (Switzerland) sent by Paderewski, the aged ex-President of the Polish Republic and celebrated pianist, which read: 'On behalf of a nation who is today defending the sacred right to remain free against a cruel and nameless tyranny, I appeal to you as one of the greatest moral authorities of the world to use your noble influence with your countrymen to gain for Poland their sympathy and friendship ....In this terrible hour when innumerable innocent women and children are massacred daily, a word of sympathy and encouragement from you, great teacher of your own nation, would profoundly move the heart of every Pole.'[55] In reply Gandhi sent his 'heartfelt prayer for the early termination of their fearful trial and for the grant of the required strength to bear the suffering whose very contemplation makes one shudder.'[56]

Though he declared that he was not much conversant with international issues his views on the rights of Palestinians showed his penetrating insight: 'Palestine belongs to the Arabs in the same sense that England belongs to the English or France belongs to the French. It is wrong and inhuman to impose the Jews on the Arabs.'[57]

World War-II and its Effect on India

The constitutional experiment which, under Gandhi's advice, the Congress had begun in July came to a sudden halt at the end of 1939. With the outbreak of the World War II, the national leadership was faced with a seemingly no-win situation. It either had to help the British in the preservation of their Empire or, by refusing co-operation, indirectly helping the Fascist powers. Initially, Gandhi was inclined to help the Allies in their war effort, but the Congress as a political organization could not subscribe to non-violence as a creed or accept Gandhi's suggestion of unconditional moral support to the British. Most of the Congress leaders were skeptical about the British protestations of fighting for democracy. The Congress Working Committee, after prolonged discussions lasting over four days, passed on September 14, 1939 a resolution drafted by Jawaharlal Nehru declaring their intention not to 'associate themselves or offer any co-operation in a war which is conducted on imperialist lines and which is meant to consolidate imperialism in India and elsewhere' and inviting the British Government to declare their war aims and to state how they 'are going to apply to India and to be given effect to in the present.'[58] In reply, the Viceroy merely reiterated the British Government's intention to help India 'attain its due place among our Dominions, promised some modifications in the Government of India Act of 1935 after consultation with representatives of the several communities, parties and interests in India, and with the Indian Princes.'[59] Gandhi characterized the declaration as 'profoundly disappointing'.[60] The subsequent debates in the two houses of Parliament and Sir Samuel Hoare's speech in the House of Commons convinced him of the 'prudence of the course adopted by the Working Committee.' Gandhi wrote a strongly worded article to counter the untruths spread in England about him that he was in favour of unconditional support to the British and was still powerful and influential enough to bring about a change in the Congress Working Committee resolution[61] that demanded a clear enunciation of the British Government's war aims. Defending Nehru's stand Gandhi, in a Statement to the Press, wrote:

> The author of the statement is an artist. Though he cannot be surpassed in his implacable opposition to imperialism in any shape or form, he is a friend of the English people. Indeed he is more English than Indian in his thoughts and make -up....And he is a humanitarian in the sense that he reacts to every wrong, no matter where perpetrated. Though, therefore, he is an ardent nationalist his nationalism is enriched by his fine internationalism. Hence the statement is a manifesto addressed not only to his own countrymen, not only to the British Government and the British people, but it is addressed also to the nations of the world including those that are exploited like India. He has compelled India, through the working Committee, to think not merely of its own freedom, but of the freedom of all the exploited nations of the world.[62]

Not that Jawaharlal Nehru needed a certificate of good intentions from Gandhi, but this statement put to rest the conjectures that

Gandhi and Nehru differed with regard to their attitude towards the British. A careful perusal of the wording would reveal how Gandhi projected Nehru as a leader who did not hate the opponent in the Gandhian tradition of satyagraha, and was not hesitant in showing the opponent his mistake. The statement also gave a cosmopolitan dimension to the issue of non-cooperating with the British.

Bid to Neutralize the Spread of Communal Ill- will

When the Congress demanded that the Indian people be allowed to work under the government created by the Constituent Assembly elected solely by the Indians, the British came up with the plea that this was not possible since the Government had obligations with reference to the Princes, the European commercial interests and the minorities. The cat was then really out of the bag and it became clear that the British had no intention of granting self-government to the Indians. They sought to undermine the nationalists by instigating the Princes and minorities to make their own separate claims on power-sharing, thus putting hurdles on the path to independence. Gandhi pleaded in vain that 'there can only be political parties and no majority or minority communities', that the 'cry of the tyranny of the majority is a fictitious cry ', for 'Hinduism is an elastic, indefinable term, and Hindus are not a homogeneous whole like the Muslims and Christians'. And in any case Hindu majority was only a 'paper majority...ineffective because (it was)...weak in military sense'. The 'so-called minorities fear,' Gandhi argued with surprising insight into the reality of the Indian situation, 'has some bottom only so long as the weak majority has the backing of the British bayonets to enable it to play at democracy'.[63]

Gandhi ruled out civil disobedience against the British at that juncture as he felt that there was division in the Congress ranks, because of which it was unable to neutralize the intransigence of the Muslim League. Civil Disobedience in such a situation would have led to communal riots.[64] The easiest method of arriving at a just solution of the communal problem was through the Constituent Assembly, he believed.[65]

Gandhi challenged the concept of British responsibilities again and again in his articles. In a statement to The *News Chronicle* which was cabled to London and which later appeared in the *Harijan* under the title 'Purely Moral Issue' Gandhi wrote thus:

> ...I fail to see why Britain's intention about India should be dependent upon Muslim, Hindu or any other opinion. The only opinion that counts is India's opinion, not even the Congress opinion. India's opinion can only be ascertained by the free vote of her people. The only true and democratic way is to ascertain their will through adult suffrage or any agreed equivalent. So far as the Congress is concerned, the people of Princes' India should be represented precisely on the same footing as those of British India. The Muslims and other accepted minorities may be represented by separate electorates, if necessary, and in the exact proportion of their numbers. They will determine what is required for their protection. In all matters of common interest a composite majority decision should prevail. If a better way than a Constituent Assembly can be found for knowing the will of the people, so far as I know, the Congress will accept it without hesitation.[66]

When the Congress Governments resigned in protest against the British policy, Jinnah exhorted the 'Mussalmans all over India to observe Friday, the December 22, 1939 as a *day of deliverance and thanksgiving*—as a mark of relief that the Congress Governments have at last ceased to function.' Gandhi asked him to wait till the report of the Governors regarding the so-called excesses by the Congress Government were properly investigated, and not to shoulder the tremendous responsibility of 'being both the judge and the accuser.'[67]

When Jinnah formed pacts with Parties that were opposed to the Congress policies and politics such as the Justice Party and Dr. Ambedkar's Party, Gandhi congratulated him for 'lifting the Muslim League out of the communal rut and giving it a national character'.[68] Jinnah, however, refused to give this meaning to his move and instead reiterated the stand that Muslims belong to a separate nation.

Such was the communal atmosphere that a Muslim member of the Congress wrote to Gandhi that it was he who was responsible for the rising communalism. He said that by making the Congress Party advocate the eradication of untouchability as one of its important programmes, he had made it a communal party. Gandhi compared the reform in Hinduism to the Congress support to the Khilafat cause which was a religious issue for Muslims. He said that these ideas were now cropping up because false propaganda has changed the mentality of both the communities.[69]

The British took full advantage of the situation. Posing as the 'fair umpire' they claimed it was their responsibility to carry out the transfer of power in a manner that did justice to all communities. By this one cunning move, the British had let loose a cat among pigeons, leaving to the Congress the well-nigh impossible task of damage control. At the annual Congress session on March 20, 1940 in Ramgarh the Party made it a part of its resolution that 'India's Constitution must be based on independence, democracy and national unity' and repudiated 'attempts to divide India or split up her nationhood.'[70] Three days later, on March 23, 1940, the annual session of the Muslim League at Lahore passed a resolution demanding that 'geographically contiguous units' in the north-western and eastern zones of India should be grouped to constitute 'independent States' in which the constituent units shall be autonomous and sovereign.[71] This was followed by a virulent attack on Gandhi by a leading light of Muslim League, Liaquat Ali Khan.[72] The stage for the Partition of the subcontinent was thus set. This Lahore Declaration created a 'baffling' situation according to Gandhi, since it created doubts in the minds of the public whether in view of the declaration Gandhi should resort to civil disobedience or not. Conceding the fact that if the civil disobedience against the foreign rule succeeded the Muslims would also benefit from it, Gandhi however, emphasized that when freedom came the 'Muslims must have the same right of self-determination that the rest of India has. We are at present a joint family. Any member may claim a division.' Gandhi made an appeal to Jinnah and his followers that they should stop harping on the exclusiveness of the Muslims, because the majority of Muslims in India were actually converts from Hindus. In Bengal the difference between the Hindus and Muslims was hard to discern as both spoke the same language, ate the same food and dressed alike. Gandhi stressed the point that men like Jinnah 'are rendering no service to Islam.'[73]

In an article entitled, 'My Answer to Quaid-e-Azam' Gandhi pointedly asked:

> Can a Hindu organization have a Muslim divine as President, and its Working Committee have four Muslim members out of 15?....I cannot understand the Muslim

> opposition to the proposed Constituent Assembly. Are the opponents afraid that the Muslim League will not be elected by Muslim voters?"[74]

Gandhi never avoided questions of controversial nature. Rather he gave them first preference in the columns of his journals. Sample the loaded question and the answer given by Gandhi:

> Q. The Muslim public need to be satisfied on a very important question. Will the Muslims be allowed to eat their national food—beef—under a Hindu-majority Government? If you can satisfy the Muslims on this all important question, a great deal of knots will be solved. You should give a straight answer to this question in your paper *Harijan*..
>
> A. I do not know how this question arises. For whilst Congressmen were in office they are not known to have interfered with the practice of beef-eating by Muslims. The question is also badly conceived. There is no such thing as a Hindu majority Government. If a free India is to live at peace with herself, religious divisions must give place to political divisions based on considerations other than religious. Even as it is, though unfortunately religious differences loom large, most parties contain members drawn from all sects. It is moreover not true to say that beef is the *national* food of Muslims. In the first place the Muslims of India are not as yet a separate nation. In the second, beef is not their ordinary food. Their ordinary food is the same as that of the millions. What is true is that there are very few Muslims who are vegetarians from a religious motive. Therefore they will take meat, including beef, when they can get it. But during the greater part of the year millions of Muslims, owing to poverty, go without meat of any kind. These are facts. But the theoretical question demands a clear answer. As a Hindu, a confirmed vegetarian, and a worshipper of the cow whom I regard with the same veneration, as I regard my mother (alas, no more on this earth), I maintain that Muslims should have full freedom to slaughter cows, if they wish, subject of course to hygienic restrictions and in a manner not to wound the susceptibilities of their Hindu neighbours.[75]

Things had come to such a pass that a petition signed by a number of Muslims was sent to various Corporation authorities to see whether previous instructions for various removal of Gandhi's portrait from all schools for Muslim boys and girls was acceded to, as it was unislamic, and if not, the institutions be boycotted. When Gandhi read about it in the newspapers he advised immediate withdrawal of his portrait. At the same time he told the leaders of the agitation that their agitation was supported by a wrong argument, 'For they surely have their own heroes. The proper and conclusive argument is that I am no longer their hero.'[76] Huge portraits of Jinnah now adorn the public offices in Pakistan and this is not considered anti-Islamic!

Gandhi's concern for Hindu-Muslim unity is well reflected in another article of the same period. He recommended to his readers a book by Atulanand Chakrabarti which showed that ever since the contact of Islam with Hinduism there has been attempt on the part of best minds of both to see the good points of each other, and to emphasize similarities rather than seeming dissimilarities.[77] Gandhi was inundated with letters after the publication of this article. He chose to deal with one written by a Khan Bahadur from Delhi, which it seems, must have been the most vehement of the lot. The writer was of the opinion that the stumbling block to any negotiations for a settlement of the communal question has been the refusal of the Congress to recognize the All India Muslim League as the authoritative and sole representative body of the Indian Mussalmans. He also urged Gandhi not to trust the Congressite Mussalmans who he characterized as the 'Mir Jafars' of the Muslim community. Gandhi replied that he could not establish the relationship between the demand for settlement and recognition of the Muslim League as the party of Muslims by the Congress. Defending the Congress Muslims staunchly, he retorted with pithy irony , 'If they become members of the Muslim League, they will become worthy Muslims!!!"[78] Similar intolerance was reflected from a research scholar from Aligarh University who claimed that since Gandhi was a non-Muslim, he had no business 'quoting the Koran for his purpose. In response to this Gandhi observed:

> It will be an evil day if the reading and interpreting of religious books are to be confined only to those who wear particular religious label. I ask my correspondent and his

companions, as their friend, to shed what in my opinion is their gross intolerance and give the same credit to others for seeing truth as they claim for themselves.[79]

After the Muslim League declared its intention to press for Partition, the communal situation worsened. Gandhi's as well as Congress' bona fides were questioned. The silver lining, however, was that while India moved to the tragic end of Partition, world public opinion expressed faith in Gandhi's method. World's first Satyagraha Army was also formed during this period.

War Shakes Faith in Efficacy of Non-violence

The barbaric War being fought in Europe, shook the faith of some of the Congress leaders in non-violence. Rajaji successfully managed to pass a resolution in the Congress Working Committee that non-violence could not be extended to defence (1940). Gaffar Khan resigned on the issue. Later when the Congress saw the attitude of the British Government with regard to their offer of assistance, the resolution was amended. Gandhi was rehabilitated and non-violence declared the creed of Congress both for internal as well as external affairs. When reports of the war started pouring in a number of Congress leaders and public men started sympathizing with the British. Gandhi, however, was emphatic. He declared:

> British people stand in no need of sympathy from subject people...they can command all they want from them. They are a brave and proud people....They are well able to cope with any difficulty that may face them. India has no say whatsoever in the manner in which she is to take her part in the war. She was dragged into the war by the mere wish of the British Cabinet. India is a dependency, and Britain will drain the dependency dry as she has done in the past. What gesture is the Congress to make in these circumstances? The greatest gesture in its power the Congress is already making. It creates no trouble in the country."[80]

In September 1940 the Congress realized that their co-operation with the British Government in the war effort did not make any difference to the policy the latter followed *vis-à-vis* India. Therefore, the All India Congress Committee passed a resolution on September 16, 1940, wherein the Congress pledged under the leadership of Gandhi to resume the movement for India's freedom. Gandhi clarified his stand in the series of speeches he delivered at the AICC meetings stating that under his leadership the movement for freedom and the reconstruction of the country after freedom would be along non-violent lines. He also reiterated his stand that Congress was not a Party of Hindus alone. Speaking on the issue of Partition, Gandhi feelingly noted:

> It is worse than anarchy to partition a poor country like India whose every corner is populated by Hindus and Muslims living side by side. It is like cutting up a living body into pieces. No one will be able to tolerate this plain murder. I do not say this as a Hindu. I say this as a representative of Hindus, Muslims, Parsis and all. I would like to say to my Muslim brethren, 'Cut me to pieces first and then divide India. You are trying to do something which was not attempted even during the Muslim rule of two hundred years.[81]

He also declared that his civil disobedience under the circumstances of war was limited to freedom of speech and action provided they are absolutely non-violent. The first satyagrahi to be arrested was Vinoba Bhave, to be followed by Nehru, Azad and others.

At this stage Gandhi had to face opposition from a very unlikely quarter. His long standing British and American friends started questioning him whether the non-co-operation at that stage when Britain was involved in a bloody war with the Nazis was not tantamount to strengthening the Nazis against the Allies.[82] 'It must not be forgotten that the Indian struggle is not anti-British, it is anti-exploitation, anti-foreign rule, not anti-foreigners', Gandhi argued.[83] Even some Congressmen asked Gandhi that while it was wrong to offer satyagraha against a person in distress why was it that the same was being offered against the British while they were in distress? 'To do what is morally necessary and beneficial is a duty and quite different from that which may not be morally defensible but calculated to vex and embarrass an opponent in difficulty', was Gandhi's considered reply.[84]

Spatc of Communal Riots: Gandhi's Response

One negative impact of the arrest of the Congress leaders and strict censorship on the Press so that they do not report on the progress of the movement, was that the communal forces raised their ugly head. The leaders of the Muslim League like Jinnah and Liaquat Ali, had already started their anti-Hindu tirade, demanding a separate Muslim state. Communal riots broke out in quick succession in Dacca, Ahmedabad, Bombay and parts of Bihar in March, April and May of 1941.These riots were very different from the previous ones. In Gandhi's words they resembled a 'miniature civil war.'[85] He could see that they were intended to 'intimidate the Congress'[86] and therefore advised the Congress not to be provoked and adhere to its policy of non-violence. He exhorted the Congressmen to sacrifice themselves for the sake of communal harmony in a non-violent manner. 'We shall never learn the art of mutual forbearance and toleration till some of us, though perfectly innocent, have staggered Indian humanity by losing our lives.'[87]

This policy was considered impracticable by some leaders and an important Congress leader, KM Munshi resigned on the issue and made a public statement that foreign help should be sought to resolve the fratricidal violence. Gandhi tried to reason with him, 'The fight for Pakistan is a fight between two brothers 'and therefore one should not mind if one brother won against the other but a foreign help would enslave both.[88] Similarly on the issue of language controversy he wrote to a friend, 'There need be no rivalry between the two but the wretched spirit which has nothing to do with the languages, pervades every department of life'.[89] Later in plain words he stated:

> I admit there is unfortunately an unbridgeable gulf between the Congress and the Muslim League. Why do not British statesmen admit that after all it is a domestic quarrel? Let them withdraw from India and I promise that the Congress and the League and all other parties will find it to their interest to come together and devise a home made solution for the Government of India. It may not be scientific; it may not be after any Western pattern; but it will be durable. It may be that before we come to that happy state of affairs.[90]

Continuing in the same vein he wrote in another article,

> Separate electorates may have resulted in the separation of hearts. They presupposed mutual distrust and conflict of interests....What conflict of interest can there be between Hindus and Muslims in the matter of revenue, sanitation,

police, justice, or the use of public conveniences? The difference can only be in religious usage and observances with which a secular state has no concern."[91]

Quoting passages of virulent attacks on Hinduism in a paper founded by Jinnah and issued under the direction of Liaquat Ali Khan, Gandhi pleaded for a 'juster estimate of men and things in papers representing the policies and programmes of the Muslim League'.[92]

In fact the deterioration of communal situation was not solely due to the resignation and arrest of Congress leaders. The Muslim League had been propagating the idea of two separate states for quite some time. Jinnah in a speech at Lucknow on October 15, 1937 had declared in no uncertain terms:

> The present leadership of the Congress, especially during the last ten years, has been responsible for alienating Mussalmans of India more and more by pursuing a policy which is exclusively Hindu, and since they have formed the governments in six provinces where they are in majority they have by their words deeds and programmes shown more that the Mussalmans can not expect any justice or fair play at their hands....
>
> ....Hindi is to be the national language of India and *Bandematram* is to be the national song and is to be forced upon all. The Congress flag is to be obeyed and revered by all and sundry. On the very threshold of what little power and responsibility is given m the majority community have clearly shown their hand that Hindustan is for Hindus; only, the Congress masquerades under the name of nationalism whereas the Hindu Mahasabha does not mince words.[93]

Gandhi had noted this transformation in Jinnah and had conveyed this in a letter to the latter when he wrote 'In your speeches I miss the old nationalist.'[94]

Temporary Suspension of Harijan, Harijanbandhu *and* Harijan Sewak *In Protest Against Press Censorship*

When the Government sent notice in November 1940 that no account of Vinoba's arrest should be reported in the *Harijan*, Gandhi announced the suspension of the journal along with the Hindi and Gujarati editions. Gandhi said, 'Let every one become his own walking newspaper and carry the good news from mouth to mouth.'[95] In retrospect one can say that the suspension of the journals proved to be of inestimable harm to the cause of keeping the nation united. For, the predominant sane voice was muted giving the rumour mongers an open field to further weaken the fragile structure of communal relations.

While Gandhi's journals were discontinued, Gandhi did not hesitate to make use of other newspapers and journals. For instance, 'The Instructions to Satyagrahis' issued by Mahadev Desai, were published by *Hitavada* (18-12-40). Another set of instructions similarly were published by the *The Bombay Chronicle* (8-1-41) which included an interesting instruction: 'A satyagrahi shall not recite slogans in an authoritative tone but in a persuasive way.'[96] The Instructions continued to be given at the meetings with Congressmen which were later published in Congress Bulletins.

Determined to silence Gandhi the Government started applying the Press censorship laws to all the dispatches sent by Gandhi to the newspapers. Hence Gandhi was obliged to write a Letter to Newspaper Editors wherein he wrote, 'for the conduct of the campaign and for the sake of keeping it within restraint I have to issue statements from time to time....I therefore appeal to the Press not to succumb to the gag but to assert its independence by publishing all the satyagraha news in its fullness.'[97] *The Times of India* responded to this by stating that Gandhi was demanding unfettered right to the freedom of speech and expression which were denied to the public even in the Congress ruled provinces, and that the demand was a device for squeezing political concessions from Britain.[98] Gandhi wrote a reply to this stating that he was not asking for the moon. It was a normal right of every citizen to demand freedom of speech and expression.[99]

Friendly papers continued publishing news of Gandhi. Thus the *The Hindu* carried an item on the 'Advice to Calcutta Satyagrahis'[100] and 'Advice to Sind Assembly Congress Party.'[101] *The Bombay Chronicle* published an interesting interview with Sankaran, the Secretary of Tamil Nadu Congress Committee. Sankaran stated that door to door anti-War propaganda by Congress Satyagrahis had been permitted by Gandhi, provided the residents do not object[102] and also that Gandhi had on November 17, 1941 spoken to him referring to the instructions to Satyagrahis advising them not to bring persons from villages into towns for offering satyagraha.[103] Thus the purpose of civil disobedience was served without attracting the breach of law. *The Hindustan Times* on 11-3-41 carried Gandhi's Instructions to Andhra and Tamil Nadu Provincial Congress Committees.[104] Gandhi, however, gave vent to his philosophical inclination vide the columns of *Sarvodaya* which was a non-political journal.[105]

The weeklies were resumed on January 9, 1942 because, as Gandhi wrote,

> ...we have arrived at a stage where it is no longer merely a question of resisting war effort. These are questions which confront war-resisters as well as war -mongers. And they can be decided only one way by both, though the approach must vary. Such are questions of dealing with scarcity of food and clothing, looting and bread-riots, etc. I have views on all these and like questions. Resumption of the weeklies is needed for the dissemination of my views on these and like matters. In the ability of the people to deal with them without fuss and even without Government effort lies the way to swaraj whose basis is non-violence. Mere Government effort cannot deal with crises affecting millions of people unless there is voluntary response from them.[106]

At another place he wrote,

> ...*Harijan* is a views paper as distinguished from a newspaper. People buy and read it not for amusement but instruction and regulating their daily conduct. They literally take their weekly lessons in non-violence.[107]

The paper was again suspended in August 1942. The ban was lifted in January 1946. Giving reasons for reviving it once again Gandhi wrote:

> Many readers including English and American, had all along felt a void, and they began to feel it more after the defeat of the Fascist Powers. The reason for the feeling was obvious They wanted my reaction, in terms of truth and non-violence, to the various events happening in India, if not in the world.[108]

This shows how the paper rose in stature because of the temporary discontinuance. People in India and abroad were keen to know about the developments in India with a correct assessment. In addition to this, *Harijan* having acquired the status of a 'viewspaper', was read avidly for the views expressed by Gandhi on matters of human importance, national as well as international.

Gandhi, the Negotiator

Quit India Movement and Negotiations for Freedom

As the tempo of the war in the Far East gained momentum, the Allies saw the defeat of the Colonial powers in their erstwhile colonies largely due to the lack of sympathy and local support. Statesmen in the USA and China therefore suggested that Britain should pay heed to the demands of the Indians voiced by the Congress Party. Unwillingly, Britain sent Sir Cripps to India on a mission more to satisfy Britain's allies than for any breakthrough in India. Holding no promise of Independence the mission exposed the hollowness of the British claim that they were fighting a war for the establishment of democracy in the world.

In India things were in a bad shape. There was division in the Congress ranks over the nature of struggle against the British and the Japanese.[109] Communal atmosphere was rife with hatred as Gandhi's remarks were mutilated and given malicious constructions.[110] Food shortages and famine ravaged Bengal. Stories of refugees from Burma poured in with harrowing accounts of how the British discriminated between Whites and Indians. Under the circumstances it became imperative to launch a movement even though the conditions were far from favourable.

Gandhi wrote to an English friend, 'My firm opinion is that the British should leave India now in an orderly manner....Britain cannot defend India, much less herself on Indian soil with any strength. The best thing she can do is to is to leave India to her fate.'[111] Similar sentiments were expressed by him in his letter to the Chinese Generalissimo wherein he confessed, 'our proffered help has repeatedly been rejected by the British Government and the recent failure of the Cripps Mission has left a deep wound which is still running. Out of that anguish had come the cry for immediate withdrawal of British power so that India can look after herself ....'[112]

Prior to the passage of the Quit India resolution Gandhi wrote an appeal 'To Every Briton', wherein he asked them to 'retire from every Asiatic or African possession and at least from India'. He believed that such a step was 'essential for the safety of the world and for the destruction of Nazism and Fascism.' He further went ahead with his request for 'a bloodless end of an unnatural domination for a new era, even though there may be protests and wailings from some of us.'[113] He also made appeals to the conscience of international leaders and common people in other countries to see the genuineness of his request for the end of foreign domination.[114]

At the AICC meeting in Bombay on August 7-8, 1942 the Quit India resolution was passed. The message that Gandhi gave to the nation was as following:

> 'Message to the Country',
>
> 'Everyone is free to go to the fullest length under ahimsa. Complete deadlock by strikes and other non-violent means. Satyagrahis must go out to die not to live. They must seek and face death. It is only when individuals go out to die the nation will survive.' *Karenge Ya Marenge.*[115]

There were genuine concerns voiced by some Englishmen that in the absence of the British, India would disintegrate. A retired English collector cabled from England:

> Please consider that India without British troops and the sure shield of the British navy would be at the mercy of Pathans, Afghans and Japan. The Constituent Assembly would all be in a concentration camp very quickly or killed. Satyagraha only works with civilized people who are gentlemen.

Gandhi's Reply to this was instructive

> The English friend gives little credit to Indian nationalists when he thinks that they contemplate a Constituent Assembly in a vacuum which can be blown to pieces by any power. If there is an honourable settlement, the Constituent Assembly will meet in the presence of the British but without any interference from them. If there is no settlement, it will

> meet after a successful rebellion, in which case India will have made herself ready to face any emergency. There is no other contingency possible in which a Constituent Assembly can meet....My friend's ignorance of the working of satyagraha is quite excusable....I can only assure him that it is not the sob-stuff he believes it to be. It is of little use if it can work only among the so-called civilized people. The partition separating the civilized from the uncivilized is very thin. Both act almost alike when their passions are roused.[116]

With the arrest of important Congress leaders including Gandhi, secrecy and sabotage entered the movement on a very large scale. Gandhi refused to condemn the popular fury which he considered was pardonable, whereas 'the vindictive and inhuman retribution [by the Government] wholly indefensible.' Again in a Press interview he refused to judge popular action by the yardstick of truth and non-violence, unless he 'could apply the same measure for Government action.'[117]

During his detention and especially during the period of his fast Gandhi wrote excellently argued letters to the then Viceroy and other Government officials against the malicious propaganda spread against him. These letters are now available but during the period under review, these were kept secret. During that period Gandhi lost his valued colleague Mahadev Desai after a short illness and his wife Kasturba. A decision to fast led to deterioration in Gandhi's health and he was released from prison. But all these tragedies, personal as well as public, did not shake his resolve. He stuck to his stand that the British should leave India. He made it clear that the Quit India resolution was not any ordinary resolution aimed at securing independence for India. The non-violent rebellion envisaged by the resolution was not 'a programme of seizure of power' it was a 'programme of transformation of relationship ending in a peaceful transfer of power...'

Acknowledging the importance and role of other forms of struggles for achieving independence, Gandhi conceded,

> In the historical process, the country will be found to have advanced towards freedom through every form of struggle, even through the August upheaval.[118]

He further dispelled doubts about the nature of the Quit India Resolution when he wrote:

> In terms of non-violence, 'Quit India, is a healthy potent cry of the soul. It is not a slogan. It means the end, through means purely truthful and non-violent, of foreign rule and domination. It does not mean the foreigner's destruction but his willing conversion to Indian life. Thus his conversion implies our conversion too. If we cease to be inferiors he cannot be our superior.[119]

He volunteered to have a talk with the Congress underground workers without evaluating them. The upshot of Gandhi's discussions with underground workers like RR Diwakar, Ananda Chowdhury, Achyut Patwardhan and Aruna Asaf Ali was that except for Achyut Patwardhan and Aruna Asaf Ali, all others surrendered themselves to the authorities or courted imprisonment by offering civil disobedience openly. A look at a letter written to Aruna Asaf Ali (which was published in the *Link* magazine in 1968 (6-10-68) gives an insight into how Gandhi would have used his persuasive power against the underground Congressmen. In the letter dated June 30, 1944 Gandhi wrote:

> Chi. daughter Aruna (written in Devanagari script),
>
> I have just read your letter. My whole heart goes out to you. I consider myself to be incapable of asking anybody, much less you of doing anything that will hurt your pride. If you surrender yourself, you would do so to raise yourself and the country with you. The surrender wont be out of your weakness but out of your strength. This struggle has been full of romance and heroism. You are the central figure. I would love to see you since you are so near. Therefore, come if you at all can. Lest you cannot, this is my advice: I do not want you to surrender unless you feel that it is the better course. I have brought myself to regard secrecy as a sin in the application of non-violence. But it cannot be followed mechanically. I am working for and in the name of the dumb and the downtrodden millions. They are strangers to the art of secrecy as I am. You must, therefore, be the best judge of what is proper And is that not the final message of the Congress in the closing sentence of the great resolution of

> 8th August, 1942? Every Congressman is the bearer, in his (or her own person, of the Congress message which he (or she) is to carry out according to his (or her) own will, remaining within truth and nonviolence....God be your sole guide and do as He bids you. This I promise: I will not judge you no matter what you do....[120]

Gandhi-Jinnah Talks

Gandhi made a determined effort to solve the communal problem through negotiation with M.A. Jinnah. On July 17, 1944, he asked for a meeting between them, but Jinnah fell ill and the meeting took place on September 9, 1944. The talks lasted eighteen days. The whole country waited in suspense, hoping for the best and fearing the worst. The talks failed. The announcement to this effect on September 27, 1944 sealed the subcontinent's fate. Inexorably history moved towards the day of India's greatest tragedy—the Partition.

Gandhi approached Jinnah guided by his vision of non-violent society, built on the 'willing consent of all its components', by 'accepting the freedom of every part'.[121] He was hopeful that Jinnah could be won over 'with trust and love.'[122] This clearly shows that Gandhi's aim was not to enter into bilateral agreement with Jinnah which could be implemented by their respective parties, but to ensure the unity of India while ensuring the freedom of every part.[123] The press however projected the issue of talks in such a manner that aroused fear in the minds of Hindus and Sikhs in Punjab and Bengal.

Jinnah was not motivated by the aim of achieving a national consensus. He was following the narrow objective of arriving at an agreement between Gandhi as the 'Hindu' representative, and he as his Muslim counterpart. Jinnah based his demand on the two-nation theory whereby Hindus and Muslims, because of their different religions, were to be treated as two distinct nations. Gandhi totally rejected this theory. This divergence of opinion created a deadlock, and the one not to give up easily, Gandhi suggested a way out. On the basis of a formula devised by C. Rajagopalachari and published in July, 1944, Gandhi suggested that the proposal for separation of Muslim majority areas would be placed specifically before and approved by the people of the areas concerned and after their decision a joint agency would regulate matters of common interests like Defence, Foreign affairs and Communications. Here Gandhi had totally misread Jinnah's intentions, who wanted nothing less than sovereign state of Pakistan with Muslim majority areas. A very interesting account of the interview is given by Pyarelal in h s book, *Mahatma Gandhi – The Last Phase*. Pyarelal reports Gandhi to have remarked, 'It was the test of my patience ....I am amazed at my own patience.' In the course of the talks Jinnah made an interesting observation about converting Gandhi to his point of view, '...if I can convert you, you will be my Ali' about which Gandhi observed later, 'It was the most revealing remark. I was meeting the prophet of Pakistan looking for his Ali'.[124]

Gandhi also suggested the democratic method of arriving at a decision by having a public discussion on the issue. Finally Gandhi informed the public through the Press regarding the breakdown of the talks. He stated, 'The breakdown is only so called. It is an adjournment *sine die* .Each one of us must now talk to the public and put our viewpoints before them. If we do so dispassionately and if the public cooperate, we may reach a solution of the seemingly insoluble at an early date.'[125] Gandhi tried hard to salvage the situation of deadlock by agreeing to Bhulabhai Desai's proposal. Bhulabhai proposed an interim Government in which both Muslim League and Congress would participate.

Things had come to such a sorry pass on the communal front that international issues were also given communal colour. Hence, when Syria and Lebanon were fighting for their independence against France in 1945 Jinnah issued a statement assuring the Syrians and Lebanese of the support of 'the hundred million Muslims of India', and also warned that 'not only the Middle East and Muslim India but also the whole of the Muslim world will flare up' if freedom was not granted.[126] Gandhi hit the nail on its head when he said, 'It pains me to think that our Muslim fellow-countrymen feel that they can effectively ask for justice to the Syrians and the Lebanese as fellow Muslims. Syrians and Lebanese are a mixed population. Their liberty is at stake not as Muslims but as a separate nation.'[127]

British Initiatives on the Constitutional Deadlock and Gandhi's Warning

The constitutional negotiations that the British initiated, after the failure of the Gandhi-Jinnah talks, unfortunately took cue from the issue on which the talks had floundered. On June 14, 1945 the Viceroy announced in a radio broadcast the release of the members of the

Congress Working Committee and the summoning at Simla of a conference of Indian leaders for the purposes of discussing the formation of a more representative Executive Council.[128] The reference to the 'principle of parity between the caste Hindus and Muslims' irked Gandhi. In a Statement to the Press, he asserted that 'there were no caste or casteless Hindus' and, giving reasons for issuing such a statement, argued, 'I would not have dwelt on the matter but for the fact that it touches the political mind of Hindus in its sensitive spot and carries with it political repercussions.'[129] Moreover, the formula worked out with Gandhi's approval, between Bhulabhai Desai and Liaquat Ali Khan, had spoken of parity between the Congress and the Muslim League[130] and the shift to communal parity would have the effect of reducing the Congress to the status of a communal organization, representing only 'caste Hindus'. This was what Jinnah had been wanting all along! Predictably, the Simla Conference, held in June-July 1945 failed to arrive at an agreement on the formation of a National Government.

With the assumption of office of the Labour Government in Britain on July 27, 1945 things looked better for India. The Government announced elections in India for Central and Provincial Legislatures. The Congress, accordingly, occupied itself with preparations for the elections, with Patel in charge. Gandhi showed no interest in these preparations and in fact made it clear in his personal letter to those who sought his intervention over election tickets etc. that he did not wish to intervene and also issued a statement to the Press in the matter.[131] In fact, earlier, the Congress Working Committee had differed with him on two important matters. First was the question of League–Congress parity in National Government, as envisaged by the Bhulabhai Desai formula where Congress had agreed to Hindu-Muslim parity at the Simla Conference. The second issue was with regard to Gandhi's offer to Jinnah for a limited Pakistan. Gandhi had to publicly acknowledge that these were his personal views.

Out of the fear of embarrassing the Government Gandhi curtailed his public activities and confined himself to writing letters to Viceroy and Government officials to show leniency to those prisoners who were in jails for their involvement in the Quit India Movement of 1942. He also pleaded to the Viceroy on behalf of the INA prisoners who were on trial. He wrote to the Viceroy and appealed for legal assistance of their choice being given to the prisoners.[132] The request was conceded, and when the trial began the defence was lead by Bhulabhai Desai with Tej Bahadur Sapru serving on the Defence Committee and Jawaharlal Nehru appearing in the court in his barrister's robe. The acceptance of Gandhi's demands proved to be a tactical blunder on the part of the British as the publicity of the trials and the involvement of the national leaders in them raised an unprecedented upsurge of popular sentiments.

Gandhi Disassociates Himself from Negotiations

Gandhi kept away from political developments and devoted most of his time to guiding constructive workers and educating the people on the responsibilities of freedom. Meanwhile Gandhi took a 45 day tour of Bengal, then toured Madras and Andhra. Gandhi's focus was on constructive work in his speeches.[133] Still it was construed by some that he had gone to Madras to set up Rajaji as Premier.[134] Seeing the hold Gandhi had over the masses the British Government had requested him to write in his journal on the food shortage and the duty of the citizens in the situation, which Gandhi did.[135]

Gandhi's Stand on Royal Indian Navy Mutiny

As is often the case when the hosts are waiting for the guests to leave, this was a period of uncertainty for Indians. The open trial of INA revived the memories of Bose and his army's heroic defiance of the British. In February 1946 there was mutiny by Royal Indian Navy men snowballing into a series of sympathetic strikes all directed against the British. Gandhi issued a strong indictment of the mutiny in the Press. He wrote:

> This mutiny in the navy and what is following is not, in any sense of the term, non-violent action. Inasmuch as a single person is compelled to shout "Jai Hind" or any popular slogan, a nail is driven into the coffin of swaraj in terms of the dumb millions of India. Destruction of churches and the like is not the way to the swaraj as defined by the Congress ...Let the known and unknown leaders of this thoughtless orgy of violence know what they are doing and then follow their bend. Let it not be said that India of the Congress spoke to the world of winning swaraj through non-violent action and belied her work in action and that too at the critical period in her life.[136]

This was clearly an announcement of disassociation of the Congress with the mutiny. It was also an appeal to the conscience of the mutiny leaders that their actions had harmed rather than furthered the national cause. The use of the word 'thoughtless' was deliberate because the naval ratings could have found a non-violent way of registering their grievance which, Gandhi thought would have been more 'manly' and effective. In the same statement Gandhi made a prophetic observation which, unfortunately, later proved to be all too true. He observed, 'A combination between Hindus and Muslims and others for the purpose of violent action is unholy and will lead to and probably is a preparation for mutual violence — bad for India and the world.'[137]

The firebrand leader of the mutiny, Aruna Asaf Ali took notice of Gandhi's statement and wrote a letter to him. While refuting her arguments Gandhi gave full publicity to her letter in the Press. The reason was not personal, Gandhi clarified,

> Except for the fact that she represents not only herself but also a large body of underground workers, I would not have noticed her refutation, if only because she is a daughter of mine not less so because not born to me or because she is a rebel ....I do not appreciate underground activity. I know that millions can not go underground ....A select few may fancy that they will bring swaraj to the millions by secretly directing their activity. Will this not be spoon-feeding?.... Real swaraj *must* be felt by all – man, woman and child."[138]

British Government's Announcement Regarding Indian Independence: Gandhi Misses the 'Big Touch'

Events on the political front were moving fast. On March 15, 1946, the British Prime Minister, Clement Richard Attlee, said in a speech in the House of Commons, 'it is worth remembering ...a nation of 40,00,00,000 people that twice sent her sons to die for freedom ...should herself have freedom to decide her own destiny'. This was followed by a Bill for setting up a Provisional Government for India. Towards the end of his speech he paid a handsome tribute to the nature of freedom struggle in India in the following words, 'In the mass of Asia, an Asia ravaged by war, we have here the one country that has been seeking to apply the principles of democracy. I have always felt myself that political India might be the light of Asia.'[139]

This speech infused a new spirit in India. HN Brailsford, a senior journalist met Gandhi to seek his reactions on the Prime Minister's speech. Gandhi was certainly not unmoved by the new development, but was cautious, 'This time I believe that the British mean business. But the offer has come suddenly. Will India be jerked into independence?' he observed.[140] Brailsford noted that though Gandhi had accepted that the British Government had done the right thing, he missed the big touch. The interviewer came back with the impression that in a way 'hard to define, one felt that this man as speaking for India,' though Gandhi had warned the journalist 'that he would be speaking only for himself and not for the Congress. Brailsford concluded his interview with the following words: 'I came away with the sense that I had been talking to a brave man who had the courage to believe that human society can be built only on moral principles. Amid our preoccupations over military perils, he stands aloof and repeats with unshaken faith his creed that safety is attainable, only when men learn to treat each other as brothers and equals. No lesser means will avail.'[141] These assets of Gandhi were to be used to the maximum in the years to come.

Gandhi the Pacifier

Prayer Meetings as Forum of Communication

In the last phase of his life Gandhi started using prayer meetings for the dissemination of his ideas. Apart from discussions on spiritual matters Gandhi discussed the outcome of his talks with Government functionaries, contents of letters addressed to him, comments on him in the Press or any idea that came to his mind at these meetings. The meetings began with recitations from the religious texts from different religions followed by *bhajans* sung by his ashram associates or at times by well-known singers like Dilip Kumar Roy or MS Subbulakshmi. In a way these prayer meetings were a barometer of the country's communal atmosphere. At times, some Muslims would walk out at the singing of Ramdhun and return later to listen to Gandhi's speech[142] or some Hindus or Sikhs would vehemently object to the recitations from the Koran. The prayer meetings were an assertion of the *sarvadharma samabhava* i.e., equal respect for all religions, concept preached by Gandhi. All these speeches were widely reported in the Press. Later some of the prayer meeting speeches were broadcast live.

People saw Gandhi as a man of prayers and felt a ring of credibility in his tone of voice. Sometimes such meetings also helped diffuse communal tensions in the region. A brief recount of the content of the prayer meetings would show the range of Gandhi's concerns and his fearlessness when broaching unpleasant issues, in front of hostile audiences, even at the risk of his life. Thus Gandhi would pass on the message of hope and fearlessness among his audiences and readers. Nehru had appropriately summed up the significance of these meetings. Speaking at a convocation address later on December 13, 1947, Nehru had said:

> Freedom came to us, our long-sought freedom, with a minimum of violence. But immediately afterwards we had to wade through oceans of blood and tears ....Horror piled on horror and a sudden emptiness seized us ....The light seemed to go out. But one bright flame continued to burn and shed its light on the surrounding gloom. And looking at that bright, pure flame, strength and hope returned to us...There was the Spirit of India, strong and unsullied, rising above the turmoil of the present....during the past four months, in a dissolving world, he has been like a rock of purpose and lighthouse of truth."[143]

Chandrakant Kaji has compiled and edited the prayer speeches of Gandhi[144] and one can see how important these prayers were in Gandhi's scheme of things. He felt that 'As body needs food and feels hungry, so the soul needs and feels hungry for prayer.' He regarded it as 'the very soul and essence of religion', and the 'very core of a man's life'.[145] The fanatics could not stand prayers from other religions the atheists were at a loss to understand how such prayers helped people in distress. Was there Anyone listening to and answering the appeals of the faithful? A correspondent challenged his supreme faith in Ramanama and conceded that young people come to his prayer meetings out of deference to the man 'who taught us a whole lot of things', and therefore are prepared to 'suffer' his 'fad'. Gandhi treated this question in one of his articles in the *Harijan*. He wrote: 'How is one to prove to a person who has never tasted sugar, that sugar is sweet, except by asking him to taste it?'[146]

In India where the majority of the people are religious Gandhi's appeal to pray with ones heart in the prayer meetings must have calmed the people. It is not without reason that medical scientists have sworn by the soothing effect of prayers on patients' nerves. Stephen Hay in the course of discussion of the value of prayers with reference to Gandhi and also taking into account the non-believers, has observed: 'It seems to me likely that heartfelt prayers, with or without spoken words, that ask not for external results but for such higher emotions and emotional attitudes as gratitude, humility, peacefulness, benevolence and courage, will continue to prove helpful and healthful to individuals in future generations—whether within or independent of any particular religious group–as they discover that the mere act of humbly requesting such gifts can actually usher them into consciousness.'[147]

Gandhi's words had great conviction because, along with prayers, he laid emphasis on a purely moral conduct through his own example. When India was on the threshold of freedom, Gandhi wrote in an article, significantly entitled, 'Let us Pray', in the *Harijan*, (14-4-46), 'There is little doubt that India is about to reach her cherished goal of political independence. Let the entrance be prayerful. Prayer is not an old woman's idle amusement. Properly understood and applied, it is the most potent instrument of action. Let us then pray and find out what we have meant by non-violence, and how we shall retain the freedom gained by its use.'[148]

In the last two years of his life Gandhi made good use of prayer meetings for communal unity.

Lady Mountbatten at one of the Prayer Meetings of Gandhi

The Final Phase

From 1946 onwards, Gandhi contented himself with guiding Congress leaders. Along with this, he continued offering well meant advice to the British representatives. He continued to educate people with all his moral might, on self rule and on fighting the menace of communalism, which had assumed dangerous proportions.

The Cabinet Mission came to India in the last week of March and issued a State Paper in May wherein it rejected the formation of a sovereign state of Pakistan explaining it to be impracticable. Gandhi had not doubts that the British were sincere about leaving the country.[149] He considered the proposals as first steps in the 'act of renunciation' something akin to 'a promissory note.'[150] The honouring of the 'note' was subject to certain pre-conditions. These preconditions were: the position of the European members of the Assemblies with regard to the Constituent Assembly; the exercise of Paramountcy in the intervening period; the withdrawal of British troops from India; and, the installation of Interim Government at the Centre.[151] Gandhi wanted the Interim Government to be formed immediately in view of the food crisis in the country as the result of the War. The Mission members, however, found themselves faced with the old insuperable difficulty of Jinnah's insistence on parity of representation between the Congress and the Muslim League. Gandhi asked the Viceroy, Lord Wavell, to bypass the parity issue and invite the Congress and the Muslim League to submit a joint list representing 'a coalition Government composed of persons of proved ability and incorruptibility. If they failed to produce a joint list, the Viceroy should examine the separate lists of the two parties and 'accept either the one or the other (not an amalgam)...'[152] Gandhi wrote again the next day, on June 13: 'You are a great soldier –a daring soldier. Dare to do the right. You must make your choice of one horse or the other...Choose the names submitted either by the Congress or the League. For God's sake do not make an incompatible mixture and trying to do so produce a fearful explosion.'[153] Gandhi's concern is well reflected in this communication. The Mission members and the Viceroy feared that a one-sided arrangement such as proposed by Gandhi either with regard to the Constitution making machinery or the composition of the Interim Government, would lead to a civil war. But both Gandhi and Patel seemed to believe that if the British were firm the Muslims would not fight.[154] Gandhi's proposal was similar to the dilemma presented before Solomon by the real and the usurper mother. Only, the British lacked the fearlessness and foresight of Solomon.

Gandhi's faith in the God fearing and law-abiding masses was great. His hope was that the masses had 'sufficiently imbibed the spirit of ahimsa' and that when the British went there might be a 'little fight here and there' and then Indians would 'settle down as brothers giving a lesson of peace to the world.'[155] According to him the very presence of the third party, pretending to be an impartial judge, encouraged the communal leaders to address their arguments to that party rather than to the common people who could be counted on to exert their own restraining influence on the extremists in either community. Charged with the sole responsibility of running the Government of the country, the Congress or the Muslim League, Gandhi was convinced, would display greater realism and take pains not to put itself in the wrong in the eyes of the masses. British representatives, including Lord Mountbatten later, failed to appreciate this reasoning behind Gandhi's suggestion to hand over power either to the Congress or the Muslim League and persisted in their efforts to bring about an artificial agreement among leaders at the top.

The Viceroy, Lord Wavell announced on June 16, 1946 a composite list drawn up by him which, while denying parity to the Muslim League, also denied to the Congress the right it claimed of including a nationalist Muslim among its nominees. Both the Congress Working Committee and the Muslim League were reconciled to the position. But Gandhi pressed the Congress Working Committee not to sacrifice its character as a national party by waiving its right, and even gave notice that if it yielded 'he would have nothing to do with the whole business and leave Delhi.'[156] His firmness, coupled with 'the general right' conceded by the Viceroy to Jinnah to have a say in the selection of names in future,[157] finally made the Committee decide against accepting the Viceroy's plan for the Interim Government. While Gandhi never doubted the sincerity of the Mission members he believed that they somehow had done a 'bad job'. Their best had fallen short of 'India's needs or India's best.'[158] For him India's needs could only be met by the welfare and paramountcy of the people, even at the cost of vested commercial interests and princely privileges.

Seeing the situation getting out of hand, the Viceroy invited Jawaharlal Nehru to send him a list of names for the Interim Government. Nehru submitted the names and thus the interim Government was sworn in on September 2, 1946. The situation had the potential of turning into a communal riot had the Congressmen or their supporters decided to celebrate their victory as the Muslim Leaguers were observing it as a day of mourning. Gandhi was cautious in his prayer meeting speech of the day. He called it a 'memorable day in the history of India' but added that it was no occasion for jubilation as the Ministers were only 'putting on a crown of thorns'. The Hindus could not join the Muslim Leaguers in observing the day as a day of mourning, but they could avoid 'illuminations, feasting and other forms of rejoicing.'[159]

Gandhi's Cautious Approach Vs the Hate Campaign of Muslim League

The Muslim League rejected Congress claim to represent the Muslims and thus disqualified itself from the Interim Government. Later it launched its programme of Direct Action to 'achieve Pakistan...and to get rid of the present British slavery.' As it turned out, the programme had little to do with the ending of the 'British slavery' and was no more than a concerted effort to incite communal riots on a massive scale all over the country. On August 16, declared by the League as Direct Action Day, Calcutta witnessed an outbreak of violence that left in its wake, according to official figures, five thousand dead and fifteen thousand wounded. Communal riots were indeed nothing new in India, but the organization behind these, their dimension and intensity, staggered and stunned the country. Gandhi put the blame for this orgy of violence squarely on the League's hate propaganda. Wishing that the violence of Calcutta did not become a signal for its spread all over India, Gandhi concluded: 'It depends on the leaders of the Muslim League, of course, but the rest will not be free from responsibility. They can retaliate or refrain. Refraining is easy and simple, if there is the will.'[160] Soon, however, Gandhi's worst fears were proved right. On October 13 rioting started in Noakhali where according to the Governor's reports 'Large bands of Muslim hooligans are moving about terrorizing Hindus and committing acts of arson, loot, murder, kidnapping and forcibly converting Hindus.'[161] Gandhi recalled and seriously considered a correspondent's suggestion that he should himself 'go to some place of riot and show ...the way of quelling riots in a non-violent manner by personal example.[162]

The atmosphere was so vitiated by the Muslim League's 'hymn of hate' that Jawaharlal Nehru who had gone on a study tour to Peshawar along with Khan Abdul Gaffar Khan and Dr. Khan Saheb was attacked by a mob on October 21, 1946.[163] Gandhi's prayer meeting was disturbed in Delhi on October 24, 1946 when a crowd of excited young men shouting slogans came to demand redress for the violence in East Bengal. Gandhi assured the audience that if the members of the interim Government were convinced that they could put a stop to the disturbances in East Bengal, by offering their lives as a sacrifice, not one of them would hesitate to make such a sacrifice.[164]

Gandhi was facing the same irony of fate as had been the lot of many a martyr in history before him who became the object of anger of the very people for whose good they had been willing to give their lives. He was accused of being partial to the Hindus when he declared his intention to proceed to Noakhali. It was the 'cry of outraged womanhood' that beckoned him to Noakhali, he reasoned with them.[165]

Gandhi Tours Noakhali to Douse Communal Flames

Gandhi set out on his healing mission and arrived in Calcutta on October 29, 1946 and started his Noakhali tour on November 9, 1946. There he met the refugees and reassured them,[166] and held discussions with Muslim League leaders telling them in plain words where their responsibilities lay.[167] He also addressed the relief workers exhorting them to sacrifice their all for the cause of communal unity. This elicited the remark, 'You have opened up a new vista before us, Mahatmaji. We feel fresh blood coursing through our veins.'[168]

Even in the most dangerous of situations Gandhi stuck to his habit of plain speaking even if it meant hurting the party concerned. Thus at a prayer meeting in Ramgung he is reported to have said that the Muslims were afraid of befriending him or the Hindus because they were not permitted to do so by the Muslim League leaders![169] The meetings had desired impact. Congress and League flags were seen flying side by side in Kazirkhil by the mid of November.[170] Men and women met him privately and put before him their fears and expectations. Gandhi would then talk to the other party and was able to effect a solution. This happy solution was then conveyed at the prayer meeting for rest of the population to know. Such incidents made him able to arrive at the decision that one good Hindu and one good Muslim of each village should take charge of the refugees and ensure their safe return to their homes and hearths.[171] Gandhi was instrumental in forming a Peace Committee comprising members of both the communities. His later speeches were appeals to people to help the Peace Committee members in maintaining communal harmony.[172] In an interview to the Press when asked about the exchange of population, with penetrating insight he said that it 'was unthinkable and impracticable.' He further elaborated, 'In every province, everyone is an Indian, be he a Hindu, a Muslim or of any other faith. It would not be otherwise even if Pakistan came in full.' The 'logical consequence' of exchange of population was too 'dreadful to contemplate', he warned.[173] By December 9, 1946, the Hindus of Srirampur had gathered courage enough to recite *Ramanama* in public and were congratulated by Gandhi for their fearlessness.[174] Muslim youths expressed gratitude to Gandhi over his work in Noakhali and promised that what happened in the past would not be repeated.[175]

Some correspondents wrote to him and certain newspapers also gave publicity to the theory that his continued presence in Noakhali was acting as a deterrent to the restoration of cordial relations between the Hindus and the Muslims for his intention was to bring discredit to the Muslim League Ministry. Gandhi proclaimed that his purpose in coming to Bengal was simply to bring about heart unity between the two communities.[176] In a letter to Vallabhbhai Patel Gandhi wrote from Srirampur, 'My truth and non-violence are being weighed in a balance which is much more accurate than any pearl merchant ever used.'[177]

Body Experiments

On November 20, 1946, Gandhi announced his decision to cut himself off from his colleagues in order to test both the power of truth and non-violence and himself. He also cut himself off from correspondence with the *Harijan* and delegated his ashram mates to look after the journal.[178]

As referred to earlier, Gandhi believed the communal tension flare up and subsequent rioting were the result of his own personal failure.[179] The entries in his diaries and the letters to close friends clearly reflect the agony of his soul. He felt that though he had overcome all kinds of violence in thought and action to a satisfactory level, he could not say the same about his sexual instinct. He still needed to be purged of it, purified. He saw the sexual act itself as a form of violence. So the extreme penance for him would be to test whether he was truly free from lust. His repeated reference to how the molestation of women in Noakhali had moved him, links the idea of his belief that probably his conduct had not been pure enough to ensure their safety.[180] This was a far-fetched link, but Gandhi was more than convinced about it. So much so that he was prepared to forego the friendship of his lifelong ashram mates and companions on the issue.[181] He wrote letters to friends seeking their views on the matter.[182] Among these letters the one written to Acharya JB Kriplani is important. Kriplani to a large extent followed the principle of brahmacharya as propagated by Gandhi in his marriage with Sucheta Kriplani. Therefore his views are of special significance in the whole issue. Kriplani wrote back a very diplomatic reply without objecting to the experiment openly. He wrote:

> ...These matters are I find, beyond my depth. Moreover I have enough to do to keep myself morally straight to sit in judgment on others and specially those who are morally and spiritually miles ahead of me. I can only say that I have fullest faith in you. Even if I had lurking suspicion I would rather distrust my eyes and ears than distrust you..."

After saying this Kriplani very cleverly put forward his objections to the experiment. Kriplani proceeded thus,

> Sometimes I thought that ...you may be employing human beings as means rather than an ends in themselves. But then I take consolation in the thought that that consideration cannot be absent from your mind and if you are sure of yourself, no harm can come to them. Then knowing you to be a great student of the *Gita* I have wondered if you are not doing violence to the principle of *lokasangraha* (conservation of social good), wisely propounded therein. But, this consideration, too, I am sure, must not be absent from your calculations, in this experiment of yours... I know your

attitude to woman is the only right attitude as you are one of those who consider her an end in herself and not merely as a means. You have never exploited her.[183]

The purpose behind quoting the above letter in full is that the same arguments were put forward by the common people when they learnt of Gandhi's experiments but their doubts and Kriplani's dilemma were two very different things. Their doubts had not the depth of understanding nor been tempered by the faith which Kriplani had for Gandhi. Gandhi sought the permission of his eighteen year old grand niece in the matter[184] and then the permission of her father.[185] All these experiments were tolerable as long as they were confined to private life. But when Gandhi started to talk about them in public[186] his old confidante, Thakkar Bapa dissuaded him from doing so for the damage it would cause to the work he was pursuing at that time. Gandhi and Manu, his partner, agreed to discontinue the experiment[187] though Gandhi refused to accept that it was in any way immoral.

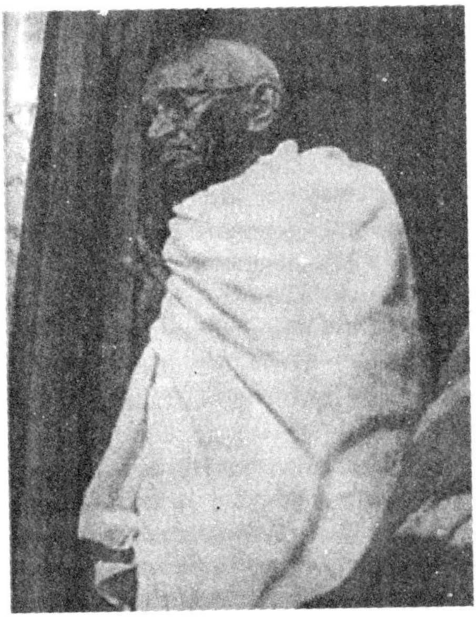

This rare photograph taken during his visit to the riot affected villages in Noakhali (1947) captures a heart-broken and sad Gandhi

Healing Touch of Gandhi's Presence in Bihar

After spending an uninterrupted three and a half months in Noakhali Gandhi moved to Bihar. In October 1946 riots had broken out in Bihar as a reaction to the happenings in Calcutta and Noakhali. Bihar was Noakhali magnified. When Gandhi learnt about the rioting that had broken out in Bihar following a hartal on October 25, 1946, he immediately sent a telegram to Jawaharlal Nehru asking him to wire particulars.[188] Gandhi was stunned and bewildered. He saw it as his personal failure. In letters written to friends he expressed his anguish over the happenings.

He went on a partial fast and threatened to go on a fast unto death unless slaughtering stopped. He wrote an open letter to 'Bihar', wherein he chastised the Hindus of Bihar for their cowardice. He asked them not to rest till every Muslim refugee came back to his home.[189] This letter did have its impact. Hindus were able to persuade Muslims to come back to their homes and even volunteered to make up for the loss of property.

Gandhi was not able to give his single-minded attention to Bihar as events moved fast in the political arena and he was twice called to Delhi for advice and guidance in the discussions which had started. On February 20, 1947, Prime Minister Attlee had announced the intention of His Majesty's Government to withdraw British authority from India by June 1948 and the appointment of Lord Mountbatten as the Viceroy in place of Field Marshall Lord Wavell to carry out the operation. The new Viceroy arrived in India on March 22 and wrote to Gandhi on the same day, inviting him to Delhi. Gandhi met Mountbatten on March 31, but in the discussions which followed he could not carry the Congress Working Committee with him in his daring 'act of faith' of entrusting Jinnah with the power and responsibility of running the nation as its first prime minister. Gandhi quietly took leave and returned to his work among the people of Bihar. One cannot help but wonder what India would have been today if Gandhi had succeeded and Jinnah had taken over as the first Prime Minister of India!

Since Bihar had a Congress Government, Gandhi was more successful in mobilizing the resources of the state for relief work. Since the aggressors in this case were his co-religionists he had threatened fast and then later was forthright in his criticism of their action. 'I remind you again that those who hurt Muslims will be hurting me.[190] The result was that he was able to collect funds for relief work largely from the Hindu population as well and was able to persuade the Hindus to go and help the rehabilitation of Muslims in their villages.'

Gandhi also managed to rope in the services of INA men like Shahnawaz Khan for relief work initially. Arriving in Patna on March 5, 1947 Gandhi toured the affected parts of the Province and heard tales of destruction from the survivors. Gandhi was outraged when he heard that people carried out the killings while shouting *Mahatma Gandhi ki Jai*[191] Gandhi devoted his prayer speeches trying to instil human sympathy and moral concern among the Hindus. 'With our overflowing love we should reassure the Muslims that the Hindus are their brothers and that there can be no difference between us'.[192]

Gandhi in Delhi: Last Stop as Pacifier

Gandhi was firm in his faith that the lasting cure to the lust for violence was in the moral transformation of human beings rather than in any institutional arrangements. He also believed that the spiritual resources to bring about this necessary and possible change were already available in the great religions of the world and that India with its tradition of tolerance and pluralism provided the most congenial soil for the active pursuit of the spiritual value of universal brotherhood. Hence his insistence on the recitation of verses from the Koran in his prayer meetings, even in those held in or near temples, and the replacement of 'Sitaram' by 'Rama-Rahim' and 'Krishna-Karim' in a popular *bhajan*. Answering the objection of those Hindus who objected to such 'defilement' of holy places and sacred hymns, Gandhi defined a Hindu as one 'who is also a good Muslim and a good Parsi.'[193]

Gandhi's prayer meetings in Delhi were marred by interruptions. The role of Rashtriya Swayam Sewak Sangh, an organization supporting militant Hinduism was the suspect in these interruptions. 'Why do you listen to those who are causing obstruction? Actually they have suffered nothing. It is we who have suffered in the Punjab-who have been wronged. But we are not preventing you. We request you to hold the prayer, if only for some time,' the Punjab refugees would implore to Gandhi,[194] when Gandhi would hint at discontinuing his meetings.

Not given to hiding facts, Gandhi shared with people the grave communal situation in the Punjab and East Bengal. Gandhi tried to pacify fanatics by all means or resources at his disposal. At a prayer meeting in New Delhi on May 30, 1947, he referred to a letter from a woman who objected to Gandhi reading from the Koran as she believed that the Koran ordained the killing of the infidels. He cited the authority of Badshah Khan, Abdus Samad Khan, Bihari Muslims and the Maulvis of Noakhali to prove his point that no such reference exists in the Koran.[195] Sometimes his guests at prayer meetings would be eminent Muslims like Badshah Khan or Sheikh Abdullah. The Muslim minority gained courage on seeing them. Gandhi also spoke of instances from history where kings like Maharana Kumbha, Ranjit Singh and Chhatrapati Shivaji showed their respect for Islam.[196]

Gandhi was well aware of the hot-blooded Hindu youth thirsting for revenge. In a talk with Dr. Rajendra Prasad he confided, 'We top leaders are getting old. Before we pass away, we should devote whatever strength God has given us to train younger people to shoulder the responsibility of building up India of our dreams, just as we trained them before as non-violent soldiers for the freedom struggle.'[197]

Gandhi strove with all his heart and soul to preserve and present the freedom movement as a world wide effort to spiritualize politics and public life, globally as well as locally. It was the tragedy of our times that others were bent on politicizing religion. Gandhi's fervent appeals in the name of common humanity of Hindus and Muslims and the true ideals of Islam, evoked no response from Jinnah and other League leaders. It was only under pressure from Lord Mountbatten that Jinnah agreed to sign a peace appeal denouncing 'the use of force to achieve political ends', but only on the condition that Gandhi alone, and no other Congress leader, should sign it with him.[198] Even this appeal was for Jinnah a political agreement, or in the Viceroy's words a 'truce'[199] to be observed conditionally by those observing it. The argument that it was unjust, inhuman and insane to retaliate against a wrong done by one community at one place by victimizing innocent members of that community elsewhere, found no echo in Jinnah's utterances. He made no serious attempt to see that the appeal he had formally signed was honoured by his followers. Gandhi's pleas for more energetic action[200] elicited nothing more than an assurance that he would do his best.[201]

During the communal upheaval, papers like *Dawn* published false or unverified reports. Gandhi brought this to the notice of the paper in one of his prayer speeches and the result was that the paper accepted Gandhi's suggestion that there would be a committee of journalists who would examine the reports of communal riots and decide what should be published.[202]

By now, it was becoming clearer day by day that the Partition of the country was the only way out. The Mountbatten Plan also suggested it. But Gandhi could not be reconciled to idea of slicing up the nation—a caesarian operation to give birth to Pakistan. Gandhi's agony is reflected in his words to Manu, his closest confidante at that point of time, 'I shall perhaps not be alive to witness it, but should the evil I apprehend overtake India and her independence be imperiled, let posterity know what agony this old man went through thinking of it. Let not the coming generations curse Gandhi for being a party to India's vivisection.'[203]

To avoid such an irrevocable step, Gandhi even suggested a transitional arrangement, that power be handed over either to the League or the Congress, but the Congress Working Committee rejected his suggestion. At this stage, there was a wide divergence of views between Gandhi and the Congress on the momentous political questions. But Gandhi did not oppose the Congress leadership. He had no desire to launch a futile struggle against what at that time seemed inevitable. A correspondent wrote to him, 'The British are quitting India but leaving it divided....In case you launch a struggle against the division of India on communal or Indian States basis .... I respectfully offer about one lakh ...disciplined volunteers to loyally carry out your orders.' Gandhi's reply was that he had no desire to launch a struggle against what promises to be an accomplished fact.[204] Hindus and Muslims also wrote to Gandhi from Ireland not to agree to the partition plan quoting the experience of Ireland, but Gandhi said he was 'helpless'.[205]

Once the Congress Working Committee accepted the June 3, Plan of Partition Gandhi defended it in public and advised the AICC to endorse it.[206] He could sense that the country was not with him but with the Congress Working Committee. In a public statement he conceded: 'When I said that the country should not be divided I was confident that I had the support of the masses. But when the popular view is contrary to mine, should I force my own view on the people?'[207] He may have reluctantly agreed to Partition, but he was dead against the partition of the Indian army. In a speech at a prayer meeting Gandhi expressed his distress over the matter when he said, 'If one country increases the army the other will also do the same. The result will be war."[208] If Britain and India could remain friends why not India and Pakistan,'[209] Gandhi wondered. He was undoubtedly sad over the turn of events. He refused to celebrate the freedom to come on August 15, 1947. He said, 'Unfortunately the kind of freedom we have got today contains also the seeds of future conflict between India and Pakistan. How can we therefore light the lamps?'[210] In a letter to an ashram inmate who reminded Gandhi of his promise to return to Sabarmati Ashram when India became free, Gandhi wrote:, 'Why so jubilant? *Purna* swaraj is far off. Have we got swaraj? Did swaraj mean only that the British rule should end? To my mind it was not so. *For me Sabarmati is far off, Noakhali is near'*(emphasis added).[211] Gandhi was very right in his observation.

On August 15, 1947 the country became free but the freedom that came was marred by barbarous outbreaks of communal violence provoked and sustained by the prolonged 'hymn of hate' which accompanied the campaign for a separate state for the Muslims. Gandhi pitted his whole soul against the madness and tried to calm both Hindus and Muslims. In Calcutta the 'One–man Boundary Force' (as Mountbatten hailed him) stopped the rioting, while 55 thousand soldiers failed to do so in the Punjab. Punjab needed the martyrdom of Gandhi to finally quell the rioting.

Gandhi agreed with the refugees who had come from Punjab that Pakistan had not kept its promise of protecting their lives and property but he also implored with them that they should not follow the Pakistani example and take revenge on the totally innocent Muslims in India. Without fear of life, Gandhi spoke from the most unlikely platforms like Gurudwaras and in front of refugees whose miseries had known no limits. He did attempt to hide from people the reports of atrocities on Muslims in Kathiawad, Jammu, and gave reassurances quoting from the speeches of Sardar Patel, Swaran Singh and Jawaharlal Nehru.

Like a mother giving bitter pills to her children, Gandhi gave to ministers, constructive workers and over zealous reformers much salutary advice, however harsh it may have sounded at that moment. He warned people that freedom was not 'suicidal anarchy', that it called for self-sacrifice and self-restraint, for everyone thinking of the whole of India, not of oneself and one's family alone[212] Refugees should learn to live together, should work for and earn their bread, clothing and shelter, keep their camps clean and 'build ideal cities.'[213] Since controls encouraged laziness and corruption (which was even worse than violence) they should be removed so that the millions would learn to be farsighted 'by making mistakes and rectifying them.'[214] In a democracy the government should trust the people and educate them in and through the exercise of freedom.[215]

Gandhi's Last Fast

Some Maulanas of Delhi saw him on January 11, 1948 and one of them asked for help to enable them to go away to England. For days Gandhi brooded over what he called his 'impotence' to give the right answer to Muslim friends who had sought his guidance. The final realization flashed upon him on the afternoon of January 12, and it made him happy. Without consulting anyone, not even Nehru or Patel, who had called on a him couple of hours earlier, he drafted a statement to be read out at the prayer meeting in the evening, announcing the commencement of an indefinite fast the following day. This was his answer to the Maulanas. The fast was to quicken the conscience and not deaden it, to turn the searchlight inwards and seek self-purification. 'No man, if he is pure, has anything more precious to give than his life. I think I have the purity in me to justify the step.'[216]

The step was indeed justified as it evoked the right response from all quarters. Numerous telegrams from Pakistan as well as India gave assurances of communal amity. On January 15, the Government of India announced the decision to release forthwith the cash balances due to Pakistan. On January 17, leader of all communities, Hindus, Sikhs and Muslims, met in Delhi and on January 18, a hundred representatives of various organizations called on Gandhi with a joint statement promising to fulfill the conditions he had laid down for breaking the fast. On January 20 the first attempt was made on his life.

Gandhi's political legacy was democracy safe in the hands of leaders like Nehru so carefully chosen and groomed by him, and Patel a realist with the determination of steel. About his other efforts, it is said: 'No such concrete success could be expected of Gandhiji's last mission of 'spiritualizing' politics and public life. Indeed there was for a moment the danger of 'politicizing' religion and so destroying it. The fast that restored Hindus to sanity averted this danger and was not the least of Mahatma's services to his mother religion.'[217]

While Gandhi put his life at stake to maintain the secular character of the nation, a section of his co-religionists were convinced that he was ignoring their interests by going out of the way to appease the Muslims. They decided that Gandhi was a threat to their religion. The apostle of non-violence was killed in cold-blood on January 30, 1948 while on his way to a prayer meeting. His sacrifice stunned the warring communities into peace.

Thus came to an end the life of epic proportions. He was reverentially given the title of the 'Father of the Nation.' It was an honour he more than deserved. For, he was the one who had toiled the most in giving it a national outlook by stressing the unity which was palpable in the maddening diversities of religions, languages, races, castes, cultures and classes. His efforts and success at assimilating the good from all cultures and his non-confrontational approach to all problems is unmatched in world history. Gandhi, in the last years of life, laid firm foundations for a functioning democracy, a healthy party-system, concept of civilian supremacy, free and responsible press and a secular polity. These healthy traditions, though now eroding, still have been largely responsible for the resilience of India's democratic polity.

REFERENCES

1. The newspapers described these writings as 'Instruments of Instructions' to which Gandhi replied that these were just 'humble notes'. 'Not Instrument of Instructions', *Harijan*, 21-8-37, *CWMG*, LXVI, p. 61.
2. Interview to the Press, *The Hindustan Times*, 20-3-37, *CWMG*, LXV, p. 8.
3. The letter runs thus: 'But this I write to tell you that I have begun to write on the function of Congress Ministries and allied topics. I hesitated but I saw it was my duty to write, when I felt so keenly. I wish I could send you an advance copy of my article for *Harijan*... When you see it, you will please tell me if I may continue to write so. I do not want to interfere with your handling of the whole situation. For, I want the maximum from you for the country. I would be doing distinct harm, if my writing disturbed you.' *Letter to Jawaharlal Nehru*, *CWMG*, LXV, p. 395.
4. *CWMG*, LXV, pp. 406-8.
5. *Harijan*, 24-7-37, *CWMG*, LXV, pp. 431-33.

6. 'Criticism Answered', *Harijan*, 31-7-37, *CWMG*, LXV, pp. 447-453.
7. 'Against Ahimsa and Untruth', *Harijan*, 14-8-37, *CWMG*, LXVI, pp. 47-48.
8. 'Discussion on Prohibition', *Harijan*, 21-8-37, *CWMG*, LXVI, pp. 59-60.
9. 'The Greatest Act', *Harijan*, 28-8-37, *CWMG*, LXVI, pp. 81-83.
10. 'Are Christians Against Prohibition?' *Harijan*, 11-9-37, *CWMG*, LXVI, pp. 118-120.
11. 'Not Impracticable', *Harijan*, 25-9-37, *CWMG*, LXVI, pp. 161 63.
12. Interview to Parsi Deputation, *Harijan*, 10-6-39, *CWMG*, LXIX, pp. 320.
13. 'Meaning of Prohibition', *Harijan*, 17-6-39, *CWMG*, LXIX, pp. 335-339.
14. 'A Dangerous Game', *Harijan*, 22-7-39, *CWMG*, LXIX, pp. 429-31.
15. 'Lack of Sense of Humour', *Harijan*, 14-10-39, *CWMG*, LXX, p. 224.
16. 'Not a Prize', *Harijan*, 7-8-37, *CWMG*, LXVI, pp. 15-17.
17. *Harijan*, 4-9-37, *CWMG*, LXVI, pp. 103-5.
18. Discussion with Pacifists, *Harijan*, 9-3-40, *CWMG*, LXVI, pp. 224-6
19. *Letter to K.F. Nariman, July 17, 1937*, *CWMG*, LXV, pp. 412-13.
20. *Harijan*, 14-8-37, *CWMG*, LXVI, pp. 45-6.
21. 'Corruption In The Congress', *Harijan*, 24-9-38, *CWMG*, LXVII, pp. 371-3.
22. 'Havoc in Orissa', *Harijan*, 25-9-37, *CWMG*, LXVI, pp. 160-1.
23. 'Red Tape', *Harijan*, 17-12-38, *CWMG*, LXVIII, pp. 193-5.
24. 'The AICC', *Harijan*, 13-10-37, *CWMG*, LXVI, pp. 292-3.
25. QuestionBox. *Harijan*, 31-3-46, *CWMG*, LXXXIII, pp. 306-7.
26. Discussion with Bengal Congressmen, *Harijan*, 23-4-38, *CWMG*, LXVII, pp. 22-24.
27. 'Accumulating Evidence', *Harijan*, 17-9-38, *CWMG*, LXVII, pp. 352-3.
28. Interview to Louis Fischer, *Harijan*, 4-8-46, *CWMG*, LXXXV, pp. 9-10.
29. On March 29-1939 Tagore wrote, 'At the last Congress session some rude hands have deeply hurt Bengal with ungracious persistence. Please apply without delay balm to the wound with your own kind hands and prevent it from festering', *CWMG*, LXIX, Fn.1, p. 99.
30. Gandhi never hid the fact from Bose that he was the one who drafted the resolution regarding the disciplinary action against him. He wrote to Bose describing him as his 'lost sheep' who Gandhi believed would return provided his [Gandhi's] love was pure, *CWMG*, LXX, pp. 84-5.
31. 'Doing not Idle Thinking', *Harijan*, 2-10-37, *CWMG*, LXVI, pp. 191-3
32. 'Self-Supporting Education,' *Harijan*, 11-9-437, *CWMG*, LXVI, pp. 123-5; 'Discussion with an Educationist', *Harijan*, 18-9-37, *CWMG*, LXVI, pp. 137-39.
33. *Ibid;* p. 141, 'Some Criticism Answered', *Harijan*, 16-10-37, LXVI, 238-41, 'Prohibition and Education', *Harijan*, 16-10-37, *CWMG*, LXVI, pp. 241-2; 'In Support', *Harijan*, 16-10-37, LXVI, pp. 243-5, 'Self-Supporting Education', *Harijanbandhu*, 17-10-37, *CWMG*, LXVI, pp. 248-9.
34. *Harijan*, 30-10-37, *CWMG*, LXVI, pp. 263-66.

35. *Notes;* 'Legalised Prostitution', *Harijan,* 25-9-37, LXVI, pp. 164-65.
36. 'Congressmen Beware!', *Harijan,* 10-9-38, *CWMG,* LXVII, pp. 323-6.
37. *Pratharthana Pravachan*-I, pp. 260-3, *CWMG,* LXXXVIII, pp. 375-6.
38. *Pratharthana Pravachan*-I, pp. 277-80, *CWMG,* LXXXVIII, pp. 424-6.
39. 'Independence', *Harijan,* 28-7-46 , *CWMG,* LXXXV, p. 33.
40. 'Scheduled Castes', Questions sent to Gandhi by Untouchables, *Harijan,* 28-7-46, *CWMG,* LXXXV, p. 18.
41. *Ibid.*
42. Interview to the 'New York Times', *Harijan,* 27-4-40, *CWMG,* LXXI, pp. 10-12.
43. *Harijan, Harijansewak,* 4-9-37. 11-9-37,*CWMG,* LXVI.
44. 'Illiterates v. Literates', *Harijanbandhu,* 3-10-37, *CWMG,* LXVI, pp. 197-8.
45. 'Civil Liberty', *Harijan,* 23-10-37, *CWMG,* LXVI, pp. 268-9.
46. 'The States,' *Harijan,* 9-7-38, *CWMG,* LXVII, pp. 157-8.
47. 'States and the People', *Harijan,* 3-12-38, *CWMG,* LXVIII, pp. 151-3.
48. 'Rajkot,' *Harijan,* 7-1-39, *CWMG,* LXVIII, pp. 274-6.
49. 'Violence and Non-Violence,' *Harijan,* 21-1-39, *CWMG,* LXVIII, pp. 300-2.
50. 'States and the People,' *Harijan,*3-12-38, *CWMG,* LXVIII, pp. 151-3.
51. 'Question of Honour,' *Harijan,* 4-3-39, *CWMG,* LXVIII, pp. 453-6.
52. *Letter to Adolf Hitler, CWMG,* LXX, pp. 20-21
53. *Letter to Adolf Hitler, CWMG,* LXXIII, pp. 253-55.
54. 'Logical Consequence', *Harijan,* 8-10-38, *CWMG,* LXVII, pp. 413-15.
55. *CWMG,* LXX, Fn.3, pp. 163-4.
56. *Cable to Paderewski, CWMG,* LXX, pp. 163-4.
57. 'The Jews,' *Harijan,* 26-11-38, *CWMG,* LXVIII, p. 137.
58. *Working Committee Resolution,* Appendix-X, *CWMG,* LXX, 412.
59. *CWMG,* LXX, pp. 416-18.
60. Notes:Disappointing, *Harijan,* 21-10-39, *CWMG,* LXX, p. 267.
61. 'Unconditional Support'?" *Harijan,* 4-11-39, *CWMG,* LXX, p. 311.
62. Statement to the Press, *Harijan,* 23-9-39, *CWMG,* LXX, p. 176.
63. 'The Fiction of Majority', *Harijan,* 21-10-39, *CWMG,* LXX, pp. 259-61.
64. *Notes: Hindu-Muslim Clashes, Harijan,* LXX, p. 265; "The Task Before Us", *Harijan,* 2-12-39, *CWMG,* LXX, p. 374.
65. 'The Only Way,' *Harijan,* 25-11-39, *CWMG,* LXX, pp. 362-65.
66. *Harijan,* 9-12-39, *CWMG,* LXXI, pp. 6-7.
67. *Statement to the Press, The Hindu, The Hitavada,* 10-12-39, *CWMG,* LXXI, pp. 18-19.
68. 'A Welcome Move', *Harijan,* 20-1-40, *CWMG,* LXXI, pp. 109-110.
69. 'My Sin',*Harijan,* 20-1-40, *CWMG,* LXXI, pp. 110-13.
70. *CWMG,* LXX, pp. 440-41.
71. Appendix-VII, *CWMG,* LXX, p. 444.
72. Appendix-X, *CWMG,* LXX, pp. 446-8.

73. 'The Baffling Situation', *Harijan*, 6-4-40, *CWMG*, LXXI, pp. 387-90.
74. *Harijan*, 30-3-40, *CWMG*, LXXI, pp. 371-2.
75. Question Box, *Harijan*, 27-4-40, *CWMG*, LXXII, p. 13.
76. *Notes, Harijan*, 25-5-40, *CWMG*, LXXII, pp. 79-80.
77. 'Hindu-Muslim Tangle', *Harijan*, 4-5-40, *CWMG*, LXXII, pp. 27-8.
78. 'Hindu-Muslim', *Harijan*, 8-6-40, *CWMG*, LXXII, pp. 131-34.
79. 'I Wonder', *Harijan*, 29-9-40, *CWMG*, LXIII, pp. 50-51.
80. 'Our Duty', *Harijan*, 25-5-40, *CWMG*, LXXII, p. 81.
81. *Speech at AICC Meeting, Bombay, Harijan Sewak*, 12-10-40, *CWMG*, LXXIII, p. 25.
82. *Discussion with English Pacifists, Harijan*, 20-1-40, *CWMG*, LXXI, pp. 108-9; 'For Englishmen', *Harijan*, 16-3-40, *CWMG*, LXXI, pp. 313-18.
83. 'For Englishmen', *Harijan*, 16-3-40, *CWMG*, LXXI, pp. 316-317.
84. *Discussion with Nagpur Congress Workers, Harijan*, 6-1-40, *CWMG*, LXXI, pp. 62-64.
85. *The Bombay Chronicle*, 27-6-41, *CWMG*, LXXIV, p. 113.
86. *Letter to Manu Subedar*, *CWMG*, LXXIV, p. 319.
87. 'Communal Riots', *CWMG*, LXXIV, p. 28.
88. *Letter to KM Munshi*, *CWMG*, LXXIV, pp. 312-13.
89. *Letter to Khwaja*, *CWMG*, LXXIV, p. 6.
90. *Statement to the Press, The Hindu*, 27-4-41, *CWMG*, LXXI, p. 14.
91. 'Communal Unity', *Harijan*, 25-1-42, *CWMG*, LXXV, p. 237.
92. *Harijan*, 8-3-42, *CWMG*, LXXV.
93. *CWMG*, LXVI, Appendix-VII, p. 468.
94. *Letter to M.A. Jinnah, The Bombay Chronicle*, 16-6-38, *CWMG*, LXVI, p. 350.
95. 'Why Suspension', *Harijan*, 10-11-40, *CWMG*, LXXIII, pp. 125-6.
96. *CWMG*, LXXIII, p. 273.
97. 28-1-41, *CWMG*, LXXIII, pp. 304-6.
98. *The Times of India*, 15-2-41, *CWMG*, LXXIII, pp. 321-24.
99. *Ibid.*
100. 26-2-41, *CWMG*, LXXIII, p. 348.
101. 1-3-41, *CWMG*, LXXIII, p. 351.
102. 5-3-41, *CWMG*, LXXIII, p. 357.
103. *CWMG*, LXXIII, p. 377.
104. *CWMG*, LXXIII, p. 370.
105. 'The Only Way towards World Peace', May, 1941, *CWMG*, LXXIII, p. 407
106. 'Why?'*Harijan*,18-1-42, *CWMG*, LXXV, p. 213.
107. 'If "Harijan" is Suppressed', *Harijan*, 19-6-42, *CWMG*, LXXVI, p. 288.
108. 'Harijan" Revived', *Harijan*, 10-2-46.
109. 'The whole nation is not with me over the non-violence question', Gandhi had remarked in an interview. *Talk with an Australian Journalist, Harijan*, 3-5-42, *CWMG*, LXXV, p. 13.

110. For instance his words, 'If the vast majority of Muslims regard themselves as a separate nation having nothing in common with Hindus and others, no power on earth can compel them to think otherwise.And if they want to partition on that basis , they must have the partition, unless Hindus want to fight against such a division. ('The Illfated Division', *Harijan,*19-4-42, *CWMG,* LXXVI, p. 29,) was considered an instigation for the Hindus to fight!
111. *Letter to Horace Alexander, CWMG,* LXXVI, p. 61.
112. *Letter to Chiang Kai-shek, CWMG,* LXXVI, p. 224.
113. *Harijan,* 17-5-42, *CWMG,* LXXVI, pp. 98-100.
114. Sent a letter to F.D. Roosevelt with Louis Fischer, *CWMG,* LXXVI, pp. 264-5; made an appeal 'To All Japanese"(this was published in three Japanese newspapers, *Nichi Nichi, Yomiur ,iMiyako* wherein he warned the Japanese "If not the Allies some other power will certainly improve upon your method and beat you with your own weapon....Our appeal to Britain is coupled with the offer of free India's willingness to let the Allies retain their troops in India. The offer is made in order to prevent you from being misled into feeling that you have but to step into the country that Britain has vacated.' *Harijan,* 6-7-42 *CWMG,* LXXVI, pp. 311-12.
115. *CWMG,* LXXVI, p. 403.
116. *Notes: 'India without the British', Harijan,* 17-2-40, LXXI, p. 202.
117. *HarijanCWMG,* LXXI, p. 405.
118. 'Discussion with a friend', *Harijan,* 10-2-46, *CWMG,* LXXVII, pp. 267-68.
119. *Harijan,* 7-4-46, *CWMG,* LXXXIII, pp. 330-1.
120. *CWMG,* LXXVII, pp. 343-4 and Letter from VS Srinivas Sastri, 'You know, as only a very few do, how in simple words to get to a man's heart. It takes a big heart to do so.' Apendix-XV, *CWMG,* LXXVI, p. 469.
121. *Letter to V.S. Srinivas Sastri, CWMG,* LXXVIII, p. 56.
122. *CWMG,* LXXVIII, p. 24.
123. *Letter to K.M. Munshi, CWMG,* LXXVIII, p. 25.
124. Vol. 1 Book., pp. 184-6.
125. *Interview to the Press, CWMG,* LXXVIII, p. 137.
126. Fn.2, *CWMG,* LXXX, p. 250.
127. *Statement on Syrian Lebanese Question, The Bombay Chronicle, The Hindu,* 8-6-45, *CWMG,* LXXX, pp. 250-51.
128. *CWMG* ,LXXX, p. 441.
129. *The Bombay Chronicle,* 16-6-45, *CWMG,* LXXX, pp. 331-333.
130. *CWMG,* LXXX, p. 406.
131. *Statement to the Press, The Hindu,* 6-8-45, *CWMG,* LXXXI, p. 74.
132. *Letter to Lord Wavell, CWMG,* LXXXI, p. 35.
133. Lure for Offices, *Harijan,* 17-2-46, *CWMG,* LXXXIII, pp. 95-6;

"Preservation of Cattle", *Harijan*, 17-2-46, LXXXIII, 106-7; 'Famine of Grain and Cloth', *Harijan*, 17-2-46, *CWMG*, LXXXIII, pp. 111-2, *Statement to the Press, Harijan*, 17-2-46, *CWMG*, LXXXIII, pp. 120-1.

134. *Speech at Vijayavada, The Hindu*, 6-2-46, *CWMG*, LXXXIII, pp. 89-90.
135. *CWMG*, LXXXIII, pp. 120-1.
136. Statement to the Press which was issued on February, 26, 1946 and later published in *Harijan*, 3-3-46, *CWMG*, LXXXIII, pp. 170-1.
137. *Ibid.*
138. *Harijan*, 3-3-46, *CWMG*, LXXXIII, pp. 182-84.
139. Clement Attlee's Speech, Appendix-XI, *CWMG*, LXXXIII, pp. 432-33.
140. *Interview to H.N. Brailsford, 'Gandhiji on New Spirit', The Hindu*, 31-3-1946, *Harijan*, 14-4-46, *CWMG*, LXXXIII, pp. 276-9.
141. fn.1, *CWMG*, LXXXIII, p. 279.
142. as in Noakhali,*Hindustan Standard,The Hindu*, 9-1-47, *Amrita Bazar Patrika*, 20-1-47, *CWMG*, LXXXVI, pp. 323-4.
143. Preface, *CWMG*, XC, p. i.
144. M.K. Gandhi, *Prayer* (Navajivan Publishing House, Ahmedabad, 1977).
145. *CWMG*, XXXVIII, p. 197, LIXII, p. 411.
146. 'Sovereign Remedy', *Harijan*, 28-4-46, *CWMG*, LXXXIV, p. 24.
147. Stephen Hay, 'Gandhi: Guide to Better Human Future,' in Anthony J. Parel (ed.), *Gandhi, Freedom and Self-Rule* (Lexington Books , Oxford, 2000) pp. 161.
148. *CWMG*, LXXXIV, p. 372.
149. Speech at a Prayer Meeting; *Harijan*, 26-5-46, *CWMG*, LXXXI, p. 162.
150. 'An Analysis', *Harijan*, 26-5-46, *CWMG*, LXXXIV, p. 171.
151. 'Vital Defects', 2-6-46, *CWMG*, LXXXIV, pp. 209-11.
152. *Letter to Lord Wavell*, *CWMG*, LXXXI, p. 320.
153. *Letter to Lord Wavell*, *CWMG*, LXXXIV, pp. 328-9.
154. *Interview with Lord Wavell and the Cabinet Mission*,Wavell, *The Viceroy's Journal*, pp. 259-60, *CWMG*, LXXXIV, p. 466.
155. Question-Box, *Harijan*, 28-4-46, *CWMG*, LXXXIV, p. 47.
156. *Speech at Congress Working Committee Meeting, New Delhi, June 19, 1946*, *CWMG*, LXXXIV, p. 347.
157. *Talk with Norman Cliff*, *CWMG*, LXXXIV, pp. 387-8.
158. *Talk with Norman Cliff*, *CWMG*, LXXXIV, pp. 383-4.
159. *Hindustan*, (in Hindi), 3-9-46, *CWMG*, LXXXV, p. 243.
160. 'What can Violence Do?', *Harijan*, 25-8-46, *CWMG*, LXXXV, pp. 186-7.
161. *Transfer of Power*, p. 743.
162. 'Heal Thyself,' *Harijan*, 4-8-46, *CWMG*, LXXXV, pp. 54-55.
163. Fn. 1, *CWMG*, LXXXVI, p. 18.
164. *Harijan*, 3-11-46, *The Hindustan Times*, 26-1046, *CWMG*, LXXXVI, p. 27.
165. *Talk with a Muslim Friend, Harijan*, 10-11-46, *CWMG*, LXXXVI, p. 65.

166. *Harijan*, 24-11-46, *The Hindu*, 10-11-46, *CWMG*, LXXXVI, pp. 96-97.
167. Pyarelal, 'Overproof is Admission', *CWMG*, LXXXVI, pp. 93-95.
168. *Harijan*, 8-12-46, *CWMG*, LXXXVI, pp. 99-101.
169. *Harijan*, 1-12-46, *CWMG*, LXXXVI, pp. 124-3.
170. *Harijan*, 8-12-46, *Hindustan Standard*, 21-11-46, *CWMG*, LXXXVI, pp. 127-8.
171. *Harijan*, 8-12-46, *CWMG*, LXXXVI1, pp. 32-33.
172. *Speech at Prayer Meeting*, *The Hindu*, 21-1-46, *CWMG*, LXXXVI, pp. 149-51.
173. *Hindustan Standard*, 4-12-46, *Harijan*, 19-1-47, *CWMG*, LXXXVI, pp. 182-3.
174. *Hindustan Standard*, 12-12-46, *CWMG*, LXXXVI, p. 212.
175. *The Hindu*, *Amrita Bazar Patrika*, 17-1-47, 19-1-47, *CWMG*, LXXXVI, p. 354.
176. *Harijan*, 19-1-47, *CWMG*, LXXXVI, p. 258.
177. *CWMG*, LXXXVI, p. 262.
178. *Harijan*, 1-12-46, *CWMG*, LXXXVI, pp. 138-9.
179. 'Have been awake since 2 a.m. God's grace alone is sustaining me. I can see there is grave defect in me somewhere which the cause of all this...' Extract from Diary, *Mahatma Gandhi: the Last Phase*, Vol. I, 115, *CWMG*, LXXXVI, p. 302.
180. Gandhi was largely influence by the Jain philosophy of extreme penance. In the Jain tradition there is a story how Lord Mahavira thought that he was not non-violent enough when he observed that the birds were afraid of coming near him. By the same logic it can be assumed that Gandhi thought that his lack of control over his sexual urges might have been responsible for the rape and molestation of women in Bengal. However, this is just a conjecture. Gandhi nowhere said or wrote so.
181. Narahari, Kishore Mashruwala, Madalsa, [Jamnalal Bajaj's daughter] for instance. Sardar Patel and Nehru also disapproved of the experiment.
182. *Letter to Satis Chandra Mukerji*, *CWMG*, LXXXVI, p. 414; *Letter to Manilal Gandhi*, *CWMG*, LXXXVI, p. 415; *Letter to Vinoba Bhave*, *CWMG*, LXXXVI, F.n 2.p. 453, who replied, that he did not agree with Gandhi on the issue as any consciousness of the difference between man and women was contrary to *brahmacharya*; *Letter to G.D. Birla*, *CWMG*, LXXXVI, pp. 465-66; *Letter to Manilal B. Desai*, *CWMG*, LXXXVI, pp. 474-5; *Letter to Balkrishna Bhave*, *ibid.*, pp. 475-6.
183. Appendix-II, *CWMG*, LXXXVII, p. 532.
184. Entry in diary of December 20, 1946...Woke up Manu at 12.45 a.m. Made her understand about her dharma. Told her to have talk with Jaisukhlal [her father and Gandhi's cousin] She could still change her mind, but once having taken the plunge she would have to run the risks. She remained steadfast. *Eklo Jano Re*, 9, *CWMG*, LXXXVI, p. 248.
185. *Letter to Jaisukhlal Gandhi*, *CWMG*, LXXXVI, p. 256.
186. *Speech at a Prayer Meeting Amishapara 2-2-47*, *Hindustan Standard*, 3-2-47, *Harijan*, 23-2-47, *CWMG*, LXXXVI, p. 420.

187. *Discussion with A.V.Thakkar, Mahatma Gandhi – The Last Phase,* Vol. I., Bk.I., pp. 224-6 *CWMG,* LXXXVII, p. 16, and *Letter to Vinoba Bhave* where Gandhi refers to Bapa's wish. *CWMG,* LXXXVII, p. 63.
188. *CWMG,* LXXXVI, p. 70.
189. *Harijan,* 10-11-46, *CWMG,* LXXXVI, pp. 81-82.
190. *Gandhiji ke Dukhi Dil Ki Pukar,* pp. 26-28, Urdu, *CWMG,* LXXXVII, p. 134.
191. *Harijan,* 23-3-47, *CWMG,* LXXXVII, p. 52.
192. *Harijan,* 23-3-47, *CWMG,* LXXXVII, p. 46.
193. *Prarthana Pravachan,* Part-I, pp. 5-11, *CWMG,* LXXXVI, p. 184.
194. *Prarthana Pravachan-I,* pp. 14-19, *CWMG,* LXXXVIII, p. 98.
195. *Prarthana Pravachan-I,* pp. 103-6, *CWMG,* LXXXVIII, p. 43.
196. *Prarthana Pravachan*-1, pp. 40-2 , *CWMG,* LXXXVIII, p. 117.
197. *Talk with Rajendra Prasad, Mahatma Gandhi–The Last Phase,* Vol. II, p. 248, *CWMG,* LXXXVIII, p. 123.
198. For text of the Joint Appeal see *CWMG,* LXXXVII, p. 261, for the "condition" see Mountbatten's message to Gandhi. *CWMG,* LXXXVII, .f.n.1., p. 277.
199. *CWMG,* LXXXVIII, p. 548.
200. In the Draft Formula that Gandhi had drafted to make the Muslim League responsible by handing over power to it the instances of Leagues active and passive support to communalism were stated along with the request that the Draft would come into force only if the League desisted from such actions. *CWMG,* LXXXVII, p. 247 When Muslim atrocities on the Hindus increased in the Frontier Provinces and the hand of Muslim Leaguers was evident in the action Gandhi said in his speech at a prayer meeting , 'If the people of the Frontier Province, even as supporters of Muslim League, do not honour the words of Jinnah Saheb, I would venture to suggest that it is his paramount duty to leave everything and work to restore peace. Why is he not following that course?' *Prarathana Pravachan,* Part-I, pp. 54-8, *CWMG,* LXXXVII, p. 395 Expressing his concern over the exodus of Hindus and Sikhs from Punjab and Bengal Gandhi again enquired of Jinnah, "Jinnah Saheb has stated that the Hindu and Sikh minorities would be absolutely safe in Pakistan and that they would not be persecuted. But why are such conditions not obtaining today?" *Prarthana Pravachan,* Part-I, pp. 59-62 *CWMG,* LXXXVII, p. 400. When Abul Hashem, Secretary of Bengal Muslim League approached Gandhi with a proposal for a tripartite division of India into India, Pakistan and Sovereign Bengal, Gandhi raised questions about the role of Jinnah and the Muslim League in the riot affected areas. He said, '...if you are loyal to the party to which you belong and for which you work, you must ask Jinnah Saheb why, after signing the peace appeal with Gandhi, he is sitting in Delhi when thousands of Hindus are dying in the Punjab, and the Frontier Province

and Noakhali and thousand s or women are being raped.' *My Days with Gandhi,* pp. 227-8, *Biharni Komi Agman,* pp. 327-8, *CWMG,* LXXXVII, p. 444, Again in an interview with Suhrawardy Gandhi reiterated that Jinnah does not do what he says. *Biharni Komi Agman,* pp. 341-3, *Mahatma Gandhi – The Last Phase,* Vol. II, pp. 182-3, *My Days with Gandhi,* p. 232 *CWMG,* LXXXVII, p. 458.

201. *Interview with Lord Mountbatten, CWMG,* LXXXVII, p. 550.
202. *Prarthana Pravachan*-I, pp. 263-6, *CWMG,* LXXXVIII, pp. 381-2.
203. *Bihar Pachhi Dilhi,* pp. 50-2, *CWMG,* LXXXVIII, pp. 51-2.
204. *CWMG,* LXXXVIII, p. 63.
205. *CWMG,* LXXXVIII, p. 64.
206. *Speech at Prayer Meeting, Prarthana Pravachan*-I, pp. 120-4, *CWMG,* LXXXVIII, pp. 73-75, *ibid.,* pp. 124-30, LXXXVIII, pp. 84-5, AICC ENDORSEMENT, *ibid.,* pp. 34-7, LXXXVIII, pp. 97-98., *Bihar Pachhi Dilhi,* pp. 142-46, *CWMG,* LXXXVIII, pp. 153-7.
207. *Prarthana Pravachan*-I, pp. 140-2, LXXXVIII, p. 118.
208. *Prarthana Pravachan*-I, 224-6, *CWMG* LXXXVIII, 287; *ibid.,* pp. 227-8, *CWMG* LXXXVIII, pp. 297, 341.
209. *Prarthana Pravachan*–I, pp. 163, *CWMG, LXXXVIII,* p. 204.
210. *CWMG,* LXXXVIII, p. 380.
211. *Letter to Hariprasad Desai, The Hindustan Times,* 28-7-47, *CWMG,* LXXXVIII, p. 418.
212. *CWMG,* LXXXIX, p. 86.
213. *CWMG,* LXXXIX, pp. 84, 186.
214. *CWMG,* LXXXIX, p. 197.
215. *CWMG,* LXXXIX, p. 344.
216. *CWMG,* LXXXIX, p. 409.
217. Preface, xvii, XC.

The Epilogue

The preceding discussion amply proves that Gandhi was a great communicator. He evolved a form of communication which today is known as 'non-violent communication'[1] communication where the both the parties are in a 'win-win' situation, where dialogue is of prime importance and no attempt is made to evaluate or berate the other.

Interestingly Gandhi had as his contemporaries two great communicators though of an entirely different order. One was Hitler whose speeches were responsible for deaths of over six million innocent Jews throughout the world. He identified an imagined enemy and rallied Germans around to fight this enemy. Another competitor of Gandhi was closer home. Jinnah appears to have been more successful than Gandhi in achieving his objective of creating a separate state of Pakistan. His 'hymn of hate' created havoc in the Indian subcontinent and seemed to have defeated the forces of sanity and nonviolence that Gandhi had so carefully cultivated. But in retrospect we know who ultimately succeeded. The Germans are as a nation ashamed of Hitler's legacy. Once using the communal card for achieving Pakistan Jinnah could not go back to his real secular self. At the most he remained a pseudo-communalist bequeathing to his country a schizophrenic identity—with the establishment remaining committed to religious identity out of both compulsion and expediency, whereas the middleclass has liberal and secular character.

Gandhi a devout Hindu, committed to creating an ethical polity, was basically against a theocratic state and wanted like his successor, Nehru, to separate organized religion from governance. Gandhi wore himself out trying to protect the secular and syncretic religious culture of India. He came out with pamphlets on Hindu-Muslim question. Especially during the period after the suspension of the Non-Co-operation Movement in 1922 Gandhi wrote several articles aimed at defusing the atmosphere of hatred created by communal minded papers and leaders. He gave sane answers to Muslim accusations of religious partiality. He brought out the facts about leaders who were suspected of spreading anti-Muslim sentiments among Hindus. He answered the criticism by Hindus and Arya Samajists that he had a soft-corner for Muslims. He implored the leaders of both communities not to disturb the harmony of the country by encouraging false rumours or writings. He pointed out the dangerous implications of the movements like the Arya Samaji's *Shuddhi*, the Muslims' *Tabligh* and, in 1930, had long discussions with both the lower caste Hindus and Christian community on the issue of conversions. Today if India boasts of its secular credentials, it is largely due to the tireless efforts of Gandhi and the leadership he groomed to take his place when he was gone.

Gandhi was incapable of penning anything except what he believed to be the truth, and possessed a fine sense of discretion and jurisprudence combined with remarkable lucidity of expression that was easily comprehensible to even the simple and ordinary folks. The wonderful harmony of thought, word and deed was responsible for Gandhi's words to carry conviction with the masses. JH Broomfield, an American academic, has described Gandhi as a great 'scribbler.'[2] Whatever came to his mind, he put on paper. That is why there was never much of a difference in the content of what he wrote and what he spoke. That is not to say that what he wrote was of inferior quality but to emphasize that, for Gandhi, who continuously practised self-control like a yogi, to get the right expression was never a problem. Being conscious of the value of time there were rarely any 'retakes', though he always revised what he wrote. It is said of Gandhi that he liberated his writings from the tradition of the word. He wrote what he spoke and he spoke only what he was convinced about.

He used the media with a well-planned strategy and with a definite sense of purpose in mind. A crusade, one might say, forms the undercurrent of the motivation that flows through his writings.

In truth, if one dare use a phrase generally denounced in today's media world, Gandhi was, in the best and noblest sense of the term, a 'committed journalist' — committed to freeing Indians of all creeds not only from the British Raj but also from their own shortcomings and weaknesses.

In answer to the question as to what initially impelled Gandhi to take to writing and were the reasons for his taking to writing different from those of the leading journalists of the times, one may say that Gandhi very soon realized that he could not physically approach all the people he intended to influence therefore he made use of print media. As mentioned in the introduction, Gandhi's life and writings had a symbiotic relationship. Through his writings he endeavoured to take his readers in a joint journey on the path to truth. He did not write just to share his thoughts. He aimed at bringing about a radical change in the lives of the people and through them, the life of the nation, and finally, the world. No doubt, at first glance it seems to be an over-ambitious plan. But the pragmatic idealist in Gandhi was quite content to just make a beginning in the direction and was optimistic that he would at least achieve partial success.

In the period in which Gandhi wrote, many leaders of the freedom movement were also journalists who used the media for the nationalist cause, according to their own light. Dadabhai Naoroji had his journal *India,* Bal Gangadhar Tilak edited *Kesari* in Marathi and *Marhatta* in English, Surendranath Bannerjee edited *The Bengalee,* Shyamji Krishnavarma published his journal, *The Indian Sociologist* from abroad, Pt. Jawaharlal Nehru was associated with *The National Herald* and so on. Thus almost all strands of freedom movement were fairly represented. Moderate views were represented through Dadabhai Naoroji and Surendranath Bannerjee. Shades of militant nationalism found expression in the writings of Tilak on the one hand and Krishavarma and Savarkar on the other. Nehru represented the new socialist thinking.

Gandhi's writings, as has been made all too clear, were a genre apart. His writings were different both in style and content from those of the other leader-journalists. Their style was usually grand and aimed at impressing the educated class of Indians (With a few exceptions, most of them wrote in English whereas Gandhi wrote in Gujarati and Hindustani as well). In contrast Gandhi's language was spare, devoid of embellishments, yet clear, straightforward and therefore, easily understandable. The content of their writings was also limited to arousing the people against the injustices they were suffering under the British rule. Only Dadabhai Naoroji, out of these, brought to light the economic condition in depth and held the British responsible for India's misery. Gandhi wrote on everything under the sun that had relevance for human beings. He dealt with contemporary political developments and laws. His writings were a crusade against the social injustice of untouchability, caste system, status of women, especially of the plight of widows. He wrote copiously on the role of religion, importance of using one's mother-tongue and the use of Hindustani as the *lingua franca* of Indians. He focussed on poverty and unemployment with practical suggestions on how to remove them. Health and hygiene also occupied an important place in his writings. He also touched upon spiritual development. The wide range of topics shows that Gandhi was aiming at not only the freedom of the country but also the building of the nation. This further differentiates him from the other leader-writers.

Gandhi's insistence on putting the minutest detail in black and white and his belief in publicity of a cause he championed shows how important print-media was to him. The hundred volumes containing his writings which include letters, notes, drafts of constitutions of organizations, speeches, articles and books is impressive in itself. But a careful study of these, however, leads one to the conclusion that the motivating factor behind all these writings was the quest for *swaraj,* the word in which Gandhi saw a multi-layered meaning. *Swaraj* meant for him freedom through self control at all levels of human existence. At national level it stood for freedom from foreign rule. In domestic politics it stood for democratic polity which was tolerant to different points of view and served the interests of the poorest of the poor. At economic level it meant sustainable development with sufficient and decent food, clothing and shelter for all. At social level it stood for equality for all members of the great human species. *Swaraj* had spiritual connotation as well. In this sense, it stood for self-control for the sake of achieving *moksha,* that is, liberation from the cycle of birth and death. It is amazing to find that Gandhi's writing revolved around the levels of the multi-layered meaning of *swaraj* alone! In South Africa, for instance, Gandhi sought to teach the lessons of self-respect and self-assertion through his writings. In India he inculcated in the people freedom from fear and mobilized them for fighting for the freedom of their motherland. In all his struggles, self-control was the underlying condition. Therefore, ultimately the goal of Gandhi's communication strategy was the spread of the concept, the message of and thereby the achievement of *swaraj*.

Largely addressed to the common man, Gandhi's simple style of writing was well-suited for the phase of the freedom movement which, by 1920 was moving towards becoming mass-based, thanks to the efforts of Bal Gangadhar Tilak. Thus one reason for the popularity of Gandhi's writings was that they answered the needs of the time. It was no accident that at one point of time, *Navajivan* (published in Gujarati) had a sale of 40,000 copies and *Young India* (English) , behind it, had the envious distinction of having a sale that equalled the sale of all the English language papers in India, put together. This was remarkable, especially since Gandhi never took recourse to sensationalism to push his sales. He consistently refused advertisements to make the journals financially viable. The journals paid for their existence through the quality of their contents. One could call it a step towards journalistic *swaraj*!

The concept of 'viewspapers' that is, using journals for the propagation of ideas was the original Gandhian idea. Here too he differed from the exclusive, one-sided propaganda press of the communists or communalists. All shades of opinion found their representation in his journals with Gandhi making an effort to discover common points of agreement. His journals were basically organs of political and social movements and discussed, with intensity and concentration, the problems that demanded immediate action. The journals also made an attempt to arrive at consensus on issues of national importance by initiating dialogue among different shades of opinion. His 'viewspapers' were assimilative-they were for the people, by the people.

Gandhi put his writing to a variety of uses – publicizing a cause; educating the people; expressing his personal viewpoint; bringing about social, political and economic changes; and, also at times as an act of defiance.

His writings served to publicize a variety of causes. In South Africa, as discussed earlier, the purpose of Gandhi's writings was to highlight the inequalities suffered by Indians so that they become aware of their rights and fight for them. In India the causes were political, social, economic and moral. Politically it was freedom from British rule and the establishment of democratic institutions and traditions. Socially it was a drive for removing man-made discriminatory rules based on caste, gender or religion. Economically, it was the cause of self-sufficiency through proper use of local resources and skills. Morally, it was the removal of untruth, corruption, lethargy and feeling of worthlessness.

In an age when pamphlet writing was uncommon, Gandhi not only wrote a number of pamphlets and circulars but created a record of sorts. The *Green Pamphlet* dealing with the plight of Indians in South Africa, had sold 10,000 copies when it was first published and still more was in demand. This was something unheard of then. His letters and interviews to important dailies in India and abroad, justified his belief that 'publicity is our only defence'. Publicity for his cause was one of the main reasons for this writings. Gandhi knew the significance of the written world in inspiring and conspiring. Therefore, he put his writings to use for educating public in the principles of democratic thinking, tolerance, moral values and highlighting their shortcomings so that they reform themselves. His journals were open fora for discussing all kinds of issues validated and enlivened by giving full coverage to criticisms and even accusations. A lawyer by profession, Gandhi wrote in simple lucid style on legal issues of concern for the understanding and education of the common man.

Gandhi put his journals to use for conducting satyagraha. They carried the programmes for the people to follow during the campaign. *Indian Opinion* was his weapon during the satyagraha in South Africa. Gandhi, the leader, talked to his 'soldiers' through the journal. The directions were issued through the journal. The advance made in negotiations with the officials was made public through the journal. The morale of the 'army' was sought to be raised by recounting heroic sacrifices of the past and present. Similarly, the *Satyagraha,* the unregistered paper of 1919 was published with the express purpose of defying the Rowlatt Bills and, through this act, British Government in India. The *Young India* and *Navajivan* were responsible for carrying out the Non-Co-operation Movement in accordance with the directions and wishes of Gandhi. *Harijan, Harijan*

Bandhu and *Harijan Sewak* initially served the cause of the backward section of people in India but later became powerful instruments of the Quit India Movement and were actively involved in the discussions for the future of India.

Writing was used as a tool for bringing about fundamental social, economic and political changes. Among the social issues of the time the one to occupy the greatest attention of Gandhi was the issue of untouchability. *Harijan* started in 1932 mainly devoted to the cause of removal of untouchability. His *Statements on Untouchability* issued from Yervada jail touched upon most of the issues related to the problem. His epic fast against separate electorate and then the publicizing of the fast, were all strategies aimed at removing the curse of untouchability from India. Perhaps no reformer has been such a relentless crusader against untouchability as Gandhi was. So powerful was the impact of his efforts in this direction that in 1930s it seemed that untouchability was on its last legs.

Gandhi devoted a large part of his writings to the question of women in India. At one level Gandhi appeared to be influenced by his patriarchal upbringing rooted in the firm belief about the traditional role assigned to women as per his understanding of the ancient Indian scriptures. At another level Gandhi emerged as a social reformer concerned about the backwardness of women in India and their status abroad. In this *avatar* he championed the rights of women as an equal partner of men. At still another level Gandhi saw women as a potential resource for the success of his movements, both political and social, and advocated their increased participation. Here too Gandhi's faith in women's power is born out of a deep spiritual understanding where he has the ideals of Sita or Savitri in mind. There are times when all the three levels merged, making his views on women an enigma.

The views of Gandhi on the women's question that irked the feminists especially are with regard to the duties he assigned to women in social life. Gandhi could not appreciate the fact of women working in factories to supplement the family income. He favoured their role as home-makers taking care of family and children.[3] He wanted them to be educated but was against imparting English education to them. He believed that English education was of no use to them because it had no application in their day to day life.[4] He had no problems with regard to co-education but believed that once the gender relations are sorted out in the Indian family, co-education will follow as a natural consequence.[5] On purely spiritual and moral grounds he was against artificial means of birth control and especially against the use of contraceptives or abortions for the purpose. He preferred sexual continence to artificial methods of birth control. On being told that this was not possible in the situation in which women are placed in India he refused to believe that women are that powerless as not to have a say in the matter.[6] The same moral high ground was reflected in his advice to women who were molested during communal riots. He asked them to either kill the culprit or kill themselves.[7]

Psychologists have tried to unravel the source of Gandhi's seemingly patriarchal views. Erik Erikson has linked this to his marital experiences and the feelings of guilt about his natural sensual needs.[8] In the last phase of his life Gandhi conducted the highly controversial 'body experiments' in order to purify his mind of sensual desires. Though at personal level he was satisfied about his spiritual evolution such experiments were not appreciated by his colleagues and friends and at the insistence of Thakkar Bapa, a revered old friend, he dropped them. The deep influence of the Jain tradition which refers to the importance of the purity of the seeker of truth in order to attract similar vibrations around him perhaps motivated Gandhi to conduct such experiments. Gandhi had been deeply hurt by news of molestation of women during communal riots and had concluded that perhaps the impurity of his mind, the leader's mind, was responsible for such happenings.

As a social reformer, Gandhi included the work for uplift of women in his Constructive Programme. He repeatedly made it clear that women were in no way inferior to men and this canard has been spread through ancient writings whose authors were men.[9] In fact Gandhi went a step further and said that in terms of capacity to suffer and belief in nonviolence women were far superior to men.[10] He advocated education to empower them.[11] He asked them to be economically self-sufficient in order to maintain their dignity. He advised them to participate in social life and contribute to moral and spiritual growth of the community. He was against the *purdah* system that cut off women from social life.[12] He was also against dowry system and exhorted the youth not to ask for dowry in their marriages. In very strong words he said, 'Any young man who makes dowry a condition of marriage discredits his education and his country and dishonours womanhood.'[13] He advocated remarriage for child widows but was not very forthcoming on the marriage of widows who had enjoyed a long married life.[14] He believed in equal rights of both men and women. He also wanted women to be represented in proportion to their population in the legislatures and panchayats and had said that he would not like to be a member of a legislature where women were not represented.[15] It was no coincidence that Sarojini Naidu succeeded Gandhi as the President of the Congress Party and the Constituent Assembly that drafted the Constitution of India had sizeable number of woman who spoke on women issues.

As an astute strategist, Gandhi soon realized the potential of woman in contributing to the success of his movements. He tried this in South Africa where the government by a piece of legislation had declared all Indian marriages solemnized outside courts as illegal. Gandhi explained the implications of such a ruling to women and they spontaneously came out in large numbers demonstrating against the evil law. In India, initially Gandhi confined the role of women to picketing and similar non-aggressive activities during the Non-Cooperation Movement. Out of a sense of dignity, he believed that the English would not like to use force against women and he did not want to misuse this sensitivity for his personal gain. Later, however, during the Civil Disobedience Movement he encouraged women to take over leadership roles. The role of Sarojini Naidu in the Dharasana Salt Depot raid during the Salt Satyagraha was reported the world over. Gandhi made it a point to report the non-violent exploits of the women leaders in the columns of his newspapers, eulogizing them in glowing terms. Women were at the forefront even in dousing communal fires. Amtulassalam accompanied Gandhi in the worst communal affected areas in Noakhali and went on fast for communal harmony.

One can say that Gandhi's views on women's question apparently appear very complex but if one goes deep into the origins of such beliefs one finds that they are born out of deep concern, respect and empathy for them. The most enlightened and forward looking women of the period, both Indian and foreign, were Gandhi's friends and confidantes. This would not have been possible had Gandhi been a close-minded man with patriarchal mind-set. Well known Gandhian scholar Mark Lindley, in the course of one of the discussions with the author pointed out an interesting facet of Gandhi's views on women. According to him Gandhi had different standards for the uneducated and the educated women of India which is clearly reflected in his interactions with them. For the uneducated the social reformist facet of Gandhi was in evidence. He empathized with their situation while admiring their capacity to suffer. Educated women were treated by Gandhi as his equals with whom he held frequent consultations and on whom he could rely fully.

Gandhi's economic ideas have a strong ring of authenticity today, especially with reference to the developing countries like India. Gandhi believed that the rich ought to put aside some part of their wealth for the society has found strong reverberation in the modern concept of Corporate Social Responsibility. The argument that Gandhi gave in his unconventional idea of 'trusteeship' was that the rich were rich not only due to their own effort. The workers and the society at large also had a great role to play in their richness. Hence the rich owed to the society some part of their wealth. Gandhi's rejection of machinery is now examined with reference to the intention behind such rejection. Appropriate technology was what Gandhi demanded and not blind following of the development pattern of the West. Schumacher, the famous economist, acknowledged the foresight of Gandhi as early as in the 1960's when he wrote his famous work with the telling title *Small is Beautiful.* Rather than considering Gandhi's economic ideas as old-fashioned and impractical scholars have praised him for this 'alternative modernity'[16] Also in the twelve cases cited by Rajni Bakshi in her book *Bapu Kuti* it becomes evident how Gandhi's ideas of village self-sufficiency and the use of local resources for development are today being recognized and put into practice by a number of devoted social workers.[17]

Gandhi was very particular about hygiene. He prided in calling himself a 'scavenger', yet he was pained to see a section of people in India bound to this work by the order of the society. Gandhi's reform in this direction has been carried to a fruitful conclusion by the Sulabh International Movement whose founder Dr. Pathak has brought about innovations in the disposal of night soil and freed such unfortunate people from the drudgery.

Gandhi emphasized the practice of morality in politics. High ethical standards were expected of the practitioners. Transparency, democratic and just conduct were also to be the hallmark of his concept of politics. For Gandhi politics was not for gaining power but for serving the people. On the eve of independence he advised the Congress party to disband and convert itself into Lok Seva Dal. These extreme views were influenced by Gandhi's experience of rule by Indians in British India after 1937. He found some of these governments suffering from the same malaise that afflicted their British predecessors and therefore was wary of power. Gandhi laid emphasis on high degree of probity in public life. Gandhi's influence was evident in our leaders who led the country after independence. Gradually the canker of corruption set in. Now India has the dubious distinction of being the fifth most corrupt country in the world, and the general perception of the rulers being a corrupt lot, *yatha raja, thatha praja* ('as is the ruler so are the subject')appears to be a truism for India. With development held hostage to corruption, the public is getting aware of its rights and the deep connection between morality and politics is being recognized. A respected politician and former Governor of Jammu and Kashmir, Jagmohan reiterated the stand of Gandhi when he wrote: 'By not following Gandhi's interpretation of religion and by despiritualising politics, the present day world is merely adding to its sickness and reinforcing its hidden inhumanities Unfortunately, it is ignoring Gandhi's warning that 'politics bereft of principles are death-traps; they kill the soul of a nation.'[18]

Gandhi also revolutionized the medium. Gandhi was a journalist of the first order. His impact on journalism was so far-reaching that his advent in journalism was hailed as 'not merely an event but a phenomenon'[19] He set down standards of journalism which are still looked upon with great respect. The restraint, the quest for truth, the duty to educate – were the hallmarks of his style. Media took on an entirely new meaning under his wings. It became a weapon in the fight against all forms of injustice. It became a teacher, a guide, a philosopher, a harbinger of new dawn, a channel between the leader and the lead, a forum for discussion on issues of public importance, a mirror of the times – all rolled in one. Realizing its immense potential Gandhi advised utmost restraint. Gandhi set the tone for responsible journalism in India. Rajkumari Amrit Kaur, a close friend and confidante of Gandhi rightly conferred on him the title of 'prince of journalists.'[20] What is more important is the type of journalism Gandhi pursued. He used simple language to communicate his thoughts, did not resort to sensationalism, verified facts before publishing a report and did not accept advertisements for the fear that these could affect the impartiality of his newspapers. He also started the practice of reporting on social issues. Gandhi was very particular about the duties of a journalist which are quoted as the model code even by journalists today. According to him 'one of the objects of a newspaper is to understand the popular feeling and give expression to it; another is to arouse in the people certain desirable sentiments, and the third is fearlessly to expose popular defects.' Referring to this statement in his Durga Das Memorial lecture the former President of India, Dr. K.R. Narayanan had said, 'There are more modern statements of Western journalists that I could quote, but I know of no statement that has spelt out so clearly and succinctly the role and duties of a journalist as this one.'[21]

What was Gandhi's unique contribution to and impact on human history? It has been said that he left behind not Gandhian civilization, but the rich legacy of 'civilizational Gandhi' which has unwittingly found root and is striving to grow all over the world. 'These strivings do not bear Gandhi's name. And perhaps this, for Bapu, would have been the best of all tributes, notes Rajni Bakshi while discussing some of these 'strivings'.[22] Many movements and individual efforts have been inspired by Gandhi's example of selfless service to humanity through non-violent methods.

Early in his life Gandhi was distrustful of the State as the state he encountered was the oppressive British State. Gandhi wrote, 'The individual has a soul but the State is a soulless machine, it can never be weaned from violence to which it owes its very existence.' In his conception of a nonviolent society, the state did not exist. A non-violent state was a contradiction in terms. If non-violence was to be the governing principle of society, one could not call it a state—it could be only called a non-violent stateless society. Such a society was the Gandhian concept of an ideal state. In such a society people would grow accustomed spontaneously to observe their social obligations without the operation of the State.

While in the ideal society of Gandhi there is no room for the military and the police, yet in the actual state there is a provision for it according to the moral level of its citizens. That is to say, a predominantly non-violent state is a practical possibility and is the second best ideal of Gandhi. Gandhi's actual state does concede the desirability of using the military and police to deal with anti-social elements and defend the country. This concession, however, does not mean that he admitted to the weakness of the doctrine of non-violence or satyagraha. He firmly believed that the fault or weakness lies in the people who practise it. As the people evolve morally so will the institutions evolve or be replaced by better institutions. As distinct from the Marxian concept the Gandhian State does not 'wither away' but evolves into a moral state and its institutions evolve accordingly. Unlike the anarchists the state does not move towards statelessness but towards an ethical and moral order. Unlike the liberals the state does not take up the responsibility of its citizens but helps them to be self-reliant. Only in such a state can people be truly free.

Gandhi did not live to realize his dream of an ideal or predominantly non-violent state but he managed to concretize a Gandhian vision of State in which human beings and not institutions are the ultimate consideration. The following are some of its features:

1. Political decentralization in the form of direct participatory democracy operating in a tier structure from base village level tier upward through the district and state and then the national, and ultimately, international level
2. Economic decentralization with distribution of wealth with villages as basic economic units
3. Minimization of competition and exploitation in the economic sphere. The idea of Trusteeship whereby the rich would act as trustees of their properties rather than their owners (reflected in modern times in the concept of Corporate Social Responsibility)
4. Production and consumption on the basis of need rather than greed. All must have the basic necessities of life before some have more than what is required
5. Recognition of dignity of labour and greater purity of village life, that is, living a life close to and in harmony with nature.
6. Emphasis on individual, village and national self reliance (Swadeshi)
7. Absence of oppression on the basis of race, caste, class, language, gender or religion

8. A deep respect for nature, necessitating an economic system based on preservation rather than destruction of the natural environment (sustainable development).

Gandhi seldom used the word 'State' for India. Neither did he use the word 'nation'. He used the terms 'swaraj', 'swadeshi', 'Indian civilization' or 'sarvodaya' singularly or collectively to describe what we now know as his concept of state.

It is clear from Gandhi's description of state that he sought to widen the jurisdiction of civil society and proportionately limit the jurisdiction of the state. He had serious misgivings about the symbols of state power—the police, the army and the bureaucracy. His emphasis on self-control was motivated by the idea of lessening the need of police in the civil sphere. In his life time Gandhi was successful to a great extent in developing a civil society in India which would help realize his ideal state or 'Ram Rajya'. Even today this civil society is active in protesting and organizing movements against the highhandedness of the state. In the field of environment, protection of civil liberties, personal freedoms, rights of women, children, dalits, the handicapped, the elderly, inhuman treatment of animals—it is the civil society that has taken up cudgels against the symbols of state power. The noted human rights activist of Pakistan, Asma Jehangir has praised the Indian civil society for its role in limiting state power.

As early as in 1918 Prof. Gilbert Murray (1866-1957), the Australia born, British scholar, writer, translator, and dramatist, was prescient enough to recognize Gandhi's 'soul power' when recounting Gandhi's movement against the South African Government he wrote:

> Persons in power should be very careful how they deal with a man who cares nothing for sensual pleasure, nothing for riches, nothing for comfort or praise or promotion, but is simply determined to do what he believes to be right. He is a dangerous enemy—because his body you can always conquer, gives so little purchase on his soul.[23]

Gandhi's emphasis on 'soul force' is being recognized more acutely in the present increasingly materialistic world. There was a time when persons with higher Intelligence Quotient (IQ) were considered superior. Over a period of time it came to be realized that what matters is Emotional Quotient (EQ) of an individual i.e., his capacity to handle inter-personal relations. Then this infant century found itself dissatisfied with just IQs and EQs . It wanted something more. It looked for and found SQ—Spiritual Quotient—without which one felt a gnawing 'emptiness in the pit of the stomach' This, in essence, is Gandhi all over again. If there is one unbreakable thread running through all of Gandhi's beliefs and teachings, it is this aspect of the human personality: that the spirit (or soul) is the pivot, the still centre, and the essence of all human life. It would appear that Gandhi's beliefs will continue to figure prominently in all such discourses for a long time to come.

REFERENCES

1. Marshall B. Rosenberg, *Nonviolent Communication. A Language of Compassion,* Puddle Dancer Press, CA, USA, 2002.
2. JH Broomfield, 'Gandhi: A Twentieth Century Anomaly', in Richard L. Park (ed), *Change and Persistence of Tradition in India: Five Lecture* (Michigan Papers on South and South East Asia, No. 2, Michigan, USA, 1971) p. 55.
3. MK Gandhi, *Hind Swaraj or Indian Home Rule,* p. 33.
4. *Harijan,* 27-2-37, in RK Prabu's compilation, *India of My Dreams,* p. 232.
5. *Harijan,* 9-11-47 in ibid., p. 233.
6. 'Interview of Margaret Sanger', *Harijan,* 21-1-36, *CWMG,* LXII, pp. 156-60.
7. 'Woman's Honour', *Harijan,* 14-1-40, in RK Prabu's compilation, *India of My Dreams,* p. 230.
8. Erikson Erik H.: *Gandhi's Truth: On the Origins of Militant Nonviolence,* (Faber and Faber Limited, London, 1970.) p. 97.
9. RK Prabhu, *op.cit.,* p. 227.
10. Talking to women workers late in April 1947, nine months before his assassination, Gandhiji was confident that 'India can proclaim that she can defend herself and make progress not through the atom bomb but through non-violence alone' and that 'women alone can take the lead in this, for God had endowed them with great power. If women resolve to bring glory to the nation, within a few months they can totally change the face of the country because of the spiritual background of the Indian women.' *CWMG,* Vol. 87, pp. 250 & 294.
11. RK Prabhu *op. cit.,* 232-233.
12. *Ibid.,* p. 227.
13. *Ibid.*
14. *Ibid.,* p. 226.
15. Statement made at Round Table Conference in 1931.
16. David Hardiman, *Gandhi in his times and ours,* Permanent Black, 2003, p. 87.

17. Rajni Bakshi, *Bapu Kuti: Journeys in the Rediscovery of Gandhi*, (Penguin Books, New Delhi, 1998).
18. Jagmohan, "Gandhi and the Removal of Spiritual Illiteracy", *The Hindustan Times*, 3.10.97.
19. RCS Sarkar, *The Press in India*, 1984, p. 28.
20. *Harijan*, 11.4.48.
21. KR Narayanan, "A Distorting Magnifying Mirror", *The Hindustan Times*, April 28, 1997.
22. Rajni Bakshi, *op. cit.*, p. 21.
23. Gilbert Murray, 'Soul as it is and How to Deal with it', The *Hibbert Journal*, XVI, January 2, 1918, p. 199, quoted in James D. Hunt, *Gandhi in London*, Promilla and Co., New Delhi, 1978, p. 191.

Appendix–I

Gandhi's Trial Speech (1922)

"My public life began in 1893 in South Africa in troubled weather. My first contact with British authority in that country was not of a happy character. I discovered that as a man and as an Indian I had no rights. More correctly, I discovered that I had no right as a man because I was an Indian.

"But I was baffled. I thought that this treatment of Indians was an excrescence upon a system that was intrinsically an mainly good. I gave the government my voluntary and hearty co-operation, criticizing it freely where I felt it was faulty but never wishing its destruction.

"Consequently when the existence of the Empire was threatened in 1899 by the Boer challenge, I offered my services to it, raised a voluntary ambulance corps and served at several actions that took place for the relief of Ladysmith. Similarly in 1906, at the time of the Zulu revolt, I raised a stretcher-bearer party till the end of the 'rebellion.' For my work in South Africa I was given by Lord Hardinge the Kaiser-i-Hind Gold Medal. When the war broke out in 1914 between England and Germany, I raised volunteer ambulance corps in London consisting of the then resident Indians in London, chiefly students. Lastly in India when a special appeal was made at the War Conference in Delhi in 1918 by Lord Chelmsford for recruits, I struggled at the cost of my health to raise a corps in Kheda. In all these efforts I was actuated by the belief that it was possible by such services to gain a status of full equality in the Empire for my countrymen.

"The first shock came in the shape of the Rowlatt Act, a law designed to rob the people of all real freedom. I felt called upon to lead an intensive agitation against it. Then followed the Punjab horrors beginning with the massacre at Jallianwalla Bagh and culminating in the crawling orders, public flogging and other indescribable humiliations.... But in spite of the forebodings and grave warnings of friends at the Amritsar Congress in 1919 I fought for co-operation and working the Montagu-Chelmsford reforms, hoping that the reforms, inadequate and unsatisfactory though they were, marked a new era of hope in the life of India.

"But all that hope was shattered.... The Punjab crime was white-washed and most culprits went not only unpunished but remained in the service, and in some cases continued to draw pensions from the Indian revenue, and in some cases were even rewarded. I saw too that not only did the reforms not mark a change of heart, but were only a method of further draining India of her wealth and of prolonging her servitude.

I came reluctantly to the conclusion that the British connection had made India more helpless than she was before, politically and economically. India has become so poor that she had little power of even resisting famines. Before the British advent, India spun and wove in her millions of cottages just the supplement she needed for adding to her meager agricultural resources. This cottage industry, so vital to India's existence, has been ruined by incredibly heartless and inhuman processes, as described by English witnesses. Little do town-dwellers know how the semi-starved masses of India are slowly sinking to lifelessness. Little do they know that their miserable comfort represent the brokerage they get for the work they do for the foreign exploiter, that the profits and the brokerage are sucked from the masses. Little do they realize that the government established by law in British India is carried on for the exploitation of masses. No sophistry, no jugglery in figures, can explain away the evidence that the skeletons in many villages present to the naked eye.

"The law itself in this country has been used to serve the foreign exploiter. My unbiased examination of the Punjab Martial Law cases has led me to believe that at least ninety-five per cent of convictions were wholly bad. My experience of political cases in India leads me to the conclusion that in nine out of every ten the condemned men were totally innocent. Their crime consisted in the love of their country. In ninety-nine cases out of a hundred justice had been denied to Indians as against Europeans in the courts of India. This is not an exaggerated picture. It is the experience of almost every Indian who has had anything to do with such cases. In my own opinion, the administration of law is thus prostituted consciously or unconsciously for the benefit of the exploiter.

"The greatest misfortune is that Englishmen and their Indian associates in administration of the country do not know that they are engaged in the crime I have attempted to describe.... They do not know that a subtle but effective system of terrorism and an organized display of force on the one hand, and the deprivation of all powers of retaliation or self-defense on the other, have emasculated the people and induced in them the habit of simulation....

"Section 124–A, under which I am happily charged, is perhaps the prince among the political sections of the Indian Penal Code designed to suppress the liberty of the citizen. Affection cannot be manufactured or regulated by law. If one has no affection for a person or a system, one should be free to give the fullest expression to his disaffection, so long as he does not contemplate, promote, or incite violence. But the section under which I am charged is one under which mere promotion of disaffection is a crime. I have studied some of the cases under it, and I know that some of the most loved of India's patriots have been convicted under it. I consider it a privilege, therefore, to be charged under that section...."

Source: CWMG, XXII, p. 280.

Appendix–II

"Declaration of Independence"

"We believe that it is the inalienable right of the Indian people, as of any other people, to have freedom and to enjoy the fruits of their toil and have the necessities of life so that they may have full opportunites of growth. We believe also that if any government deprives a people of these rights and oppresses them, the people have a further right to alter or to abolish it. The British Government in India has not only deprived the Indian people of their freedom, but has based itsefl on the exploitation of the masses, and has ruined India economically, politically culturally and spiritually. We believe therefore that India must sever the British connection and attain *purna* swaraj or complete independence.

India has been ruined economically. The revenue derived from our people is out of all proportion to our income. Our average income is 7 pice (less than two pence) per day, and of the heavy taxes we pay, twenty per cent are raised from the land revenue derived from the peasantry and 3 per cent from the salt tax, which falls most heavily on the poor.

Village industries, such as hand-spinning, have been destroyed, leaving the peasantry idle for at least four months in a year, and dulling their intellect for want of handicrafts, and nothing has been substituted, as in other countries, for crafts thus destroyed.

Customs and currency have been so manipulated as to heap further burdens on the peasantry. The British manufactured goods constitute the bulk of our imports. Customs duties betray clear partiality for British manufactures, and revenue from them is used not to lessen the burden on the masses but for sustaining a highly extravagant administration. Still more arbitrary has been the manipulation of the exchange ratio which has resulted in millions being drained away from the country.

Politically, India's status has never been so reduced as under the British regime. No reforms have given real political power to the people. The tallest of us have to bend before foreign authority. The rights of free expression of a opinion and free association have been denied to us, and many of our countrymen are compelled to live in exile abroad and cannot return to their homes. All administrative talent is killed, and masses have to be satisfied with petty village office and clerkships.

Culturally, the system of education has torn us from our moorings and out training has made us hug the very chains that bind us.

Spiritually, compulsory disarmament has made us unmanly, and the presence of an alien army of occupation, employed with deadly effect to crush in us the spirit of resistance, has made us think that we cannot look after ourselves or put up a defence against foreign aggression, or even defend our homes and families from the attacks of thieves, robbers and miscreants.

We hold it to be a crime against man and God to submit any longer to a rule that has caused this fourfold disaster to our country. We recognize, however, that the most effective way of gaining our freedom is not through violence. We will therefore prepare ourselves, by withdrawing, so far as we can, all voluntary association from the British Government, and will prepare for civil disobedience, including non-payment of taxes. We are convinced that if we can withdraw our voluntary help and stop payment of taxes without doing violence, even under provocation, the end of this inhuman rule in assured. We therefore hereby solemnly resolve to carry out the Congress instructions issued from time to time for the purpose of establising *purna* swaraj."

Appendix–III

"Eleven Points"

(Demands submitted to Lord Irwin by Gandhi)

1. Total Prohibition.
2. Reduction of the ratio to 1s. 4d.
3. Reduction of the land revenue to at least 50 per cent and making it subject to legislative control.
4. Abolition of the salt tax.
5. Reduction of the military expenditure to at least 50 per cent to begin with.
6. Reduction of the salaries of the higher grade service to one half or less to suit the reduced revenue.
7. Protective tariff on foreign cloth.
8. The passage of the Coastal Traffic Reservation Bill.
9. Discharge of all political prisoners save those condemned for murder or the attempt thereat by ordinary judicial tribunal, withdrawal of all political prosecutions, abrogation of Section of 124–A, the regulation of 1818 and the like, and the permission to all Indian exiles to return.
10. Abolition of C.I.D. or its popular control.
11. Issue of licences to use firearms for self-defence subject to popular control.

Bibliography

PRIMARY SOURCES

Collected Works to Mahatma Gandhi, Hundred Volumes, Publications Division, Ministry of Information and Broadcasting, Government of India, New Delhi, 1958-83.

Gandhi, M.K., *Story of My Experiments with Truth,* Vol. I, (Tr. By Mahadev Desai from Gujarati) and Vol. II Tr. (By Mahadev Desai and Pyarelal Nair (sic) from Gujarati) Navajivan Press, Ahmedabad, 1927-29.

Gandhi, Mohandas, K. *Hind Swaraj, or Indian Home Rule,* Navajivan Publishing House, Ahmedabad, 1931.

Gandhi, M.K., *Ethical Religion: Neethi Dharma,* (Tr. By A. Rama Iyer from Hindi) S. Ganesan, Madras, 1930.

Gandhi, M.K., *Satyagraha in South Africa,* Navajivan Publishing House, Ahmedabad, India, 1972.

Gandhi, M.K., *Constructive Programme: Its Meaning and Place,* Navajivan Publishing House, Ahmedabad, Revised and Enlarged Edition, 1945.

Gandhi, M.K., *The Bhagvadgita,* Orient Paperbacks, Delhi, 1998.

Gandhi, M.K., *Delhi Diary,* (Prayer Speeches from 10-9-47 to 30-1-48), Navajivan Publishing House, Ahmedabad, 1948 (Written in third person and corrected by Gandhi).

Journals Edited by Gandhi

Indian Opinion

Young India

Navajivan

Harijan

SECONDARY SOURCES

Books

Agarwala, B.R., *Trials of Independence (1858-1946)*, National Book Trust, India, 1991.

Ahluwalia, B.K., (ed.)., *Facets of Gandhi*, Lakshmi Book Store, New Delhi, 1968.

Alexander, Horace G., *Gandhi Through Western Eyes*, Asia Publishing House, Bombay, 1969.

Ambedkar, B.R., *What Congress and Gandhi Have Done to the Untouchables*, Thacker and Company Limited, Bombay, 1945.

…………………, *Annihilation of Caste*, Blumoon Books, New Delhi, 2000, p. 96.

Andrews C.F., *Mahatma Gandhi' Ideas*, George Allen and Unwin, London, 1929.

Ashe, Geoffrey, *Gandhi: A Study in Revolution*, Heineman, London, 1968.

Athalye, D.V., *The Life of Mahatma Gandhi*, Revised and enlarged edition Aryabhushan Press, Poona, 1923.

Azad, Maulana Abul Kalam, *India Wins Freedom, The Complete Version*, Orient Longman, New Delhi, 1988.

Bakshi Rajni, *Babu Kuti*, Penguin Books India (P) Ltd., New Delhi, 1998.

Bandopadhya, Anu, *M.K. Gandhi: Author, Journalist, Printer, Publisher*, Navajivan Publishing House, Ahmedabad, 1994.

Bandopadhyaya, Jayantanuja, *Social and Political Thought of Gandhi*, Allied Publishers, Bombay, 1969.

Barnes, Margarita, *The Indian Press: A History of the Growth of Public Opinion in India*, George Allen and Unwin, London, 1940.

Bernays, Robert, *"Naked Fakir"*, Victor Gollancz Limited, London, 1931.

Bhargava, Motilal, *Role of the Press in the Freedom Movement*, Reliance Publishing House, New Delhi, 1987.

Bhattacharya, Bhabani, *Gandhi: The Writer (The Image As It Grew)*, National Book Trust, New Delhi, 1969.

…………………, *Mahatma Gandhi*, Arnold Heineman Publishers, New Delhi, 1977.

Bhattacharya, Sabyasachi, *The Mahatma and the Poet*, National Book Trust, India, 1999.

Bhattacharya, S.N., *Mahatma Gandhi, The Journalist*, Asia Publishing House, Bombay.

Birla, G.D., *In the Shadow of the Mahatma*, Orient Longman, India, 1953.

…………………, *Bapu, A Unique Association*, Four Volumes, Bharatiya Vidya Bhavan, Bombay, 1977.

Bolton, Glorney, *The Tragedy of Gandhi*, George Allen and Unwin Limited, London, 1934.

Bondurant, Joan V., *Conquest of Violence: The Gandhian Philosophy of Conflict*, Princeton University Press, New Jersey, 1988.

Bose, Nirmal Kumar, *My Days with Gandhi*, Orient Longman Limited, New Delhi, 1974.

Brailsford, Henry N., *Rebel India*, Leonard Stein, London, 1931.

Brock, Peter, *Gandhi as a Linguistic Nationalist*, South Asia Publications, New Delhi, 1996.

Brown, Judith., *Gandhi's Rise to Power: Indian Politics 1915-22*, Cambridge University Press, 1972.

......................., *Gandhi and Civil Disobedience: 1928-34*, Cambridge University Press, 1977.

......................., *Gandhi: Prisoner of Hope*, Oxford University Press, Delhi, 1992.

Bush, Catherine, *Mahatma Gandhi*, Burke Publishing Company Limited, London 1940.

Cargill, Oscar, *Henry David Thoreau: Selected Works on Nature and Liberty*, Liberty Arts Press, New York, 1952.

Case, C.M., *Non-Violent Coercion*, George Allen and Unwin, London, 1923.

Chadha, Yogesh, *Redicovering Gandhi*, Century Books Ltd., London, 1997.

Chandra, Bipan, *et al.*, *India's Struggle for Independence, 1857-1947*, Viking, New Delhi, 1988.

Chatterjee, Partha, *Nationalist Thought in the Colonial World*, London, Zed Books, 1986.

Chaudhary, Ramnarayan, *Bapu As I Saw Him*, Navajivan Publishing House, 1959.

Choudhari, Manmohan, *Exploring Gandhi*, Gandhi Peace Foundation, New Delhi, 1990.

Collins, Larry, and Lapierre, Dominique *Freedom at Midnight*, Vikas Publishing House Private Limited, New Delhi, 1978.

Cousins, Norman, (ed.) *Profiles of Gandhi*, Indian Book Company, Delhi, 1969.

Copley, A., *Gandhi*, London, 1987.

Dalton, Dennis, *Gandhi's Power: Non-Violence in Action* (First published by Columbia University Press, 1993) Oxford India Paperbacks, 1998.

Dandavate, Madhu, *Marx and Gandhi*, Popular Prakashan Bombay, 1977.

Das, Durga (ed.), *Sardar Patel's Correspondence*, Six Volumes, Navajivan Publishing House, Ahmedabad, 1972.

Deluca, Anthony R., *Gandhi, Mao, Mandela, and Gorbachev: Studies in Personality, Power, and Politics*, Praeger, London, 2000.

Desai, Mahadev, *Day to Day with Gandhi*, Ten Volumes, Edited by Parikh, N.D., Sarva, Sewa Sangh Prakshan, Varanasi, 1961-73.

......................., *Diary* (15 Vol.).

......................., *The Epic of Travancore*, Navajivan Publishing House, Ahmedabad, 1937.

......................., *The Story of Bardoli: Being a History of the Bardoli Satyagraha and Its Sequel*, Navajivan Publishing House, Ahmedabad, 1929.

......................., *A Righteous Struggle*, [A Chronicle of Ahmedabad Textile Labourers' Fight for Justice] Translated by Dave Somnath P., and edited by Kumarappa Bharatan, Navajivan Press, Ahmedabad, 1951.

Desai, M.V. and Ninan, Sevanti (ed.), *Beyond those Headlines*, The Media Foundation, Allied Publishers, New Delhi, 1996.

Devanesan, Chandran D.S., *The Making of the Mahatma*, Orient Longman, New Delhi, 1969.

Doke, J.M., *M.K. Gandhi: A Patriot in South Africa*, Publications Division, Ministry of Information and Broadcasting, 1994.

Dua, M.R. *Themes in Indian Communication*, Metropolitan, New Delhi, 1980.

Edwardes, Michael, *The Myth of the Mahatma: Gandhi the British and the Raj*, Constable, London, 1986.

Elwin, Verrier, *Gandhiji, Bapu of His People*, Shillong, Assam Government Press, 1950.

Erikson Erik H., *Gandhi's Truth: On the Origins of Militant Non-Violence*, Faber and Faber Limited, London, 1970.

Fischer, Louis, *The Life of Mahatma Gandhi*, Jonathan Cape Thirty Bedford Square, London, 1951.

......................., (ed.), *The Essential Gandhi*, George Allen and Unwin, London, 1962.

Fisher, Fredrick B., *That Strange Little Brown Man*, Orient Longmans, Delhi, 1970.

Galtung, Johan, *The Way is the Goal: Gandhi Today*, Gujarat Vidyapith, 1992.

Gandhi, Manu, *Last Glimpses of Bapu*, Shivlal Aggrawal and Co., Delhi, 1962.

Gandhi, Prabhudas, *My Childhood with Gandhi*, Navajivan Publishing House, Ahmedabad, 1957.

Gandhi Rajmohan, *The Good Boatman*, Viking, New Delhi, 1995.

......................., *Mohandas*, Penguin Viking, New Delhi, 2006.

Gangrade, K.D., *Gandhi's Autobiography: Moral Lessons*, Gandhi Smriti and Darshan Samiti, New Delhi, 1998.

Ghose, S.L., *Motilal Ghose,* National Book Trust, India, New Delhi, 1979.

Ghosh, Hemendra Prasad, *The Newspaper in India,* The University, Calcutta, 1952.

Ghosh, Sudhir, *Gandhi's Emissary,* Rupa and Company, Calcutta, 1967.

Green, Martin, *Gandhi: Voice of a New Age Revolution,* Continuum, New York, 1993.

Gregg, Richard B., *The Power of Non-Violence,* Navajivan Publishing House, 1934.

"Harijan" A, *Gandhi or Ambedkar,* Gandhi Era Publications, Madras, 1946.

Hardiman David, *Gandhi in his Times and Ours,* Permanent Book, 2003.

Heath, Carl, *Gandhiji: Satyagraha or Non-Violent Resistance,* S. Ganesan, Madras, 1930.

......................., *Gandhi,* George Allen and Unwin, London, 1944.

Horsburgh, *Non-Violence and Aggression: A Study of Gandhi's Moral Equivalent to War.*

......................., *Mahatma Gandhi,* Lutterworth Press, London, 1972.

Hoyland, Johan S., *The Cross Moves East: A Study in the Significance of Gandhi's "Satyagraha",* George Allen and Unwin, London, 1931.

Hunt, James D., *Gandhi in London,* Promilla and Co., New Delhi 1978.

......................., (ed.) *Winston S. Churchill his Complete Speeches,* New York, 1974.

......................., *Gandhi and the Non-Conformists,* Promilla and Co., New Delhi, 1986.

Hutchins, Frencis, Co., *Spontaneous Revolution: The Quit India Movement,* New Delhi, 1971.

Iyengar, A.S., *All Through the Gandhian Era,* Hind Kitabs Ltd., Bombay, 1950.

Iyengar, K.R. Srinivas, *Indian Writing in English,* Asia Publishing House, Bombay, 1962.

Iyer, Raghavan, N., *The Moral and Political Writings of Mahatma Gandhi,* Three Volumes, Oxford University Press, 1987.

James R., (ed.) *Winston S. Churchill His Complete Speeches,* New York, 1974.

Jones, Stanley E., *Mahatma Gandhi,* London, 1948.

Jordans, J.T.F., *Gandhi's Religion: A Homespun Shawl,* Macmillan Press Ltd., London, 1998.

Kamath, M.V., *Professional Journalism,* Vikas Publishing House, New Delhi, 1980.

Kapur, Sudarshan, *Raising Up A Prophet: The African-American Encounter with Gandhi,* Oxford University Press, New, Delhi, 1993.

Karkhanis, Sharad, *Indian Politics and the Role of Press,* Vikas Publishing House, New Delhi, 1998.

Keer, Dhananjay, *Dr. Ambedkar: Life and Mission,* Popular Prakashan, Bombay, 1954.

......................., *Mahatma Gandhi: Political Saint and Unarmed Prophet,* Popular Prakashan, Bombay, 1973.

Khare, Prem Shankar, *Press and Public Opinion in India (1857-1918),* Piyush Prakashan, Allahabad, 1964.

Kishore, Giriraj, *Pehla Girmitiya,* Jnanapith Prakashan, New Delhi, 2000.

Khosla, Gopal Das, *Stern Reckoning,* Bhawanani and Sons, New Delhi, 1949.

Kothari, M.M., *Critique of Gandhi,* Critique Publications, Jodhpur, 1996.

Koontz, Harold and Weihrich, Heniz, *Essentials of Management,* McGraw-Hill Book Co., Singapore, 1990.

Kriplani, Krishna, *Gandhi: A Life,* National Book Trust, New Delhi, 1993.

Kumar, Mahendra and Low Leter, (ed.) *Legacy and Future of Non-Violence,* Gandhi Peace Foundation, New Delhi, 1996.

Kumar, Satish, *Mahatma Gandhi: The Man and Writer,* Prakash Book Depot, Bareilly, India, 1983.

Lester, Muriel, *Entertaining Gandhi,* Ivor Nicholson and Watson, London, 1932.

Limaye, Madhu, *Mahatma Gandhi and Jawaharlal Nehru: A Historic Partnership 1916-48,* Four Volumes Gandhi Media Centre, New Delhi, 1989.

Lindley, Mark, *Gandhi and the World Today (1998),* Centre for Gandhian Studies, Kerala, 1999.

Lovett, Pat, *Journalism in India,* (Aharchandra Mookerjee Lectures April 1926), Banne Publishing Company, Calcutta, (Year of Publication not mentioned).

Manubehn, *Bapu, My Mother,* Navajivan Publishing House, Ahmedabad, 1949.

McQuail, Denis, *Mass Communication Theory,* Sage Publications, London, 1994.

Meer, Fatima, *Apprenticeship of a Mahatma: A Biography of Mahatma Gandhi 1869-1914,* Gandhi Hindustani Sahitya Sabha, New Delhi, 1997.

Mehta, D.S., *Mass Communication and Journalism in India,* Allied Publishers Private Limited, Bombay, 1979.

Mehta, Naresh, *Prarthana Purush (Hindi),* National Publishing House, New Delhi, 1975.

Mehta, Ved, *Mahatama Gandhi and His Apostles,* Penguin Books, 1976.

Menon, Narayana, *The Communications Revolution,* National Book Trust, New Delhi, 1976.

Mira, *Gleanings, Gathered at Bapu's Feet,* Navajivan Publishing House, Ahmedabad, 1949.

Mujumbar, Ammu Menon, *Social Welfare in India: Mahatma Gandhi's Contribution,* Asia Publishing House, London, 1965.

Mukherjee, Hiren, *Gandhiji, A Study,* National Book Agency Private Ltd., Calcutta, 1958.

Mukherjee, Subrata, and Ramaswamy, Sushila, (ed.), *Facets of Mahatma Gandhi,* Four Volumes, Deep and Deep Publishers, New Delhi, 1994.

Munshi, K.M., *Gandhi: The Master,* Rajkamal Publications, Delhi, 1948.

......................., *Gujarat and its Literature,* Longmans, Green and Co., Ltd., Calcutta, 1935.

Murti, V.V. Ramana, *Gandhi: Essential Writings,* Gandhi Peace Foundation, New Delhi, 1970.

Nair, Gopalakrishnan, N., *Mahatma Gandhi and the Indian Writers,* Gandhi Smriti and Darshan Samiti, New Delhi, 1996.

Nanda, B.R., *Mahatma Gandhi: A Biography,* George Allen and Unwin Ltd., London, 1958.

......................., *Mahatma Gandhi: A Pictorial Biography,* Publications Division, New Delhi, 1972.

......................., *Gokhale, Gandhi and the Nehrus,* George Allen and Unwin London, 1976.

......................., *Gandhi and his Critics,* Oxford University Press, Delhi, 1985.

......................., *Gandhi, Pan-Islamism, Imperialism and Nationalism,* Oxford University Press, New Delhi, 1989.

......................., (ed.), *Mahatma Gandhi: 125 Years,* ICCR, Wiley Eastern Ltd., New Age International Publishers, 1995.

Narain, Jai, *Gandhi's View of Political Power,* Deep and Deep Publications, New Delhi, 1987.

......................., *Economic Thought of Mahatma Gandhi,* Sehgal Publishing Service, 1991.

Narasimhan, Bharati, (ed.) *Making of Great Communicator, Gandhi,* National Media Centre, New Delhi, 1997.

Narayan, Shriman, (ed.), *Selected Works of Mahatma Gandhi,* Six Volumes, Navajivan Publishing House, Ahmedabad, 1968.

Narsimhaiah, C.D., *The Writers Gandhi,* Punjabi University, Patiala, 1967.

Natrajan, S., *A History of Press in India,* Asia Publishing House, Bombay, 1962.

Nayar, Sushila, *In Gandhiji's Mirror,* Oxford University Press, New Delhi, 1991.

........................, *Mahatma Gandhi's Last Imprisonment, The inside Story,* Haranand Publishers, New Delhi, 1996.

Nehru, Jawaharlal, *An Autobiography,* John Lane, London, 1936.

........................, *The Discovery of India,* Asia Publishing House, 1960.

Pandhikattu, Kuruvilla, *The Meaning of the Mahatma for the Millennium,* Maadhyam Book Services, Delhi, 2000.

Parekh, Bhikhu, *Gandhi,* (Past Masters, General Editor: Keith Thomas), Oxford University Press, 1997.

........................, *Gandhi's Political Philosophy, A Critical Examination,* Macmillan, New Delhi, 1989.

........................, *Colonialism, Tradition and Reform: An Analysis of Gandhi's Political Discourse,* Sage Publications, New Delhi, 1999.

Parel, Anthony J., (ed.), *Hind Swaraj and Other Writings,* Cambridge Texts in Modern Politics, Cambridge University Press, New Delhi, 1997.

........................, J. (ed.), *Gandhi, Freedom and Self Rule,* Oxford 2000.

Park, Richard L., *Change and Persistence of Change in India,* Five Fectures Michigen, USA, 1971.

Parthsarthy, Rangswami, *Basic Journalism,* Macmillan India Ltd., New Delhi, 1984.

Patel, Jehangir P., and Sykes, Marjorie, *Gandhi: His Gift of the Fight,* Friends Rural Circle, Rasulia, India, 1987.

Payne, Robert, *The Life and Death of Mahatma Gandhi,* The Bodley Head, London, 1969.

Pinto, Vivek, *Gandhi's Vision and Values: The Moral Quest for Change in Indian Agriculture,* Sage Publications, New Delhi, 1998.

Prasad, Rajendra, *Satyagraha in Champaran,* Navajivan Publishing House, Ahmedabad, 1949.

........................, *At the Feet of Mahatma Gandhi,* Asia Publishing House, Bombay, 1961.

Polak, Henry S.L., *M.K. Gandhi: A Sketch of His Life and Work,* Ganesan and Co., Madras, 1918.

........................, *Speeches and Writings of M.K. Gandhi,* Ganesan and Co., Madras, 1919.

Polak, Millie Graham, *Mr. Gandhi: The Man,* Vora and Company, Bombay, 1949.

Pyarelal and Nayar, Sushila, *Mahatma Gandhi: A Biography,* Ten Volumes, Navajivan Publishing House, Ahmedabad, 1965.

Pyarelal, *The Epic Fast,* Mohanlal Maganlal Bhatt, Ahmedabad, 1932.

........................, *A Pilgrimage for Peace: Gandhi and Frontier Gandhi Among North West Frontier Pathans,* Navajivan Publishing House, Ahmedabad, 1950.

Radhakrishnan, N., *The Quest for Tolerance and Survival*, Gandhi Smriti and Darshan Samiti and Gandhi Media Centre, New Delhi, 1995.

........................, *The Gandhian Concept of Sustainable Development and New World Order*, Gandhi Museum, Madurai, 1997.

........................, *The Sparks of Non-Violence*, Gandhi Smriti and Darshan Samiti, New Delhi, 1998.

Radhakrishnan, S., *Mahatma Gandhi: Essays and Reflections on His Life and Works*, George Allen and Unwin, London, 1939.

........................, (ed.) *Mahatma Gandhi: 100 Years*, Gandhi Peace Foundation, New Delhi, 1968.

Raghavan, G.N.S., *PTI Story: The Origin and Growth of the Indian Press and the News Agency*, PTI, New Delhi, 1987.

Rajagopalachari, C., and Kumarappa, J.C., *The Nations Voice: Being a Collection of Gandhiji's Speeches in England and Sjt. Mahadev Desai's Account of the Sojourn*, Navajivan Press, Ahmedbad, 1931.

Ranjeet, Swami, *A Hidden Side of Mahatma Gandhi*, Gandhi Smriti and Darshan Samiti, New Delhi, 1995.

Rau, Chalpathi M., *The Press*, National Book Trust, New Delhi, 1974.

........................, *The Press in India*, Allied Publishers Private Limited, Bombay, 1976.

Reddy, E.S., *Gandhiji's Vision of a Free South Africa*, Sanchar Publishing House, New Delhi, 1995.

Reynolds Reginald, *The True Book About Mahatma Gandhi*, Educational Publishers, Bangalore, 1966.

Rolland, Romain, *Mahatma Gandhi, The Man Who Became One with the Universal Being*, (Tr. from French by Catherine D. Groth), Publications Division, Ministry of Information and Broadcasting, Government of India, New Delhi, 1990.

Rosenberg, Marshall B., *Nonviolent Communication*, A Language of Compassion, CA. USA, 2002.

Rothermund, Dietmar, *Mahatma Gandhi: An Essay in Political Biography*, Manohar Publications, New Delhi, 1991.

Roy Chaudhury, P.C., *Gandhi and His Contemporaries*, Sterling Publishers Private Limited, New Delhi, 1972.

Ruben, Brent D., *Communication and Human Behaviour*, Macmillan Publishing Company, New York, 1984.

Rudolph, Susanne Hoeber and Rudolph Lloyd I., *The Modernization of Tradition: Political Development in India*, University of Chicago Press, Chicago and London, 1967.

......................., *Gandhi, The Traditional Roots of Charisma,* Orient Longman India, 1987.

...................., *Postmodern Gandhi, and other Essays,* Orient Longman India, 1987.

Runbold, Algernon, *Watershed in India* London, 1979.

Sarkar, R.C.S., *The Press in India,* Sultan Chand and Company Limited, New Delhi, 1984.

Sengupta B. and Chowdhary R., *Mahatma Gandhi and India's Struggle for Swaraj,* Calcutta, 1932.

Sethi, J.D., *Gandhi Today,* Vikas Publishing House, New Delhi, 1978.

Shankhdhar, B.M., *Pioneers of Social Change in India,* Deep and Deep, New Delhi, 1986.

Shankhdhar, M.M., *Understanding Gandhi Today,* Deep and Deep, New Delhi, 1996.

Shannon, Claude E., and Weaver, Warren., *The Mathematical Theory of Communication,* University of Illinois Press, USA., 1949.

Sharp, Gene, *Gandhi Wields The Weapon of Moral Power,* Navajivan Publishing House, Ahmedabad, 1960.

......................., *Gandhi Faces the Storm,* Navajivan Publishing House, Ahmedabad, 1961.

......................., *Gandhi as a Political Strategist with Essays on Ethics and Politics,* Porter Sargent Publisher, Inc., Boston, USA, 1979.

Sheean, Vincent, *Lead, Kindly Light,* Random House, New York, 1949.

......................., *Mahatma Gandhi, A Great Life in Brief,* Publications Division, Ministry of Information and Broadcasting, New Delhi, 1954.

Shridharani, Krishnalal, *War Without Violence,* Bharatiya Vidya Bhawan, Bombay, 1962.

Shourie, Arun, *Worshipping False Gods: Ambedkar and the Facts which Have Been Erased,* ASA Publications, New Delhi, 1997.

Shukla, Chandrashanker, (ed.), *Gandhiji as We Know Him,* Vora and Company Publishers, Bombay, 1945.

......................., *Incidents of Gandhiji's Life,* Vora and Company Publishers, Bombay, 1949.

......................., *Reminiscences of Gandhiji,* Vora and Company Publishers, Bombay, 1951.

Slade, Madeleine, *The Spirit's Pilgrimage,* Coward-McCann, New York, 1960.

Sonnlietner, Michael W., *Gandhian Nonviolence: Levels of Satyagraha,* Abhinav Publications, New Delhi, 1985.

Spratt, P. *Gandhism,* The Huxley Press, Madras, 1939.

Tandon, P.D., and Wolseley, Roland E., *Gandhi: Warricr of Non-Violence*, National Book Trust, New Delhi 1969.

Tarlo, Emma, *Clothes Matter: Dress and Identity in India*, Viking Penguin India, New Delhi, 1997.

Tendulkar, Dinanath G., *Mahatma Gandhi: Life of Mohandas Karamchand Gandhi*, Eight Volumes, Publications Division, Ministry of Information and Broadcasting, Government of India, New Delhi, 1960-63.

Thiaga Rajan, S.P., *History of Indian Journalism*, The Columbia House, Thanjavur, 1966.

Thoreau, Henry D., *Life Without Principle*, London, 1905.

......................., *On the Duty of Civil Disobedience*, London, 1903.

......................., *Selected Writings on Nature and Liberty*, Cargill, Oscar, Liberty Arts Press, New York, 1952.

Tolstoy, Leo, *The Kingdom of God and Peace Essays*, London, 1936.

......................., *Tolstoy's Writings on Civil Disobedience and Non-Violence*, Peter Owen, London, 1968.

P. Van den Dungen, *Essays on Gandhian Politics*, R. Kumar (ed.) Oxford, Clarendon Press, 1971.

Upadhayaya, J.M., *Mahatma Gandhi as a Student*, Publications Division, Ministry of Information and Broadcasting, New Delhi, 1965.

......................., *Mahatma Gandhi: A Teacher's Discovery*, Vallabh Vidyanagar, Ahmedabad, 1969.

......................., (compiled)., *Gandhiji's Early Contemporaries and Companions*, Ahmedabad, 1971.

Verma, M.M., *Gandhi's Technique of Mass Mobilization.*, R.K. Gupta and Co., New Delhi, 1998.

Walker, Roy., *Sword of Gold*, Orient Longman, New Delhi, 1969.

Watson., Francis, *Talking of Gandhi*, London, 1957.

Weber, T.A., *Gandhi*, Pallas Publishing Company, London. (Year of Publication not mentioned.)

Weber, Thomas *Conflict Resolution and Gandhian Ethics*, Gandhi Peace Foundation, New Delhi, 1991.

......................., *Gandhi's Peace-Keeping Army: The Shanti Sena and Unarmed Peacekeeping Army*, Syracuse, New York, 1996.

Wellock Wilfred, *Gandhi as Social Revolutionary*, 1950.

White, Margaret Bourke, *Halfway to Freedom*, Bombay, 1957.

Wolport Stanely, *Nine Hours to Rama*, Hamish Hamilton, 1990.

......................., *Gandhi's Passion, The Life and Legacy of Mahatma Gandhi*, Oxford University Press, New York, 2001.

Wolseley, E. Roland, (ed.), *Journalism in Modern India*, Asia Publishing House, Bombay, 1953.

Woodcook, George, *Gandhi*, Fontana, New York, 1972.

......................., *Who Killed the British Empire*, New York, 1974.

Yogananda, Paramhansa, *Autobiography of a Yogi*, The Philosophical Library, New York, 1946.

Zakaria, Rafiq, *Gandhi and the Breakup of India*, Bharatiya Vidya Bhavan, Mumbai, 1999.

Periodicals and Journals

Gandhi Marg, Gandhi Peace Foundation, 221-223, Deen Dayal Upadhyaya Marg, New Delhi.

Journal of Gandhi Smriti and Darshan Samiti, Gandhi Smriti and Darshan Samiti, New Delhi.

Journal of Peace and Gandhian Studies, A Quarterly of Gandhi Media Centre, Delhi.

Articles

"Special Issue on Hind Swaraj", *The Aryan Path*, September, 1938.

Dasgupta, Swapan, and Koppikar Smruti, "Nathuram Godse on Trial Again," *India Today*, August 3, 1998, pp. 22-28.

Porter, William E., "Journalism", *International Encyclopedia of Social Sciences*, Vol. 8, pp. 265-271.

Patel, Avaan, "Gandhi on Canvas", *The Hindu*, New Delhi, Sunday, March 28, 1999.

Pinto, Vivek, "Gandhi: Writing for Change", *Folio: Reaching Out, The Hindu*, Chennai, April 8, 2001, pp. 16-17.

Sundaram, Geeta, "The Gandhi Oberschule", *The Hindu*, New Delhi, Sunday, January 3, 1999.

Varma, Ravindra, "Godse's Testament", *The Hindu*, New Delhi, August 30, 1998.

Balachandran, P.K., "Godseism Without Gandhi", Reflections: *The Hindustan Times*, New Delhi, August 16, 1998.

Brown, Judith, M., "Gandhi: Will He Be Relevant?", *A Future Past and Present, The Hindustan Times, Special Issue*, 2001, New Delhi, January, 2001.

Chowdhry, Kamla, "Gandhi Failed, Like All Saints", *The Hindustan Times*, New Delhi, January 30, 1998.

Cole, Kris, "Ten Steps to Good Communications for Managers", *Careers, The Hindustan Times*, New Delhi, December 8, 1998.

Dalmia, Yashodhara, "The Mahatma As Muse", *The Hindustan Times, HT City*, New Delhi, July 28, 1999.

French, Patrick, "Gandhi was My Number One Hero", *The Hindustan Times, Sunday Magazine,* New Delhi, January, 25, 1998.

Ganguli Amulya, "The Mahatma in Sepia" *The Hindustan Times,* New Delhi, September 27, 1997.

.........................,"The Spectre of Godse", *The Hindustan Times,* New Delhi, July 27, 1998.

Inder Jit, "Parliament Ignores Gandhi," *The Hindustan Times,* New Delhi, October 1, 1997.

Jagmohan, "Gandhi and the Removal of Spiritual Illiteracy", *The Hindustan Times,* New Delhi, October 3, 1997.

Khan, Maulana Wahiduddin, "The Gandhi I Knew", *The Hindustan Times,* New Delhi, January 30, 1996.

Madan, T.N., "Victory Without Fulfilment", *The Hindustan Times,* New Delhi, December, 28, 1997.

Mukherjee, Subrata, "Gandhi's Theory of the State", *The Hindustan Times,* New Delhi, 2, 1999.

Nanda, B.R., "Gandhi and the West", *The Hindustan Times,* New Delhi, January 30, 1998.

Narayanan, V.N., "Dumbing Down of a People", *The Hindustan Times, Sunday,* New Delhi, February 1, 1998.

Padgaonkar, Lalita, "A Lifetime of Tolerance", *Interview of Narayan Desai, Recepient of 1998 UNESCO-Madanjit Singh Prize of the Promotion of Tolerance and Non-Violence, The Hindustan Times,* New Delhi, November 1, 1998.

Salil, Kuldip, "Gandhi is Glad" (a poem) in Singh, Khuswant, "With Malice Towards One and All" *The Hindustan Times,* New Delhi, 30, 1999.

Singh, Natwar, K., "The Eternal Pilgrim", *The Hindustan Times, Sunday Magazine,* New Delhi, January 25, 1998.

Sharp, Gene, "The Gandhian Way Today", *The Hindustan Times,* New Delhi, January 30, 1999.

Narayanan, K.R., "Media: A Distorting, Magnifying Mirror," *The Hindustan Times,* New Delhi, April 28, 1997.

Polak H.S.L., "Gandhiji As I Knew Him", *Nostalgia, The Hindustan Times,* New Delhi, January 26, 1995.

Kumar, Ravinder, "A Prophet of Modernity?", *The Hindustan Times,* New Delhi, January 30, 1999.

Bakshi, Rajni, "A Tale of Two Yogis", *The Times of India,* New Delhi, February 24, 1999.

"Candidus" survey of 1947, *Times of India,* January 1, 1948.

The SGI Newsletter/Special, Tokyo, 1996 "Gandhi: A Tireless Speaker and Writer", pp. 8-9.

Sharma, Jai Narain, "The Great Nuclear Debate: A Gandhian Persp ective", *The Tribune,* Chandigarh, May 27, 1998.

Naipaul, V.S., "Christianity Didn't Damage India Like Islam", *Outlook, Milleneum Special,* November 15, 1999, pp. 48-56.

Special Issue on Gandhi as a Journalist Vidura, Journal of the Press Institute of India, New Delhi, Vol. 35, Issue No. 1, January-March, 1998.

Gandhi Memorial: Peace Number, Vishwa Bharati Quarterly, Shantiniketan, 1949.

News Items

"Gandhi Corners' to Come up in Schools", *The Hindu,* New Delhi, September, 24, 1999.

"Mahatma Gandhi's Rare Letters to Be Auctioned", *The Hindustan Times,* New Delhi, July 8, 1998.

"Too Late, But SA Honours Gandhi", *The Pioneer,* July 24, 1997, p. 1.

Brochures

The Sulabh Movement: Human Development Approach to Sanitation, Brochure issued by Sulabh International Social Service Organisation, New Delhi.

Index